PERU

NATIONAL GEOGRAPHIC

TRAVELER

PERU

by Rob Rachowiecki
photography by Vance Jacobs

National Geographic
Washington, D.C.

CONTENTS

Pages 2–3: High Andes landscape
Left: A young girl and her alpaca near Chivay

TRAVELING WITH EYES OPEN

Alert travelers go with a purpose and leave with a benefit. If you travel responsibly, you can help support wildlife conservation, historic preservation, and cultural enrichment in the places you visit. You can enrich your own travel experience as well.

To be a geo-savvy traveler:

- Recognize that your presence has an impact on the places you visit.

- Spend your time and money in ways that sustain local character. (Besides, it's more interesting that way.)

- Value the destination's natural and cultural heritage.

- Respect the local customs and traditions.

- Express appreciation to local people about things you find interesting and unique to the place: its nature and scenery, music and food, historic villages and buildings.

- Vote with your wallet: Support the people who support the place, patronizing businesses that make an effort to celebrate and protect what's special there. Seek out local shops, restaurants, and inns. Use tour operators who love their home—who love taking care of it and showing it off. Avoid businesses that detract from the character of the place.

- Enrich yourself, taking home memories and stories to tell, knowing that you have contributed to the preservation and enhancement of the destination.

That is the type of travel now called geotourism, defined as "tourism that sustains or enhances the geographical character of a place—its environment, culture, aesthetics, heritage, and the well-being of its residents." To learn more, visit National Geographic's Center for Sustainable Destinations at *www.nationalgeographic.com/maps/geotourism.*

NATIONAL GEOGRAPHIC TRAVELER

PERU

ABOUT THE AUTHOR & THE PHOTOGRAPHER

■ British-born **Rob Rachowiecki** is an award-winning guidebook author with a master's degree in ecology. An active member of the Society of American Travel Writers, he has traveled extensively and frequently throughout Peru since his first visit in 1982 when he fell in love with this hugely diverse and stunningly lovely country. Rachowiecki has written numerous books about Peru and has worked there as an adventure travel guide, leading treks in the High Andes and cruises on the upper Amazon. When not on the road, he makes his home in the American Southwest.

■ **Vance Jacobs** is an award-winning photographer whose work has been exhibited in galleries and museums throughout the world. He's based in San Francisco, but travels widely, and has shot assignments in 12 countries and counting. You can see more of his work at *www.vancejacobs.com*.

■ Portions of the History & Culture and Amazon chapters were written by **Joe Yogerst.** California-based Yogerst is the co-author of *Traveler's Companion Peru* and has contributed to a number of National Geographic books about South America, including *Long Road South: A Journey Along the Pan American Highway, Enduring Treasures: National Parks of the World,* and *Sacred Places of a Lifetime.*

CHARTING YOUR TRIP

From arid Pacific coastal deserts to dripping Amazonian rain forests, from the highest navigable lake on the planet to its most spectacular tropical mountain ranges, Peru has an enviable and varied abundance of scenery and climate, while hidden within the mountains, forests, and deserts lie the remnants of dozens of ancient cultures.

Opportunities Abound

Visitors have a daunting array of things to do and places to see. It seems almost unthinkable not to visit Machu Picchu, but there's so much else to do that some travelers somehow miss this stunning archaeological highlight. Wildlife-watchers might spend their entire visit ensconced in a rain forest lodge looking for toucans, turtles, and tapirs. Students can take courses in Spanish or Quechua or try their hands at some of the indigenous crafts such as weaving. Outdoor enthusiasts can scale the highest peaks and surf off the wildest beaches. Visitors of all ages can learn to dance a sensual salsa or taste a spicy salsa to accompany the fabulous gastronomy that is slowly emerging onto the world's culinary scene. You don't have to do what everyone else does, but what most people do is well worth doing!

A Week-Long Visit

If this is your first visit to Peru, and you have just a week but feel ambitious, it is possible to cover the highlights of Cusco, Machu Picchu, and the southern Amazon in just seven days. Understand that all international flights from North America or Europe arrive in Lima, so plan from there. Note that the best way of getting around in-country is often by bus; service is frequent and reasonably efficient.

Here's a way to do it: If your flight arrives in early morning, fly on to Cusco on **Day 1.** Be aware of the high altitude (10,913 feet/3,326 m), and walk slowly; perhaps take a short nap after arrival.

Ceramic from a Barrio Santa Ana gallery in Ayacucho

Cusco, famed for superb colonial buildings, was erected on top of ancient Inca foundations. The population mirrors the country's, most of which can claim at least some indigenous heritage mixed with the blood of the Spanish conquistadores. The first afternoon buy the Cusco *Boleto Turístico* (tourist ticket), which you'll need to visit most of the sights in and around the city (it is sold at Dircetur tourist info points). Walk around the Plaza de Armas, stop in the cathedral, and visit the Museo Inka (not included in the cumulative ticket).

On **Day 2,** visit by foot, bus, or taxi some of the many archaeological sites in and around Cusco especially Sacsayhuamán, and either Pisac or Ollantaytambo. If you are in Pisac on Sunday or Thursday, make sure you enjoy some time at the traditional farmers and crafts market.

On **Day 3** take the train to Aguas Calientes (see p. 139), where you can overnight and arrange a dawn visit to nearby Machu Picchu (buy advance tickets in Cusco) on **Day 4.** None of Peru's ancient sites is better known than this, the iconic Inca city built in the 15th century on a mountainous, cloud-forested ridge and then forgotten until its rediscovery in 1911. The afternoon train back will get you to Cusco for the night.

The next morning board a flight to Puerto Maldonado in the southern Amazon, your destination for **Days 5** and **6.** Several lodges will accommodate two-night stays, giving you a quick glimpse of the rain forest and its burgeoning flora and fauna before taking your flight back to Lima on **Day 7.**

If two nights in the rain forest doesn't appeal, an excellent alternative is to take the six-hour bus ride from Cusco to Puno on Lake Titicaca on **Day 5,** spend **Day 6** on an all-day tour of the inhabited islands on the lake, and fly from nearby Juliaca to Lima on **Day 7.**

If this plan seems too rushed, by all means take it slower or spend the entire week in the Cusco area.

If You Have More Time

The biodiversity of the Amazon rain forest and the luminescence of Lake Titicaca, as well as the ancient non-Inca

Visitor Information

PROMPERÚ, the Peruvian Tourist Promotion Commission, has an efficient information and guidance system for tourists called iPerú (*tel 01/574–8000, e-mail: iperu@ promperu.gob.pe*), with 42 offices present in the major cities in the country and at the international airport of Lima and a 24-hour telephone assistance service (recently also via WhatsApp at *944492314*).

The official tourism portal, *www.peru.travel,* offers useful information on interesting sites, cities, itineraries, hotels, and restaurants.

sites that date back more than five millennia and represent dozens of different cultures offer ample opportunities for your second week.

After your visit to the Amazon, you could spend a couple of days at Lake Titicaca exploring the lake's many islands on **Day 7/8.** On **Day 9,** take the six-hour bus ride from Puno, on the lake's west end, to Arequipa over the bleak, high altiplano. Take a walk through Arequipa's colonial center and visit the city's other important sights on **Day 10,** especially the Monasterio de Santa Catalina and Museo Santuarios Andinos.

Fly to Lima on **Day 11,** transferring to a flight north to Trujillo and spend **Day 12** visiting the Chan Chan World Heritage site and the Huaca de la Luna—the Moche Temple of the Moon. On **Day 13,** a three-hour bus ride takes you to Chiclayo, which acts as a base for visiting northern Peru's best museum, Museo Tumbas Reales de

■ **The Inca trail to Machu Picchu is an adventurous trek through history and ancient culture.**

Drinking Water

Perhaps the main challenge that most travelers to Peru face is avoiding sickness caused by drinking the water. Tap water is not suitable for drinking anywhere in Peru. Filtered, bottled water is available everywhere in different bottle sizes, including 2.5 liters and 600 mL. Carbonated water (*agua con gas*) is generally safer than natural water (*agua sin gas*). Many hotels provide large water coolers where you can fill your own bottle for free. Restaurants usually buy or produce ice with filtered water. If you are in remote places you can treat the local water through boiling (for at least 5 min.), or with sterilizing tablets or portable filtering systems.

Sipán, followed by a visit to the site of Sipán itself—the recently excavated, 1,700-year-old Moche tomb of the Lord of Sipán, considered the richest burial site ever unearthed in the Americas. On **Day 14** fly back to Lima from Chiclayo.

Alternatively, if you want to skip Trujillo and the north coast, you can head back to Lima from Arequipa via buses along the coast, stopping in the high southern desert to book a flight over the famous Nazca Lines. Made during the flowering period of the Nazca civilization, between 300 B.C. and 500 A.D., they can only be appreciated from the air. Or pause in Pisco for a boat trip to watch huge colonies of sea lions and seabirds in the Islas Ballestas.

Other Possibilities

You can visit the spectacular thousand-year-old fortress of Kué-lap, in the northern highlands. Difficult to get to, it was set amid the remote cloud forest by the poorly understood Chachapoyas people, who built many marvelous strongholds that are still being discovered. Or consider the city of Caral on the north coast, where studies undertaken in 2001 have extended our understanding of Peruvian culture to its origins around 5,000 B.C.

Or, you can skip the cities and historic sites and take advantage of the wide range of outdoor activities—mountain climbing, white-water rafting, surfing, trekking, or bird-watching—available countrywide from the high peaks of Parque Nacional Huascarán to the dry forest of Reserva Ecológica Chaparri. Enjoy Peru!

Dealing With Cusco's Altitude

Most travelers are able to acclimatize to Cusco's altitude without any problems beyond a headache. Those who know they'll have difficulties in acclimatizing can transfer from the Cusco airport to Urubamba (9,416 feet/2,870 m), which has several good hotels and is a convenient base to visit many sites including Machu Picchu. Ollantaytambo (9,187 feet/2,800 m) is another option.

HISTORY &
CULTURE

Paragliding in the Miraflores district of Lima

PERU TODAY

Peru—a nation of several personas—defies easy description. Large urban centers thrive alongside the timeworn traditions of the Andean country-side; vast deserts give way to deep-green rain forest, regions so remarkably different you might think they were separate countries. Together they form the unique mosaic which makes Peru an absolutely extraordinary country.

The pedestrian shopping along Jirón de la Unión extends for several blocks.

The name may have changed over the years; the Inca called their realm *Tahuantinsuyo*, or Land of the Four Quarters, while the Spaniards originally dubbed their new colony Nueva Castilla. And the national capital may have been established in mountain-bound Cusco before its relocation to coastal Lima. But the European colonials, homegrown liberators, and local republicans who have governed Peru over the last 500 years kept the country essentially intact. In fact, most of what now lies within Peru's borders has been continuously ruled by one central government since the 15th century, when the Inca Empire reached its zenith, making Peru the oldest nation-state in the Americas.

Given this continuity, it's not surprising that many things typically associated with South America are, indeed, quintessentially Peruvian. Take the humble potato, for

example, which probably originated in the high plains around Lake Titicaca. There it grew wild until the ancient nomadic peoples of Peru settled and began to cultivate what would become the world's most popular tuber. Around 6,000 years ago, these same indigenous cultures domesticated the llama and alpaca, slowly moving away from hunting and gathering to an economy based on herding. This shift in turn gave rise to the weaving industry that produces the hats and ponchos that nearly every tourist seems to bring home from South America.

Cultural Legacy

The characteristic sights and sounds of the continent also have Peruvian roots. The haunting music played on panpipe instruments like the *zampoña,* and now heard in clubs and on street corners worldwide, has its roots in the pre-Inca cultures that thrived in the high Peruvian Andes. And, other than Christ the Redeemer hovering over Rio de Janeiro in Brazil, only one other sight instantly conjures the image of South America in the minds of millions of people around the globe: cloud-shrouded Machu Picchu high in the Andes. In recent years, Peru has also begun to make inroads in Hollywood, whose filmmakers, enthralled with the rich history and culture of South America, often turn to Peru for filming and story ideas.

With a varied landscape of rain forests, deserts, mountains, glaciers, swamps, and beaches, Peru exemplifies the continent's reputation as a land of stark contrasts. Even its cities flaunt their differences. In colonial Trujillo, echoing old Spain, bullfighting and equestrian traditions still flourish, and the Plaza de Armas remains a fulcrum of urban life. Much still goes on behind the high, whitewashed walls and closed doors of quiet, secretive Arequipa, a desert city, while Cusco buzzes with the high-mountain energy brought by the eclectic blend of people who congregate in the Andean metropolis— bright-eyed tourists and indigenous craftsmen, scientists on their way to the Amazon, and clergy clad in the cassocks of a bygone era. And, with a population large enough to rival that of London or Paris, Lima is huge, diverse, and often surprising in its modernity.

■ A young resident of Taquile Island in Lake Titicaca

One Country, Many Peoples

With a population exceeding 30 million, Peru is the fourth most populous nation in South America. About 45 percent of Peruvians are indigenous, the second highest percentage in the Western Hemisphere after Bolivia. The rest are primarily divided between those of mestizo, or mixed, ancestry (37 percent) and those of European origin (15 percent). There are also African and Asian ethnic groups.

Quechua speakers, who trace their origins to the Inca and other native peoples who lived in the Andes at the time of the Spanish conquest, dominate Peru's indigenous population. More than three million Peruvians, mostly in the central and northern Andes, consider Quechua their first language. Because of migration from the country-side to Peru's urban centers, this statistic also includes an increasing number of people in the nation's coastal cities. About half a million people in the region around Lake Titicaca and along the Bolivian border speak Aymara, another ancient Andean language.

Dozens of Amerindian groups call the Amazon Basin home, including the Aguarana, Machigenga, Shipibo, Urarina, and Yagua. In addition to their own languages, many of these rain forest dwellers also have distinct traditions and customs inspired by the pre-Columbian and Iberian cultures of highland and coastal Peru. The jungle groups, some of which number no more than a couple thousand people, have varying degrees of contact with the outside world. Some are well integrated into the urban societies of jungle cities like Iquitos and Puerto Maldonado, while others continue their nomadic ways and have little or no contact with the world beyond their range.

Peruvians of Spanish descent have dominated the nation's political and economic life since the time of Pizarro. Although the indigenous and mestizo populations have made great strides in the 21st century—including the election of Alejandro Toledo as the first indigenous president in 2001—the European primacy continues and likely will for many decades to come.

Urban Influences

Of all Peruvian cities, Lima has the most European populace, especially in wealthy coastal districts like Miraflores, San Isidro, and Barranco. Other large cities like Arequipa in the south and Trujillo in the north are also Eurocentric. But Peruvians with European descent are not limited to the nation's city centers. Here and there in the countryside you will come across enclaves of Europeans—particularly Germans, Italians, French, and British—who have migrated to Peru over the last century and a half. Traditions such as Alpine architecture and the wearing of lederhosen, as out of context as they may seem, persist in small towns like Pozuzo, which was established in the 1850s in the Pasco region of the Andes by settlers from Austria and Prussia.

Found mostly in the coastal communities north and south of Lima, Afro-Peruvians constitute about 3 percent of the population. They originally arrived from Africa as servants to the conquistadores; later they came as slaves, bought and shipped to Peru to serve the mining and agriculture industries. The slave trade persisted until the 1850s. Among the more celebrated black communities are the port of Callao near Lima and the south coast town of Chincha, known for its homegrown Afro-Peruvian music. A number of prominent Peruvians have African roots, including the 17th-century San Martin de Porres, international soccer star Teófilo Cubillas (b. 1949), and Grammy-winning singer Susana Baca (b. 1944).

Peru boasts the largest Asian population of any Latin American nation, with about 5 percent descended from Japanese and Chinese émigrés. Like elsewhere in the Americas, many Asians first arrived in Peru in the 19th century as contract laborers hired to work for the country's plantations and mines. Over the decades, they have

Eiffel's Architectural Influence on Peru

Although many talented Peruvian architects have burst onto the international scene in recent years, the architect with the greatest impact on the nation wasn't Peruvian at all. In the 1870s and 1880s, Frenchman Gustave Eiffel (1832–1923)—who excelled at designing metal structures— worked extensively with clients throughout South America. A full decade before he rose to worldwide fame with the completion of his iconic tower in Paris, Eiffel designed steel bridges, buildings, and fountains in the Amazon and Atacama. The main plazas in both Tacna and Moquegua bear his trademark fountains. Another one of his distinctive creations, the two-story Casa de Fierro (House of Iron), once the home of a rubber baron, still stands in Iquitos. But Eiffel left his most indelible mark on the desert city of Arequipa, where he designed the old Bolívar Bridge (near the train station) and the original San Camilo Market.

■ **Young, would-be sailors in a small fishing harbor near Pisco**

slowly but steadily prospered in business, education, the arts, and even politics. Elected to the Peruvian presidency in 1990, Lima-born Alberto Fujimori—the son of two Japanese immigrants—became the first person of East Asian heritage to lead a government in Latin America.

Around 90 percent of Peruvians identify themselves as Roman Catholics, although the Catholicism you find in the Andes, laced with shamanism and indigenous tradi- tions, differs substantially from what predominates among Euro-Peruvians along the coast. Increasing numbers of foreign missionaries—today the most active are Mormons, Seventh-Day Adventists, and Evangelical Christians—play a vital role in the religious mix of the Altiplano and Amazon forest, where many tribes adhere still to animist traditions.

Plantation Economy to Modern Capitalism

Like many developing nations, modern Peru revolves around a two-tier economy with feet in both the 19th and 21st centuries. The wealthy, and increasingly the middle class, live in much the same manner as their counterparts in other Latin American nations. They live in single-family homes or apartments in the city, own their own cars, send their children to private schools, work in white-collar jobs or have their own businesses. They watch American movies, wear European fashions, and can easily navigate their way around the Internet. Lower-class

Peruvians often live in poor rural villages or poverty-stricken shanties on the outskirts of big cities; they walk or ride public transit, work in fields or factories, and
their children don't get much of an education.

In the colonial era, Peru based its economy almost
entirely on plantation agriculture (in particular, sugar and
cotton) and mineral extraction, a trend that continued well
after independence. Despite moves toward industrialization
at the end of the 19th century, the country didn't really make
the leap into modern business and industry until the 1990s,
when government economic reforms sparked more foreign
investment as well as the development of a service sector and
manufacturing.

Five hundred years after the conquistadores fleeced the Inca
of their treasures, minerals remain the nation's most important
export item and foreign-exchange earner. The extraction and
shipment of copper, silver, gold, iron, zinc, molybdenum, and
lead account for more than half of all
Peruvian exports and attract around three and half billion dollars
a year to the economy.

> **Five hundred years after the conquistadores fleeced the Inca of their treasures, minerals remain the nation's most important export item and foreign-exchange earner.**

The largest and most successful mines operate in the southern desert and central
Andes, in places like Cerro Verde near Arequipa and Antamina near Huascarán,
where giant pits carved into the earth reach the mineral deposits.

Important ingredients of Peru's economic mix, the agriculture and fishing industries
not only feed the populace but also provide valuable exports. Although traditional com-
modities like cotton and sugar have declined over the past 20 years, other agricultural
exports have surged, especially coffee, fruits, and vegetables. The wide variety of farm

EXPERIENCE: Travel Peru, the Geo-savvy Way

In June 2007, the National Geographic
Society joined governmental and other
agencies in Peru in promoting a new kind
of authentic—and sustainable—travel experience called "geotourism." At dozens of
town-hall-style meetings, more than 2,000
Peruvians gathered to share their thoughts
about visiting the Sacred Valley and the
area around Machu Picchu. Their recommendations aim to transform the typical
tourist itinerary into a rich and varied
introduction to the region's culture, heritage, and natural environment while also
preserving or enhancing the well-being of
local residents and the character of the
area. So follow the path of the geotraveler
(consult the proposals for private tours in the
Sacred Valley of the Incas, www.national
geographic.com/expeditions/destinations/
south-america/private/private-expedition-
peru). Gaze up a terraced mountainside at
a mysteriously uncompleted citadel. Tour a
potato park in six highland villages to celebrate the diversity of the tuber tribe.
Then stop in nearby Pisaq, where a communal oven serves up empanadas filled
with—yes!—potatoes. Above Calca, relax in
the restored thermal baths. In Chinchero,
hear weaver Nilda Callañaupa tell that
wool dyed with natural colors is one of the
precious gifts of Pachamama, Mother
Earth. And, of course, see Machu Picchu.

products that Peru now ships overseas includes mangoes, asparagus, black-eyed peas, artichokes, tomatoes, and onions. The country's primary markets are other South American nations, but, since the passage of the U.S.-Peru Trade Promotion Agreement in 2006, the United States has started to purchase far more Peruvian produce.

For all its recent growth, however, commercial agriculture in Peru now pales in comparison to the flourishing tourist trade. American archaeologist Hiram Bingham unwittingly spawned Peru's tourism industry in 1911, when he rediscovered Machu Picchu. From that moment, embarking on a pilgrimage to the ancient mountaintop city has become de rigueur for anyone making a grand tour of South America. The mysterious Nazca Lines became another darling of global travelers, especially after the 1968 publication of Erich von Däniken's book, *Chariots of the Gods,* which attributes the mysterious desert artworks to prehistoric extraterrestrial visitors. And by the

■ **Former president Ollanta Humala came to power in 2011 after a long military career.**

1970s, avid backpackers from around the world had deemed the Inca Trail hiking route through the central Andes one of their favorites.

But tourism in Peru really didn't reach fever pitch until the end of the 20th century, when the variety of attractions available in Peru began to draw a large number of tourists eager for the chance to explore the Amazon, Andes, and ancient ruins without ever having to cross a border. At the same time, the advent of boutique hotels and rain forest lodges, better domestic air service, and a new luxury train through the Andes improved the country's developing tourism infrastructure. There's still plenty of room for growth however. A number of Peru's most compelling sights—Cañón del Colca and its resident condors, the ancient mud-brick cities of the north, the Huascarán glaciers, Lake Titicaca, and many of the best Amazon parks—continue to lie well off the main tourist trail.

> **After several centuries as a marginal player on the global scene, Peru has increased its influence in a number of fields.**

Peru's Global Profile

After several centuries as a marginal player on the global scene, Peru has increased its influence in a number of fields. These include politics, sports, and cuisine.

Since the early 1990s, a series of strong presidents—Alberto Fujimori, Alejandro Toledo, Alan García Pérez, and Ollanta Humala—has helped move Peru out of its traditional isolation and remake the nation into a well-respected economic and political power. Peru's most renowned diplomat, Javier Pérez de Cuéllar (1920-2020) served as Secretary General of the United Nations from 1982 to 1992, during which time he played a key role in negotiations over international conflicts in the Falkland Islands, Namibia, and Central America.

In the sports world, Teófilo Cubillas and Juan Varga are among more than a dozen homegrown soccer players who have played at the premier level for leading European club teams like Hamburg SV in the German Bundesliga and Atalanta in Italy's Serie A. Several world-class tennis players have also emerged from the prestigious Club de Tenis Las Terrazas in Miraflores, including 2008 French Open doubles champion Luis Horna.

Peruvians have even excelled at sports that are fairly rare in their own country. Edgar Prado, one of only a handful of jockeys who have won more than 6,000 career races, rode legendary Barbaro to victory at the 2006 Kentucky Derby and reached the winner's circle twice at the Belmont Stakes. Among the megastars on the global surf circuit, Lima's Sofía Mulánovich was the first South American of either gender to win a world surfing championship, reach number one in the world tour rankings, or get elected to the international Surfing Hall of Fame. ■

PERU'S MANY-SPLENDORED FESTIVALS

With an annual calendar that includes a heavy dose of religious rituals, harvest celebrations, and historical observances, it's a good bet that on any given day there is at least one festival unfolding somewhere across the country. The Catholic holidays, the most flamboyant of public celebrations, blend Spanish customs and indigenous custom into something uniquely Peruvian.

■ Traditional dancers perform in front of the Iglesia de la Compañía de Jesús, in Cusco.

Religious Celebrations

Taking its cue from other Latin American nations, Peru's pre-Lenten **Carnaval** has become increasingly boisterous, with parades and parties in just about every town and city. It also includes one practice not found anywhere else: water pranks. If you visit in the weeks before Easter, be prepared to get soaked!

The final week of Lent leading up to Easter Sunday is called **Semana Santa** (Holy Week). Although celebrated throughout the country, Holy Week is especially cherished in

the Andean cities of Cusco, Huaraz, Tarma, Puno, and especially Ayacucho, where music, street markets, horse racing events, and a running of the bulls complement the religious ceremonies. In Cusco, the **Fiesta del Señor de los Temblores,** a colorful Easter Monday procession and fireworks display dedicated to the Lord of the Earthquakes, takes place during this time. The holiday dates back to 1650 when the city was hit by a catastrophic earthquake. The festivities blend aspects of Catholic and ancient Inca tradition.

Between October 31 and November 2, the three-day holiday of **Día de los Muertos** (Day of the Dead) blends sacred and secular into a colorful new whole. Like elsewhere in Latin America, Peruvians flock to cemeteries to eat, drink, sing, and even sometimes sleep around the graves of their dearly departed. On the other hand American-style Halloween costumes and trick-or-treating are increasingly popular in Lima. October 31 also marks the **Día de la Canción Criolla,** a celebration of Creole music, with concerts and shows organized by Afro-Peruvian communities. If you visit the country during the Christmas period, do not miss Cusco on December 24, the largest handicraft fair in Peru is held in the local Plaza de Armas. Known as the **Santuranticuy** (Saints for Sale), the market specializes in intricately carved Nativity scenes. On Christmas, traditional festive drinks are hot chocolate and ponche, a powerful rum-based punch.

Peruvians commemorate their own **St. Rose of Lima**—the first person from the Western Hemisphere to be canonized as a saint—with a festival on August 30. Born Isabel Flores De Oliva in 1586, the Dominican nun demonstrated extreme devotion (including self-flagellation) and impressed everyone with her charitable work with the poor. The holiday is especially important in her hometown of Lima and surrounding villages. Lima, Arequipa, and Junín celebrate her feast day with Masses and processions.

Inca Holidays

At the opposite end of the Peruvian holiday spectrum is the Inca religious ceremony **Inti Raymi,** which takes place around the time of the winter solstice (*June 21*). Dedicated to the ancient sun god, the festival plays out amid the ruins of Sacsayhuamán, on the outskirts of Cusco, with folklore performances and a procession with thousands of participants clad in ancient Inca dress.

Another festival that harks back to ancient days, **Qoyllur Rit'i** occurs in late May or early June, when as many as 10,000 pilgrims make their way to the secluded Sinakara Valley near Cusco to pay tribute to Christ and the indigenous mountain gods (*apus*). Villages from all around the Peruvian high country send troupes of dancers and musicians to participate. The name derives from the local belief that a sacred snow star is buried inside nearby Mount Colquepunku; one of the highlights of the festival is an early morning trek to gather holy ice from the mountain.

EXPERIENCE: See the Winter Solstice in Iquitos

The San Juan Festival in Iquitos, the city's biggest annual party, honors St. John the Baptist, patron saint of the Amazon Basin. Celebrated over three days during the winter solstice (around June 21), the festivities begin with a ritual dip in the Amazon that both purifies the soul and cools the body from the jungle heat. According to tradition, anyone who bathes in the river at this time will be blessed with great health and good fortune for the rest of the year. Visitors are welcome if they wish to participate in the community ritual bath and enjoy the music and dance that animate the following stages of the celebration. Typical "jungle foods" are all the rage, especially *juanes*—spicy rice balls with chicken or fish wrapped in a dark-green leaf and served with yucca fries. Although the celebration draws its origin from the most ancient Christian traditions, aggregative events like snake dances, chain-saw demonstrations, and bikini contests give the San Juan Festival a thoroughly modern vibe.

| FOOD & DRINK

With a human history so tested by time, and with a geography and ecology diverse enough for the successful cultivation of many crops, Peru flaunts one of Latin America's most delectable and surprising culinary cultures.

According to the ancient Inca creation myth, the supreme being Viracocha sent his sons to Earth to teach the people how to sow crops. Since then, Peru, a land of culinary bounty and variety, has never wanted for food. From *cuy* (guinea pig) to ceviche (marinated raw seafood), from the pisco sour cocktail to bright yellow Inca Kola, much of what you find in Peru is unique to the country. But Peruvian menus also offer many familiar foods, in particular potatoes, corn, and chili peppers, all of which have roots, literally and figuratively, in the Andes.

Staples

Peru may have as many as 5,000 different types of potato, a plant that likely originated in the altiplano highlands around Lake Titicaca. Available large or small, and in various colors (brown, beige, red, purple, yellow), potatoes are served in a variety of ways, from baked, mashed, and pureed to modern French fries. Peruvians rarely eat their potatoes plain, preferring instead to cover them with cheese, *ají* chilis, garlic, onions, fried eggs, lime juice—or whatever else they can find.

Just as ubiquitous, corn probably originated in Mexico or Central America but has been cultivated in the Andes for several thousand years. Today it is one of the savory staples of the Peruvian diet and essential for making tamales. You can enjoy corn barbecued on the cob or smothered in butter and cheese. You might also see Peruvians snacking on fried kernels (*canchas*) or using them to make ceviche. Corn is also the main ingredient of *chicha*, a mildly alcoholic beverage drunk by indigenous peoples of the Andes.

Today's Dining

Peruvian meals usually center on meat, poultry, or fish. While the thought of barbecued guinea pig may not stimulate your taste buds, plenty of dishes do feature chicken, beef, or pork. One of the most popular is *lomo saltado*, a delicious beef stir-fry with garlic, onions, chilis, and potatoes. Other favorites include *pollo asado* (roast chicken) and *lechón* (roast pork). Because there are fewer cattle in Peru compared to other South American countries, the quality of Peruvian steaks normally doesn't approach the excellence of those you might find in Argentina.

Seafood is another matter, however. The upwelling of the Peru Current creates one of the Pacific's richest fishing grounds. The bounty includes tuna and sea bass (*corvina*), lobster and crab, oysters and mussels, octopus and squid, all baked, grilled, fried, poached, or used as the main ingredient of a ceviche seafood cocktail. Many of Lima's eateries specialize in seafood. The Peruvian craving for fish extends into the Andes and Amazon, where mountain trout and giant arapaima are delicacies.

Most of Peru's grapes are harvested and fermented into wine in the oasis-like Ica Valley in the southern desert. More than 60 wineries in the valley open their

■ **Dining outside is a pleasant option in Arequipa.**

cellar doors to visitors, but don't expect a posh Napa ambience even at the more established wineries like El Catador and Vista Alegre. The industry has been around for hundreds of years but has yet to reach the sophistication, in taste or in marketing, of the wine regions of Chile or Argentina.

Nevertheless, the local wines are worth sampling. The whites are heavy and sweet, similar to the white port of Portugal, while the reds are dry and a tad on the bitter side. Some Peruvian vintners also distill their grapes into sangria and pisco, a type of clear grape brandy that can be consumed either straight (for those with a cast-iron gullet) or used to form the basis of a pisco sour cocktail. Delicious, wicked, and quite addictive, pisco sour is Peru's national cocktail.

Regional & National Favorites

All of Peru's major geographic regions boast their own culinary specialties. Northern favorites include *pato a la naranja en almíbar* (honey-glazed duck in orange sauce) and *cabrito al horno* (roast goat). Among the local dishes in Arequipa and the southern desert you will find *ocopa arequipeña* (boiled potato slices in a slightly spicy cheese sauce) and *rocoto relleno* (stuffed bell peppers). Mountain cities like Ayacucho and Huancayo are renowned for their hearty stews and creative dishes made from animal organs, like *mollejitas* (chicken innards) and *anticuchos* (beef hearts). *Cuy* is largely confined to the Andes, where you might see guinea pigs roasting on spits on the side of the road.

Peru's Asian immigrants have added both pizzazz and variety to the nation's culinary heritage. A familiar sight in every city, *chifas* are restaurants that serve Chinese food, often cooked with traditional Latin American ingredients and methods. Lima alone may have more than 6,000 chifas, the greatest number of them concentrated in a century-old Chinatown centered around Calle Capón in the old town. While fried rice and *sopa wantán* are among the more popular dishes, chifa cuisine

Glossary of Peruvian Foods

Ají: chili peppers; found in many Peruvian dishes, although they do vary from mild to superhot

Alfajores: pastry dessert filled with honey or sweet milk caramel

Anticuchos: grilled beef hearts marinated in chili sauce

Ceviche: uncooked seafood marinated in lime juice and chili peppers and served with onions and cold potatoes

Charqui: dried meat, often alpaca or beef, sometimes llama

Chicharrón: fried pork

Chifa: Chinese food or restaurant

Chupe: traditional soup or stew

Corvina: white sea bass

Cuy: guinea pig

Lechón: roast pork

Lomo saltado: sautéed beef mixed with potatoes, onions, and/or chili

Mate: coca leaf tea, used to treat altitude sickness in the Andes

Pachamanca (Earth Pot): traditional Andean mix of meats, vegetables, and spices cooked underground

Pisco: grape brandy

Pulpo: octopus, popular along the Peruvian coast

Salsa criolla: hot sauce made from chili, onions, cilantro, and lime juice

Seco de cabrito: goat stew

Tamales: rolls prepared with a dough made from cornmeal stuffed with meat or other ingredients, served wrapped in banana leaves or corn cob.

Fish, the main ingredient in ceviche, can be purchased at Lima's Mercado Central.

also entails strange fusion food like *chi jau cuy* (Chinese-style guinea pig). With their natural passion for raw fish, Peruvians have also taken to Japanese food, introduced by the country's largest Asian group.

Ceviche—raw, marinated fish served with cold potatoes and corn on the cob—is undoubtedly the iconic Peruvian dish. The fish "cooks" in the marinade, made from lime and pepper. Often eaten for lunch along the coast, ceviche is usually made with ocean fish like *lenguado* (sole, flounder) or *corvina* (white sea bass), and it can be served along with a variety of seafood (squid, shrimp, octopus, shellfish). Trout is popular in the highlands, and in the Amazon, various river fish are used, especially the giant arapaima (also called the *paiche*).

Peru also boasts a wide variety of beverages. Launched in 1935, Inca Kola was allegedly based on an ancient drink flavored with the leaves of the lemon verbena shrub. Despite the advent of foreign sodas and local competition, the sweet yellow concoction remains Peru's most popular soft drink and a source of national pride. Peruvian beers likewise inspire fierce loyalty, and there is a long and spirited rivalry between the cities of Cusco and Arequipa over who brews the better beer—Cusqueña or Arequipeña. ∎

EXPERIENCE:
Learning to Cook in Peru

Incas del Peru (*José Galvez 400, Huancayo, tel 064/393–298, e-mail: incas delperu@gmail.com, www.incasdelperu. org*) can arrange a variety of cultural classes, ranging from Spanish language to cooking. **Peruvian Cooking Experience** (*tel 054/213–975, www. peruviancookingexperience.com*) offers two-hour classes in Arequipa. They also offer market tours to sample and buy ingredients.

LAND &
ENVIRONMENT

As the geographical linchpin of South America, Peru boasts just about every ecosystem for which the continent is known. From the High Andes and the Amazon rain forest to the Atacama Desert and the enigmatic altiplano, the nation magnificently unfolds as a remarkable mosaic of landscape, weather, and wildlife.

Stretching between the Pacific Ocean and the Amazon Basin, Peru is the third largest nation in South America (after Brazil and Argentina) and the sixth largest in the Western Hemisphere. About twice the size of Texas, it encompasses around 500,000 square miles (1.3 million sq km). More than 70 percent of Peru's entire population of 31 million lives in cities, leaving much of the countryside virtually uninhabited. Throughout the country, vast tracts of mountain, desert, and rain forest remain much as they were a hundred, or even a thousand, years ago.

For many generations, Peruvians have divided their land into four great geographic regions: the sierra (Andes mountains), the *selva* (Amazon Basin), the altiplano (high plains), and *la costa* (the desert-like strip along the coast).

Andes & Altiplano

The longest mountain range in South America, the Andes are the country's most prominent landscape feature and one of the cradles of ancient Peruvian civilization. A classic example of plate tectonics, the range was born around four million years ago, when the underwater Nazca plate began burrowing beneath the South America plate, lifting the crust to great heights.

North of Lima, mount Huascarán rises 22,206 feet (6,768 m) high in the Cordillera Blanca, a perpetually snowcapped peak that is Peru's highest point and bears the extra added distinction of being the world's highest tropical mountain. This range is also home to the rare and endangered tropical glacier. Meltwater from the glaciers has created hundreds of glacial lakes and lagoons around the base of the Cordillera Blanca.

Given its position astride one of the planet's most active geological zones, Peru is plagued by frequent earthquakes. A 7.7-magnitude quake struck northern Peru in 1970, killing around 70,000 people and still ranks as the most deadly natural disaster ever to

Quelccaya Ice Cap

The largest glaciated region in all the tropics—the Quelccaya Ice Cap—lies in south-central Peru. Located in the Cordillera Oriental about 100 miles (160 km) east of Cusco, the frozen cap once covered around 17 square miles (44 sq km). It has retreated appreciably over the past decade, probably because of global warming. A dramatic 180-foot (55 m) ice cliff marks one edge of Quelccaya with horizontal bands that clearly show centuries of snow and ice accumulation. The Qori Kalis Glacier grows out of the cap, its melt creating a pea green glacial lagoon.

■ **Beach dunes adorn Peru's north coast.**

hit the Western Hemisphere. In 2007, an 8.0-magnitude quake destroyed Paracas, Pisco, and other coastal towns south of Lima. Unlike other Andean nations, however, Peru has relatively few active volcanoes. Misti, the highest at 19,101 feet (5,822 m) last erupted in 1784.

In southern Peru, the Andes gradually give way to the altiplano, an area of high plains that flaunts its own haunting beauty. With an altitude of about 11,000 feet (3,300 m), this region bears its own distinct climate and vegetation. Although bright blue skies predominate, the weather is arid and windy, with temperatures that can plunge below freezing even in the height of summer. Short grasses and shrubs cover the ground.

Lake Titicaca—which Peru shares with Bolivia—is all that remains of a vast lake thought to have once covered the entire region. It is both the largest lake in South America and the world's highest navigable freshwater body, with steamboats and ferries plying a route between the Peruvian city of Puno and ports along the Bolivian shore.

Coastal Plain & Desert

The Peruvian coast stretches roughly 1,500 miles (2,414 km) between Ecuador and Chile. Arid, barren, and thoroughly forbidding, the coastal plain averages 10 to 100 miles (16–160 km) in width. Technically speaking, this is merely an extension of the Atacama Desert, but in Peru, this arid sliver running between the mountains and the ocean has its own name—the Sechura Desert. Often overlooked by travelers, the stunning desert offers forests of cardon and candelabra cactus, giant sand dunes that plunge into the sea, strange cryptogamic *lomas* vegetation fed by moisture from coastal fog, and ancient seabeds with the fossils of prehistoric sharks and whales.

■ Fishing in the Amazon Basin, downriver from Iquitos

EXPERIENCE: Climb Misti & Other Mountains

The best climbing is north near Huaraz, but don't dismiss the Arequipa region to the south. Loose volcanic soil makes the route to the top of Misti difficult, yet it is still the most popular with today's climbers. Once you reach the glaciated summit at 19,102 feet (5,822 m), you will need an ice axe and, possibly, crampons.

At 21,080 feet (6,425 m), **Coropuna** is the tallest mountain in southern Peru, and the four-day trek to its summit requires moderate climbing skills. Coropuna's guides require that you first prove yourself on 19,932-foot-high (6,075 m) **Chachani.** Other mountains in the area include 18,609-foot (5,672 m) **Ubinas,**

one of the easiest; **Mismi,** the 18,363-foot (5,597 m) source of the Amazon; and **Solimana,** one of the harder climbs at 20,068 feet (6,117 m).

Although Peru is perfect for beginning climbers, the high elevations, steep routes, poor footing, and severe, changeable weather conditions mean that everyone should take these ascents seriously. Good equipment is essential, and, since many routes are not clearly marked, hiring a guide is recommended. Guided climbs start around $80 per person, depending on the mountain, group size, and services such as transportation. (See Travelwise p. 307.)

Dozens of rivers wash snowmelt down from the Andes and across the coastal plain, creating pockets of fertility that supported Peru's earliest civilizations. These include the Rímac, the Chili, and the Moche. Only in the far north around Tumbes does the coastal desert finally peter out in favor of mangroves and dry tropical forest that provide a haven for many endemic bird species.

Peru's offshore islands are small and uninhabited yet rich with wildlife, including seabirds and sea lions. About 100 miles (160 km) offshore, the continental shelf ends abruptly with the Peru-Chile Trench, at 26,460 feet (8,065 m) below sea level, one of the deepest spots in all the world's oceans.

The Amazon

Every bit as wild and rugged as the rain forests of Brazil and Ecuador, the largely uninhabited Peruvian selva, or Amazon, takes up about a third of the country's land area. It slopes down gradually from the cool cloud forest on the eastern flank of the Andes to the sweltering low-altitude flatlands around Iquitos in the northeast.

> " Dozens of rivers wash snowmelt down from the Andes and across the coastal plain, creating pockets of fertility that supported Peru's earliest civilizations. "

Although typically considered a single region, the selva does contain two distinct subregions. In Peru, the southern Amazon tends to be drier, marked by foothills rambling down from the Andes and vast tracts of forest that rarely flood. Precipitation and runoff are much greater in the northern Amazon, where some areas lie underwater for six months or more. Today, many different factors—such as logging, mining, oil and gas exploration, hunting, ranching, and ever increasing human habitation—threaten the survival of the Amazon rain forest in Peru. Sanctuaries like Parque Nacional Manú and Reserva Nacional Pacaya-Samiria work to protect large swaths of this national treasure.

El Niño: The Stormy Christmas Mystery

One of the world's most talked about and least understood natural phenomena, El Niño (also called the Southern Oscillation) is an intermittent disruption of the weather and water conditions in the tropical eastern Pacific. Peruvian fishermen first detected the change in the 19th century, when they noticed a current of warm water flowing south from the Equator and blunting the much cooler Humboldt Current. Because it always arrived around Christmas time, they dubbed the mysterious current El Niño (The Little Boy) after the Christ Child.

In the 1980s, scientists discovered that the periodic oscillation impacted weather patterns all around the Pacific Basin, causing increased rainfall in Peru and the southern United States and drought conditions in Australia and Indonesia. El Niño can occur every year, or every three to four years, but no one has yet to determine its pattern, if indeed there is one, or even why it exists at all.

Climate

Determined by altitude and ocean currents, Peru's climate varies every bit as much as its landscapes. On any given day, you may find perfect weather along the Pacific shore, freezing temperatures and snow in the Andes, and torrential Amazonian downpours. All of which makes packing for a trip to Peru that much more difficult.

The famed Peru Current sweeps up the South American coast from the Antarctic, bringing with it cooler air along the shore and cold water that wells up to form rich fishing grounds. It also helps create the layer of mist or fog (garúa) that usually appears along the coast in winter (May–Nov.). Every few decades, the legendary El Niño Current (see sidebar above) unexpectedly drops down from the equatorial Pacific. Although the dreaded fog dissipates and rains fall on the coastal desert, the arrival of El Niño frequently causes flash floods and mudslides.

Latitude can affect Peru's highland weather, but in the Andes and altiplano, altitude is more important. Blue skies and panoramic views bless the sierra dry season (May–Oct.), which, as a result, is also the major tourist season. However, thin mountain air year-round makes sunscreen essential. The Amazon follows roughly the same pattern, but heat and humidity are a fact of life and precipitation can appear at any time.

Wildlife & Conservation

No other nation in South America has such an incredible range of wildlife, animals fit for jungle, mountain, desert, and coastal survival. The numbers are astounding: around 1,800 different bird species, more than 400 species of mammal, and more than 680 species of reptiles and amphibians (more than half of them are frogs). And their populations are often larger than elsewhere in the world.

Typical sierra animals include the giant condor, the llama, the spectacled bear, and the puma or mountain lion, all of which dwell in Parque Nacional Huascarán in the central Andes. Another denizen of this region is an extremely rare mountain deer called the north Andean huemul. Although more known for its adventure sports and stark desert scenery, Cañón del Colca in the south is a good place to spot condors, especially at the overlook called Cruz del Cóndor, where they like to float on the updrafts.

Coastal Peru presents a much different menagerie, creatures drawn to the area by an abundance of food produced by the upwelling of the Peru Current. Beneath the surface lurk whales, dolphins, sea turtles, hammerhead sharks, and manta rays.

Colonies of seabirds and marine mammals can be found at dozens of spots along the coast, but their greatest haven is the Reserva Nacional de Paracas near Pisco, an eclectic sanctuary that includes beaches and bays, coastal mountains, and sunbaked desert. The birdlife is astounding: thousands of cormorants, boobies, terns, petrels, gulls, and other seabirds; flights of pelicans soaring over the beach and flamingos stepping gingerly through salty lagoons behind the shore; egrets and herons and strange little feathery creatures like the burrowing owl. South American fur seals and sea lions monopolize many of the shoreline rocks and islands, but especially the Mirador de Lobos. Sea otters, desert foxes, and Humboldt penguins are also part of the Paracas wildlife mosaic.

The Amazon Rain Forest

Of course, the Amazon rain forest is Peru's great wildlife treasure. By occupying 40 percent of South America and containing an estimated 20 percent of the world's freshwater, the basin remains one of the Earth's great stores of biodiversity. Peru's slice of Amazonia represents about one-sixth of the total, second only to Brazil.

From top-of-the-food-chain predators like the jaguar and anaconda to more than two million insect species, the Amazon is home to an incredible array of living things. Peru counts more than 20 different species of monkey, including extremely rare species like the pigmy marmoset. Freshwater dolphins, the Amazon manatee, the caiman crocodile, and the notorious (but largely harmless) piranha are among the denizens of the region's rivers. About 120 endemic bird species have thus far been identified

La Isla de los Monos (Island of the Monkeys) is about one hour from Iquitos on the Amazon River.

in Peru, a majority of which call the Amazon home. And from bushmasters and coral snakes to the dreaded fer-de-lance, there are plenty of serpents that pack lethal venom.

Peru's most important rain forest reserve—and perhaps the best in all the Amazon— is Parque Nacional Manú. Accessible only by boat, the park and adjacent sanctuaries protect a huge chunk of native woods and wetlands. Reserva Nacional Pacaya-Samiria is another natural treasure, the world's largest protected flooded forest according to the Nature Conservancy. Sprawling across an alluvial plain between the Ríos Marañón and Ucayali, the park is often flooded for half the year. ■

PERU'S HISTORY

Peru has the greatest number of historic sites of any country in South America. These include not only the famed "lost city of the Incas" but also a bewildering array of cities, fortresses, towers, pyramids, tombs, and temples that date back more than 4,000 years *before* the Inca.

The Earliest Peoples

Although some believe that people may have occupied the region thousands of years earlier, the earliest evidence we have of a human presence in Peru lies in the caves at Pikimachay near Ayacucho, where archaeologists have discovered bone arrowheads that date to 12,000 B.C. As in other parts of the New World, the people who made them were nomadic hunter-gatherers.

Between 7000 and 4000 B.C., the nomads settled down. They learned how to plant and raise crops such as beans, squash, potatoes, chili beans, and corn. Simple agricultural techniques like weeding and watering kept them attached to one specific area year-round. They also domesticated llamas, alpacas, and guinea pigs. Fishing and shell collecting became important activities, and the cultivation of cotton soon followed.

During this era, now termed the Pre-ceramic Period, the earliest Peruvians had not yet developed pottery; they did their cooking over open fires or using hot rocks. By 2900 B.C., organized groups had begun to build burial structures and simple mud-brick pyramids, such as the ones recently excavated near the north coast at Caral, now considered the oldest city in the Americas.

The first Peruvians began to make pottery during the Initial or Formative Period (2000–1000 B.C.), starting with rudimentary pots and then developing elaborately sculpted and colored vessels. They also improved their irrigation systems, constructed the first agricultural terraces in the highlands, and built large and increasingly complex ceremonial sites along the coast. One of the most important, Sechín, dates back to around 1600 B.C. Built by a warlike people of whom we know little, Sechín is famous for its fierce, life-size carved reliefs of warriors eviscerating their enemies.

Cultural Expansion

After 1000 B.C., numerous Peruvian cultures appeared and developed rapidly, leaving us with massive monuments and intricately designed ceramics and textiles. The first of these was the Chavín (ca 1000–300 B.C.), whose fabulous temple in the Andes, Chavín de Huántar, features complex underground passages.

Termed a "horizon" society because its art and religion had such widespread influence over the civilizations that followed, the Chavín adorned their temples along much of the Peruvian coast with trademark feline carvings. They also decorated their temples, pots, and ornaments with images of deities that were part-human and part-animal. Because some of the featured animals live only in the Amazonian lowlands, historians have speculated that at least some of the Chavín people may have migrated to the coast from the rain forest.

■ **Machu Picchu—the most recognizable archaeological site in South America**

Metalworking (especially with gold, silver, and copper), and increasingly fine ceramic and textile production, gave rise to commerce, as people began trading cloth, pots, and other items between the coast and the Andes, and even into the Amazon. This trade helped fuel the spread of the Chavín cult, unifying disparate geographical zones for the first time. Over the next thousand years, several different cultures emerged contemporaneously and replaced the waning Chavín.

On the south coast, the Paracas culture produced what many consider the finest pre-Columbian textiles, including one with a record-breaking 398 threads per linear inch. The Nazca culture constructed the enigmatic Nazca Lines in the coastal desert while decorating their distinctive polychrome pottery with images of food items and human activity that lend historians valuable insight into daily life.

Meanwhile, along the north coast, the Moche erected massive temple mounds and pyramids near modern Trujillo and Chiclayo. At the most famous site, Sipán, archaeologists found an exceptionally rich tomb in 1987 that is now considered the most valuable burial site ever discovered in the Americas. The Moche crafted metal and ceramics with exceptionally fine techniques, and their pottery is considered the best in ancient America. Tens of thousands of their pots—sculpted into human faces, animals, plants, musical instruments, and a variety of human activities including agriculture, warfare, and sexual practices—can be seen in museums throughout Peru.

Peruvian Time Line

20,000–7000 B.C.	Early peoples
7000–4000 B.C.	Nomads & settlers
1000–300 B.C.	Chavín cult
300 B.C.–A.D. 200	Paracas culture, south coast
200 B.C.–A.D. 600	Nazca culture, coastal desert
100 B.C.–A.D. 850	Moche, northern coastal plains
A.D. 600–1100	Tiahuanaco & Wari cultures
A.D. 750–1375	Sicán culture, northern coastal areas
A.D. 800–1547	Chachapoyan culture
A.D. 1000–1400s	Chancay culture, central coast, & Colla culture, shores of Lake Titicaca
A.D. 900–1470	Chimu culture, Trujillo region
A.D. 1200–1533	Inca culture, from modern Chile to Ecuador, capital in Cusco
A.D. 1533–1821	Spanish rule
A.D. 1821–	Independent Peru

Highland Cultures

Around A.D. 600, two important highland cultures emerged. The religious Tiahuanaco erected important temples in the region around Lake Titicaca and developed extensive trade routes, while the warlike Wari culture, with its capital in the Ayacucho area, extended its influence throughout the central Andes and along the north coast. Unlike the relatively peaceful cultures that preceded them, the Wari waged military campaigns and conquered extensive regions through violence, leading directly to the collapse of the Moche culture.

By A.D. 1000, Wari influence had waned, replaced by several regional states. The best known, the coastal Chimu kingdom, flourished in the Trujillo area and left us with Chan Chan, the largest mud-brick city in the world. Farther north, the remnants of the Moche culture evolved into the pyramid-building Sicán society near Chiclayo, while to the south, near Lima, the Chancay people made exquisite textiles. In the highlands, the

Chachapoyan culture constructed the massive fort of Kuélap. Higher still, the Colla people built the idiosyncratic funerary towers of Sillustani near the shores of Lake Titicaca. Numerous other cultures existed all over Peru.

In hindsight it is not surprising how easily these divided regional societies were conquered by a more aggressive group, a small tribe from the Cusco area: the Inca. Once the military expansion was complete, the Inca Empire would become the largest kingdom in the New World.

The Inca Empire

The Inca trace their origins to about A.D. 1200, when Manco Capac (r. 1200–1230) founded Cusco (Q'osqo in the Quechua tongue) and became the first Inca (the Quechua word for "king" and eventually the name for the people as a whole). For more than two centuries, the Inca held sway over the Cusco area, fighting sporadic battles against their main enemy, the Chanka, and expanding only slowly.

The balance of power changed dramatically in 1438, when great numbers of Chanka attacked Cusco. The eighth Inca, Viracocha (r. 1410–1438), retreated, but his third son, Yupanqui, remained to fight what is chronicled as a desperate battle against the Chanka, one in which legend says the stones themselves rose up to battle alongside him. After an unexpected victory, Yupanqui changed his name to Pachacutec (Quechua for "changer of the world"), assumed the Inca throne (r. 1438–1471), and set out to conquer other Andean peoples. Along the way, he supervised the construction of some of Cusco's major Inca sites.

By the time of his death in 1471, Pachacutec had conquered most of the Peruvian Andes, joined in battle by his warrior son Túpac Yupanqui, who continued his father's expansionist traditions as the tenth Inca king (r. 1471–1493). During his reign, the Inca Empire grew to cover the territory from northern Ecuador to northern Chile and Bolivia, and from the Pacific coast into the Amazon lowlands.

The Inca needed barely half a century to grow into the greatest empire of the New World. However, they were as benevolent as they were fierce. Tribes that acquiesced quietly were treated well and welcomed into the sophisticated Inca social system. The victorious conquerors spread their sun-worshipping religion and Quechua language to the far corners of the empire but allowed less troublesome groups to enjoy some autonomy in language and clothing. Those who resisted found their spirits sorely tested by banishment to distant parts of the realm.

■ **A portrait of Manco Cápac**

A decimal-based administrative system helped the Inca maintain social and economic control over their vast territory. Ten workers would have one leader; ten leaders would have their own head, and so on. About 20,000 miles (32,000 km) of new roads ran through the empire, and a system of *chasquis* (runners) was developed for communication. The Inca strictly managed resources such as food and clothing and used knotted strings called *quipus* for accounting purposes.

Citizens were expected to work hard, but in return, they received adequate food and clothing. They attended elaborate fiestas at regular intervals, during which plentiful amounts of food and *chicha* (maize beer) were consumed. Sayings like "*Ama shua, Ama LL'ulla, Ama Q'el*"—"Don't steal, don't lie, don't be lazy" encouraged good citizenship.

Huayna Capac (r. 1493–1525) solidified the empire's hold of Ecuador and added parts of Chile and Argentina. But upon his death from smallpox, a disease brought by the Europeans, the Inca Empire divided between his two sons— Atahualpa (1502–1533) in the north and Huáscar (1503–1532) in the south. The bloody civil war that followed severely weakened the empire and made it vulnerable to the attacks by foreign invaders who were about to appear from the north.

The Legendary Founding of Cusco

A popular Peruvian legend has it that Manco Capac, the first Inca, emerged from Lake Titicaca and that the sun god Inti entrusted him with a gold staff. Even today, Puno Festival (November 5) celebrates a ceremony in which Manco Capac arrives by raft. Accompanied by his sister-wife Mama Ocllo and his brothers, Manco Capac began searching for the *q'osqo* (navel of the world), where the Earth would swallow the gold staff. At the place where this finally happened, in a valley in the high Andes, Manco founded Cusco as the capital of the Inca civilization.

Conquest

It is difficult to fathom what the Inca must have thought about the sudden arrival of the Spanish in 1532, an alien invasion force that not only looked and acted like nothing the Inca had ever seen before, but who also fought with fearsome weapons of previously unimaginable fury and levels of destructiveness.

Venturing down the west coast of South America on his third journey to the New World, Francisco Pizarro (ca 1471–1541) marched his small but eager band of conquistadores into what is now northern Peru. Turning inland, Pizarro and his troops made their way to Cajamarca, where they arranged an audience with Atahualpa, who had recently become supreme leader of the Inca realm in the aftermath of the civil war against his brother Huáscar.

Atahualpa believed he had no reason to fear the Spaniards; they had shown no previous hostility, and after all, he was the leader of the greatest empire—and army— ever seen in South America. But his overconfidence played right into Pizarro's hands. The Spaniards ambushed the Inca party and took Atahualpa hostage, insisting they would release the emperor only after the Inca had paid a huge ransom. According to legend, the amount of gold that eventually arrived in Cajamarca was enough to fill the room in which the emperor was held captive. But fearing a vicious Inca counterattack if Atahualpa was released, Pizarro ordered the emperor's execution.

The Spaniards had little trouble subduing the rest of Peru and marched south to Cusco, where they installed a puppet emperor. Greed plagued them, however. The

Pizarro capturing the last Inca emperor, Atahualpa, in a painting by John Everett Millais (1845)

ongoing feud amongst the various conquistador factions eventually resulted in Pizarro's murder at the hands of Spanish assassins in 1541. By then the Spaniards had already established their own capital at Lima (1535), a coastal location that offered a much milder climate than the high Andes. The favorable new city had a constant source of freshwater and a fine natural harbor that allowed for easy communication with Spanish bases in Panama. Within a few decades of its founding, the thriving seaport had become the seat of the Spanish viceroy and the most important European settlement in all of South America, a city of imposing palaces and churches and cobblestone streets flanked by colonial mansions.

The tumultuous struggle between the European invaders and indigenous groups continued inland for another century. What remained of the Inca elite fled into the jungle on the eastern side of the Andes, where they established a new military and religious center at Vilcabamba. The rebel state endured until the 1570s, when the ruthless viceroy Francisco Toledo sent an army to capture the mountaintop retreat. Dynamic rebel leader Túpac Amaru and his generals fled into the Amazon, but were eventually captured and executed in 1572, an event which modern historians use to mark the end of the Inca Empire.

Colonialism

By the close of the 16th century, Peru had evolved into one of the crown jewels of the Americas, a land dominated by its new European masters that sent a vast amount of wealth back to the motherland. As elsewhere in the New World, the twin pillars of early Spanish rule were the institutions of *encomienda* and *reducciones.*

The policy of encomienda rewarded the conquistadores by granting them land and trusteeship over the indigenous peoples who occupied that land. As a reward for keeping the peace and converting the Inca to Christianity, the *encomenderos* could tax their indigenous tenants and force them to work, although ultimately, the Spanish crown retained ownership. The practice quickly evolved into a brutal feudal system in which the indigenous peoples were little more than slaves.

Attempting to moderate the abuses of encomienda, the crown established a completely different system called reducciones, the forced resettlement of rural indigenous populations to newly established European-style towns and cities. The new policy placed the indigenous peoples under the guardianship of the local Catholic Church, but it, too, led to widespread suffering and abuse. Some estimate that more than one million indigenous Peruvians were forced off their ancestral lands. Millions more probably died from widespread disease that followed the arrival of the conquistadores. As a result, the Spaniards began to import slaves from Africa to supplement the dwindling labor pool.

By the end of the 17th century, the first generation of Peruvian-born Spanish (creoles), as well as mestizos (people of mixed blood), dominated Lima and other lowland cities. Wealthy and often well educated, they formed the core of a thriving colonial society that valued fine art, good food, and deep faith. Like other elites in the Americas, they were inspired by the liberal philosophical and intellectual ideas of Enlightenment Europe. The successful rebellion in Britain's American Colonies and the revolution that overthrew the French monarchy set the stage for similar political upheaval in Peru.

Independence

Spanish possessions in the New World got the spark they needed in 1808, when Napoleon invaded Spain. After three centuries of answering to a higher authority on the other side of the globe, Peru and the other colonies found themselves suddenly on their own politically, economically, and to some extent, culturally.

Peruvian nationalism had been growing for some time and, along with general discontent over heavy-handed Spanish colonial rule, had set the tone for the birth of an independence movement that worked hand in hand with similar movements in Argentina, Chile, and Colombia. However, royalist sentiment also remained strong, especially in Lima. As a result, Peru achieved emancipation only after the invasion of rebel armies from elsewhere in South America. After liberating his native Argentina and then Chile from Spanish control, José de San Martín (1778–1850) came ashore with his army at Paracas in 1819 and initiated Peru's war for independence. Two years later, after taking Lima without firing a shot and sending the royalist armies retreating into the Andes, San Martín proclaimed Peru's independence.

The civil war continued for another two years. It wasn't until Simón Bolívar (1783–1830) and Antonio Sucre (1795–1830) led another army of liberation south from Colombia that the Spanish were permanently routed. The final battle took place at Ayacucho in December 1824. Despite a resounding defeat, the Spaniards refused to recognize Peru's independence. (Four decades later, they launched an ill-fated attempt to regain the colony, an affair that ended with another humiliating Spanish defeat at the Battle of Callao.)

Bolívar stepped into the power vacuum created by the end of Spanish rule and assumed the presidency, dragging Peru into his Andean Confederation (which also included Colombia, Venezuela, Ecuador, and Bolivia). After several years of dictatorial rule, the famed liberator was forced into exile and his constitution revoked. In his wake followed Gen. Andrés de Santa Cruz (1792–1865), the first in a long line of military rulers and juntas that would dominate Peruvian government for more than a century. Reflecting the political turmoil that plagued much of Latin America during this period, the caudillos, as they were called, were sometimes elected but more often seized power via a coup d'état.

■ The red and white Peruvian flag was formally adopted in 1825.

Here and there emerged capable and progressive rulers, such as Gen. Ramón Castilla (1797–1867), elected to the presidency four times between 1844 and 1863. In addition to introducing a new, moderate constitution, Castilla emancipated the slaves and abolished lingering vestiges of the encomienda system. During the Castilla era, Peru experienced buoyant economic growth, with booming exports of sugar, cotton, and guano-based fertilizer.

Another natural resource—nitrate deposits in the Atacama Desert—sparked the War of the Pacific (1879–1883) that pitted Peru and its ally Bolivia against the far superior military might of Chile. Victorious on land and sea, the Chileans annexed part of southern Peru, and all of coastal Bolivia, and occupied Lima for two years. The war ended with the Treaty of Anco but to this day remains a sore point between Peru and Chile.

The long war bankrupted Peru. British financiers assumed the nation's $50 million foreign debt in return for control over transportation and natural resources. London-based Peruvian Corp ran the nation's railroad lines and lake ferry service, as well as the guano industry. With a military dictator in Lima and an economy controlled by foreigners, Peru entered the 20th century little advanced beyond the days of Spanish colonial rule.

The 20th Century

Despite its long and glorious history and the manifest wealth of its land, Peru entered the 20th century as one of the world's least progressive independent nations. Elsewhere, however, military *juntas* failed to prevent capitalism from flourishing. As a matter of fact, while Argentina, Brazil, Chile, and Venezuela all prospered between the turn of the century and the 1950s, Peru found itself mired in economic and political stagnation.

U.S. investment and influence gradually supplanted British clout, but a strongman still sat in the presidential palace and a handful of wealthy monopolized business and industry. Elected president in 1908, sugar baron Augusto Leguía (1863–1932) was the first member of the bourgeoisie to hold the nation's highest office. Under his influence, the vast majority of Peruvians—especially the indigenous population—had little or no chance to rise above abject poverty. And Peru found itself virtually isolated from global affairs, a nation largely forgotten and forsaken.

The Tello Obelisk is one of the most important discoveries in Peruvian archeology.

Leguía was finally deposed in 1930, just as the Great Depression came crashing down, ending whatever chance the country had of digging itself out of the mire. Indigenous revolts in the jungle, labor unrest in the cities, and a peasant revolt in the north that was bloodily suppressed by the military junta only added to Peru's woes.

One thing did prosper in Peru during the first half of the 20th century: archaeology. When Yale professor Hiram Bingham (1875–1956) discovered the "lost" city of Machu Picchu in 1911, he set off a wave of exploration in the region. In the mid 1920s, Alfred Kroeber (1876–1960) of the University of California made the first survey of the Túcume pyramids, and another archaeologist discovered the Nazca Lines while flying over the coastal desert south of Lima in 1927. Four years later, another aerial survey uncovered the Great Wall of Peru near Chimbote, and Peruvian archaeologist Julio C. Tello (1880–1947) discovered the ancient city of Sechín Alto in 1937.

With no allegiance to either side and little in the way of strategic resources, Peru stood on the sidelines during World War II but was affected nonetheless. The U.S. government funded the construction of the Pan American Highway (Panamericana) down the west coast of South America as a means to convey troops and supplies. As a result, many Peruvian towns and cities were connected by highway for the first time, a revolutionary step in the development of modern communications and commerce.

Elected to the presidency in 1963, Fernando Belaúnde (1912–2002) introduced far-reaching social and economic changes such as the dissolution of the haciendas that had dominated rural Peru since colonial times. Although he was deposed in 1968, his reforms continued under a military junta. Since 1980, when Belaunde returned from exile to serve a second term, Peru has been governed by fairly elected civilian leaders and has become one of the Western Hemisphere's more stable democracies.

Poverty & Strife

Despite political stability, chronic rural poverty, combined with hardships caused by natural disasters such as the 1970 violent earthquake, provoked more social unrest and rebellion. For much of the 1980s, leftist groups like the Movimiento Revolutionario Tupac Amaru (MRTA) and Sendero Luminoso (Shining Path) besieged the government and business community. Their message of class warfare resonated with Peru's indigenous majority, who saw armed conflict as the only way to close the economic gap with the European minority. Almost 70,000 civilians died in atrocities committed during the Terror Years.

When Alberto Fujimori (b. 1938) became president in 1990, the state took a more proactive stance against the guerillas and eventually crippled both groups. Fujimori modernized the economy and attracted foreign investment before accusations of human rights abuses and corruption sent him into exile in 2000; he later returned, was tried, and is now serving a 25-year prison sentence. In 2001, Alejandro Toledo (b. 1946) became the first indigenous president and had an unprogressive term as head of state. In 2006, Alan García Pérez (b. 1949) returned to the presidency after an economically disastrous first term from 1985 to 1990. His second term featured controversial mineral rights policies, which led to strikes and deadly demonstrations. Former army officer Ollanta Humala (b. 1962) was elected to the presidency in 2011 and he also faced criticism about the country's mining policy. In 2016, Pedro Pablo Kuczynski defeated Keiko Fujimori, daughter of the former president, who was granted pardon in 2017. In March 2018, Kuczynski was forced to resign after allegations of exchanging votes for money and favors and was succeeded by his deputy, Martín Viczarra. ∎

THE ARTS

While the history of art in Peru stretches back centuries to the ancient cultures of the Andes and coastal plains, today's artists are far from being stuck in the past. Drawing on European traditions as well as the latest trends, Peruvian painters, writers, filmmakers, and musicians have created a national scene that is beginning to make some international noise.

Art

From indigenous ceramics and weaving to European-style painting and sculpture, Peruvian art takes many different forms. Although not much of its art remains, one of the earliest and most influential civilizations was the Chavín, which flourished in the northern Andes from about 1000 to 300 B.C. Its abstract human forms and geometric motifs heavily influenced 20th-century European artists, particularly Pablo Picasso, who said, "Of all the ancient civilizations that I admire, Chavín amazes me the most."

> **Escuela Cusqueña is now regarded as the first artistic movement to appear in the New World after the European conquest.**

Among other early masters, the Moche in the northern desert valleys produced an incredible array of pottery between 100 B.C. and A.D. 850, much of it modeled on actual humans. Noted for their erotic ceramics, the Moche were also skilled at metalwork and weaving, as the royal tombs at Sipán reveal.

The Inca excelled at architecture and industry but were not innovative artists and relied primarily on methods and motifs learned from the societies they conquered. As a result, because of them we know about many older traditions, such as the intricate handles and semicircular blades of ceremonial *tumi* knives.

After the Spanish conquest, indigenous and European artistic traditions coalesced in a uniquely Peruvian style called Escuela Cusqueña or the Cusco school. Escuela Cusqueña is now regarded as the first artistic movement to appear in the New World after the European conquest. In subject matter, Cusqueña art is predominantly European and Catholic but heavily influenced visually by Andean elements, including a lack of perspective, brighter than usual colors, and the appearance of native flora and fauna.

The Cusqueña masterpieces that decorate Cusco Cathedral demonstrate a fusion of Iberian and Inca artistic traditions. In amongst the Catholic saints carved into the huge entrance doors is a puma head. And if you look closely at "The Last Supper" by Marcos Zapata (1710–1773), you will notice that Jesus and his apostles have been served *cuy.*

The post independence era suffered from a certain lack of artistic creativity. The Catholic Church continued to patronize painters and sculptors, but the religious artists of the 19th century relied mostly on old baroque traditions rather than break new ground. However, new-wave European movements such as Romanticism did find their way into the secular art scene. Generally regarded as the greatest Peruvian painter of

■ Weaving is one of Peru's national arts.

this period, Ignacio Merino (1817–1876) is perhaps best known for his series on the life of Christopher Columbus. He also painted romantic landscapes and many vibrant portraits.

Peruvian art took a sharp turn toward the modern in 1919, when the National Academy of Arts was founded in Lima. Over the next half century, many of the country's leading artists either learned their craft or taught at the school, among them Carlos Quizpez Asin (1900–1983), whose work spanned cubism to magic realism, portraitist Daniel Hernández Morrillo (1856–1932), and José Sabogal (1888–1956), whose moody surrealistic portraits helped inspire the country's modern indigenous art movement.

Literature

Spanish accounts of discovery and conquest, as well as nonfiction works on local life and culture, dominated early colonial writing in Peru. One of the era's most notable works, *El primer nueva corónica y buen gobierno* (*The First New Chronicle and Good Government*) details the oppression of indigenous peoples and the destruction of local culture by corrupt colonial authorities. Written over a 15-year period by Felipe Guaman Poma de Ayala (1534–1615), an indigenous Peruvian, this powerful 17th-century manuscript began life as a lengthy and comprehensive letter (totaling nearly 1,200 pages) to the king of Spain.

> **Spanish accounts of discovery and conquest, as well as nonfiction works on local life and culture, dominated early colonial writing in Peru.**

By the time of independence in the 19th century, European-style neoclassical writing and Romanticism were all the rage in Lima and other cities. But Peru didn't produce its first bard of global renown until the advent of Cesar Vallejo (1892–1938), an avant-garde author who clashed with the establishment and later sought exile in Europe. The best known writer of the postwar period was Julio Ramón Ribeyro (1929–1994), who laced his gritty tales of everyday Peruvian life with the pointed irony and humor popular throughout Latin America at the time. Winner of the Juan Rulfo Prize for Latin American and Caribbean literature, the prolific Ribeyro worked in many different forms, including short story, novel, play, and essay. Among his few works translated into English is *Chronicle of San Gabriel* (1960).

Ribeyro and other urban realists set the tone for the emergence of Mario Vargas Llosa (see sidebar opposite) and other modern Peruvian authors who have found an audience at home and abroad. Jaime Bayly (b. 1965) is perhaps the nation's best known contemporary author. His first novel, *No se lo digas a nadie* (1994), and a later work, *La mujer de mi hermano* (2002), were both made into films.

Foreign authors have also found food for thought in Peru. Hiram Bingham kicked off the trend when he penned *Lost City of the Incas* after his rediscovery of Machu Picchu in 1911. Published right after World War II, *The Condor and the Cows* by Christopher Isherwood is an entertaining and evocative account of traveling through Peru in the late 1940s. Peter Mathiessen's classic *At Play in the Fields of the Lord* could be the best book ever written about modern missionaries in the Amazon, a fictional (yet highly realistic) account of the challenges faced by several American families in the rain forest. *The Celestine Prophecy,* James Redfield's New Age blockbuster, was also largely set in Peru.

Cinema

In days past, few outside Peru saw any of the nation's films. Today, however, Peru's small but dynamic film industry is starting to burst on to the international scene, the result of a new generation of talented young directors coming out of television (especially the *telenovela* or soap opera), the increasing sophistication and lower cost of video cameras, and cable or satellite outlets like HBO Latino that push for innovative and interesting Spanish-language programming.

The early classics of Peruvian cinema included silent black-and-white films like *Negocio al agua* (1913) and *Luis Pardo* (1927), about the Chilean sea captain who helped rescue Ernest Shackleton's men from the Antarctic. Even though the studios in Lima continued

Peru's Living Legend—Mario Vargas Llosa

Born in 1936 in the southern city of Arequipa, Mario Vargas Llosa stands as one of the lions of modern Latin American literature alongside Colombia's Gabriel García Márquez and Mexico's Carlos Fuentes. Having made the transition from pen to politics, he has had an impact far beyond literature and may be the world's best known Peruvian.

The politics is a natural outgrowth of his starkly realistic writing, novels and essays that often dwell on the plight of ordinary people and the trials and tribulations of everyday life. Vargas Llosa's formative years were spent in the northern coastal city of Piuru, where he attended school and worked as a journalist.

La ciudad y los perros (titled *The Time of the Hero* in English), his first novel, was published in 1963 and set the tone for his later life, a work that transformed him into a literary star and a thorn in the side of the generals who dominated politics at that time. His 1965 novel, *La casa verde* (*The Green House*), was a critical and financial success throughout Latin America.

Vargas Llosa's writing has always had an underlying social or political theme, but he didn't enter active politics until the 1980s when he helped found the Liberty Movement political party. He lost the 1990 presidential election to Alberto Fujimori. In recent years he has split his time between homes in London and Lima.

to make movies over the following years, Peru's first great director didn't emerge until the 1960s. Born in New York City, Armando Robles Godoy (1923–2010) moved to Peru at the age of ten and became the nation's greatest filmmaker. Starting with *Ganarás el pan* (1964), Godoy produced a string of movies that were well received both at home and abroad. His stories often deal with the daily struggle between ordinary people and the environment, both urban and rustic. Released in 1970, *La muralla verde* (*The Green Wall*), one of his biggest hits, gives a fictionalized account of Godoy's own attempt to homestead the Amazon rain forest; it proved his biggest overseas hit. Another leading director, Francisco José Lombardi (b. 1947), has made a name for himself by adapting popular Peruvian novels like *No se lo digas a nadie* (1998) by Jaime Bayly and Mario Vargas Llosa's *Pantaleón y las visitadores* (1999). In 1991, Lombardi won a Goya (Spain's version of the Oscar) for *Caídos del cielo*.

Leading the charge into the 21st century is a whole new generation of filmmakers like Claudia Llosa (b. 1976), who in 2006 transformed the magic realism of *Madeinusa*, in which an urban sophisticate encounters rural tradition in the Cordillera Blanca, into a

■ **The Arequipa Cathedral faces onto Plaza de Armas.**

minor international hit. Peru has also ventured down the road of 3D animation in recent years with movies like *Piratas en el Callao* (2005), about a 17th-century Peruvian lad who battles buccaneers off the coast of Lima's seaport.

Architecture

As the birthplace of so many ancient civilizations, Peru served as one of the key architectural fulcrums of the Western Hemisphere. Drawing mostly from the materials at hand—mud brick along the coast and stone in the Andes—the first Peruvian builders and their workers built impressive cities, of which it is still possible to admire the ruins. The vast metropolis of Túcume contains 26 pyramids, including the towering Huaca Larga, one of the largest adobe structures in Peru and one of the biggest on the planet. Rising beside the Panamericana, the ceremonial city was erected by the Sicán people between A.D. 800 and 1200. Although impressive, few of Túcume's architectural details actually survive. Luckier is Chan Chan, where geometric patterns, zoomorphic figures, and friezes fashioned nearly a thousand years ago adorn the adobe walls of various palaces and temples. Located on the outskirts of Trujillo, Chan Chan was built by the Chimu civilization between 1100 and 1470.

The Inca wrote their architectural history in stone, a substance not as pliable as mud brick but certainly more enduring. The magnum opus of Inca structural design and engineering, the incredible mountaintop sanctuary of Machu Picchu features stone terraces, temples, and even an ancient astronomical observatory. But it's certainly far from being the only Inca masterpiece. Even more impressive is the stonework of the ancient fortress of Sacsayhuamán near Cusco, where the walls are almost like a jigsaw puzzle, made of interlocking stones of different sizes and shapes with smooth facades and rounded corners. Historians still do not quite understand how the Inca craftsmen managed to get the stones to fit together so perfectly.

More Inca buildings would still survive in Cusco today if the conquistadores hadn't been so proactive about "borrowing" the Inca stonework for their own constructions. Although we should definitely mourn the loss, we shouldn't lose sight of the equally stunning results of Spanish scavenging. Erected over more than a hundred years spanning the 16th and 17th centuries, Cusco Cathedral—an over-the-top church designed to intimidate and impress—blends Gothic, Renaissance, and baroque elements. In the desert oasis city of Arequipa, where Moorish designs influenced the colonial architecture, stand buildings with brickwork arches and whitewashed domes, such as the Monasterio de Santa Catalina and Santo Domingo church.

By the early 1800s, the European-inspired neoclassical style known as republican design came to dominate the Peruvian architectural scene. Later, a homegrown Spanish colonial revival produced structures like the Palacio Municipal (City Hall), Palacio de Gobierno (President's Palace), and Palacio Arzobispal (Archbishop's residence) around the Plaza de Armas in Lima. Trujillo boasts some of the finest surviving examples of republican architecture, like the blue pastel Casa Urquiaga, where Simón Bolívar once resided.

Peru's postmodern architectural wonders are mostly limited to Lima. One of the city's more intriguing structures, the Tanatorio Chapel and Crematorium inside the Jardín de la Paz cemetery, a startling glass-and-concrete design, recalls the work of the legendary American architect Louis Kahn.

Locally born architect Bernardo Fort-Brescia (b. 1951), who cofounded the cutting-edge Arquitectonica design firm in Miami, created several of Lima's most modern and highest structures. Conceived of as an abstract version of a traditional Spanish colonial courtyard building, the Banco de Crédito headquarters boasts Inca ruins inside its elliptical glass-block atrium. Fort-Brescia also helped create the Lima Marriott Hotel in Miraflores, which resembles a giant green-glass arch overlooking the sea.

Peru's Best Art Museums

Peru boasts a number of incredible art collections, including the ancient treasures at the new **Museo Tumbas Reales de Sipán** in Lambayeque (see pp. 211, 215).

Lima's **Museo Larco** (see p. 72)—housed in an 18th-century Spanish colonial palace—boasts perhaps the country's finest collection of pre-Columbian art and artifacts, spanning everything from gold jewelry to erotic ceramics. Unlike most museums, this one lets visitors explore the pieces kept in the storeroom.

The nuns of Cusco's **Convento de Santa Catalina** (see pp. 127–128) oversee a superb collection of painting and sculpture from the Escuela Cusqueña. Other examples are displayed at the nearby **Museo de Arte Religioso** in the old archbishop's palace, where a noteworthy painting of arrow-filled San Sebastián includes Inca onlookers.

The **Museo de Arte de Lima** (see pp. 66–67) has Peru's most eclectic art collection. Its artworks range from pre-Columbian and Spanish colonial to republican and contemporary works of the 20th century.

Once the nation's tallest, the wedge-shaped Cho-
cavento Tower office building rises 351 feet (107 m) high.
But the 30-story Westin Libertador Hotel, in the capital's
swank San Isidro District, shattered that record at 394
feet (120 m) in 2010, before it, in turn, was topped by
the 433-foot (132 m) Edificio Banco Continental in 2011.

But Peru's most dramatic 21st-century building actually lies hundreds of miles north of the capital, in the
heart of one of the ancient architectural zones. Inspired
by the design of ancient Moche pyramids, the Museo
Tumbas Reales de Sipán in Lambayeque, a modern
abstract pyramid, glistens bloodred beneath the desert
sun.

Music

Nothing evokes the enduring culture of the Andes
more than the sound of Peruvian flute-and-drum music,
which ranks with Argentine tango and Brazilian samba
as one of the iconic sounds of South America. Although
no one knows for certain when the genre originated,
archaeologists have discovered examples of ancient
flutes and drums in more than 2,000-year-old tombs,
making this one of the oldest musical traditions in the
Americas, if not in the entire world.

The most emblematic instrument is the *zampoña* or
siku, a single or double-rowed panpipe. In more modern
times, the *charango* (a ten-stringed lute or mandolin
fashioned from an armadillo shell) has rounded out the ensemble. There's nothing quite like hearing the unmistakable sound of flute-and-drum music played well
at traditional village fairs and festivals. But if that's not possible, any old *peña* (folk
club) will usually do.

Five Favorite Peruvian Music Collections

*Afro-Peruvian Classics—The Soul of Black
Peru* (Luaka Bop) An exceptional compila-
tion of Andean-influenced interpreta-
tions of Afro-Peruvian music.

Mountain Music of Peru (2 vols., Smithson-
ian Folkways) Features *huaynos*, Andean
folk songs with pre-Columbian roots,
played with *zampoñas* (panpipes), *quenas*
(bamboo flutes), drums, and other traditional instruments.

Peru, Kingdom of the Sun: The Inca Heritage
(Nonesuch Explorer) Live field recordings
of highland musicians.

Susana Baca (Luaka Bop) by Susana Baca.
The finest Afro-Peruvian singer working
today, she often tours the United States.

The Rough Guide to Music of the Andes
(World Music Network) A more contemporary collection of Andean music.

In Arequipa the restaurant Dejavu draws in both locals and tourists.

Peru's musical heritage has been hard won. Indigenous music had to weather the brutal Spanish conquest and the imposition of European music into both sacred and secular settings. It then had to brave the arrival of various musical forms from outside Peru in the 20th century. Yet somehow the flute-and-drum tradition survived, helped along by roving bands of Peruvian musicians who carried the music overseas to clubs and street corners, from Tokyo to Paris. Popular songs like "El Cóndor Pasa," written in 1913 by Peruvian composer Daniel Alomía Robles (1871–1942), and then later covered by Western artists as diverse at Perry Como and Simon and Garfunkel, also kept this distinctive Andean style of folk music alive.

Spanish colonial folk music has passed into the 21st century as *música criolla,* a spirited genre that combines European, Andean, and African traditions into something new but thoroughly Peruvian. Developed mainly in the coastal cities, música criolla has several distinct subgenres, including a Peruvian style of blues called *landó* and the fast-paced *polquita,* which traces its origins to the polka dances of bygone immigrants from Europe. Peru's small but influential African population also developed its own musical form, the wildly popular *música negra* found along the coast. While salsa and other Latin genres enjoy widespread popularity in Peru, there is a lively modern rock scene led by the group Libido, which has earned a large fan base both at home and overseas. ∎

The nation's capital—a place to visit for its nightlife, classic and modern art, recreation, fine cuisine, and pre-Inca sites

LIMA & ENVIRONS

Lima high-rises along the Pacific coast

LIMA & ENVIRONS

Almost a third of Peru's population lives in metropolitan Lima, the nation's huge and bustling capital. A historic and vibrant city, Lima is home to superb colonial architecture, world-class but still largely unknown cuisine, scintillating nightlife, exceptional museums, and even some pre-Inca archaeological sites.

Lima has a decidedly atypical climate for being a tropical city located 505 feet (154 m) above sea level and at a latitude 12 degrees south of the Equator. From June to August, in fact, the cold Humboldt Current goes up from Antarctica bringing with it a gray and dense haze, the *garúa,* which remains suspended over the central coastal areas of Peru. This particular climatic condition causes high humidity and causes temperatures to drop in the winter. From the end of December to March, the warmer central Pacific current pushes the cold current south: The *garúa* thins out, the sun reappears, the temperature rises, and the *limeños,* the inhabitants of Lima, pour onto the beaches. For most of the year, in any case, temperatures remain between 59°F and 77°F (15–25°C), with little rainfall if the phenomenon of *garúa* is excluded. The urban area of the city of Lima has almost nine million inhabitants, more than ten

million taking into account the metropolitan area, suffering from overcrowding and poverty. Millions of people, many of them migrant workers, crowd into the city's *pueblos jóvenes* (young towns), neighborhoods that began with no electricity or running water and developed slowly over time.

Yet Lima, once thought of as a dreary, gray city that travelers should pass over quickly, continues to improve, cultivating a reputation for culture, cuisine, and nightlife that are second to none in Peru.

Today, most travelers to Lima enjoy downtown, the political heart of the nation and home to colonial buildings and the presidential palace. They also flock to the fine hotels, restaurants, and seaside parks of chic Miraflores and the lively arts and nightlife communities in Barranco. San Isidro, an upscale residential area and Peru's most exclusive business center, draws corporate travelers and first-class tours.

Each of the city's districts has a distinctively different vibe, but all are well policed and have benefited from a decade of refurbishing. No matter where you choose to spend your time, you are sure to find a wealth of activities and plenty of ways to escape the city's frenetic traffic. ■

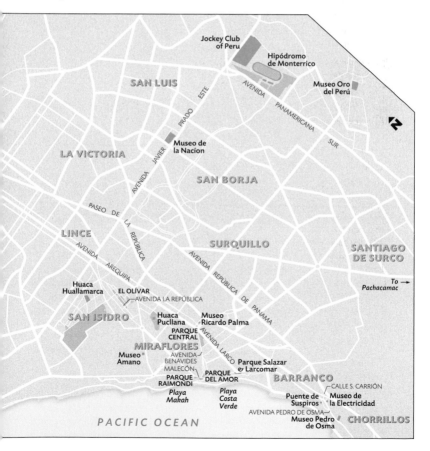

CENTRAL LIMA

The ancient sites that lie scattered around Lima date back nearly 2,000 years; it is likely that older ones existed but have been destroyed by the modern city. Despite such a strong connection to the past, or perhaps because of it, Lima continues to look toward the future, offering visitors a wealth of historical treasures as well as the best in modern recreation.

Basílica y Convento de San Francisco in the heart of colonial Lima

Lima

Map pp. 54–55

Visitor Information

Plaza de Armas Municipalid

iPerú, Aeropuerto Internacional Jorge Chávez (3 information offices)

01/574-8000

E-mail:
iperulimaaeropuerto
@promperu.gob.pe

Lima's History

The capital of the Inca empire was the city of Cusco, high in the Andes, but the seafaring Spaniards found its location unsuitable. So on January 5, 1535, Francisco Pizarro founded a new coastal city elegantly named Ciudad de Los Reyes (City of Kings) in honor of the Catholic feast of the Epiphany, when the Magi visited the infant Jesus. With a sheltered port at Callao, a large plain, and a year-round supply of water from the Río Rímac, the city sat in an ideal place. Pizarro only enjoyed it for a few years, however, before his assassination in 1541. You can visit his tomb in the city's cathedral (see p. 59).

In 1542, Spain declared Lima the capital of its Viceroyalty of Peru, a region that covered most of the continent of South

America. The city soon became the leading Spanish colonial port in the New World, a distinction it held until the dissolution of the colonies following independence in the early 19th century. The founding of a university in 1551, followed by the arrival in 1570 of the Spanish Inquisition, cemented the importance of the City of Kings. The city adopted its present name, a Spanish corruption of the Quechua word *rímac* (speaker), in the late 16th century.

Famed British sailor Francis Drake attacked and plundered the port of Callao, 7 miles (12 km) from central Lima, taking by surprise the Spanish colonists unprepared for the assaults of buccaneers and pirates, who until that time had never come up from the waters of the Pacific Ocean. The city of Lima, following that event, built a defensive wall, the remains of which are still visible in the Parque de la Muralla (see p. 62).

Post-1746 Quake: In 1687, an earthquake caused considerable damage in Lima, but a much more violent one in 1746 destroyed most of the city, killing tens of thousands of people and swamping the port of Callao with a tsunami that followed. Most of the buildings standing today date after 1746; the Basílica y Convento de San Francisco (see pp. 64–65) is one of the few structures to survive. The reconstruction began immediately, relying on African and indigenous slave labor to put up many of the city's glorious buildings.

Although Lima continued its role as Spain's main trading outlet in the New World, its power began to wane with the creation of viceroyalties in Buenos Aires and Bogotá. During the wars of independence in the 1820s, Lima remained a royalist stronghold, and the population suffered and declined during years of battles between forces loyal to the

Catching Lima's Buses

Lima has no central, long-distance bus station, although dozens of companies have terminals around town, especially near central Lima. Along Avenida Javier Prado Este, in the La Victoria district, you will find the main operators: Cruz del Sur, Ormeño, and Tepsa. The modern Metropolitano electric bus service (*tel 01/203–9000, www.metropolitano.com.pe*) has 35 stops centered on Paseo de la República and is the fastest way to get from Lima to San Isidro, Miraflores, and Barranco. Riders must buy a *tarjeta inteligente* card (S/5 for activation plus the price of the single trip)

at the self-service ticket offices. The journey along the main street on the Paseo de la República costs S/2.5. Access the line from the overpasses that cross the multilane highway. For short hauls around the city, many bus lines offer *combis* and *micros* (minibuses). Instead of numbers, look for a placard in the windshield listing the main streets on which the bus travels. Board the bus at any street corner, and ask to get down (*"Baja!"*) at any street corner.

You may find the system complicated and seemingly confusing, but locals and drivers are usually willing to help.

Spanish crown and those bent on liberty and self-rule.

Beyond Independence:

After independence, Lima enjoyed a few decades of renewed prosperity, due in part to the growth of Peru's guano industry (see p. 83). The continent's first railway opened in 1851, connecting Lima with Callao, and soon after, trains began to run between Lima and Miraflores, then a coastal village separated from the capital by farmland and a popular relaxation spot. These decades of growth and success culmi-

peace treaty was signed.

The census of 1919 reveals that, by the early 20th century, Lima was still a small city with a population of just 173,000. With a steady influx of rural poor from the Peruvian highlands looking to improve their lives, this number would soon change—dramatically.

Within two decades, Lima's population had tripled, and by the 1980s, six million people lived in the shantytowns around the city. They traveled into the center to work as *ambulantes* (street vendors), selling anything from shoelaces to sunglasses in

Enjoying Lima's Spectator Sports

As in the rest of South America, *fútbol* (soccer) is the leading spectator sport in Lima, which has numerous teams, including Universitario ("La U") and Alianza Lima. There are two seasons each year, *Apertura* (Opening), from February to June, and *Clausura* (Closing), from July to December. The major stadium, Estadio Nacional, lies off the seventh to ninth blocks of Paseo de la República at the south end of central Lima. You can buy tickets at Wong supermarkets.

Lima's second most loved spectator sport, bullfighting, begins in late October and lasts until early December. International matadors perform in the Plaza de Acho ring at the north end of central Lima (see p. 66). The Jockey Club of Peru sponsors horse racing on Thursday to Sunday afternoons at Hipódromo de Monterrico (*Ave. El Derby s/n puerta N°3, Santiago de Surco, tel 01/610–3000, www. hipodromodemonterrico.com.pe*). Enter the members' stand with your passport.

nated in the Lima Exposition of 1872.

The War of the Pacific, between Peru and Chile over mineral rights, devastated Lima. The Chileans won and invaded Lima, looting its churches, libraries, and mansions during a two-year occupation that forced the Peruvian government out. Lima began to recover only after the

an effort to make ends meet.

During this period, the capital suffered from great poverty and hardship exacerbated by the economic chaos caused by weak political leadership and the civil war with the Sendero Luminoso guerrilla movement (see sidebar p. 165). Bombings and blackouts had free rein regularly in the city, and petty

The Changing of the Guards at the Palacio de Gobierno in the Plaza de Armas

thieves ran the streets. In 1986, city authorities imposed a curfew from 1 a.m. to 5 a.m. that lasted several months. With the 1992 capture of Abimael Guzmán, the leader of Shining Path, as well as the strong-arm and austere policies of President Alberto Fujimori (1990–2000), order finally returned in the 1990s.

In 1996, Lima Mayor Alberto Andrade Carmona created great public works, making the city an important cultural center of South America. He launched a successful restoration campaign in the historic center. City laborers scrubbed and painted the city's streets and buildings and undertook an ambitious project to renovate the beautiful but badly dilapidated colonial balconies. Today, the center has become increasingly attractive and secure, although it remains overcrowded and noisy.

Plaza de Armas

Forming the heart of the city, the Plaza de Armas originated with Lima's foundation in 1535. Its oldest attraction, the central bronze fountain, dates to 1651.

On the northeast side of the plaza, fire and natural disaster have destroyed the **Palacio de Gobierno** several times since Pizarro constructed the city's first government building here in the 1530s. The current palace, which takes up the entire block, was completed in 1937. The changing of the guard draws a small crowd daily at noon.

The **Catedral** dominates the southeast side of the plaza. Finished in 1755, in the place where a church once stood, it was demolished in the 1746 earthquake but was constructed in the original Renaissance fashion. Its facade and interior—with

(continued on p. 63)

Palacio de Gobierno

🅰 Map p. 61
✉ Plaza de Armas
☎ 01/311–3900 or 01/311–4300

www.gob.pe/presidencia

Catedral

🅰 Map p. 61
✉ Plaza de Armas
☎ 01/427–9647 or 01/426–7056
💲 $

A WALK THROUGH CENTRAL LIMA

This walk shows off the best of old Lima with a variety of attractions, including glorious churches, historical plazas, and colonial architecture. The tour also includes a visit to several monuments and public museums, free or low cost.

From San Isidro or Miraflores head north by taking a micro along Avenida Arequipa or the Metropolitano bus along Paseo de la República (*see Bus in Lima, p. 57*) to the **Parque de la Exposición,** which extends north of Avenida 28 de Julio, near the Estadio Nacional and Parque de la Riserva. Inside this large park you will find walking paths, a Japanese garden, an outdoor amphitheater, occasional cultural events, and the **Museo de Arte de Lima ❶** (see pp. 67–68). About a hundred yards (92 m) east of the museum is Plaza Grau, named

NOT TO BE MISSED:

Museo de Arte de Lima
• Museo del Banco Central
de Reserva • Iglesia de San
Pedro • Plaza de Armas •
Monasterio de San Francisco

after a Peruvian and naval officer of the War of the Pacific, Adm. Miguel Grau.

Head north along Paseo de la República for 200 yards (183 m) to the **Museo de Arte Italiano ❷** (*Paseo de la República s/n, tel 01/321–5622, closed Mon., $*). Donated by local Italians in 1921 (Peru's independence centennial), the museum has lovely exterior mosaics and a nice neoclassical facade, an impressive collection of European paintings, drawings, and sculptures, and an exhibit of modern Peruvian artists.

Continue north along the wide Paseo de la República, past the huge Hotel Sheraton on your left and the elegant Palacio de Justicia to your right. Here you'll pass the entrance to the Estación Central del Metropolitano underground bus terminal. At the T-junction with Avenida Roosevelt, turn left and then immediately right onto northbound Jirón de la Unión, and follow it for two long blocks to **Plaza San Martín ❸**, with a massive equestrian bronze of liberator José de San Martín erected for Peru's centennial. At the base there is another enchanting statue depicting the *Madre Patría* (motherland), commissioned in Spain with the request to portray her with a *corona de llamas* (crown of flames). The

A statue of José de San Martín stands in the middle of the Plaza San Martín.

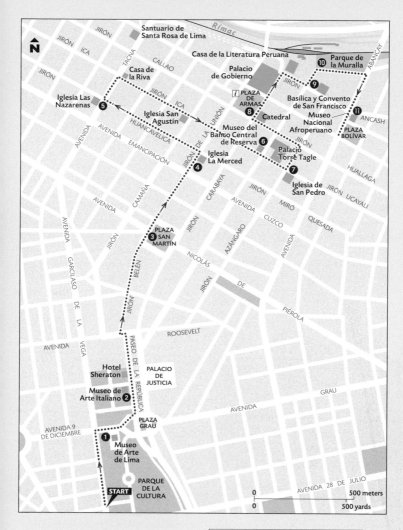

Santuario de
Santa Rosa de Lima

Casa de la Literatura Peruana

Parque de
la Muralla ⑩

JIRÓN ICA

JIRÓN

JIRÓN

TACNA

CALLAO

Palacio
de Gobierno

Casa de
la Riva

ABANCAY

⑨

Iglesia Las
Nazarenas ⑤

JIRÓN ICA

ℹ PLAZA
DE
ARMAS
⑧

Basílica y Convento
de San Francisco

Museo
Nacional
Afroperuano

⑪

Iglesia San
Agustín

HUANCAVELICA

Catedral

ANCASH

PLAZA
BOLÍVAR

AVENIDA

AVENIDA

EMANCIPACIÓN

Museo del
Banco Central
de Reserva ⑥

JIRÓN DE LA UNIÓN

Iglesia
La Merced

Palacio
Torre Tagle

JIRÓN

④

⑦

HUALLAGA

CAMANÁ

CARABAYA

Iglesia de
San Pedro

JIRÓN

MIRO

JIRÓN UCAYALI

AVENIDA

AVENIDA

QUESADA

JIRÓN

CUZCO

AZÁNGARO

PLAZA
SAN
MARTÍN ③

AVENIDA

GARCILASO

JIRÓN

BELÉN

JIRÓN

NICOLÁS

JIRÓN

DE

DE

AVENIDA

PIÉROLA

LA

VEGA

PASEO DE LA REPÚBLICA

ROOSEVELT

AVENIDA

Hotel
Sheraton

PALACIO
DE
JUSTICIA

Museo de
Arte Italiano ②

GRAU

AVENIDA

PLAZA
GRAU

AVENIDA 9
DE DICIEMBRE

①

Museo
de Arte
de Lima

AVENIDA 28 DE JULIO

START

PARQUE
DE LA
CULTURA

0   500 meters

0   500 yards

sculptor, not knowing how to interpret the term
llama (flame), which in Spanish has two meanings,
placed a small blade, still visible, on the head of the
female figure.

Jirón de la Unión, the long pedestrian
walkway that crosses eleven blocks extending to Plaza de Armas, houses 19th- and early
20th-century buildings and some of the oldest
churches in Lima. On the corner with Jirón Santa

🔺 See also area map pp. 54–55
➤ Museo de Arte de Lima
🕐 2 hours (not including stops)
↔ 3 miles (5 km)
➤ Museo Nacional Afroperuano

Rosa (formerly Jirón Miró Quesada), recently
renamed to mark the 400th anniversary of
the death of the city's patron saint, **Iglesia La**

Merced ❹ (*tel 01/427–8199*) dates back to the founding of Lima, although the actual structure has been destroyed by earthquakes, burned, and rebuilt several times. Most of today's church dates to the 18th century. Opposite, you can buy numerous Catholic paraphernalia, such as ornamental candles, tiny medallions, fragrant incense, Bibles, icons, and statuettes.

Turn left and walk four blocks northwest along Jirón Huancavelica to the intersection with Avenida Tacna. There you will see the 18th-century **Iglesia Las Nazarenas** ❺ (*tel 01/423–5718*), built around a mural of the Crucifixion (*Señor de los Milagros*) that survived the 1655 earthquake and the next one. The church marks the starting point of the fervent and incredibly crowded pro-

The Plaza de Armas is a favorite place to relax and people watch.

cessions celebrating the highly venerated sacred image in October.

Turn northeast on Tacna and walk one block to Jirón Ica, the center of small printing enterprises. Note the old presses working alongside modern computers. Turn right, passing the colonial **Casa de la Riva** (*Jr. Ica 426*) on the left, an elegant 18th-century structure: Note its Nicaraguan cedar door and Spanish tiles. Often closed, **Iglesia San Agustín** (*Jr. Ica & Jr. Camaná,*

tel 01/427–7548) has an early 18th-century churrigueresque facade that is one of Lima's finest.

After crossing Jirón de la Unión, Ica becomes Jirón Ucayali. Walk two blocks to the **Museo del Banco Central de Reserva** ❻ (*Jr. Ucayali & Lampa, tel 22655/6, closed Sun.–Mon., www.bcrp.gob.pe/ museocentral.html*). Show your passport to enter this well-curated display of pre-Columbian ceramics and gold and Peruvian art from independence to the present.

Continue southeast past the **Palacio Torre Tagle** (*Jr. Ucayali 363*) on your left. Built in 1735, the building now houses the Ministry of Foreign Affairs and is closed to the public, although you can see its splendid Moorish-influenced, carved mahogany balcony from the street. The sumptuous 17th-century Jesuit **Iglesia de San Pedro** ❼ (*Jr. Azángaro 451 & Ucayali; tel 01/428–3010, closed 12:30 p.m.–5 p.m., www.sanpedrodelima.org*) was built in neoclassical style and houses altars covered in gold leaf and an important reliquary with the remains of many saints, some of whom were sent from Rome.

Continue northeast for one block along Jirón Azángaro, then turn left for two blocks on Jirón Huallaga to **Plaza de Armas** ❽ (see pp. 59, 63), where you can enjoy the **catedral** and **Palacio de Gobierno.**

Leave the square by Jirón Carabaya on the right side of the building; turn right after one block to Jirón Ancash in front of the ancient Estación de Desamparados, home of the Casa de la Literatura Peruana. Continue one block to the **Basílica y Convento de San Francisco** ❾ (see pp. 64–65). Behind the monastery you will find the **Parque de la Muralla** ❿ (*tel 01/433–1546*), so called for the remains of the colonial walls of the city. Built along the Río Rímac, the park has a small museum explaining the history of Lima's growth, a restaurant, labeled sections of the wall, an equestrian statue of Francisco Pizarro, play areas for children, and lawns with benches.

Exit at the park's east end and head south along wide, busy Avenida Abancay three blocks to Plaza Bolívar. Along the road (*Jr. Ancash corner*) you will find the **Museo Nacional Afroperuano** ⓫ (see p. 66).

intricately carved wooden choir stalls, silver-plated altars, and religious artwork—enjoyed a complete restoration in the 18th and 19th centuries. The body of Francisco Pizarro, for centuries buried in the crypt, now rests in a chapel to the right of the main entrance. The religious art museum inside the cathedral displays paintings and vestments. On the last Friday of each month it is possible to visit the structure in the evening at a reduced price (*from 5 to 10 p.m., ticket: S/2*). The superbly carved balconies immediately to the left of the cathedral belong to the archbishop's palace.

On the northwest side of the plaza, the Municipalidad (Town Hall) has a local tourist information office (*Pasaje Nicolás de Ribera El Viejo 145, tel 01/632–1542, e-mail: infoturistica@ munlima.gob.pe*).

Colonial Lima

A block from the plaza, **Iglesia de Santo Domingo** was founded by the Dominican friar Vicente de Valverde, who accompanied Pizarro when Inca Atahualpa was captured in Cajamarca (see p. 38). Constructed in the 1540s, the church has since been rebuilt, although the ceiling and the older of the two cloisters date to the early 17th century. Limeños revere the church because it contains the remains of three local saints: Rose of Lima (1586–1617), the first Catholic saint of the Americas; Martin de Porres (1579–1639), the patron saint of barbers and one of the few black saints; and Juan Macias

■ Iglesia de Santo Domingo

(1585–1645), a Dominican missionary to Peru. You can see the reliquaries to the right of the main altar.

A few blocks away, the **Santuario de Santa Rosa de Lima** marks the spot where St. Rose was born and lived her short life. Contemporary accounts claim that she was a beautiful girl and her parents expected her to marry well. She was a dutiful daughter, but defied her parents' desires of marriage, wanting to remain a virgin in service of God. She opened a room in her house to care for the homeless, elderly, sick, and orphans. Believing in penance, Rose wore uncomfortable devices such as a studded headband to emulate Christ's crown of thorns, slept on a wooden bed without bedding, and prayed for long hours

Iglesia de Santo Domingo

✉ Jr. Camaná 170 & Jr. Conde de Superunda

☎ 01/427–6793

Santuario de Santa Rosa de Lima

✉ Ave. Tacna 100

☎ 01/425–1279

Casa de la Gastronomía

✉ Jr. Conde de Superunda 170

☎ 01/426–7264

🕐 Closed Mon.

💲 $

Casa Aliaga

✉ Jr. de la Unión 224

Basílica y Convento de San Francisco

✉ Jr. Ancash & Jr. Lampa

☎ 01/426–7377

💲 $$

www.museocata cumbas.com

without sleep. Her death on August 30 is an important feast day in Lima.

The 19th-century building between the Iglesia de Santo Domingo and the Palacio de Gobierno houses the **central post office,** the Peruvian Postal and Philatelic Museum and, since 2011, the **Casa de la Gastronomía,** which illustrates the variety and development of culinary styles from all over Peru. On the north side of the block stands **Casa Aliaga,** the oldest inhabited private residence in Lima. Built on land given by Pizarro to his lieutenant, Jerónimo de Aliaga, it has been in the family ever since. The plain exterior belies a splendid interior, decorated with colonial art and furnishings and adorned with tile and woodwork of the period. Visits can

Buying Maps in Peru

For a topographical map, visit the **Instituto Geográfico Nacional** (*Ave. Aramburú 1190, Corpac, San Isidro, tel 01/475–3030, www.ign. gob.pe, closed Sat.–Sun.*). Prices begin at $15.

Lima 2000 (*Ave. Arequipa 2625, Lince, tel 01/440–3486, e-mail: info@lima2000.com.pe, lima2000.com.pe*) has excellent street maps of Lima, Cusco, and Arequipa for sale.

be arranged only through Lima tour agents.

Two blocks away, eastward, about three dozen Franciscan monks still occupy one of the city's most interesting churches, the **Basílica y Convento de San Francisco.** One of the oldest continuously used churches in Lima, it survived the 1746 earthquake in reasonably good shape. Built during the mid-17th century to replace an older adobe-and-wood church, the building consists of earthquake-resistant materials called *quincha,* thick canes, reeds, or slim twigs made into a framework and covered with mud and plaster. An impressive pair of baroque belfries overlook a lovely paved courtyard surrounding a fountain. Painted canary yellow, this is one of Lima's most photographed churches.

Inside, it is worth visiting the ossuaries of the catacombs and the remarkable library, which contains 25,000 volumes, including maps and old books, some dating back to the 16th century. An attractive, plant-filled cloister is surrounded by patios with walls covered in European tiles and topped by carved wooden ceilings.

The catacombs were used as a cemetery in colonial times because Lima did not have a graveyard until the early 19th century. Nobility and the rich were buried in the floors of churches or in niches in side chapels, while the majority of corpses were placed into large pits full of lye within the catacombs. From these mass graves, archaeologists have excavated bones belonging to about 7,000 people, now rather morbidly arranged by type, with femurs piled in one pit and skulls in another. In some pits, the bones have been rearranged in macabre patterns. One part of the catacombs has a series of coffin-size niches still used for burials but reserved for the Franciscans serving in the monastery.

The catacombs, library, cloister, and religious art collection can be entered only on guided visits, which are offered at the entrance. Tours are in Spanish and English, last about 45 minutes, and are included in the modest entry fee. Entry to the church itself is free.

Rímac District

North of the Palacio de Gobierno and Basílica y Convento de San Francisco, the Río Rímac formed the natural boundary of early colonial Lima. Apart from the panoramic point of Cerro San Cristóbal, two sites of interest lie beyond the river, but the Rímac district is a poor one so taking a taxi is suggested.

Named for the barefooted (*descalzo*) Franciscan friars who founded it in the late 16th century, **Convento de los Descalzos** boasts several hundred colonial paintings of the Cusqueño, Quiteño, and Limeño schools, many in excellent condition. More interesting for many visitors is the kitchen, where you can examine 17th-century winemaking equipment. Or visit the

infirmary, apothecary, refectory, and monks' cells.

The entrance fee includes a guided tour, and unlike crowded monumental complex San Francisco, this convent is rarely visited and you are likely to have a semiprivate tour; an offer is appreciated. Most guides speak a little English; if you are lucky, you may even get to walk around with one of the friars.

■ **Door knocker at the Basílica y Convento de San Francisco**

The Lima bullfighting season is a short one, but Limeños are proud of the tradition. Held in the Plaza de Armas in early colonial times, events now take place in Rímac's **Plaza de Acho,** the oldest bullring in

Convento de los Descalzos

✉ Alameda de los Descalzos 278

☎ 01 / 481–0441

🕐 Closed Mon. Mar.–Dec.; Sun. Jan.–Feb.

💲 $

Museo Taurino

✉ Jr. Hualgayoc 332

☎ 01/481–1467

⊕ Closed Sun.

💲 $

Museo Nacional Afroperuano

✉ Jr. Áncash 542, Cercado de Lima

☎ 01/426–0689

⊕ Closed Sun.

the Americas. Adjoining the ring, the **Museo Taurino** displays the costumes of famous matadors, memorabilia, and artwork of Goya and Picasso, famous bullfighting fans.

Plaza Bolívar

Crossing back over the Río Rímac and continuing several blocks on Avenida Abancay will lead you to the **Plaza Bolívar,** at the intersection of Avenidas Abancay and Junín. Named after the Venezuelan liberator, Simón Bolívar, who was also the sixth president of Peru (1824–1826), the plaza contains Peru's Congress building. On the site of the first university of the Americas is Universidad de San Marcos, founded by decree of the emperor Charles V in 1551. Today, the university has several campuses scattered across the city.

One block away from the square, to the north, is the **Museo Nacional Afroperuano,** inaugurated on June 4, 2009. It is housed in the Casa de las Trece Monedas, an 18th-century building. The museum is divided into 9 rooms. The stages of migration from Africa are illustrated, the travel routes, the treatment received on arrival in Peru, and the customs adopted by migrants once they settled in the country. The museum displays objects dating back to the colonial era and various documents from the republican era, such as the rights papers.

Once the most important produce market in the city, the **Mercado Central,** one block south at Ucayali and Ayacucho, is still a bustling affair.

It takes up an entire city block and offers everything from sunglasses to squash, a good introduction to the typical Peruvian central market of small stalls crammed with household essentials, fresh fish, and piles of potatoes. Visitors should be careful of pickpockets who often take advantage of the chaotic situation.

Next to the market, you will find Lima's small but immediately recognizable **Barrio Chino** (Chinatown), with several excellent Chinese restaurants and shops selling Asian paraphernalia. On Ucayali at Andahuaylas, the arch known as the **Portada China** (Chinese Doorway) marks the barrio entrance. Immigrants from China began to arrive in Peru in the mid-19th century, working in agriculture and later on the railroads. Their descendants form the largest Chinese community in South America, and they have had an important influence on Peruvian cuisine. Every town in Peru has a *chifa* (Chinese restaurant); the most authentic are in Lima.

Parque de la Exposición

Look for the entrance to the **Museo de Arte de Lima** (MALI), the capital's leading art museum, off 9 de Diciembre (Paseo Colón) through a gate into the park. This

■ **Lima has the largest Chinatown in South America.**

building was designed by the Italian Antonio Leonardi. The construction of the iron columns is attributed to Eiffel's signature (see sidebar p. 17), who created many structures throughout Peru. The structure was completed in 1872 to host the Lima Exposition. Since then it has been home to the **Sociedad de Bellas Artes** and has hosted a hospital, a history museum, and the Ministry of Public Works.

In 1961 it was transformed into the current Lima Museum of Art. It exhibits pieces ranging from pre-Columbian to modern pieces, including exceptional colonial furniture, clothing and silverware, ancient ceramics and textiles from several cultures, and paintings from the 16th century to the present. Signs are in English, and guides are available.

The **Museo Nacional de la Cultura Peruana** (National Museum of Peruvian Culture) has the country's most important collection of popular arts and crafts from all regions of Peru. It exhibits contemporary and traditional artifacts from all regions of Peru with examples of handicrafts of high quality and pre-Columbian products that provide a historical context for many of today's craft forms. ■

Museo de Arte de Lima

✉ Paseo Colón 125
☎ 01/204-0000
🕐 Closed Mon.
💲 $$$ (additional fee for special exhibits, Nuevo Soles)

www.mali.pe

Museo Nacional de la Cultura Peruana

✉ Ave. Alfonso Ugarte 650
☎ 01/321-5626
🕐 Closed Sun.–Mon.
💲 $

SUBURBAN LIMA

With more than 50 districts and constantly growing, suburban Lima can be quite complicated, but never disappointing. This area boasts numerous attractions such as museums, parks, and archaeological sites scattered throughout the territory. Many visitors usually frequent the exclusive districts of Miraflores, Barranco, and San Isidro, but you will have to move much farther if you want to take full advantage of the multiple cultural offerings of the capital.

Surfing at Playa Punta Roquita in the Miraflores District

Miraflores

Map p. 55

Visitor Information

iPerú, Plaza Gourmet Nivel 1 – stand 211, Centro Comercial Larcomar, Miraflores

01/234-0340

E-mail: iperularco mar@promperu. gob.pe

The best way to get around is by taxi. Buses take you everywhere, but it's difficult to trace a route unless you speak Spanish: Get a good map and be prepared to take more time and travel with the locals—which can be rewarding.

Some bus information for the easier destinations to reach is given here.

Miraflores

In the 1930s, affluent Limeños used Miraflores primarily as a beach resort and pleasant rural getaway. Today this bustling, modern, and trendy suburb is anything but rural, but it still has some remarkable parks. Foremost among them is **Parque Central,** a triangular-shaped plot of greenery south of El Óvalo, the traffic circle at the south end of Avenida Arequipa. Also known as Parque Kennedy, the moderate-size park has a bust of President John F. Kennedy located at its center.

Parque Central holds outdoor crafts and local artists' markets most evenings and on weekends. It also stages frequent changing outdoor cultural exhibits, some of them exceptionally impressive. The playground will delight children, while the park's amphitheater draws crowds Thursdays through Sundays for evening performances of Peruvian music; musical genres range from traditional folk music to salsa and rock. On the southeast side of the park, pay a visit to the **Municipalidad** (*Ave. Larco & Ave. Diez Canseco*), which has an art gallery with free changing exhibits.

Less than a mile (1.6 km) south of Parque Central, along Avenida Larco, **Parque Salazar** boasts lovely clifftop views of the Pacific Ocean. Much of this park has been developed into the upscale **Larcomar,** a popular, modern shopping mall with a multiscreen cinema and restaurants and shops overlooking the ocean.

Southwest of Parque Central along Avenida Diagonal, or a half mile (0.8 km) northwest along the coast from Larcomar, **Parque del Amor** (Park of Love) has a famed statue ("El Beso") of a couple kissing. Colorful mosaic walls overlook the ocean, and this seems to be the perfect place for a romantic date, proposal, or wedding photo.

A few minutes north of Parque del Amor is **Parque Raimondi,** where paragliders launch their adrenaline-fueled flights.

EXPERIENCE: Pursue Lima's Adventure Sports

Lima may be a capital city, but within a short distance of the metropolis, lovers of the outdoors will find plenty of adventure:

Horseback Riding: You can ride Peruvian *paso* horses near Pachacamac, 18 miles (30 km) south of Lima. Check with Cabalgatas (*tel 944/806–152, e-mail: informes@cabalgatas.com.pe, www.cabalgatas.com.pe*).

Paragliding: Aeroxtreme (*tel 999/480–954, e-mail: info@aeroxtreme.com, www.aaroxtreme com*). Your flights begin at Parque del Amor above the cliffs of Malecón Cisneros in Miraflores.

Scuba Diving: Peru Divers (*Ave. Defensores del Morro, Chorrillos, Lima, tel 01/251–6231, www.perudivers.com*) sells and rents equipment, issues PADI certifications and organizes various excursions.

Surf: For a list of beaches, visit *www. perusurfguides.com* or the "Peru adventure" section of the website *www.peru.travel.* You can visit the shop of the most famous surfboard manufacturer in South America, Wayo Whilar (*Alameda Las Garzas Reales, Mz.FA-7, Chorrillos, Lima, tel 994/042–280, e-mail: wayowhilar@gmail. com, www.wayowhilar.com.pe*), active since the late 1960s, or take lessons in the surf school named after the ex-national champion Magoo de la Rosa (*www.magoosurfperu.com*).

You can walk between the two parks along the paved, clifftop Malecón *Cisneros* (beach walk), although the beach itself is several hundred feet below.

■ Humboldt penguins at the zoo

Museo Amano
✉ Calle Retiro 160, Miraflores
☎ 01/441–2909
$ $$$
www.museoamano.org

Huaca Pucllana
✉ Calle General Borgoño s/n, cuadra 8
☎ 01/617–7148
⏲ Closed Tues.
$ $$
huacapucllana miraflores.pe

Museo Ricardo Palma
✉ Calle General Suárez 189, Miraflores
☎ 01/445–5836
⏲ Closed Sat.–Sun.
$ $
ricardopalma. miraflores.gob.pe

The **Museo Amano** offers a unique experience. It displays the most beautiful collection in Peru of pre-Columbian fabrics made by 10 different populations, including Chavín, Huari, and Chancay. The little-known Chancay culture existed on the coast north of Lima for several hundred years prior to the emergence of the Inca.

The raw materials and equipment room also illustrates the textile production process. Generic or specialized guided tours are available. To know the rates for groups of more than 10 people, it is advisable to contact the museum in advance.

Nearby to the east, **Huaca Pucllana** belongs to the Lima culture (A.D. 200–700). Located in the center of the Miraflores district, the adobe and clay complex was an important center for religious rituals, but it seems that administrative activities were also carried out here. The exploration and excavations are still ongoing. A night visit is recommended (*7 p.m.–10 p.m. Wed.–Sun.*) and can be combined with a delicious dinner in the exclusive restaurant named after the site.

Back near Parque Central, the **Museo Ricardo Palma** resides in the house of this Peruvian author (1833–1919). Its collection showcases period furniture and offers an homage to Palma's life and writing.

Barranco
South of Miraflores along the coast stands Barranco. A seaside village popular with Limeños as far back as 300 years

ago. It developed a reputation in the 19th century as an artists' and writers' district. Later, it became a fashionable place. Today, the center of Barranco—especially Avenidas Pedro de Osma and Sánchez Carrión, which branch off from Plaza de Barranco—has become well known for its nightclubs and typical peñas. The area remains sleepy during the day, however.

With its history as a rural coastal village, Barranco does not have a clear checkerboard layout; indeed every map seems to have different names for the same streets. Never mind. The center is small and tight; if you get lost, you are only a few minutes' walk away from the plaza (also called the *parque*). And the streets are pleasantly quiet, so getting briefly lost can actually be a delight.

Barranco's most famous sight is the not very exciting **Puente de los Suspiros** (Bridge of Sighs), a wooden footbridge that spans a couple of blocks west of the plaza. Resourceful tour guides relate various love legends concerning it. And the bridge certainly sits in a pretty area of the metropolis. Between the plaza and the bridge, an area of food stalls comes alive on weekends, especially in the evenings to feed hungry barhoppers.

More interesting, and just off the southwest corner of the plaza, the **Museo de la Electricidad** has a small exhibition that outlines the history of

the development of electricity in Lima.

Across the street you will see the electric train, now restored, that used to join Barranco with Miraflores and Lima. Its modern route encompasses just a few blocks, but train enthusiasts can go for a ride by buying tickets at the museum.

Also worth a look is the **Museo Pedro de Osma,** housed in a well-preserved 19th-century mansion. Its superb collection includes colonial art, furniture, sculpture, and silverware. A few steps from here you will also find the **MATE,** a museum founded in 2012 by the Peruvian Mario Testino, an internationally renowned fashion photographer. You can admire his works exhibited in the permanent collection and discover Peruvian and international contemporary art in temporary exhibitions.

In the northern area of the Barranco district you can visit the **Museo de Arte Contemporáneo (MAC),** inaugurated in 2013, which houses works by Peruvian, Latin American, and European exponents of the currents of abstract expressionism, conceptual art, constructivism, and pop art. The collection covers a time span from the 1950s to the present day. The entrance ticket also includes the guided tour.

San Isidro & North

The most interesting site in San Isidro is the **Huaca Huallamarca,** a Maranga pyramid built in A.D. 200 and still in use

Museo de la Electricidad

✉ Ave. Pedro de Osma 105, Barranco

☎ 01/708-3232

museodela electricidad. blogspot.com

Museo Pedro de Osma

✉ Ave. Pedro de Osma 421, Barranco

☎ 01/467-0063

🕐 Closed Mon.

💲 $$$ ($$$$ cumulative ticket with MATE e MAC)

www.museopedro deosma.org

MATE

✉ Ave. Pedro de Osma 409, Barranco

☎ 01/200-5400

🕐 Closed Mon.

💲 $$

www.mate.pe

MAC

✉ Ave. Miguel Grau 1511, Barranco

☎ 01/514-6800

🕐 Closed Mon.

💲 $

www.maclima.pe

Huaca Huallamarca

✉ Ave. Nicolás de Rivera 201, San Isidro

☎ 01/222-4124

🕐 Closed Mon.

💲 $

Museo Larco

✉ Ave. Bolívar 1515, Pueblo Libre

☎ 01/461-1312

💲 $$$

www.museolarco.org

Museo Nacional de Arqueología, Antropología e Historia

✉ Plaza Bolívar, Pueblo Libre

☎ 01/321-5630

💲 $

mnaahp.cultura.pe

Parque de las Leyendas

✉ Ave. de las Precursores, San Miguel

☎ 01/644-9200

💲 $$

www.leyendas.gob.pe

Fortaleza Real Felipe

✉ Plaza Independencia, Callao

☎ 01/429-0532

💲 $$

www.realfelipe.com

in Inca times. The structure has been restored and is known locally as Pan de Azúcar (meaning "sugar loaf"). A small site museum exhibits masks and household objects excavated here.

A 15-minute walk away, off of Avenida La República, the delightful and quiet park of **El Olívar** surrounds a grove of ancient olive trees. The park itself dates back to early colonial days.

To the north in Pueblo Libre, enthusiasts of Peru's ceramics should not miss the private **Museo Larco.** Some buses from Miraflores along Arequipa labeled "Todo Bolivar" will pass the museum, which is housed within an 18th-century mansion, itself built on 7th-century ruins.

Inside, the museum has a limited collection of excellent textiles and exceptional gold work, but its main focus is ceramics. The museum owns tens of thousands of pieces, and its main exhibit hall shows the finest of them. A separate room dedicated to erotic pottery displays a number of pots that explicitly illustrate the remarkably imaginative sexual practices of the ancient Peruvians.

About a 15-minute walk back to the southeast, you'll find the **Museo Nacional de Arqueología, Antropología e Historia.** Really, two adjoining museums are housed in the colonial home of some of Peru's viceroys. The liberators, José de San Martín and Simón Bolívar, also stayed here, and visitors can tour their rooms. The museums show a little bit of everything, from 14,000-year-old Stone Age objects to 19th-century art. Some of their archaeological pieces were moved to the Museo de la Nación (see opposite) in the 1990s, but the remaining collection is still varied, impressive, and worthwhile. Highlights include the Raimondi Stele belonging to the Chavín culture (see p. 195) and a scale model of the archaeological site of Machu Picchu. To the west of the Larco Museum extends the **Parque de las Leyendas** zoo. It is organized in three areas that represent the three major regions of Peru—coast, highlands, and rain forest. The majority of the exhibits are centered around Peruvian animals, but there is a sprinkling of international creatures on display as well. Spend some time wandering around the grounds of the zoo, and explore the **Huacas de Maranga,** a pre-Inca site first occupied in A.D. 200.

Travel a few miles west of the zoo to Callao, home of Lima's port and airport. Here visit the **Fortaleza Real Felipe,** a fort built in 1747 at the entrance of the La Punta peninsula overlooking the port. Originally constructed to defend the port against pirates, this is where royalist soldiers made their last stand during the battles of independence. A military museum now marks the site. It includes dungeons and watchtowers that you can visit with a Spanish-speaking military guide.

The Puente de los Suspiros, in the suburb of Barranco

Southeast Districts

The **Museo de la Nación,**
Peru's national history museum,
is located southeast of central
Lima along Avenida Javier Prado
Este. The rooms dedicated to
the exhibition of the country's
archaeological activity–over
3,000 years of Peruvian history represented by ceramics,
fabrics, metal artifacts, and
scale models of archaeological
sites–are under renovation. On
the sixth floor of the building,
on the other hand, it is possible
to visit an exciting exhibition,
however sad, entitled *Yuyanapaq*
("remember" in Quechua).
Here is illustrated the civil war
with Sendero Luminoso, which
took place in the 1980s (see p.
165). About 80,000 Peruvians,

INSIDER TIP:

In Barranco, there is a
cevicheria called Canta
Rana, which is adorned
with *fútbol* [soccer]
memorabilia from the
owner's days as an
Argentinian player—
well worth the visit.

–KENNY LING
National Geographic contributor

mostly *campesinos* (peasants), lost
their lives. Their killing was the
work of both terrorists and the
Peruvian army.

   South of the Hipódromo de
Monterrico (the horse-racing
track), the **Museo Oro del Perú**

**Museo de la
Nación**

✉ Ave. Javier
Prado Este
2465, San Borja

☎ 01/476–9878

⊕ Closed Mon.

Museo Oro del Perú

✉ Jr. Alonso de Molina 1100, Monterrico

☎ 01/345–1292

$ $$$

www.museoroperu.com.pe

Pachacamac

✉ Antigua Carretera Panamericana Sur ᴋᴍ 31.5, Lurín

☎ 01/321–5606

$ $$

pachacamac.cultura.pe

houses a private collection and includes two museums. In the basement, a wonderful assortment of gold ornaments from various pre-Columbian cultures fills many rooms behind an armored door. So much has been made of reports in 2001 that many of the gold pieces were in fact elaborate fakes that each of the thousands of pieces has since been authenticated and many reproductions removed. It's still worth a visit; you won't see more gold in one place anywhere else in Peru.

Upstairs is an incredible **small arms collection,** said to be the largest in the world. Ancient blunderbusses, colonial-era muskets, and 19th-century pistols and rifles form the majority of the collection. Most of the exhibits are poorly labeled in Spanish, so using the English audio tour is recommended. Consider spending some time on the museum grounds, which include a grassy woodland with deer, where you will also find a café and a number of shops with upscale souvenirs.

South Beyond Lima

Southeast of Lima, the Panamericana Sur passes **Pachacamac,** the most important and most interesting archaeological site in the Lima area. Begun around A.D. 200, it reached its apex with the Wari culture (A.D. 600–1100), and archaeologists believe it may have served as a place of pilgrimage.

The Inca enlarged the site with their own buildings, most notably the Palacio de las Mamacuñas (House of the Chosen Women), which has been extensively restored.

Wear comfortable shoes and be prepared to walk for a couple of hours. Today near the site there is also a new futuristic museum, inaugurated in February 2016. The museum preserves and exhibits precious artifacts found on the

Taking Taxis

In Peru, anyone can slap a TAXI sticker in the windshield and moonlight as a cab driver. Taxis don't have meters, so settle the fare before entering the vehicle. If your Spanish is limited, have the address of your destination written down.

Hailed on the street, a short ride costs $1 to $2; rides between most districts run $2 to $4; to the airport $8 to $12. (Drivers do not expect tips.) Taxis called by phone have fixed rates that are almost twice street cabs. The most expensive are *remisse* taxis: smart-looking cabs stationed in front of the city's best hotels.

For a ride from the airport—10 miles (16 km) to most areas in the city—official taxis with a desk outside the arrivals gate charge $15 to $25. (See Travelwise p. 270.)

Pachacamac site in the last 75 years: masterpieces of pre-hispanic art from the second to the sixteenth century, expression of the Wari, Ychma, and Inca cultures. The ceramic collection includes 6,590 pieces. The area will become an important museum center

South of Lima you will find the best beaches for surfing and, in the summer, for swimming. **Punta Hermosa** (see sidebar p. 69) has good surfing and some places to stay.

Pucusana, 40 miles (64 km) from Lima, is a colorful fishing village with simple but

■ Pachacamac, just outside Lima, contains both Inca and pre-Inca structures.

in view of the imminent construction of the new Museo Nacional de Arqueología in the district of Lurín. The facility will be completed by 2021. Ideal for day trips, Pachacamac also offers beautiful ocean views.

Travel agencies can arrange tours, or take a minibus labeled "Pachacamac" from the corner of Jr. Ayacucho and Ave. Grau in central Lima. Tell the driver you want to get off at "*las ruinas de Pachacamac*" or you'll end up in a small village about 0.6 mile (1 km) past the site.

adequate accommodations. The province of **Cañete** lies 90 miles (145 km) south at the point where Highway 24 turns inland to the village of **Lunahuaná,** known as the entry point for river rafting down the Río Lunahuaná. Local outfitters can set you up for an adventurous trip. Try Río Cañete Expeditions (*KM 33.4 Carretera 24 Cañete-Yauyos, Lunahuaná, tel 01/284–1271, www.riocanete.com*), which also offers a camping area by the river. ■

A region rich in wildlife, delicious wines, recreational activities—
and even a few unsolved mysteries

SOUTHERN LOWLANDS

The mysterious Nazca Lines were created by the pre-Inca Nazca culture.

SOUTHERN LOWLANDS

Stretching 827 miles (1,330 km) from Lima to the Chilean border, the Panamerican Highway South (La Panamericana Sur) forms the backbone of the southern lowlands. It runs along the arid coast then cuts far inland to pass through oases formed long ago, playing witness to sudden and dramatic changes in landscape that draw a sharp line between lush fields and the dusty barrenness of Peru's southern deserts.

■ Wildlife-watching boat tours from Paracas

The frigid waters of the Peru Current, also called the Humboldt Current, flow north from Antarctica, making the coastal waters very cold. However, the current stirs up nutrients from the ocean floor, forming the basis of a rich food chain that supports abundant wildlife along the coast (see pp. 82–83).

Overland travelers have traditionally used the Panamericana as the gateway to Arequipa, Lake Titicaca, and Cusco, making their way along what has become known as the "gringo trail." Frequent buses wend their way along the highway, and transportation is easy to find. Visitors who choose to fly from Lima to Cusco miss out on a remarkably different experience of Peru. This region is part of the driest desert in the world, an area where stunning sand dunes slowly roll wherever the wind blows,

giving rise to the local sport of sandboarding—snowboarding on sand.

Ancient Civilizations & the Nazca Lines

The ancient civilizations of the southern lowlands often lived inland, where they could reach water; the few oases in the region have been known since pre-Inca times. Only a small number of the rivers that flow from the western Andes reach the ocean. The coastal strip is narrow, yet despite the short distance from mountains to sea, most rivers are quickly swallowed up by the parched earth. Some flow underground and form aquifers that the Peruvians have tapped for irrigation.

None of the archaeological sites in the region match the great size and distinctiveness of the Nazca Lines. Created about 2,000 years ago over a period of several hundred years, the lines were made by the Nazca people, who simply pushed aside the top layer of dark-colored stones to expose the lighter, gypsum-laden soil underneath. Numerous "lines" form geometric patterns stretching over many square miles of high desert. Others represent birds, animals, and insects, covering the length of a football field and observable only from the sky. Local tour operators offer flights over the lines, and for this experience

NOT TO BE MISSED:
Colonies of seabirds and sea lions on the Ballestas Islands 81–83
Sandboarding on desert dunes 87
Tasting samples of wine and pisco at a bodega near Ica 87
A visit to the newly excavated pyramids of Cahuachi 88–89
Centuries-old skeletons buried in desert cemeteries 89
An unforgettable flight over the mysterious Nazca Lines 89
The traditional wattle-and-daub architecture and cobblestoned streets of Moquegua 90–91

alone it is worth venturing into this sparsely populated area.

The most important city in the southern lowlands, Ica, was once the capital of the Nazca people. Today it is at the center of Peru's main grape-growing region. Watered by irrigation canals fed by the Río Ica, the area's fertile vineyards produce some of Peru's highest quality wines as well as the clear brandy known as pisco. Produced in the region since the early 17th century, pisco is the uplifting spirit at the heart of Peru's national cocktail. Travelers can tour the small wineries near the city and visit some of Ica's many pisco makers, sampling the products and learning about traditional methods of winemaking. ∎

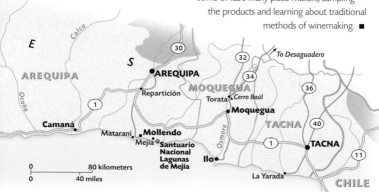

PARACAS & THE BALLESTAS ISLANDS

Located 4 miles (7 km) west of the Panamericana and 145 miles (235 km) south of Lima, the port of Pisco is this region's major town. Although the 2007 earthquake devastated the city, tourism is now recovering.

Templo Belén on Plazuela Belén in Pisco, months after the 2007 earthquake

Pisco

Map p. 78

Pisco is Quechua for "bird" and was so named in Inca times because of the great amount of birdlife in the region. The nearby Bahía de Paracas (Bay of Paracas), sheltered by the eponymous peninsula, gives rise to one of the best natural harbors on the south coast. In early colonial times, the Spaniards considered Pisco as a possible capital before settling on Lima.

In the 19th century, wine and brandy from Ica were exported through Pisco. The brandy, with its distinctive sharp, smoky flavor and slightly viscous consistency, was known as "liquor from Pisco," and eventually, simply "pisco."

Sedimentation forced authorities to close the port in 1969 and replace it with Puerto San Martín to the south. The new port's main export is fish meal.

Sightseeing in post-earthquake Pisco can be a very somber experience. The San Clemente colonial cathedral on the Plaza de Armas has been replaced by a new modern building. Ask anyone where they were on August 15, 2007, and you're bound to hear some

Recovering From the 2007 Quake

The southern lowlands are part of the Ring of Fire that encircles the Pacific Ocean. The subduction of the Nazca plate beneath the South American plate causes minor tremors almost every day and major quakes every few years.

On August 15, 2007, an earthquake with a magnitude of 8.0 devastated Peru's south coast. Its epicenter—90 miles (145 km) southeast of Lima and 25 miles (40 km) off the coast—strongly affected the Ica Department. More than 550 people were killed, about 2,000 injured, and nearly 100,000 buildings destroyed. Hardest hit was the town of Pisco, where the 19th-century cathedral collapsed, killing more than 100 worshippers inside.

Most of the city's buildings were so badly damaged that they had to be razed.

In Ica, the tower of the iconic church of Señor de Luren collapsed, along with many other buildings. The city of Chincha was also hit hard by the quake, and the Panamericana was closed, partially cutting off the region in the immediate aftermath of the quake. The 2007 earthquake was one of the most devastating for Peru in recent decades. Immediately after the disaster, many international aid organizations offered help. Today the southern coast of Peru is once again ready to welcome tourists, and local residents invite travelers to return to visit the region enjoying all it has to offer.

INSIDER TIP:

For a fun trip into the Paracas reserve, contact Paracas Explorer [paracasexplorer.com], which offers package trips for adventurers and sightseers. Don't miss the dune buggies.

—CELIA CACERES
National Geographic grantee

heart-wrenching stories.

Catch a *combi* at the Plaza de Armas for the 7-mile (12 km) ride to the Paracas Peninsula, the small fishing port of **El Chaco** (also called Paracas). Since the 2007 earthquake, the number of simple, small waterfront hotels in El Chaco has grown, some new and some replacing old hotels damaged during the quake. Wherever you

stay, it is advised to use taxis at night and not to walk along deserted streets during the day.

Half-day tours to the **Islas Ballestas**—where the spectacle of seabirds and sea lions rivals that found on the Galápagos Islands—are easily arranged at the dock in El Chaco and well worth your while. Tours are conducted by speedboats that depart early every morning, when sea conditions are best. Landing on the islands is prohibited, but the boats come within a stone's throw of beaches filled with sea lions and cliffs covered with dense colonies of birds (see pp. 82–83).

During the journey to and from the islands, you might glimpse groups of large jellyfish, small groups of dolphins, and even a few whales, especially during the summer (January to March).

Bird-watchers may scope out petrels and shearwaters

Islas Ballestas

Map p. 78

(continued on p. 84)

WILDLIFE OF THE DESERT COAST

Peru's coastline is primarily desert dotted with oases. Yet, because the Peru Current flowing up the Pacific coast from Antarctica stirs up nutrients from the ocean floor, this seemingly inhospitable environment teems with wildlife. In the waters live vast amounts of tiny plankton, the bottom of a food chain that supports fish (particularly anchovies), squid, seabirds, and marine mammals in spectacular numbers. The Ballestas Islands afford the single best place to view the spectacle.

From the boat to the Ballestas you can get close-ups of the baby sea lions.

Birds

Tens of millions of seabirds inhabit the desert coastline, although their numbers decline dramatically in warmer El Niño years, when normally thriving populations of plankton and fish shrink. The species endemic to the desert coast of Peru attract bird-watchers eager to extend their life lists.

Black, with white throat, breast, and belly, yellow feet and bill, and a conspicuous red eye patch, the **Guanay cormorant** is the most abundant of the species and the main producer of commercial guano. These birds reach about 29 inches (74 cm) in length, but despite their large size, they live in dense colonies of 15 birds per 0.4 square foot (1 sq m).

Of similar size is the endearingly named **Peruvian booby,** the second most important guano producer. White with dark wings and black face masks, boobies gather in soaring flocks and perform a splashy aerial ballet as they dive for schools of fish. **Peruvian pelicans** also plunge dive for their food. At 6 feet (2 m) in length, and flying in distinctive V-shaped formations, they are a remarkable sight.

Many visitors here favor the **Humboldt penguin,** Peru's only penguin species and a year-round inhabitant of the Ballestas Islands. At 28 inches (72 cm) in length, they are amazing swimmers and can stay underwater for two minutes, reaching depths of 250 feet (80 m).

The most handsome of the coastal birds, the 16-inch-long (39 cm) **Inca tern,** has a slate blue body set off with striking white handlebar moustache feathers, its legs and bill a distinctive bright red.

The **Andean condor** occasionally makes its way to the coast, where its unmistakable 10-foot-wide (3 m) fingered wingspan can be seen gliding along beaches looking for food. The pink **Chilean flamingo** is also a highland bird, but sometimes visits the coast, usually from June to August each year.

Mammals

Large colonies of **South American sea lions** inhabit the Ballestas Islands. The larger colonies are usually composed of females, which reach 6 feet (2 m) in length and can weigh up to 330 pounds (150 kg). Males, with a short rusty mane, are twice as heavy and grow about 2 feet (0.7 m) longer. Often illegally hunted, sea lions compete with local fishermen for food.

Smaller colonies of the rarer **southern fur seal,** distinguished from sea lions by pointed rather than broad snouts and hoarse rather than barking calls, are scattered along the south coast. **Common dolphins** and **bottlenose dolphins** frequently swim alongside boats in coastal areas.

Guano Gold

Guano (seabird droppings) covers the coastal islands and cliffs of Peru in a thick, odoriferous, white layer. Derived from the Quechua word *huanu* (manure), guano has been used as a natural, nitrate-rich fertilizer

Peruvian boobies, among the guano-producing birds on the islands

since pre-Inca times. The sunny atmosphere of the coast bakes in the nitrates, and lack of rain ensures that the droppings are not washed away. During the 19th century, Peru's guano was recognized as the world's best, and by 1850, it had become the nation's main export, with nearly a million tons harvested annually.

By the early 20th century, the supply of guano had been almost completely depleted, so in 1908, the Peruvian government established the Guano Administration to manage the resource. Today Peruvians continue to harvest guano on about 30 islands and coastal headlands. Destined primarily for domestic markets, the guano is removed the traditional way, by hand, using buckets and shovels. Laborers live in tents on the islands during harvest season, which occurs approximately every seven years. When they leave, these places are once again deserted except for millions of seabirds.

**Museo Julio
C. Tello**

✉ Carretera
Pisco Puente
San Martin KM
27, Reserva
Nacional de
Paracas

☎ 056/234–383
(ext. 103)

💲 $$

**www.cultura.gob.pe/
es/ddc/ica**

skimming the waves. The boats pass a 420-foot-high (128 m) candelabra-shaped design etched into the north side of the Paracas Peninsula. Why it was constructed remains a mystery, although most researchers agree it dates to pre-Columbian times.

Bilingual guides will help you identify the seabirds and remind you to stow your camera when the boat is speeding through sprays.

Museo Julio C. Tello, named after the Peruvian archaeologist who discovered some of the most important burials in the area, is located at the reserve entrance and offers interpretations of the excavated remains. Damaged in the 2007 earthquake, the museum has been renovated and improved.

The quake also destroyed roads leading into the peninsula,

▪ Plaza San Martín in Pisco

Paracas Peninsula

Extend a morning visit to the Ballestas into a full-day tour with an added visit to the **Paracas Peninsula** ($, tours are limited; check locally for updates) in the afternoon. Located southeast of the Ballestas, the peninsula is part of a national reserve created to protect coastal biodiversity as well as many small archaeological sites. For those who are interested, the

cutting off most of the beaches favored by bird-watchers, sea lion viewers, and picnickers. Also destroyed was the famed natural rock arch known as the Cathedral, now a pile of rubble.

Other Sites

The Inca site of **Tambo Colorado** ($$) lies 30 miles (48 km) inland from Pisco along the paved road to Ayacucho. An administrative

Paracas Culture

Paracas, Quechua for "sandstorms," is an apt name for a culture buried beneath drifting coastal sands for two millennia or more. In 1925, Peruvian archaeologist Julio C. Tello (1880–1947) discovered 420 mummies in the large Wari Kayan necropolis, also known as Paracas necropolis (300 B.C.–A.D. 200), yielding some of the finest ancient textiles yet discovered.

Woven from cotton and wool, the pieces of cloth were intricately embroidered with repeating designs, often of a zoomorphic nature.

Tello also discovered a group of skulls in the necropolis that demonstrated two fascinating practices for which the Paracas culture is known: deformation and trepanation. The Paracas aristocracy deformed the malleable skulls of their young children by compressing them between tightly bound wooden boards, believing that elongated skulls signified nobility. Young warriors sometimes suffered blows to the head, which resulted in cranial swelling; the pressure was relieved by trepanning (surgically opening) the skulls. You can see excellent examples of both practices at the Museo Regional de Ica (see p. 87).

The necropolis lies near the Museo Julio C. Tello (see opposite). Visit local museums to see the best textiles recovered from the site.

---

and communications center that once controlled the Pisco Valley, Tambo Colorado has many adobe walls still standing, some of which show traces of the reddish paint that give the site its name. Hire a guide in Pisco for a tour.

Badly damaged in the 2007 earthquake, **Chincha**—located 20 miles (32 km) north of Pisco just off the Panamericana—is the heart of the largest concentration of Afro-Peruvians in the country. The district of El Carmen, 8 miles (13 km) southeast of town, draws hip young Limeños for long nights of traditional dancing during the festivals of La Virgen del Carmen de Chincha (Dec. 27), Verano Negro (late Feb.), and some national holidays.

To the east of Chincha, the vast 17th-century **Hacienda San José** in the past depended almost entirely on the work of slaves, who were locked up in the

INSIDER TIP:

During the boat crossing to the Islas Ballestas wear a light jacket to guard against wind and spray. A wide-brimmed hat protects against seabirds squirting guano.

—LARRY PORGES
*National Geographic
Travel Books editor*

---

catacombs and in the chambers of punishment, which can be visited on the guided tour. Today it is possible to stay overnight in the structure. The restaurant and its Afro-Peruvian music and dance shows are open on weekends. The *hacienda* also includes a chapel, a museum, 12 suites, 15 bungalows, and an outdoor swimming pool. ■

**Hacienda
San José**

✉ Panamericana
Sur KM 203,
El Carmen,
Chincha

☎ 056/313–332

$ $$$

**casahacienda
sanjose.com**

INLAND

South of Pisco, the Panamericana climbs inland through a seemingly inhospitable desert landscape on its way to the departmental capital of Ica and the thriving little town of Nazca. It then drops to the coast, passing through small fishing villages and port towns before swooping back inland toward Arequipa and the southern highlands. Staying inland, it passes through the sleepy town of Moquegua and Peru's most southerly city, historic Tacna.

 The sand dunes of Pozo Santo, on the road to Ica

Ica

Map p. 78

Ica's Winemaking Country

The desert landscape changes abruptly as you approach the Río Ica Valley. Water pumped through irrigation canals from an aquifer 260 feet (80 m) below the city allows local farmers to produce asparagus, most of which is exported to the United States. Other crops include cotton, paprika, and grapes—this last the basis of Ica's thriving wine and pisco industries.

Dozens of bodegas, shops often run by families or small companies, allow visitors to sample Ica's wines and piscos. The locals label the production of these handcrafted drinks *artesanal,* made by an artisan.

Home to the city's patron saint, Ica's neoclassical sanctuary, **El Señor de Luren** (*Calle Ayacucho 1057*), has drawn crowds of pilgrims for more than a century. Sadly, the church's tall, tapering spire came crashing down in the 2007 earthquake, crushing several people. After years of renovations, the sanctuary has reopened in 2019. Many other buildings in Ica were also destroyed or damaged in the quake, including some of the colonial structures around the Plaza de Armas.

Briefly closed after the quake, the useful little **Museo Regional de Ica "Adolfo Bermúdez Jenkins"** interprets the prehistory of the region. Exhibit highlights include skulls that have been trepanned in various ways, such as by drilling, sawing, and filing. Some skulls had been operated on three times, and healing of the bone indicates that the patients survived the primitive surgeries. Also look for children's skulls deformed to achieve the elongated look so prized by the upper class (see sidebar p. 85).

The museum's collection also includes pre-Inca mummies, which scientists have studied using x-rays and other techniques. Trophy heads, fossils, pottery from various cultures, and the finely woven textiles of the Paracas people are also on display. Allow an hour to visit.

The Dunes of Huacachina

Just 3 miles (5 km) from Ica you will find the sleepy oasis of **Huacachina,** with towering sand dunes tumbling around a palm tree-lined lagoon. Most travelers use this tranquil spot as a base for touring Ica and the region's bodegas, which can be arranged through local hotels. You can also go jeeping into the dunes directly from your hotel. Take sandboards with you; your driver or guide will soon show you how to go careening down the dunes like an expert.

The dunes and fields of marine **fossils** west of Ica and Huacachina indicate that this area once lay underwater. Beyond lie some of the region's most deserted and remote beaches, forming the southern reaches of the Paracas reserve. Hardy visitors can connect with wilderness tours in 4WD vehicles to combine sandboarding, fossil hunting, and fishing and camping on the coast.

In Huacachina, Desert Adventures (*tel 056/228–458, www.desertadventure.net*) arranges all-day and overnight expeditions.

Museo Regional de Ica "Adolfo Bermúdez Jenkins"

✉ Ave. Ayabaca, cuadra 8 s/n

☎ 056/234–383 (ext. 103)

💲 $

www.cultura.gob.pe/ es/ddc/ica

EXPERIENCE:
Making & Tasting Wine

If you are a wine lover, consider visiting Ica during the *vendimia* (wine harvest), a two-week festival held annually in early March, when you can watch colorful parades and beauty pageants, attend traditional dance shows and performances of the Peruvian *caballos de paso* (saddle horses), shop for local crafts, and, of course, sample local products. In full swing at that time of year, artisanal wine and pisco producers encourage everyone—from the newly crowned pageant queen to international travelers—to join in the stomping of freshly harvested grapes. Be sure to book a hotel in advance.

While you can't stomp grapes year-round, you can visit the numerous small, family-run bodegas on wine-tasting tours offered by many of the local hotels and travel agencies ($$$$$). Tours typically combine trips to large local factories that produce the well-known brands of **Ocucaje** (*ocucaje.com*), **Tacama** (*www.tacama. com*), and **Vista Alegre** (*www.vistaalegre. com.pe*) along with visits to the city's friendly bodegas, so that you can compare industrial and artisanal production.

Nazca

🗺 Map p. 78

Museo Arqueológico Antonini

✉ Ave. de la Cultura 600, Nazca

☎ 056/523–444

E-mail: info@ progettonasca.org

www.progetto nasca.org

Planetarium Maria Reiche

✉ Jr. Bolognesi, Nazca

☎ 056/522–050 or 980/767–955

💲 $$

A local fisherman will show you how to use a hand line to catch fresh fish for ceviche. In Ica, Roberto Penny Cabrera (*e-mail: roberto@icaaeserttrip.com*), an experienced guide, can arrange archaeological expeditions.

Nazca

The Panamericana next heads southeast from Ica through the orange-growing center of **Palpa,** past the Nazca Lines. Located 86 miles (141 km) from Ica and 1,935 feet (590 m) above sea level, Nazca avoids the coastal *garúa* (sea mist) and is clear and sunny year-round. Most travelers come to see the lines (see sidebar opposite), but other sites of interest are nearby.

Called the world's largest sand dune, **Cerro Blanco,** a mountain 6,847 feet (2,078 m) in height, overlooks Nazca. Although it is generally more difficult to sandboard on Cerro Blanco than in the Huacachina dunes, you can arrange it. All local tours, including

flights over the Nazca Lines, are best booked through hotels.

For more information about Nazca culture, visit the **Museo Arqueológico Antonini,** a small, high-quality private museum. Its collection includes fine ceramics, mummies, exceptionally well-preserved panpipes, and textiles. Ask for an English-language booklet for a self-guided tour. The museum director, Giuseppe Orefici, is also the archaeologist in charge of excavations at the Cahuachi pyramids (see below).

Planetarium Maria Reiche offers a 45-minute program that describes the astronomical significance of the Nazca Lines. The program is projected onto the domed ceiling every day at 7 p.m. After the show, visitors can stargaze through telescopes.

The huge site of **Cahuachi,** 15 miles (24 km) west of Nazca, comprises some 34 pyramids scattered over 9.5 square miles (24 sq km). The largest stands 125 feet (38 m) tall. For good

Nazca Culture: Reading Between the Lines

The Nazca (200 B.C.–A.D. 600) flourished on the central south coast in the centuries after the Paracas declined. Unlike their contemporaries the Moche, the Nazca left little behind but mysteries. The biggest is the Nazca Lines, mile after mile of amazing illustrations constructed on the flat desert ground.

The construction of the lines was a simple matter. The Nazca methodically pushed aside the small dark stones on the surface of the desert, exposing the lighter colored soil beneath, to construct vast spirals, glyphs, and animal shapes visible

only from the air. How they maintained perspective in areas larger than a football field and kept miles of lines perfectly straight and aligned with one another is still unclear to scholars.

German mathematician Maria Reiche (1903–1998) spent more than 50 years studying the lines and concluded that the Nazca used the lines as an astronomical calendar. Other theories abound, however, the most recent being that the Nazca Lines played an important role in the veneration of the single most important substance in the desert—water.

views of this impressive pyramid, whose interior is closed, follow the trail that leads part of the way up the left side.

The Nazca probably used Cahuachi (200 B.C.–A.D. 450) for ceremonial and religious purposes. Near the tops of the pyramids, archaeologists have discovered some burials whose artifacts have been transferred to the Antonini museum in Nazca. At present, the dirt road to Cahuachi is in poor condition, but improvements are planned; admission to the site may be charged in the future.

Approximately 4 miles (7 km) east of Nazca, the aqueducts of **Cantalloc** ($) provide a fascinating example of 1,500-year-old Nazca ingenuity. Still in use today, more than 30 underground aqueducts— each lined with stonework—are linked together and fed by a spring. They can be reached by 20 large spiral, walk-in wells. Today farmers use the wells to clean the canals, but the Nazca probably used them for rituals. Guided tours and entry fees ($) include less well-preserved sites.

Most travelers visit the **Chauchilla Cemetery** ($$), 19 miles (30 km) south of Nazca. Twenty years ago, bones and skulls from Nazca burials lay scattered haphazardly across the desert, the work of grave robbers. At Chauchilla, archaeologists have assembled the funerary remains and reconstructed several burial pits similar to those used by the Nazca. A tiny on-site museum has three mummies and some photos, as well as an interesting 550-yard (0.5 km) trail around the burials.

EXPERIENCE:
Fly Over the Nazca Lines

A 40-foot-high (12 m) observation tower north of Nazca gives foreshortened views of three of the famous designs, but to see the most impressive shapes you must take to the air. This necessity gave rise to the dubious theory that the Nazca made hot-air balloons from cotton and reeds so that they, too, could see the spiral-tail monkey, the hummingbird in flight, the whale, and the spider.

Easily booked from Nazca hotels, light aircraft leave from Nazca airport daily on 30-minute flights ($$$$$) over the lines. You can arrange for a longer flight in Ica or Lima. Most of the flights leave in the morning to avoid treacherous afternoon winds. The planes make tight turns to view the lines, however, so passengers prone to travel sickness should avoid eating before the flight.

Other Places

While in Nazca, arrange a tour of **Reserva Nacional Pampas Galeras.** Although not in the southern lowlands, this highland reserve is only about 55 miles (89 km) from Nazca and best reached via the paved road to Cusco. A sanctuary for the endangered vicuña (see pp. 104–105), the reserve stages a three-day roundup and shearing ceremony in June that is worth a visit. Some tours offer a mountain-biking option for all or part of the downhill descent back to Nazca.

The pre-Columbian port of **Puerto Inca** once supplied fresh seafood to the Inca in Cusco. The site and part of the Inca road are in good condition and reached via a

Santuario Nacional Lagunas de Mejía
☎ 968/218–434
💲 $$$
www.sernanp.gob.pe/lagunas-de-mejia

Moquegua
🗺 Map p. 79

Museo Contisuyo
✉ Calle Tacna 294
☎ 053/461–844
💲 $
www.museoconti suyo.com

2-mile (3 km) side road at KM 603 of Carretera Panamericana Sur, 6 miles (10 km) northwest of the fishing village of Chala. The southbound Panamericana then drops to the coast and passes **Chala** about 107 miles (170 km) from Nazca.

The Panamericana follows the coastline heading southeast past the town of **Camaná,** 134 miles (220 km) from Chala, where you will find simple hotels and a beach nearby. It then climbs inland for 92 miles (150 km) to the junction of **La Repartición.** Here you can choose between three different routes:

■ The dunes in Pozo Santo are popular for riding.

continuing north-east to Arequipa (see pp. 96–103), 30 miles (50 km) away; going south-west to the port of Mollendo, 50 miles (80 km) away; or continuing south-east for another 90 miles (150 km) along the Pan-American Highway to Moquegua.

Once the main port of Arequipa, **Mollendo**—quiet for most of the year—bustles with Arequipeño beachgoers during the hot summer months (*Jan.–Mar.*). Admire the

old-fashioned wooden houses as you descend down the steep streets toward the ocean, or sit and relax in one of the town's pleasant plazas.

Bird-watchers should follow for 10 miles (16 km) southeast of Mollendo the paved road to the **Santuario Nacional Lagunas de Mejía.** Encompassing the mouth of the Río Tambo and surrounding coastal scrublands and lakes, this bird refuge, where about 80 species have been recorded, is among the best places in Peru to see both resident and migrant birds from all over the Americas. The sanctuary includes a visitor center, 4.5 miles (8 km) of foot trails, and several viewing platforms. Bring insect repellent and be prepared to wade through water along some trails.

Moquegua

Moquegua, which means "silent place" in Quechua, is the dusty, dry capital of the department of the same name. Set in Peru's most arid desert, the city survives quite well on the agriculture based on the Río Moquegua. Foremost among its products are grapes and fine pisco; avocados, corn, wheat, potatoes, and fruit are also important.

The **Plaza de Armas,** with a fountain attributed to Gustave Eiffel (see sidebar p. 17), is the focus of some notable buildings. The **Museo Contisuyo** is housed behind the main wall of the Iglesia Santa Catalina de Alejandria, which was the principal church in Moquegua until its collapse during the 1868 earthquake. The museum has a display, labeled in Spanish and English, of local artifacts from the Stone Age to Inca times. It also provides visitors with information about local history and colonial houses.

Opposite, the **Casa Tradicional de Moquegua,** inside which a bistro has been opened offering traditional meat-based dishes and wines from the area, boasts an 18th-century wooden balcony. Also on this block, the partially restored 18th-century jail houses the **Dirección Regional de Cultura,** which displays local documents and art. The **Post Office** (*Ave. Ayacucho 560, closed Sun.*) is in an 18th-century house. Some buildings on this block have typical steep-sided Moqueguan roofs.

Formerly a monastery, the **Catedral de Santo Domingo** became the city's cathedral after the collapse of Iglesia Santa Catalina. One altar venerates the supposed remains of Santa Fortunata, whom locals claim was a virgin saint martyred around A.D. 300, buried in Rome, and exhumed and transported to Moquegua in 1798.

Several colonial buildings in varying states of repair stand along calle Moquegua and calle Ayacucho, both crossing from the Plaza de Armas. Many of the walls are made of *quincha* (cane and mud), which holds up well in earthquakes but suffers long-term damage from the elements. The steeply gabled roofs are rounded, a style called *mojinete.* To sample the local pisco, head to **Bodega Norbertho Villegas** (*Calle Ayacucho 1370, closed Sun.*), which makes its own.

A spectacular, but lonely, 183-mile-long (300 km) paved road leads from Moquegua to Desaguadero on Lake Titicaca,

on the border between Peru and Bolivia. Along the way, stop at **Cerro Baúl,** an early Wari city (see sidebar p. 168) near the village of Torata, 15 miles (24 km) east of Moquegua, city where you can plan a visit to the archaeological site and reserve a taxi.

INSIDER TIP:

Try to visit San Fernando Bay and reserve, 37 miles [60 km] south of Nazca; it's one of the best sites on the coast to see wildlife.

—CHRISTOPHER AUGER-DOMÍNGUEZ
National Geographic International Editions photographer

Tacna

Located about 30 miles (48 km) from the Chilean border, **Tacna,** Peru's southernmost city, was occupied by Chile from 1880 to 1929, after the War of the Pacific. The Plaza de Armas has an arch dedicated to the war heroes and another fountain designed by Gustave Eiffel, who also designed the cathedral.

One of the oldest buildings in Tacna, the early 19th-century **Casa de Zela** was home to Francisco Antonio de Zela (1768–1819), who in 1811 gave the city its first voice of independence. It is an archaeological museum. The **Museo Histórico** (*Calle Apurimac 202, tel 052/428–486, closed Sat.–Sun., $*) has a collection pertaining to the War of the Pacific. **Museo Ferroviario** displays pieces of old railroad rolling stock and train enthusiasts' paraphernalia, as well as postage stamps featuring trains. ∎

Casa Tradicional de Moquegua
- ✉ Calle Ayacucho 540, Moquegua
- ☎ 981/581–820
- 🕐 Closed Sun.
- 💲 $$ (bistrò)

Dirección Regional de Cultura
- ✉ Calle Ayacucho 530, Moquegua
- ☎ 053/461–691
- 🕐 Closed Sat.–Sun.

Catedral de Santo Domingo
- ✉ 6th block of calle Ayacucho, Moquegua
- ☎ 053/462–011

Tacna
- 🗺 Map p. 79

Casa de Zela
- ✉ Calle Zela 542, Tacna

Museo Ferroviario
- ✉ Calle Gregorio Albarracin & calle 2 de Mayo, Tacna
- ☎ 965/074–455
- 💲 $

An area of deep canyons, imperial mountains, and one majestic lake, with an enchanting colonial city at its heart

SOUTHERN HIGHLANDS

◼ Misti towers above Arequipa.

SOUTHERN HIGHLANDS

Peruvians will tell you that the southern highlands are like nowhere else in the world. Indeed, this sprawling, wild region is filled with spectacular natural scenery as well as one of Peru's loveliest cities. Until recently, unpaved roads made travel in the region difficult. Today, despite the fact that a major paved highway serves this area, the southern highlands still retain a sense of cultural and political independence.

Residents of the Uros Islands in Lake Titicaca

The southern highlands of Peru are home to the two deepest canyons in the world, the little-known Colca and Cotahuasi. Whether you decide to take in the spectacular views from the top or venture out onto the rushing waters below, you're in for the adventure of a lifetime. The Andean condor, the largest flying bird in the world, calls this region home, as do many other highland birds including flamingos, hummingbirds, and ibises, species often associated with the tropics but which have adapted well to the high altitude here. You can even catch a glimpse of the rare vicuña, the prettiest of the Andean camelids, at the Salinas y Aguada Blanca nature reserve.

Beautiful Arequipa—a kaleidoscope of graceful colonial buildings and fast-paced modern culture—is the world's largest colonial city constructed of volcanic rock. Still active today, the violent volcanoes looming over the city bear witness to the ancient sacrifices of young Inca women, their bodies left frozen on the summits for centuries. Recently discovered by mountaineering archaeologists, the mummified maidens are now on display at the Museo Santuarios Andinos in Arequipa.

First ascended by Inca wearing simple sandals, the region's peaks—Coropuna, Misti, Mismi, Solimana, and others—now attract climbers the world over with the irresistible opportunity to make some of the highest nontechnical ascents in the world. Anyone with plenty of stamina and an experienced guide can enjoy the satisfaction of climbing to 19,000 feet (5,791 m) and beyond.

Located a breathless 12,507 feet (3,812 m) above sea level, Lake Titicaca is the highest navigable lake in the world. It is also South America's largest lake and the largest body of water in the world located more than 6,500 feet (2,000 m) above sea level. Local boat operators provide residents and tourists with regular passenger services across its tranquil waters. The border between Peru and Bolivia runs right through the lake

There is no better way to experience the otherworldly thrill of Titicaca than to watch the sun rise and set from one of the dozens of islands dotting the lake. Some of the islands are inhabited by people whose way of life has changed little in centuries. Recently, however,

these tough, self-sufficient highlanders have opened their doors to travelers who want to spend a night or more on this luminous lake. ∎

NOT TO BE MISSED:

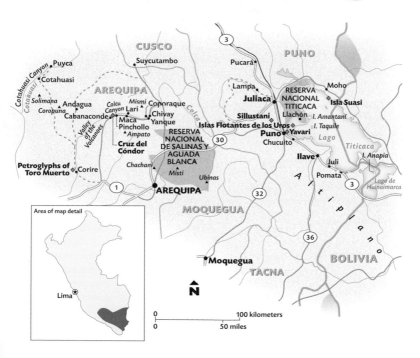

AREQUIPA

Arequipa sits in a fertile valley in the western Andes dominated by volcanic peaks that soar to almost 20,000 feet (6,096 m). Prettily perched at 7,808 feet (2,380 m) above sea level, this colonial city enjoys a year-round spring-like climate, with little rain and plenty of sun. Because many of its historic buildings were made from a light-colored volcanic stone called sillar, Arequipa—which sparkles like a pearl in the sunlight—is known throughout Peru as *la ciudad blanca*, the white city.

■ The Plaza de Armas in Arequipa

Arequipa

🗺 Maps pp. 95 & 99

Visitor Information

✉ iPerú, Plaza de Armas, Portal de la Municipalidad 110

✉ 054/223–265

E-mail: iperuare quipa@prom peru.gob.pe

"Ari, quepay"

According to legend, the city's name dates to the 14th century, when the fourth Inca, Mayta Capac, traveled to the region. When his soldiers, enamored of the climate and productive soil, asked if they could stay, he replied in Quechua, *"Ari, quepay*–Yes, stay."

The Spaniards refounded Arequipa on August 15, 1540—the Catholic feast day of the Lady of the Assumption. She is now the city's patron saint, and residents mark the date with several days of processions and parties.

At first, the Spaniards erected adobe buildings, but they soon discovered that sillar lent itself better to construction and carving. In 1600, a major earthquake destroyed most of the city. To prevent future destruction, locals developed a distinctive architectural style characterized by squat, thick buildings graced with carvings etched deeply into the soft rock. Earthquakes have shaken Arequipa regularly since 1600. Nevertheless, although they frequently damaged the outskirts of the city, the earthquakes have largely spared the low, colonial-era structures.

INSIDER TIP:

Impress your friends and toast *"¡Provecho!,"* Peruvian slang for "Enjoy your meal!" before digging into some ceviche.

–SARAH SHAW
National Geographic contributor

A proud supporter of the wars of independence in the early 1820s, Arequipa had little contact with the rest of Peru until a railroad connected it to the coastal city of Mollendo in 1870. Afterward, Arequipa grew into southern Peru's commercial center. With a current population exceeding 800,000, Arequipa is considered Peru's second most important city, but even today, Peruvians still joke that Arequipeños are a people unto themselves.

Arequipa's Colonial Heart

Most of the city's famed colonial buildings are within walking distance of the splendid

Plaza de Armas. Filled with palm trees, flowery gardens, and relaxing benches arranged around a central fountain, the white stone plaza is famed as Peru's most elegant. The city's block-long cathedral defines the north side of the plaza, while lazy arcades of sillar line the others. The plaza's key points are surprisingly distant; the extensive glaciated mountain of Chachani rises beyond the cathedral, and to its right, Misti's perfect cone beckons climbers.

The long, storied history of the **Catedral de Arequipa** begins in 1544, when the city's authorities ordered its construction. A series of earthquakes, fires, and volcanic eruptions repeatedly damaged the church, which was finally destroyed by fire. The current, elaborately designed neoclassical cathedral was built in 1844 then rebuilt in 1868 after

(continued on p. 100)

Catedral de Arequipa

- ▲ Map p. 99
- ✉ Plaza de Armas
- ☎ 054/213-149
- 🕐 Closed Sun. (museum)

www.museocatedral arequipa.org.pe

Mario Vargas Llosa House Museum

The city of Arequipa boasts the home of Mario Vargas Llosa, an internationally renowned Peruvian writer, awarded the Nobel Prize for Literature in 2010. Following a major renovation, in 2014 the building was transformed into an interesting interactive museum. The 17 exhibition halls illustrate the life of the writer by describing his journey from childhood to the achievement of the Nobel Prize, in an immersive multimedia journey with holograms and 3D videos. *(Ave. Parra 101, tel 054 / 283-574, closed Sun.)*

A WALK THROUGH COLONIAL AREQUIPA

Despite several devastating earthquakes, Arequipa's colonial heritage—most grandly demonstrated in its architecture—remains one of the city's main attractions. Solidly built structures with thick, low walls made of white volcanic sillar have enabled centuries-old buildings to survive, while recent reconstruction efforts have brought them proudly back to life.

Shimmering gold altar, Iglesia de la Compañía

NOT TO BE MISSED:

Museo Santuarios Andinos • Casa de Moral • Monasterio de Santa Catalina • Santa Teresa

Leave the palm-filled **Plaza de Armas** (see p. 97) at its southeast corner. At the intersection of Calles Morán and Álvarez Thomas stands the 17th-century Jesuit church, **La Compañía ❶** (see p. 100), whose gold-covered altar and side chapels demand attention.

A few steps east, the church's **cloisters** elegantly retain their religious air while discreetly housing boutiques selling top-quality alpaca goods. Two more blocks along Morán will bring you to **Santo Domingo ❷** (*tel 054/213–511*). Frequently damaged by earthquakes, this 16th-century church has been rebuilt several times. Return the way you came, turning left on Calle San Juan de Dios. When you reach bustling Calle Palacio Viejo, turn right.

At the first intersection, turn left on Calle Álvarez Thomas. Here you will find the **Museo Arqueológico UNSA ❸**, managed by the Universidad Nacional de San Augustín, which houses 14,000 artifacts including Nazca, Huari, and Inca ceramics (*tel 054/288–881, www.unsa. edu.pe, closed Sat.–Sun.*). Go one block before turning right onto Calle Consuelo. The solid, 17th-century facade of **Casa Arango** (*Calle Consuelo bet. Calles Álvarez Thomas & La Merced, closed to public*) will impress. At La Merced, turn left and walk to **Iglesia de la Merced ❹** (*La Merced 303, tel 054/213–233*). Construction on Arequipa's second oldest church began in 1551; it has been rebuilt several times since then and houses a remarkable colonial library.

Retrace your steps along La Merced crossing Consuelo and visit **Casa Goyeneche ❺** (*La Merced 201, tel 054/212–251, closed Sat.–Sun.*), a 16th-century mansion occupied by the Banco Central de Reserva since 1970. The building has spacious courtyards surrounded by several rooms that house colonial and republican art and period furniture. The Goyeneche family, whose coat of arms embellishes the facade, owned the building from 1782 until 1945. Its most famous member, Bishop José Sebastián Goyeneche (1784–1872), was instrumental in rebuilding the cathedral.

Go north along La Merced past **Museo Santuarios Andinos ❻** (see p. 100) and cross the Plaza de Armas to visit the **Catedral de Arequipa ❼** (see pp. 97, 100). From the northeast corner of the plaza, head north a few doors to **Casa Tristán del Pozo** (*Calle San Francisco 115, tel 054/215–060,* *closed Sun.*). Owned by the Banco Continental, the classic colonial courtyards and austere early 18th-century rooms now bustle with the incongruous sight of 21st-century bankers.

Cross the street to enter Pasaje Catedral, a pedestrian alley filled with high-quality shops. When you reach Calle Santa Catalina, proceed left to **Complejo cultural Chávez de la Rosa** (*Calle Santa Catalina 101, closed Sat.–Sun.*). This colonial house now hosts art shows under the auspices of Universidad de San Agustín.

Walk a block west along Calle San Agustín until you see the 18th-century facade of the church of **San Agustín** on the left. Turn right onto Calle Bolívar and head north. Then make another right on Calle Moral and pay a visit to **Casa de Moral** ❽ (see p. 102), Arequipa's most interesting colonial mansion. Continue east to Calle Santa Catalina, turn left, and walk a block to the city's most famous attraction, the **Monasterio de Santa Catalina** ❾ (see pp. 100–101).

Continue north on Santa Catalina; turn right on Calle Zela and walk a block to the church and museum of **San Francisco** ❿ (see p. 101). Continue east for three blocks to the fascinating church and museum of **Santa Teresa** ⓫ (see p. 101).

⊠ See also area map p. 95
▶ La Compañía
⟷ 1.75 miles (2.8 km)
🕒 1.25 hours
▶ Santa Teresa

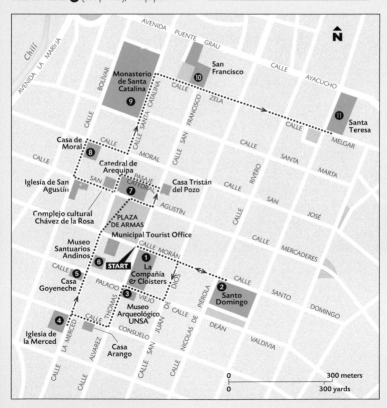

La Compañía

🗺 Map p. 99

✉ Calle Móran
  & calle Álvarez
  Thomas

☎ 054/212–141

www.jesuitasaqp.pe

Museo Santuarios Andinos

🗺 Map p. 99

✉ Calle La Merced 110

☎ 054/215–013
  054/286–614

🕐 Closed early Sun.

💲 $$ (guide not included)

www.ucsm.edu.pe

suffering substantial additional earthquake damage. It lost one of its towers in the 2001 quake but has since been repaired.

Marked by high vaults, the cathedral's uncluttered interior has a universal flavor, with an altar of Italian marble, a Spanish chandelier, an enormous, ornate pulpit carved in France, and one of the largest organs on the continent, donated by Belgium in 1870. The cathedral is one of only 70 basilicas in the world entitled to fly the yellow-and-white flag of the Vatican. The flag flies to the left of the main altar, near an alcove dedicated to Sister Ana de los

The Church of La Compañía in Arequipa

Angeles (1604–1686). Beatified by Pope John Paul II in 1985, Ana lived in the local Santa Catalina Monastery until her death.

Built in 1654, the Jesuit church of **La Compañía** stands just off the southeastern corner of the plaza. Its facade, added

in 1698, is one of Peru's finest examples of the intricate Latin American baroque style known as churrigueresque. Don't miss the church's main altar, and several of its side chapels, all covered in gold leaf, or the unique **San Ignacio chapel** ($). Located to the left of the main altar, the chapel features a polychrome cupola covered with murals of tropical plants and animals interspersed with angels and warriors.

Inca Mummies

While near the plaza, take an hour for the guided tour of the university-run **Museo Santuarios Andinos.** The tour—the only way to see the museum's collection—begins with a 20-minute National Geographic film recounting the 1995 discovery of Inca children sacrificed and buried on the 20,700-foot-high (6,310 m) glaciated summit of Ampato. It continues with a look at Inca clothing and artifacts, an explanation of where archaeologists found the bodies, and a respectful viewing of the most famous mummy, Juanita, now carefully preserved in a refrigerated case. (*Jan.–Apr. Juanita is replaced by less well-preserved Sarita.*)

Religious Sanctuaries

Arequipa's most famous colonial religious building, the **Monasterio de Santa Catalina,** was founded in 1580 by María de Guzmán, a wealthy widow who donated her riches and became a nun. At times the building housed nearly 200 Dominican sisters and their servants. Since the nuns took vows of isolation, they never left the convent, which became a virtual city-within-a-city. Opened to the public in 1970, the convent now gives a fascinating glimpse at early religious architecture, painting, furniture, and lifestyle. Hire one of the multilingual guides, or go it alone along the maze of

church. The Virgin, her body encompassed by a halo draped with cherubs, stands atop a globe with angels and the four evangelists worshipping at her feet. Adjoining the church, the **Museo de San Francisco** features cloisters, religious art, and a colonial library.

The convent of **Santa Teresa** was founded as a Carmelite

Monasterio de Santa Catalina

🅰 Map p. 99

✉ Calle Santa Catalina 301

☎ 054/221–213
054/221–234
054/221–235

🕐 Open daily till 5 p.m. & till 8 p.m. Tues. & Wed.

💲 $$$$

www.santacatalina.org.pe

Traveling on Arequipa's Buses

Most long-distance buses leave from the Terrapuerto (*Ave. Arturo Ibánez s/n, tel 054/348–810*) or the larger adjacent Terminal Terrestre (*Ave. Cáceres & Calle Arturo Ibánez, tel 054/427–792*), about 2 miles (3 km) south of the city center.

The longest direct journey is to Lima (*14–18 hrs., $$$–$$$$$*). Other key destinations include Tacna (*5–6 hrs., $–$$$*), Puno (*5–6 hrs., $–$$$*), Cusco (*10–12 hrs., $$$$–$$$$$*), and Chivay (*3–4 hrs., $*).

Buses leave once or twice a day for Cabanaconde, Corire, Andagua, and other villages in the Colca Canyon region beyond Chivay.

Among the companies, **Civa** (*tel 054/432–208*), **TEPSA** (*tel 054/424–135*) and **Cromotex** (*tel 054/451–555*) reach the main Peruvian cities such as Lima and Cusco while **Reyna** (*tel 054/425–812*) and **Ormeño** (*tel 054/427–788*) operate in the area surrounding Arequipaa.

brilliantly colored streets that open onto cloisters and cells, kitchens and laundries, chapels and classrooms. About 30 nuns still live in a private part of the convent, making the soaps and pastries sold in the convent's gift shop and café.

The redbrick columns and arches of the nearby church of **San Francisco** contrast sharply with its white sillar walls. Inside, 25 panels of brightly painted biblical scenes top the altar; cracks in the cupola attest to the region's seismic activity. A fantastic float of Arequipa's patron saint, the Virgin of the Assumption, rests in the left rear of the

monastery in 1710. Since 2005 part of the structure has housed the **Museo de Arte Virreinal.** An introductory display explains the early development of painting in the region as well as the techniques used to carve religious statues and apply gold leaf.

Among the museum's highlights, the exquisite monstrance crafted by Arequipeño masters in the 1730s glitters with diamonds and other gems, including an emerald the size of a Brazil nut. The priceless piece has a security camera hidden in its center, surrounded by golden leaves and ears of wheat. Don't miss the extraordinary

San Francisco

🅰 Map p. 99

✉ Calle Zela & Calle San Francisco

Museo de San Francisco

✉ Calle Zela 103

☎ 054/223–048

☎ Closed Sun.

💲 $

Santa Teresa

🅰 Map p. 99

✉ Calle Melgar 303

☎ 054/281–188

🕐 Closed Sun.

💲 $$

museosantateresa.org

Casa del Moral

△ Map p. 99
✉ Calle Moral 318
☎ 054/285–371
🕐 Closed Sun.
💲 $

Convento de la Recoleta

✉ Calle Recoleta 117
☎ 054/270–966
🕐 Closed Sun.
💲 $

18th-century nativity chest, which opens into a 6.5-foot-wide (2 m) diorama filled with intricately carved reliefs of well-known biblical scenes.

Three blocks southwest of the Monasterio stands the **Casa del Moral.** Built in 1733, and named after a 200-year-old mulberry tree within the main patio, Arequipa's best-preserved colonial mansion features a baroque entrance with cantuta blooms (Peru's national flower) carved into the lintels. The 1868 earthquake destroyed the roof but left the walls standing. The building stayed in poor condition until 1948, when the English consul, Arthur Williams, bought and restored it.

Today, the Banco de Crédito owns and operates the mansion as a museum of Arequipeño colonial architecture. Its exhibits include period Peruvian and imported furniture, alpaca-wool carpets, paintings by the Cusco school of artists, and 18th-century maps, as well as frequently rotating shows of work by local artists.

Away From the Center

Several interesting colonial sites located in what used to be the *campiña* (countryside), now part of the city's suburban sprawl, lie just a short cab ride ($–$$) from Arequipa. Small buses known as *combis* ($) can also get you to these places. It is best to ask at the tourist office (see p. 96) or your hotel for recommended routes.

Founded in 1648, the red-steepled **Convento de la Recoleta** stands on the west side of the Río Chili. Although the Franciscan church has been added to numerous times over the centuries, its four cloisters remain an unmistakably colonial island of peace. Recently built sections include a fabulous library of more than 20,000 volumes, the oldest of which was printed in 1494. Bibliophiles may enter for a short visit accompanied by a monk or site guide (*offer*). The museum exhibits a diverse collection of objects, including religious art, pre-Columbian mummies and masks, and fascinating Amazonian artifacts collected by the Franciscans on their missionary forays into the jungle.

About 1 mile (1.6 km) northwest of Arequipa's city center, beyond the Puente Grau (Grau Bridge), lies the neighborhood of **Yanahuara,** whose central plaza boasts a 19th-century mirador with a series of sillar-stone arches that beautifully frame Misti and parts of the city—a perfect photo-postcard opportunity.

Also in the plaza, the mid-18th-century **Iglesia San Juan Batista** features a late churrigueresque facade and a side altar venerating La Virgen de Chapi, whose image is proudly paraded through the town on her feast day of May 1. Admission to the church is free but the opening hours are erratic. Combine a visit to the plaza with lunch at the Sol de Mayo restaurant (see Travelwise p. 282), just five blocks away.

Inca terraces mark the outskirts of **Sabandía,** which was once a village in its own right and is now a suburb of Arequipa located about 5 miles (8 km) southeast of the city. Be sure to visit the 18th-century flour mill, **El Molino de Sabandía,** which you can watch at work upon request. Perfect for picnics, the grassy areas around the mill offer splendid views of the volcano.

Climbing Misti

Although the area around Arequipa is perfect for beginning climbers, the high elevations, steep routes, and severe, changeable weather mean that everyone should take these ascents seriously. Good equipment is essential, and, since many routes are not clearly marked, a guide is recommended. Guided climbs start around $80 per person, depending on the mountain, group size, and services such as transportation.

Loose volcanic soil makes the route to the top of Misti (19,102 feet/5,822 m) difficult, yet it is a popular climb. Other peaks around Arequipa include Coropuna (21,080 feet/6,425 m), the tallest in southern Peru, and Mismi (18,363/5,597 m), the source of the Amazon River. ∎

El Molino de Sabandía
☎ 959/839–545
$ $
**www.elmolino
desabandia.com**

EXPERIENCE: Enjoy the Southern Highlands' Fiestas

You'll find fiestas throughout Peru, but to experience real fervor, join the festivities in the Colca Canyon and Lake Titicaca regions where locals celebrate with gusto.

Tierra Santa (*3rd Thurs. in Jan.*) Amantaní Island

Día de San Sebastián (*Jan. 20*) Pinchollo

Virgen de la Candelaria (Candlemas; *Feb. 2*) Festivity that combines elements of the Catholic religion with the Andean traditions. It takes place in the city of Puno, where hundreds of costumed musicians and dancers perform in the *morenada*, a typical form of dance-theater of the Aymara culture that stages the transfer of black slaves from the silver mines—where they were initially employed and to whom conditions could not survive—to the Bolivian plantations. In 2014 the event was proclaimed Intangible Cultural Heritage of Humanity by UNESCO.

Semana Santa (Holy Week; *Mar./Apr.*) Candlelight procession on Good Friday in Puno; fiesta on Taquile Island

Día de San Juan (*Mar. 7–8*) Processions in Puno

Las Cruces (Crosses Festival; *May 2–4*) Music and dance on Taquile Island

Día de San Antonio (*June 13*) Yanque and Maca

Día de Santiago (*July 25*) Held on Taquile Island, Lampa, and Coporaque

Virgen de la Asunta (Patron Saint of Chivay; *Aug. 15*) Weeklong festival

Día de Puno (Puno Week; *Nov. 5*) Celebrated following Inca Manco Capac's legendary rise from Lake Titicaca

Inmaculada Concepcion (Immaculate Conception; *Dec. 8*) Traditional dances, including the *wititi*, held over five days in Chivay and Yanque

SOUTH AMERICAN CAMELS

Unique to the continent, the four South American camelids (in the same family as Old World camels) exist in greater numbers in the Peruvian highlands than anywhere else in the Andes. Two of them, the familiar llama and alpaca, have been domesticated, while the vicuña and guanaco are essentially wild.

The llama's banana-shaped ears help to distinguish it from the similar alpaca.

Llamas

Domesticated in the Lake Titicaca region more than 6,000 years ago, the llama (*Lama glama*), at 250 to 400 pounds (114–182 kg) and up to 6 feet (2 m) tall, was the largest domesticated animal on the continent until the Spaniards arrived with their horses and cattle.

Historically used for the transportation of goods, the llama still works today as a pack animal, capable of carrying up to 50 pounds (22.5 kg). To the amazement of the Inca, early Europeans attempted to ride these diminutive beasts. The llamas, distressed by the extra weight upon them, would twist their necks and spit at the riders, leading to the popular myth that llamas generally spit at people. In fact, llamas are more likely to spit at rivals during mating season than at humans.

INSIDER TIP:

In order not to damage the trails of the southern highlands, take a llama; their feet have leathery pads that don't need metal shoes.

–ROB RACHOWIECKI
National Geographic author

The indigenous peoples of Peru, who regularly ate the llama's tough meat, also used the animal's coarse fur for ropes or rough yarn and its dried dung as fuel. A vital part of everyday life, llamas were sacrificed to Inti, the Inca sun god, and to other gods by pre-Inca cultures.

EXPERIENCE:
Take an Alpaca Tour

Watch how farmers raise alpacas, and learn about the history of the alpaca textile industry in Peru, on a tour offered by **Colca Explorer** (*Calle Mariscal Benavides 201, Selva Alegre, tel 054/282–488, e-mail: ventas@ colca-explorer.com, www.colca-explorer.com*). Based at the Colca Lodge (*colca-lodge. com*) where you can also stay overnight, the trip offers participants the opportunity to feed, and even shear, alpacas.

Alpacas

Domesticated soon after the llama, alpacas (*Lama pacos*) were raised for their fine wool. Softer than most sheep wool, alpaca fleece is sought-after the world over, and alpaca farms have sprung up in North America, Europe, and Australia. About 80 percent of the world's estimated four million alpacas live in the highlands of southern Peru, where they form a major part of the economy of highland campesinos (peasants). Formerly eaten only by poor campesinos, alpaca meat—high in protein, low in fat and cholesterol—has recently earned a place in the fashionable *novo-Andino* (New Andean) cuisine.

Vicuña & Guanaco

Peru's smallest camelid, the delicate and skittish vicuña (*Vicugna vicugna*), has the finest wool in the world, and its golden coat and white belly make it the prettiest of the four species. Its wool is sheared during *chaccus* (ceremonial roundups) in late May or June, after which the animals are released back into the wild. In Inca times, only nobles wore the luxurious wool. After the Spanish conquest, however, the wool was more widely used and the animals began to dwindle. By the mid-20th century, the vicuña was in real danger of extinction. As a result, reserves

such as **Pampas Galeras** (see p. 89) above Nazca and **Salinas y Aguada Blanca** (see p. 107) near Arequipa established conservation programs. By 1995, the number of vicuña had recovered sufficiently to permit shearing once again, which in turn aided the growth of local economies profiting from the sale of the wool. Today there are more than 100,000 vicuñas in Peru.

Already extinct in Ecuador and Colombia, the guanaco (*Lama guanicoe*) is the scarcest of the camelids in Peru (larger populations exist in Bolivia and Chile). The wool of the guanaco is not fine enough to use in the manufacture of clothing and other items, but its meat is edible, thus in recent years hunting has decimated the small Peruvian population.

■ The llama grazes on native plants and grasses and can exist in either lush or arid conditions.

CANYONS & VOLCANOES

With snowcapped mountains, numerous active volcanoes, and the world's deepest canyons, the spectacular countryside surrounding Arequipa is not an easy place to build highways. Visitors to this wild and remote area must rely on rough, unpaved roads that can quickly turn into quagmires during the rainy season (Jan.–April). However, marvelous scenery, friendly inhabitants, and extreme adventure opportunities await the intrepid traveler.

Terraces along the walls of Colca Canyon in the southern highlands of Peru

Cañón del Colca

🗺 Map p. 95

Boleto Turístico (Tourist Ticket)

💲 $$$$$

cosituc.gob.pe

An excursion to Cañón del Colca (Colca Canyon) begins at Chivay, 100 miles (160 km) north of Arequipa. The canyon reaches its maximum depth in the Huambo region, where the bed of the Río Colca is 3,200 feet (1,000 m) above sea level while, a few tens of miles southeast of Cabanaconde, the Ampato volcano rises more than 19,000 feet (6,000 m) of altitude. The village of Chivay (3,630 m) is located in the center of the Cañón del Colca. Unspoiled Andean villages lie along both rims, where you

will find pre-Inca terracing and colonial churches.

Within the canyon, foot trails make their way through the sprawling high-desert scenery, passing cactuses and oases hosting palm trees. Road bridges cross the upper canyon of the Río Colca on the north side of Chivay, between Yanque and Coporaque and between Lari and Maca.

Human History

About 2,000 years ago, the Collagua and Cabana peoples inhabited the Colca region.

INSIDER TIP:

Ask before you take people's pictures. You might offer a few cents; be gracious and they will appreciate the courtesy. Stop taking pictures if local people object.

—JAMES DION
National Geographic Society, Director Tourism Programs, Maps Division

Their modern descendants, who speak a form of Aymara, still live here and they continue to maintain centuries-old agricultural practices. The women wear traditional broad, embroidered skirts and heavily sequined blouses. Cabana women wear brightly sequined felt hats, while the Collagua prefer straw boaters bedecked with ribbons.

The men no longer wear traditional clothes but retrieve them during the Fiesta de la Inmaculada Concepción (Feast of the Immaculate Conception) on December 8, when they perform the ancient *wititi* dance in Chivay, proclaimed Intangible Cultural Heritage of Humanity by UNESCO in 2015. It is a form of ritual courtship that marks the transition to adult life. The men, wearing flashy female costumes, cavort with the women, trying to kidnap one: They call it *danza de amor* (love dance).

Condor-watchers

Many visitors, eager for a glimpse of an Andean condor, travel to the Colca region, where they watch these giants glide by at close quarters. The most popular spot, **Cruz del Cóndor** (see p. 108), lies about 19 miles (30 km) west of Chivay on the canyon's south rim. Your best chance to see the birds is around 9 a.m. during the dry months (May–Dec.), when the canyon thermals begin to rise over the rim. The dry months are also best for viewing flamingos in the altiplano (high Andean flatlands) en route to Chivay.

Hiking in Colca Canyon

Typical tours of the canyon begin by taking Highway 30 out of Arequipa to **Reserva Nacional de Salinas y Aguada Blanca,** famed for its vicuñas and volcanoes, including Misti, Chachani, and Ubinas. The route turns off the highway and follows a rough road that reaches a height of nearly 15,750 feet (4,800 m), so travelers should acclimatize in Arequipa for a few days before making the trip. On the way, you may spot a flamingo here and there, but generally the terrain is bleak.

The dirt road switchbacks down from the nature reserve to **Chivay,** where you will be able to find an inexpensive hotel for the night. You can also reach Chivay easily by public bus from Arequipa (see sidebar p. 101). A five-minute walk from the plaza, on the south side of town, Chivay's bus terminal has several

Reserva Nacional de Salinas y Aguada Blanca

🅰 Map p. 95

☎ 054/257–461

www.sernanp. gob.pe

Museo de Yanque

✉ Plaza de Armas

☎ 054/764–969

🕐 Closed Sat.–Sun.

💲 $

www.ucsm.edu.pe

daily buses to Cabanaconde and less frequent bus services to several other destinations.

Walk or take a minibus ($) from the market on the north side of the main plaza to **La Calera** ($$), Chivay's hot mineral springs. Located 2.5 miles (4 km) northeast of the city center, the springs—known for their curative properties—have been diverted into clean pools with changing rooms and showers. Upscale **Colca Lodge,** near the hamlet of Coporaque, has the best thermal pools ($$$$$) in Peru. **Coporaque** lies just over 6 miles (10 km) west of Chivay on the north side of the canyon and boasts the oldest church in the region, but few other services (see Travelwise pp. 282–283).

Villages of the Colca

Most tours of Colca Canyon continue from Chivay along the unpaved road on the south side of the canyon, passing through extensive terracing and tiny villages, the best known of which is **Yanque,** 5 miles (8 km) west of Chivay. An 18th-century church still stands in the town plaza, and nearby the informative **Museo de Yanque** has exhibits on ancient and modern life in the countryside. You can hire a Spanish-speaking guide, or buy one of the booklets that explain the exhibits in English. From the plaza, walk 1.5 miles (2.4 km) to the local hot springs ($).

The dirt road continues through the village of **Maca.** Although nearly destroyed by recent earthquakes, Maca's churrigueresque church of Santa Ana has been repaired and is open. The village of **Pinchollo**—with a good mountain lodge, the 17th-century church of San Sebastián, and a January fiesta—is linked by a trail with a hanging bridge to **Madrigal** on the north side. Then comes **Cruz del Cóndor** (3287 m), where most canyon tours end.

EXPERIENCE: Touring Colca Canyon

While it is possible to see Colca Canyon briefly on a day-long tour from Arequipa, a minimum of two days is recommended, and three-day tours are now becoming increasingly common. Longer tours often involve trekking inside the canyon. Independent travelers can take one of the public buses from Arequipa; however, departure times change often, and delays occur frequently during the rainy season, so ask locally.

Standard two-day tours cost $35–$80 per person, depending on accommodations, and include transportation and a guide; most meals and admission costs ($$$$$ *for boleto turístico/tourist ticket*) are additional. First-class, two-day tours, which include all of the above with the addition of upscale accommodations, meals, and admission costs, can reach up to $300 per person; deluxe tours that include a stay at the luxurious Belmond Las Casitas (*www.belmond.com*) inside the canyon are more expensive. Dozens of tour companies operate in Arequipa, and hotels in the region also arrange tours (see Travelwise p. 307). Be sure to ask exactly what the price includes.

■ **Looking for condors on the rim of Colca Canyon**

There are no services, but on most dry season mornings many people gather hoping to view the local population of Andean condors. With luck, these carrion-eating vultures will swoop close; at other times you will need binoculars.

The Río Colca runs 6,500 feet (2,000 m) lower than the observation point, while snowcapped **Volcán Mismi** rises 2 miles (20 km) to the north. In 2000, the members of a National Geographic expedition discovered that Mismi is the farthest source of the Amazon River. From a cliff near the summit, dripping glacial water streams into the Amazon watershed, finally reaching the Atlantic Ocean 3,900 miles (6,275 km) away.

Cabanaconde village, some 11 miles (18 km) beyond Cruz del Cóndor, is a base for trekking into Colca Canyon (see below). After crossing the canyon, hikers pass through the **Valley of the Volcanoes,** with more than 80 cinder cones along a single fault line. The highest mountain in southern Peru, 21,080-foot-tall (6,425 m) **Coropuna,** dominates the area. Buses from Arequipa to Andagua (*10–12 hrs., $$$$*) pass through this 40-mile-long (64 km) valley daily.

Three hours from Arequipa, the village of **Corire** is the entry point to the **Petroglyphs of Toro Muerto,** the world's largest petroglyph field. The petroglyphs, engraved between 500 and 1300 A.D. and covering 3 square miles (5 sq km), include stylized plants, animals, people, and geometric designs. If you catch an early bus from Arequipa, you can make the trip in a day. Otherwise, join a tour from Arequipa or stay overnight in Corire. Walk or take a taxi (*$$$$$, round-trip including wait time*) from there.

Five-Day Trek

Colca Canyon is perfect for all kinds of walks, from a leisurely two-hour stroll to more

■ A condor soars above Colca Canyon in the southern highlands.

challenging multiday hikes. A detailed map is also a necessity before you start out. Pick one up at the information center in Arequipa.

The classic five-day trek takes you from Cabanaconde on the south rim, across the river, and over a 16,732-foot-high (5,100 m) pass to the finish at Andagua.

Leave **Cabanaconde** (10,785 feet/3,287 m), where there are simple hostals and mule rentals, along the main path located on the plaza's west side (ask locals for route to Choco). Descend the path and, after 45 minutes, cross an (often dry) streambed, then climb through stone-walled fields for another 45 minutes until a new road appears below.

Walk north along the road for almost a mile (1.6 km) until it begins zigzagging down. Before the switchbacks, find the path again, heading west. The route continues mainly west, with the path alternating with the road. Five or six hours from Cabanaconde,

you will reach **Puente Colgado** (5,906 feet/1,800 m), an Inca footbridge across Río Colca. Camp beyond the bridge.

On the second day, it will take you about 3.5 hours to climb the path to the friendly hamlet of **Choco** (8,114 feet/2,473 m), which has plenty of water and places to sleep and camp. From there, the northbound trail follows Río Chalza, crossing the river several times. Five to six hours of climbing beyond, you will reach **Miña** (11,812 feet/3,600 m); ask the villagers about camping. You may wish to rent a baggage mule (*$$$$$ for arriero/wrangler, $$$ per mule*) for the next day's climb.

Northwest of the plaza, the stepped trail out of Miña climbs briefly before dropping to the river. Follow the water for ten minutes, then climb south past a field and through a gate. Continue southwest through grasslands and rocky areas to a flat-topped ridge three hours from Miña. Descend to the north from the 14,765-foot

(4,500 m) ridge for almost an hour to **Río Achacota** (14,436 feet/4,400 m). Climb northwest away from the river, staying on the southwest side of the Achacota Valley. After two or three hours, the route climbs west, levels briefly, then steeply climbs loose scree to **Paso Cerani,** four hours above Río Achacota and, at 16,733 feet (5,100 m), the trek's highest point. A slippery hanging trail descends the west side of the pass heading toward a pond on the valley's left side. Rock piles mark the steep descent beyond the pond heading west-northwest

---

INSIDER TIP:

No matter which route you take to Colca Canyon, carry plenty of water: The desert canyon has few watering points.

—NEIL SHEA
National Geographic writer

---

toward the **Río Cerani Valley** (14,929 feet/4,550 m), two hours from the pass. Camp here.

On the fourth day, follow the trail west for 1.5 hours to a 15,322-foot-high (4,670 m) saddle. Descend north on faint trails to **Quebrada Ayaviri,** then move southwest to corrals at **Umapallca,** 90 minutes away The trail continues downhill to the west-southwest through open puna. At 12,468 feet (3,800 m) it passes by a large cross, 1.5 hours below Umapallca, where more vegetation appears and the path

becomes clearer. You will catch a glimpse of the town of **Chacas** (10,023 feet/3,055 m), which is reached via switchbacks through cactus, 2 hours from the cross. You can camp here or rent a bed in a house on the plaza (*$*).

From Chacas, a rough little-traveled road runs west to **Andagua** (11,769 feet/3,587 m). Walk along the road for about seven hours. The route passes just north of the Valle de los Volcanes (Valley of the Volcanoes), a stunning fissure in the earth marked with many cinder cones and lava fields. Snowcapped Coropuna should be in view as you approach the city. Buses leave Andagua for Arequipa every day.

Cotahuasi Canyon

More remote than Colca and rarely visited, Cañón del Cotahuasi (**Cotahuasi Canyon;** *12 hrs. by bus from Arequipa, $$$*) lies northwest of Andagua. With a depth of 10,975 feet (3,345 m), Cotahuasi is one of the world's deepest canyons. Hop a minibus in Cotahuasi to visit nearby villages, hot springs, archaeological sites, and steep trekking trails suitable only for hardy backpackers. Amazonas Explorer (*Ave. Collasuyo 910, Urbanización Miravalle, Cusco, tel 084/252–846, e-mail: info@ amazonas-explorer.com, www. amazonas-explorer.com*) leads rafting trips on the river. Because they include several days of Class IV and V rapids, the expeditions are designed for experienced rafters only. ■

LAKE TITICACA & THE ALTIPLANO

Surrounded by altiplano, the world's highest navigable lake. Its almost surreal brightness pays testimony to the great height and openness of the area. Because of the altitude, travelers are advised to acclimatize at lower elevations, such as in Arequipa or Cusco. If arriving by air from Lima, allow at least a day of rest before attempting any physical activity.

Lake Titicaca, the world's highest navigable lake and South America's largest

Juliaca

Map p. 95

Visitor Information

Aeropuerto Inca Manco Cápac – Juliaca 1.25 miles/2 km W of town

051/328–974 or 051/322–905

E-mail: iperupunoapto@ promperu.gob.pe

The unmatched attractions of Lake Titicaca, as well as the region's dynamic and historic fiestas, promise a unique perspective on Peru. Although days of energetic dancing at nearly 2.5 miles (4 km) above sea level may seem daunting, don't hesitate to join the locals, if your breath sustains you, as they sway and stomp their way enthusiastically.

Towns Around Lake Titicaca

The region's largest city and home of the only commercial airport, **Juliaca** is an important

business and transportation hub, but has few sights of interest to travelers, who quickly move on to the lakeside city of Puno, 28 miles (44 km) away. *Colectivo* taxis and minibuses leave for Puno (*$*) from the centrally located Plaza Bolognesi at frequent intervals (*1 hr, $*). The airport offers flights to Cusco, Arequipa, and Lima.

A visit to the attractive little colonial town of **Lampa** (*50 mins., $*), 20 miles (32 km) northwest by unpaved road, makes an excellent day trip. Minibuses leave Juliaca from Avenida 2 de Mayo near the market, best reached by mototaxi. Known as La Ciudad Rosada (The Pink Town), Lampa has many buildings painted a rosy hue. **Iglesia de la Inmaculada** looks over the town. Built of local river boulders, the lovely 17th-century church has a fairy-tale appearance. Inside, you will find a wonderfully carved wooden pulpit, colonial art pieces, extensive catacombs with a bone-filled mausoleum (*tip caretaker to show you around*), and a copy of Michelangelo's "Pietà." In case you find the church closed, ask at the Municipalidad (Town Hall) on the main plaza for someone to open it.

Another good day trip, **Pucará** is located about 40 miles (64 km) northwest of Juliaca on paved Highway 3. Buses (*1 hr, $*) leave from the 12th block of San Martín. Pucará is famed for its rustic pottery, particularly the pairs of earthenware *toritos* (little bulls), placed along the roof ridges of highland houses for good luck.

The **Museo Lítico** has a fine display of stone stelae and monoliths carved into anthropomorphic shapes, many of which come from the 2,000-year-old Tiahuanaco culture. Some of the stelae were collected from the Pucará **archaeological site,** about a mile (1.6 km) above town and reached via the same road as the museum. Behind the museum stands a fine colonial church.

Puno

Capital of its department and the area's main center of tourism, Puno sits on a bay at the western end of Lake Titicaca. The charm of this otherwise cold and drab city lies in its fantastic views of the lake and its constant stream of foreign visitors. Visit the spartan **Catedral**

Museo Lítico
- ✉ Plaza de Armas
- ☎ 051/328–278 or 051/363–662
- 🕐 Closed Mon.
- 💲 $

Puno
- 🅰 Map p. 95
- **Visitor Information**
- ✉ iPerú, Plaza de Armas, Calle Lima 549
- ☎ 051/365–088
- **E-mail: iperupuno@ promperu.gob.pe**
- **www.regionpuno. gob.pe**

Yavari—the Oldest Ship on Lake Titicaca

In 1861, the Peruvian government commissioned the construction of two ships—the *Yavari* and the *Yapura*—for use on Lake Titicaca. The ships were built in pieces in Britain then shipped to Chile. After traveling by mule over the Andes to Peru, the pieces were assembled in Puno.

Launched on December 25, 1870, the *Yavari* was the Peruvian navy's first steel ship to sail on Lake Titicaca. Powered first by coal then llama dung, the ship's engine was finally converted to diesel fuel in 1914. The *Yavari* served as a passenger and cargo vessel until the 1970s, when she was beached and abandoned. British Peruphile Meriel Larken publicized the fantastic story of the *Yavari* in 1982. With the support of Britain's Prince Philip, who had seen the ship 20 years earlier, she was determined to save her. In 1999, after years of restoration, the *Yavari* steamed out of Puno under the power of its original diesel engine, the oldest and largest of its kind still working.

Today the *Yavari* is moored in front of the Sonesta Posada del Inca hotel (see Travelwise p. 284) and can usually be visited. You can stay overnight, taking advantage of the bed & breakfast service and excursions organized by the staff (*tel 01/467–6609, www.yavari.org*). The crew provides interesting information on the history of the *Yavari* and other boats on the lake. The boat is currently being renovated and is closed to the public. Check the website for updates.

Casa del Corregidor

✉ Deustua 576, Puno

☎ 051/355–694

www.casadelcorregidor.pe

Museo Carlos Dreyer

✉ Conde de Lemos 289, Puno

🕐 Closed Sun.

💲 $$

Museo de la Coca y Costumbres

✉ Jr. Ilave 581, Puno

☎ 051/209–420

💲 $

www.museodelacoca.com

in the city's **Plaza de Armas;** its baroque façade was completed in 1757. A block away, the 17th-century **Casa del Corregidor** is now a library, coffee shop, travel agency, and cultural center that exhibits old photographs of Puno and changing art exhibits. Around the corner, you will find a good collection of archaeological artifacts and colonial art and riches at **Museo Carlos Dreyer.**

On the corner of the plaza, the iPerú information office offers free maps of the city and information for tourists. A pedestrian-only street for three blocks between the plaza and Parque Pino, **Calle Lima** contains many of Puno's better restaurants and travel agencies. Two blocks beyond Parque Pino, the small, family-run **Museo de**

la Coca y Costumbres has a permanent exhibition on the use of coca in Peru, and presents videos of regional dances as well as tra-

---

INSIDER TIP:

If you go to the floating islands in Lake Titicaca, be prepared for the strange odor of the decomposing island reeds.

–ROB RACHOWIECKI
National Geographic author

---

ditional costumes for fiestas (you can try one on). The museum director speaks English and may read coca leaves if asked politely.

Beyond Puno

The *chullpas* (funerary towers) of **Sillustani** ($$), the area's most important archaeological site, lie 21 miles (34 km) northwest of the city and are best visited by guided group tour (see Travelwise p. 307; $$$–$$$$) or taxi ($$$$$, *round-trip, including wait*). Erected by the Aymara-speaking Colla people who dominated the area before and during the expansion of the Inca around A.D. 1400, the chullpas of Sillustani are the best preserved, most dramatic, and easiest to visit in the region. The site adjoins Lake Umayo, known for its wide variety of aquatic birds.

The cylindrical towers reach 39 feet (12 m) in height and are made of carved, perfectly fitted, stone blocks. Each one has a small

---

EXPERIENCE:
Kayak on Lake Titicaca

From April to November, rent one- or two-person sea kayaks for guided paddling trips along the shores of Lake Titicaca. Available daily, the tours last two or five hours and require a minimum of two people. You can also request overnight excursions, including a trip across the lake to the islands as well as camping or hotel accommodations; life jackets and thermal tops are provided. The trips leave from Llachón, a tiny village on the tip of the Capachica Peninsula (the north peninsula of Bahía de Puno).

Contact Titikayak (*Jr. Bolognesi 334, Puno, tel 051/367–747, www.titikayak.wordpress.com*) or **Valentín Quispe** (*Llachón, tel 951/821–392*), who can arrange your accommodation with local families. Several other tour agencies in Puno also offer kayaking adventures.

entrance facing east, through which visitors can peek. The chullpas once held the remains of local families, their members entombed with food, clothing, and other belongings. None of the human remains have survived. The towers' circular shape, with the diameter at the top greater than at the base, remains a puzzle for archaeologists.

Frequent buses from Puno's Terminal Zonal travel along Highway 3 to the small lakeside towns southeast of the city. Surrounded by picturesque hills, **Chucuito,** 12 miles (19 km) south of Puno, has two beautiful colonial churches, **La Asunción,** located near the plaza, and, on the east side of town, **Santo Domingo** (*hours vary*). **Inca Uyo** (*$*), locally dubbed the Templo de la Fertilidad (Fertility Temple), is less a temple than an ancient outdoor gathering spot for women eager to increase their fertility. Huge carved stone phalluses fill the grounds, but scholars are unsure of their exact origins. Local guides (mainly kids expecting tips) offer their own entertaining accounts. You can find Inca Uyo near Santo Domingo.

The bleak highway continues inland through the commercial town of Ilave before returning to the lake at **Juli,** 50 miles (80 km) from Puno. Juli manages to cram in four colonial churches in various states of repair. The best preserved is **San Pedro** on the main plaza. **Pomata** lies 15 miles (24 km) beyond Juli and features the church of **Santiago,** visible on a hill as you enter town. Built

> ## Taking Buses & Trains From Puno
>
> **Frequent buses from Puno's main Terminal Terrestre** (*Primero de Mayo s/n, tel 051/364–733*) **service Cusco** (*7 hrs., $$$*), **Arequipa** (*6 hrs., $*), **Lima** (*18–22 hrs., $$$$$*), **and Tacna** (*10 hrs., $*).
>
> **Buses to nearby towns leave from Terminal Zonal** (*Ave. Simón Bolívar s/n*). **Inka Express** (*Jr. Tacna 346, tel 051/365–654, www.inka express.com*) **runs buses to Cusco** (*10 hrs., $$$$$*) **that include English-speaking guides and stops at local sites along the way.**
>
> **From November to March trains leave for Cusco at 8 a.m. on Monday, Thursday, and Saturday.** (*Puno station, La Torre 224, tel 084/581–414 for reservations with credit cards, www.perurail.com, 10 hrs. and 30 mins., $$$$$*).

of sandstone, with translucent alabaster windows and an elaborate interior, it is the most interesting church on the southeast shore.

Islands of Lake Titicaca

Take one of the public boats from Puno's dock in the early morning to visit the islands that dot Lake Titicaca. Ask carefully to distinguish local boats from tour boats; be sure to pay only the captain. Passengers should bring water and sun protection. Boat fares range from $3 to $8 depending on destination; day tours start at $10 and overnight tours start around $20. Islands charge a nominal entrance fee.

Los Uros: The *islas flotantes* (floating islands) of **Los Uros** lie just over 3 miles (5 km) from Puno. The Uros fled from the Colla and Inca peoples and used totora reeds (see sidebar p. 207) to construct their islands and dwellings. Today, they live on floating islands and sustain themselves through fishing and tourism.

The islands are self-sufficient, with elementary schools and stores with basic supplies, but inhabitants must travel to the mainland for essentials. Some of the islands are staged, open to tourists with small towers for viewing the lake, totora boats for brief rides on the water, exhibit rooms with stuffed lake birds, and more souvenir stalls than you need. You pay a small fee for just about everything, though, including photos.

Taquile: Nearly 2,000 people reside on Taquile, 22 miles (35 km) and three hours from Puno. The 3.5-mile-long (5.5 km) island, famed for its weaving and knitting, has several hilltop archaeological remains and wonderful views of Bolivia's snowcapped Cordillera Real across the lake. There are no roads or vehicles and only erratic electrical service. Be prepared to climb more than 500 breathlessly steep steps to reach the upper part of the island, where most of the people live.

The Aymara Language

About a million people in Peru and Bolivia speak Aymara, Peru's third most popular language after Spanish and Quechua. They are the descendants of those who resisted the imposition of Quechua after the Inca conquest in the 15th century. Even after the arrival of the Spanish, Aymara continued to thrive and remained the first language for many people in the southern highlands. The area around Colca Canyon and Lake Titicaca is especially rich. The islanders on Taquile and Amantaní in Lake Titicaca speak Quechua, but the Aymara speakers on the mainland far outnumber them.

Residents of the Uros Islands, the floating islands on Lake Titicaca, still use totora reed boats.

EXPERIENCE: Stay With an Island Family

Day-trippers often overrun Taquile and Amantaní, especially during the high season (June–Aug.). To avoid the crowds, why not stay overnight and really get to know the locals. Take a boat from the Puno dock to either island, where you'll be met by islanders who will arrange a cheap place to stay with a family. If you stay on Amantaní, don't be too surprised if your hosts take you dancing and encourage you to dress in the traditional clothing of the region.

Private rooms on the islands are basic but clean, and you will find plenty of coarse blankets to use, although you may prefer to bring your own sleeping bag. Electricity is erratic or nonexistent, toilets are usually outhouses, and washing water comes in buckets, warmed for you only by request.

Small restaurants serve lunch, but you should arrange to eat breakfast and dinner with your hosts or another local family. They will provide you with simple meals; staple foods include potatoes, rice, eggs, fish, and tea.

If you prefer a guided tour, the most comfortable and widespread solution, rely on a tourist agency or any hotel in Puno, who will organize a visit to the islands with overnight accommodation included (see Travelwise p. 307). Always check what the tour price includes, as the cheaper agencies in Puno may provide just boat and bed and offer a minimal profit for the islanders. Better agencies give islanders a bigger share.

Both Taquile and Amantaní have recently opened small guesthouses with such comforts as private bathrooms and a restaurant. Rates start at $20 per person including dinner and breakfast. On Taquile, ask for **Hospedaje Intika Pachamama** (tel 932/922–262); on Amantaní, try **Kantuta Lodge** (tel 951/636–172 or 950/034–908, ask for Segundino Cari, www.kantutalodge.com).

As you walk around, you will see the local men spinning wool or knitting the typical floppy woolen red caps. Along with the black calf-length pants, white shirts, and waistcoats, the caps give the men a dashing appearance. The women wear voluminous skirts and beautifully embroidered blouses. You can learn more about their traditional clothing at the museum and crafts store in the main plaza.

Other Islands: Less touristy than Taquile, **Amantaní**, 3.5 hours from Puno, is larger with a population of 4,000 people whose livelihood depends on farming, fishing, and selling locally made baskets. The archaeological ruins on the island's two main peaks, **Pachata** (Father Earth) and **Pachamama** (Mother Earth), are worth a visit. Pretty gardens, vibrant wildlife, walking trails, and a luxurious little hotel (see Travelwise p. 285) make tiny **Isla Suasi,** near the north shore town of Moho, an ideal getaway. Because Suasi is difficult to reach, it is best visited on a complete package tour that includes guided visits to other islands.

The rarely visited island of **Anapia** lies in Titicaca's far southeastern reaches. An ongoing program encourages tourists to stay and work alongside the locals. All Ways Travel (see Travelwise p. 307) can arrange multiday visits and provide travel information. ∎

Cusco's colonial buildings, the markets of the Sacred Valley, and the secrets of Machu Picchu—three iconic images of Peru

CUSCO REGION

■   The central plaza and the residential district of Machu Picchu

CUSCO REGION

The ancient Inca capital of Cusco was once the heart of the greatest pre-Columbian empire in the New World. Today the city and the area around it is a primary focal point for travelers to South America. Nowhere else on the continent will you find such a close concentration of incredible scenery, graceful colonial buildings, stunning ancient sites, or warm, friendly people eager to share their way of life with visitors.

■ A family-run store selling woven blankets and hats northeast of Cusco's central plaza

Cusco draws every kind of tourist from every corner of the world, from backpackers on a tight budget to sophisticated travelers looking to splurge on art and wine, from tour groups wandering together through the major sites to hearty hikers eager to experience some of the little-seen wonders in the back country.

Few who come will ever forget the unmistakable image of Machu Picchu, that ancient stone city built entirely by hand, then, somehow, forgotten for 400 years. It sits perched on top of a vertiginous saddle in the southeastern Andes, overlooked by an impossibly steep mountain of cloud forests that often shroud the city in mist. The most photographed of Peru's archaeological sites, Machu Picchu continues to yield its secrets, but reluctantly.

Although the Inca built the city of Cusco, very few original buildings remain. Most were dismantled by the Spaniards after their 16th-century conquest, the stones used to construct new and exquisitely detailed colonial buildings, especially churches. Despite the devastating earthquakes that hit Cusco in 1650 and 1950, and to a lesser extent in 1986, many of the city's colonial buildings still stand thanks to well-orchestrated restoration efforts. Its walls, however, needed no such attention; erected by the Inca, they withstood the quakes admirably.

Anyone interested in history or archaeology will find several weeks' worth of sites to explore in the countryside around Cusco. Many of the sites, which are primarily Inca, sit in the Río Urubamba Valley, an area so full of significant historical places that it has been dubbed El Valle Sagrado (Sacred Valley). Visiting the sites will expose you to not only centuries of history but also the wonders and adversities of modern rural life in the Andes.

NOT TO BE MISSED:

Here campesinos dressed in traditional blouses, ponchos, and hats work their fields by hand and carry their produce to the colorful markets in Pisac, Chinchero, and other towns nearby.

As elsewhere in Peru, the highland peoples of the Cusco region work hard and have a lot of fun during their lively and unique local fiestas. During Inti Raymi (the sun festival), it may seem as if all of Cusco has turned out to watch the dancing and singing processions that follow the statue of the first Inca as it is carried from Qorikancha, through the Plaza de Armas, and up to Sacsayhuamán. This major event attracts travelers from all over the world and has become somewhat commercialized. At the other end of the spectrum is Q'ollyoriti. This ice festival, held on the glaciated flanks of mighty Ausangate, involves a difficult, lantern-lit pilgrimage at night above the snow line.

The Sacred Valley also offers hiking and trekking, including the famed trek along the Inca Trail and many others. With so much to offer, it is little surprise that many visitors spend their entire Peruvian vacation in this Inca heartland. ∎

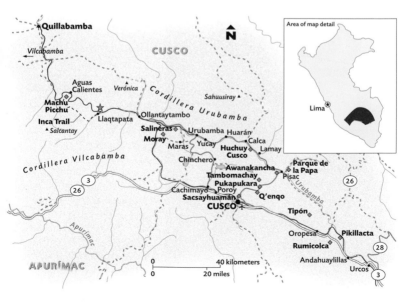

CUSCO

Founded around A.D. 1200 by the legendary first Inca, Manco Capac, Cusco is the longest continuously inhabited city in South America. For centuries it served as the spiritual and administrative center of the continent's greatest empire. Today many pieces of the history of the Inca capital have disappeared; however modern Cusco still offers extraordinary glimpses of the past.

■ A cobblestoned street in the San Blas neighborhood

According to Inca mythology, the sun god Inti told Manco Capac to go in search of the center of the world. Manco Capac traveled far and wide until one day he happened on a place more beautiful than any he had yet seen. He plunged a long, golden rod into the soil, proving it deep and fertile. Satisfied, he called the spot Q'osqo, Quechua for "navel of the world." In the centuries that followed, generations of Inca filled the city with ornate palaces and temples.

When the Spaniards arrived, they found the city's temples, particularly the iconic Qorikancha (see pp. 134–135), covered with precious metals or decorated with gold. By November 8, 1533, when Francisco Pizarro reached Cusco, the Inca had already stripped and carried away much of the treasure in a fruitless attempt to ransom the Inca Atahualpa.

Pizarro installed Atahualpa's half brother, Manco, as a puppet ruler over the Inca. Manco played along until 1536, when he gathered about 100,000 soldiers and laid siege to Cusco from the ramparts of Sacsayhuamán. Manco and his men fired flaming arrows onto the thatched roofs and nearly succeeded in burning out the Spaniards. Eventually the

---

INSIDER TIP:

Think twice about taking the bus from Lima to Cusco, as you cross three 13,000-foot [3,962 m] passes.

–KAI TIEDEMANN
National Geographic grantee

Spaniards stormed the fortress of Sacsayhuamán and barricaded themselves there. Meanwhile the revolt had also reached Lima. It was the length of the conflict that defeated the Inca, part-time soldiers who had to return to cultivate the fields. Forced to retreat, Manco fled to the nearby town of Calca then Ollantaytambo before finally fleeing to the cloud forests of Vilcabamba. After their victory, the Spaniards began to dismantle much of the city, using the stones to build their own new city atop the Inca foundations. With Lima as the capital of the viceroyalty, Cusco withered into a colonial backwater of churches and mansions.

In 1780, another indigenous uprising, led by the self-styled Inca Túpac Amaru II, failed to retake the city.

In the late 19th century, the development of the railway system that connected Cusco with Quillabamba in the jungle, and the coast via Juliaca and Arequipa, helped prepare the city for the rapid developments of the 20th century. The rediscovery of the lost city of Machu Picchu led to the development of a small tourism industry that has since

Cusco

🗺 Map p. 121

Visitor Information

Dircetur

✉ Portal Mantas 117–A (S corner of Plaza de Armas)

☎ 084/222–032

🕐 Closed Sun.

dirceturcusco.gob.pe

Direccíon Regional de Cultura Cusco

✉ Calle Garcilaso

☎ 084/582–030

🕐 Closed Sun. & holidays

www.machupicchu.gob.pe

iPerú

✉ Cusco Airport, Ave. Pachacutec cuadra 1 s/n

☎ 084/237–364

Boleto Turístico

The official Boleto Turístico del Cusco (BTC, Cusco Tourist Ticket, *www. boletoturisticocusco.org*) includes 16 attractions, including some of the city's museums and all of the region's major archaeological sites except Machu Picchu.

Valid for ten days, the nonrenewable BTC allows entrance to each site only once. Currently the cost is $47 (*free for children up to 10 years old; reduced to $18 for students: 10–17 years old showing an identity document, 18–25 years old with a university card or a valid ISIC card—International Student Identity Card*). To visit just some of the sites, buy a partial BTC (*$25, cash only, no student discount*) valid for one or two days depending on the route. BTC Circuit 1 covers the nearby sites of Sacsayhuamán, Q'enqo, Pucapucara, and Tambomachay. BTC Circuit 2 is valid for some sites in Cusco, Tipón, and Pikillaqta, while BTC Circuit 3 allows access to the Sacred Valley (Pisac, Ollantaytambo, Chinchero, and Moray). You can buy the BTC at the **COSITUC general office** (*Ave. El Sol 103–Galerías Turísticas, Municipalidad de Cusco, tel 084/261–435, cosituc.gob. pe*), at **DIRCETUR** tourist office (*Portal Mantas 117–A, 084/222–032, closed Sun., dirceturcusco.gob.pe*), in travel agencies, or at all attractions included in the tourist ticket except the Museo de Arte Contemporaneo and the Pachacutec monument. Keep in mind that the BTC does not include the entrance to the cathedral of Cusco.

Flags & the Coat of Arms

Two flags fly over Cusco's Plaza de Armas. The red-white-red motif of the Peruvian flag dates back to the early days of independence. According to the story, liberator José de San Martín landed on the coast near Paracas and took a nap on the beach. Upon awakening, he gazed up and saw a flamboyance of flamingos soaring overhead; their outstretched red wings and pale bodies inspired his choice of national colors. The second flag, the rainbow banner of Tahuantinsuyo (the

Inca name for the four corners of their empire), was adopted as an official banner of Cusco in 1978.

Granted by the king of Spain in 1540, Cusco's macabre coat of arms shows a stone tower bordered by eight condors. It represents the 1536 battle at Sacsayhuamán, where the Spaniards killed so many thousands of Manco Inca's warriors that the mass of corpses attracted large flocks of carrion-eating Andean condors.

become the city's economic mainstay.

Orientation

In the time of the Inca, Cusco had a huge central plaza that covered the modern **Plaza de Armas** and the nearby Plaza Regocijo. Today, the spacious Plaza de Armas forms the heart of the city, and it is impossible to spend any time in Cusco without passing through it several times. Impressive colonial churches, such as the cathedral on the northeast side and La Compañía to the southeast, dominate the square. Behind the colonnaded sidewalks that surround the plaza lie balconies, restaurants, shops, and travel agencies. The city's authorities have banned garish signs from the city center, so the plaza retains a stately colonial air despite large crowds.

Northeast of the Plaza de Armas, behind the cathedral, lies the district of **San Blas,** with a wonderful church and many workshops and galleries. Cusco's

two best museums—the Museo Inka (see pp. 128–129) and the Museo de Arte Precolombino (see pp. 130–131)—are located nearby, as are numerous hotels and a mix of restaurants. They stretch along some of the city's steepest and most narrow streets and alleyways, perfect for llamas but difficult for cars. Even walking can be tough; make sure your body has acclimatized before taking a stroll.

Northwest of the Plaza de Armas, backpacker hangouts and tourist traps line the pedestrian alley of Procuradores, nicknamed **Gringo Alley.** Plateros, which has some of the city's most popular bars, parallels Gringo Alley and continues on to the main road to Sacsayhuamán and the nearby archaeological sites.

West and south of the plaza you will find the city's terrain flatter. Pretty little **Plaza Regocijo** has some small museums, pleasant hotels, and the Municipalidad (City Hall). A block beyond lies the second largest plaza in the city center, **San Francisco,** with a large, ascetic-looking church. Farther on is the central San Pedro market.

The most modern street in the city center, **Avenida El Sol,** is just off the south corner of the Plaza de Armas. A long thoroughfare of banks and businesses, the avenue passes Qorikancha, the main post office, and the Wanchaq train station. It ends at El Ovalo Pachacutec, where you can pick up the road to the bus terminal or the airport.

Note that most of Cusco's streets change their name on every block, and many are just as likely to be called by their Quechua name as their Spanish one, which can make navigating your way through the city confusing. A good map is indispensable.

Plaza de Armas' Churches

Construction of the plaza's Renaissance-style **Catedral**

began in 1550 and took nearly a century to complete. The cathedral, which boasts one of the most notable interiors of any church in Peru, was built with blocks that once formed the palace of Inca Viracocha and Sacsayhuamán. To its left stands **Templo de la Sagrada Familia** (1733) and, to the right, **Iglesia del Triunfo** (1536), Cusco's oldest church, which now forms a side chapel annexed to the cathedral. Since the interiors of the three churches interconnect, you can visit the whole, recently restored complex at one time.

Entrance to the cathedral is permitted through the door of the Templo de la Sagrada Familia, where guides at the entrance will happily show you around for an offer. Statues and paintings of Jesus, Mary, and Joseph adorn the church's extremely lavish main altar. In order to

Catedral
- ✉ Plaza de Armas
- 💲 $$

▪ **The cathedral and Templo de la Sagrada Familia on Cusco's Plaza de Armas**

Iglesia de La Compañía

✉ SE side, Plaza de Armas

💲 $$

attract worshippers from the local indigenous population, the church's builders covered the altar with sumptuous gold ornament and the two small altars opposite with numerous mirrors.

Look near the connecting arch between Templo de la Sagrada Familia and the cathedral for the oldest painting in Cusco. It shows the citizens parading with a crucifix during the earthquake of 1650; the painted layout of the city is recognizably similar to the center today. Peru's most revered crucifix is also found here, it is called **El Señor de los Temblores** (Lord of the Earthquakes). Having saved Cusco from certain destruction, he became patron saint of the city and is carried in procession on Easter Monday through the streets, starting Semana Santa (Holy Week).

On the far right wall of the cathedral above the sacristy entrance, the famed painting of the "Last Supper" bears evidence of local culture. Jesus and the Apostles have been served guinea pig, and Judas is a likeness of Pizarro. Portraits of every bishop of Cusco, from Vicente de Valverde, who accompanied Pizarro, to the present archbishop, decorate the walls; more than 400 paintings from the Cusco school of art (see sidebar p. 131), many in excellent condition, adorn the cathedral.

You can find the original wooden altar at the back of the cathedral. In front of it stands the current altar, made of silver and dating to the late 18th century. The current altar faces a fabulously wrought wooden choir decorated with carved images of dozens of saints and martyrs.

Back outside in the Plaza de Armas, look up at the cathedral's left-hand **bell tower,** which holds the largest bell in Peru. Made in 1659, the bell weighs about 6 tons (5.4 mT) and took three tries before it was successfully cast. On the third attempt, María Angola, a local black woman, threw 25 pounds (11 kg) of gold into the molten metal; since then the bell

---

INSIDER TIP:

The lively streets of Cusco provide more magic than any museum. Just wander in all directions from the Plaza de Armas, especially "upward" to the north.

—GREGORY DEYERMENJIAN
National Geographic grantee

---

is known as La María Angola. Indigenous locals say that an Inca noble stands trapped inside the tower's bricks. Should the tower ever fall, they claim, he will escape and free his people. So far, the tower has withstood several quakes.

In 1571, the Jesuits built the **Iglesia de La Compañía** on the grounds of the palace of Inca Huayna Capac. After an earthquake destroyed it in 1650, the church was rebuilt with a superb baroque facade more ornate than

EXPERIENCE: Making Music in San Blas

Everyone understands the language of music, say the musicians and craftsmen of San Blas (see pp. 129–131), some of whom produce instruments and give music lessons. Many welcome music lovers of all kinds to their shops and studios.

The talented **Sabino Huaman** (*Tandapata 370, e-mail: sabinohuaman@gmail.com*) handcrafts ten-string *charangos* (small, 10-stringed lutes invented in the Andes), guitars, *zampoñas* (panpipes), *quenas* (wooden notched flutes), and *cajones* (drum boxes, an instrument which Peru's Ministry of Culture has declared a national cultural patrimony). He also makes the 16-string *bandurria* typical of the region south of Cusco, which is available in three sizes, the *marimacho, medio-marimacho,* and the smallest, simply called the bandurria. He offers classes for all of his instruments.

Professor Jaime Arias Motta (*e-mail: jaimearias22@hotmail.com, www.facebook.com/jaime.ariasmotta, tel 958/251–508*), who specializes in wind instruments, particularly the quena, teaches music at the **Instituto Superior de Música Leandro Alviña Miranda** (*Calle Tocuyeros 562, San Blas*). Conducted in Spanish, his classes introduce students to folk music. Motta also makes quenas and zampoñas and gives private lessons.

In recent years, San Blas has become a very active nightlife district, where the visitor can hear popular Andean fusion and Latin American music such as salsa and pachanga, as well as rock and roll, reggae, and blues on most nights.

the cathedral's. The city's bishops complained vociferously that the church now outshone the cathedral. When word of the quarrel reached the Vatican, Pope Paul III agreed with the bishop's point by the time his ruling reached Cusco, construction had nearly finished on La Compañía, which has stood in defiance ever since.

The Jesuits had a priceless collection of icons and artwork but took much of it with them when they were expelled from Peru in the 18th century. They left behind two large, 17th-century paintings that today hang near the main entrance of La Compañía. Interesting for their period details, they show marriages between Spanish men and Inca noblewomen. The church's extravagant gold altar is often brilliantly illuminated.

Loreto

The narrow pedestrian alley of Loreto runs past the left side of La Compañía, heading southeast from the plaza along an 820-foot-long (250 m) block. The longest unbroken **Inca wall** in Cusco runs along most of the block's left side. Behind the wall stood the *acllahuasi* (meaning "house of the chosen women"), where highly respected women, who were imprisoned, were educated to perform ceremonial and religious functions. Some of them, called "Inca wives," were destined to become real concubines.

In 1605, part of the acllahuasi became **Santa Catalina,** a cloister belonging to a cloistered order of nuns that is still active today. To enter Santa Catalina, return to the Plaza de Armas then take Calle

Museo del Monastério De Santa Catalina De Siena

✉ Calle Santa Catalina Angosta s/n

☎ 084/260–893, 984/999–803, or 984/002–734

🕐 Closed Sun.

💲 $

Museo Inka

✉ Cuesta del Almirante 103 & Calle Ataúd

☎ 084/237–380

🕐 Closed Sun.

💲 $

museoinka.
unsaac.edu.pe

Santa Catalina Angosta from the far eastern corner of the plaza.

The **Museo del Monastério De Santa Catalina De Siena** has an excellent collection of 17th- and 18th-century art from the Cusco school. The works are grouped by theme, style, and period; it's worth accompanying one of the guides available at the entrance (some speak English; *offer*) for a mini-lesson about the history and development of this important school of art. The collection also includes murals, statues, furniture, carpets, silverwork, vestments, and other items. The most celebrated piece, a large wooden trunk, opens to display intricately modeled religious scenes used by missionaries to illustrate stories from the Bible.

The beautiful colonial church adjoining the convent opens for Mass in the morning; the nuns attend services in a heavily grilled back room, out of public sight.

Museo Inka

Located a steep block northeast of the Plaza de Armas, the Palacio Almirante (Admiral's Palace) houses the Museo Inka. This fine colonial mansion, originally owned by Almirante Francisco Aldrete Maldonado, was damaged in the 1650 earthquake and rebuilt by Count Pedro Peralta de los Ríos, whose crest adorns the entrance. Above the main door, in front of a corner window, look for a pillar shaped like a naked woman; from inside, the same pillar appears to be in the shape of a bearded man.

In the museum's central courtyard, Quechua women often give traditional **weaving demonstrations** and sell their high-quality work. Around the courtyard, some **introductory exhibits** trace the region's cultural development. Cusco's most extensive and comprehensive public assembly of **Inca artifacts**—including the world's largest collection of *qeros* (wooden

EXPERIENCE: Learning to Weave

The techniques used to weave the belts, ponchos, and shawls worn by Andean peoples today—one of Peru's most important cultural traditions—have changed little over the past two millennia.

The **Centro de Textiles Tradicionales del Cusco** (*Ave. El Sol 603, tel 084/ 228–117*) is an exceptional resource for learning more about this living heritage. Its beautifully designed museum showcases weaving history, methods, significance, and geographical variety. Enlightening labels explain the exhibits, and craftspeople are usually on hand to give practical demonstrations. At the museum, you can take a weaving class given by an expert from one of the local villages or arrange a homestay in the village of Chinchero.

The museum also offers top-quality pieces for sale.

Acclimatization in Cusco

Your body needs to acclimatize to Cusco's elevation of 11,150 feet (3,399 m). Most visitors begin to feel the effects of *soroche* (altitude sickness) soon after arrival. The most immediate symptom is shortness of breath, so walk slowly. Being young and fit will not spare you; soroche can affect anyone and some people are more prone to it than others.

Most visitors find that they can manage the symptoms—which include headache, loss of appetite, insomnia, dizziness, dehydration, general malaise, and edema (puffiness) of the face—after a few hours of rest. You should avoid exertion during the first two days and stay well hydrated. Almost every hotel offers free *maté de*

coca (coca-leaf tea), which may alleviate symptoms. Drink plenty of water if you don't like the tea. To prevent symptoms altogether, some travelers get a doctor's prescription of Diamox (acetazolamide), a sulfa drug that may cause allergic or other reactions.

A good way to limit the effects of soroche includes acclimatizing at lower altitudes, for example, at Arequipa, at 7,808 feet (2,380 m), on the way to Cusco. Alternatively, after arrival from Lima, immediately descend from Cusco to nearby Urubamba at 9,416 feet (2,870 m) or Ollantaytambo at 9,187 feet (2,800 m) in the Sacred Valley, and begin your Cusco-area sojourn from there.

Inca drinking vessels)—waits at the top of the wide stone stairway guarded by mythological beasts. Highlights include tiny turquoise funeral offerings found at the nearby site of Pikillacta (see sidebar p. 137), purposely deformed and trepanned skulls, and mummies in a reconstructed tomb. Textiles, ceramics, gold, metalwork, and jewelry are also on display and labeled in Spanish. While examining the exhibits, look up also at the ornate ceilings of this former colonial residence. You can enlist the help of an English-speaking guide (*tip*) at the entrance.

San Blas

Most travelers reach attractive San Blas by heading northeast from the plaza up breathlessly steep Calle Triunfo, along the right side of Iglesia del Triunfo. After one block, the street narrows into **Hatun Rumiyoc**

(Quechua for "great stone street"), famed for the 12-angled stone set in the wall on the right side as you ascend. An actor clad as an Inca often poses here for photos. The third and steepest block, Cuesta San Blas, finally emerges at the Plaza San Blas, where you will find artisans' workshops. This route includes plenty of souvenir shopping.

The pedestrian alley of Almirante (also called Tucumán) offers another route up to San Blas. It climbs from the Plaza de Armas, along the left side of the cathedral, past the Museo Inka, to the Plaza de las Nazarenas.

The famous 12-angled stone of Hatunrumiyoc is set in one of the best-surviving Inca walls in Cusco. Today the wall is part of the **Palacio Arzobispal** (Archbishop's Palace), which was built atop the 15th-century palace of the sixth Inca, Roca. When you enter the

Palacio Arzobispal

 Calle Hatunrumiyoc & Jr. Herrajes

 $$$

Iglesia de San Blas

✉ Plaza San Blas

🕐 Closed Sun.

💲 $$$ or CRA

Museo de Arte Precolombino

✉ Plazoleta Nazarenas 231

☎ 084/595–092

💲 $

mapcusco.pe

Archbishop's Palace, note the brass door knockers; they are much too high for you but just within reach of an officer on horseback. The collection of religious art inside includes works by Diego Quispe Tito (1611–1681), a Cusqueño of Inca descent who became a master of the evolving Cusco school. A notable early Cusqueño edifice, the building bears Moorish-style carved doors and cedar ceilings.

Iglesia de San Blas, a small 1562 adobe church, is one of the

human skull, its identity unknown.

One of Peru's premier museums, the **Museo de Arte Precolombino** was originally a church built on Inca foundations. The Cabrera family bought the building in the 17th century. By the 20th century, the mansion had fallen into disrepair and stayed that way until the Banco Continental bought it in 1981 and restored it. The museum, which opened in 2003, showcases a limited number of the finest ceramics from Peru's major cultures, beginning with the

■ **An Inca wall along calle Hatun Rumiyoc**

first built outside the city center. After the 1650 earthquake, it was strengthened with thicker walls and slowly became a repository of important Cusqueño art. Inside you will find a baroque, gold-leaf altar and a pulpit that may be the world's best example of colonial wood carving. Made from a single cedar trunk, the pulpit is covered with a maze of faces, fruits and flowers, branches and birds, and carved columns topped by a

formative period (1250 B.C.).

The bulk of the pieces came from Lima's Museo Rafael Larco Herrera (see p. 72). Mounted as works of art rather than archaeological artifacts, they give the viewer a refreshing perspective of pre-Columbian culture. One particularly beautiful pair of Mochica vessels subtly expresses the busy beaks and gracefully stretched necks of cormorants. Other galleries display shells, gold and silverwork, Inca qeros, wood carvings, and 16th- and 17th-century art. The detailed labels are in Spanish, English, and French, and the entire collection is greatly enhanced by printed comments about indigenous art from some of the world's greatest artists, such as the British sculptor Henry Moore (1898–1986) and the French painter Henri Matisse (1869–1954).

In the museum courtyard, Quechua women weave and sell textiles by an outlet store of the **Centro de Textiles Traditional del Cusco** (see sidebar p. 128). Stop by the museum's excellent café for a light meal.

Outside the museum, the **Plaza de las Nazarenas** offers a restful little corner with benches and shade trees. It is named after Convento de las Nazarenas, which is now an annex of the luxurious Belmond Hotel Monasterio and stands on the site of the monastery of San Antonio Abad. The courtyard and the baroque church to the left of the hotel welcome visitors.

West of the Plaza de Armas

Built between 1657 and 1680, **Iglesia de la Merced,** considered Cusco's third most important colonial church, is a block and a half southwest of the Plaza de Armas. Enter the museum and monastery at the back of a small courtyard on the left side of the church. Highlights include La Custodia, a monstrance inlaid with precious gems, including 1,500 diamonds

Cusco School of Art

In the 16th century, the Spaniards introduced the concept of painted canvases to Peru's indigenous populations. Almost exclusively religious and didactic, the European art they imported to the new colony was designed to introduce the native peoples to Christianity. The city's artists learned to paint by copying these works of art but soon began to inject their own works with local elements such as the Virgin Mary breast-feeding Jesus, parrots instead of doves, and a heavy use of reds, yellows, and earth tones. This combination of European subject matter and Andean imagery characterized the Cusco school of art, a movement paralleled in other Spanish colonial cities.

and 1,600 pearls. Made of solid gold, the piece weighs 48 pounds (22 kg) and stands 51 inches (1.3 m) tall. The church contains the graves of Gonzalo Pizarro (ca 1506–1548), the half brother of Francisco Pizarro, and his lieutenant, Diego de Almagro (ca 1475–1538).

Plaza Regocijo: In Inca times, Cusco's main plaza included both what is now the Plaza de Armas and the smaller Plaza Regocijo, a short block to the southwest. Here, you'll

Iglesia de la Merced

✉ Plazoleta Espinar, Calle Mantas 121

☎ 084/224–567

🕐 Closed Sun.

💲 $

Performing traditional dances in front of Iglesia de la Compañía

Museo Histórico Regional

✉ Calle Garcilaso & calle Heladeros

☎ 084/223–245

💲 BTC

cosituc.gob.pe

find the **Museo Histórico Regional,** also known as the Casa Garcilaso de la Vega. One of the chroniclers of Inca life, Garcilaso de la Vega was born in Cusco in 1539 to an Inca princess and Spanish captain. The museum has a little bit of everything, ranging from Stone Age arrowheads to colonial furniture, but labels are minimal. A guide (*offer*) available at the door will make your visit more meaningful.

Also on the Plaza Regocijo, the **Museo de Arte Contemporaneo,** inside the Municipalidad, has a small display of local and, occasionally, international artists.

Plaza San Francisco: From this plaza, Calle Garcilaso heads southwest to spacious Plaza San Francisco and **Iglesia San Francisco.** Founded in 1645, the church has a superbly carved choir, crypts containing human

bones, and a large collection of colonial art, including a 30-by-39-foot (9 x 12 m) painting that many claim is the largest in South America. Created by Juan Espinoza de los Monteros, who worked in Cusco from 1638 to 1669, it shows the family tree of San Francisco de Asis.

The 16th-century **Iglesia Santa Clara,** half a block southwest of Plaza San Francisco, opens rarely except for Mass (*6 a.m.–7 a.m.*). It's worth rising early for a peek at the unique interior, almost entirely covered with tiny mirrors. The church's cloistered nuns attend morning Mass hidden behind a metal grille at the back of the church.

One block southwest, the huge San Pedro Market or **Mercado Central,** sells everything from chicken feet and coca leaves to umbrellas and underwear. This is not a crafts or souvenir market; working-class Cusqueños shop here. One of Cusco's more intriguing museums is located two blocks northwest of Plaza San Francisco. **Museo Irq'i Yachay** (formerly Andean Children's Art Museum) is presented by the Aylluy Yupachay Cultural Association, an organization founded in 1991 to expand

---

INSIDER TIP:

The central marketplace opens a door to the living past, with every indigenous product imaginable arrayed amid a timeless cacophony of Andean humanity and wares.

–CHRISTOPHER AUGER-DOMÍNGUEZ
National Geographic International Editions photographer

---

primary education in more than 30 extremely remote highland villages in the Cusco Department. The association sponsored teaching expeditions to the villages, where the Quechua children had never seen art before. The little ones learned the basics of how to mix paint and use brushes and then created their first paintings. A short video at the museum explains the teaching process and the interactions with the communities. The project produced thousands of paintings, the most interesting of which are now displayed in the museum, grouped

by theme. Signs in English and Spanish explain the artworks. The museum's collection also includes the director's personal collection of 350 *ch'uspas* (little woven bags used by men to carry coca leaves).

Along Avenida El Sol, stop by the **Museo de Arte Popular** on the avenue's first block to see a worthwhile exhibit of pieces by several of the artists who work in San Blas, including Hilario Mendivil's distinctive long-necked statues, crèches ornamented

Museo Irq'i Yachay

✉ Ave. Regional 820
☎ 084/241–416
🕐 Closed Sat.–Sun.
www.aylluyupaychay.org

Museo de Arte Popular

✉ Ave. El Sol 103, basement
☎ 084/258–089
🕐 Closed Sun.
💲 $$ or BTC

Peru's Iconic Plants

In the Cusco area, two museums pay homage to some of the symbolic plants of the Andes. The **Museo de la Coca** *(Plaza San Blas 618, tel 084/501–020, $)* offers a small but fascinating exhibition focusing on the history of this plant, whose leaves are infused in every hotel in Cusco and chewed for centuries by the inhabitants of the Andes. The exhibition also illustrates the most recent commercial uses relating to the production of Coca-Cola and cocaine. The **Choco Museum** *(tel 084/244–765, Calle Garcilaso 210, www.chocomuseo.com, $)* introduces cacao, the basis of chocolate. The museum runs 2.5-hour chocolate- and truffle-making workshops *($$$$)* daily, and runs tours to organic cacao and coffee plantations in the Machu Picchu area.

Iglesia Santo Domingo

✉ Plazoleta de Santo Domingo

☎ 084/249–176

🕐 Closed Sun. a.m.

💲 $

www.conventosanto
domingocusco.pe

in gold leaf by Antonio Olave, and Santiago Rojas' masks and dancers. The display also features photographs of Cusco in the early 20th century, including some by the man widely acknowledged as the father of Cusqueño photography, Martín Chambi.

Qorikancha: Every visitor to Cusco should see this Inca site, which forms the base of **Iglesia Santo Domingo.** View the combined structure from Avenida El Sol. The 20-foot-high (6 m) wall of Qorikancha (or Coricancha)

features smooth curves, a very unusual characteristic for Inca architecture, which typically relies on trapezoidal and rectangular patterns. The odd shape suggests that this was a significant structure.

Once decorated with hundreds of sheets of solid gold and silver, Qorikancha ("golden courtyard" in Quechua) contained gardens of corn plants, llamas, and sculptures of people made from precious metals. Today, nothing of these treasures remains. The conquistadores

Bus & Train Travel

Long-distance buses leave from the large **Terminal Terrestre** (*Ave. Vallejos Santoni cuadra 2, tel 084/224–471*) a few blocks off Avenida El Sol, 1.5 miles (2.4 km) southeast of the Plaza de Armas. The terminal has ATMs, Internet, pharmacy, and snack shops. Buses leave for Lima (*20–22 hrs.*), Puerto Maldonado (*10 hrs.*), Arequipa (*9–11 hrs.*), Puno (*6–7 hrs.*), and other destinations.

Tour Buses

Puno: Inka Express (*Ave. Alameda Pachacuteq 499–A, tel 084/634–838, www.inkaexpress.com*) has comfortable coaches (*8–9 hrs., $$$*), stops at villages and archaeological sites en route, and lunch.

Buses to Nearby Towns: Small coaches and minibuses (*colectivos*) service nearby towns frequently and cheaply. Departure points may change, so confirm locally.

Calca via Pisac: Local buses leave every 15 minutes (*45 mins., $*) from Calle Puputi just north of Avenida de La Cultura. Several companies are based in this area.

Urubamba: Transportes Urubamba (*Ave. Grau & Pavitos, alo-urubamba.com*) buses via Chinchero leave every 15 minutes (*90 mins., $*). A few go to Maras or change in Urubamba for shared taxis. Minibuses also serve Urubamba from Avenida Huascar south of Avenida de La Cultura.

Ollantaytambo: Travel to Urubamba and change there.

Urcos: Companies opposite the Regional Hospital on Avenida de La Cultura have buses or shared taxis to Urcos passing Tipón, Pikillacta, and Andahuaylillas, leaving every 30 minutes (*1.5 hrs, $*).

Trains

Cusco has two, unconnected train stations. **Estación Wanchaq** (*Ave. Pachacutec near Ave. El Sol, tel 084/581–414, www.perurail. com*), the main ticket sales center, has trains to Puno on Wed., Fri., & Sun. a.m. from 7:30 to 7:50, first-class carriages only including lunch (*10 hrs., $$$$$*). Daily trains to Machu Picchu Pueblo (Aguas Calientes) depart from **Poroy** station, 20 mins. by car from the center of Cusco (see p. 139).

melted everything down, leaving behind little but some of the finest stone walls of the Inca period.

Climb up the street of Santo Domingo to the church's side entrance, which gives access to the entire complex. Since the interior features few signs, it's worth enlisting the help of a guide ($).

In the entrance, note the photographs taken before and after the 1950 earthquake; the church was badly damaged but the Inca walls withstood the worst of the shaking, as they did during the 1650 earthquake, which destroyed the original church on the site. Inside, a **cloister** surrounds a bare courtyard containing an octagonal font that, according to the Spanish chroniclers, was once covered with 121 pounds (55 kg) of gold.

Turn right and head past a wall of colonial paintings portraying the life of Santo Domingo (St. Dominic) to reach the area known as the **Temple of the Moon.** Made with perfectly fitted stones and trapezoidal shapes, these rooms are among the best examples of exact stone joints in the Inca world. Behind the temple you can see the other side of the curved wall visible from Avenida El Sol; it forms part of the Temple of the Sun.

Opposite the Temple of the Moon, across the courtyard, another fine series of Inca rooms makes up the **Temples of Lightning, Thunder, and Rainbows.** Each of the three rooms has a trapezoidal window aligned with the next room; stand in exactly

■ **Dining out in Cusco is a warm, communal experience.**

the right place and you can see through them all. At ground level, small pebbles surface the Inca floors, and drains pass through the walls to the street outside. The function of the drains is unknown; they may have been used in ceremonial *chicha* sacrifices, to channel rainwater, or simply as speaking tubes.

Other Stops: Back on the avenue, in front of Santo Domingo, the small, underground **Museo del Sitio de Qorikancha** has a small exhibit of artifacts and photos dealing with the landmark. But to understand any of what is displayed, you need to have visited Qorikancha first.

At 7 p.m. nightly, the theater known as **Centro Qosqo de Arte Nativo** stages a show of local dances performed in traditional costumes and music.

Museo del Sitio de Qorikancha

✉ Calle Ahuacpinta 192

☎ 084/249–176

$ $$ o BTC

🕐 Closed Sun. a.m.

www.museo qorikancha.pe

Centro Qosqo de Arte Nativo

✉ Ave. del Sol 872

☎ 084/227–901

$ $$–$$$$ or BTC

centroqosqo deartenativo.com

Monumento al Inca Pachacutec

✉ Óvalo Pachacutec

💲 $ or BTC

Monumento al Inca Pachacutec, a 73.5-foot-high (22.4 m) stone tower, stands in the traffic circle on Avenida El Sol, about 1 mile (1.6 km) from the Plaza de Armas. A 38-foot (11.5 m) bronze statue of the 15th-century Inca leader—overlooking the city with his arms held aloft—tops the tower. Inside, walk beyond the exhibits up the stairs to take in the sights from the tower's viewing platform.

main road, but there are longer hiking trails in the area. Otherwise, you will find no shortage of tours and taxis from Cusco (*$$$ to Tambomachay, $$$$$ for half-day tour*). At each site, traditionally dressed people with llamas will pose for photos for a tip (*$*), vendors sell handicrafts, and guides offer their services.

Sacsayhuamán: If you are short on time, do not miss

Looking down on Cusco from Sacsayhuamán, 800 feet (244 m) above the city

Nearby Sites

The four Inca sites closest to Cusco—Sacsayhuamán, Q'enqo, Pukapukara, and Tambomachay—can easily be seen in a day. All require the BTC. The cheapest way is to catch a morning bus bound for Pisac, alight at Tambomachay, then return to Cusco on foot (5.5 miles/9 km), visiting the other sites en route. Most travelers return along the

Sacsayhuamán, the largest and most impressive of the sites. Acclimatized travelers can hike to the entrance, about 800 feet (250 m) above the city. There are several routes. One takes the stairs of Resbalosa Street to the church of San Cristóbal; turn right on the main road to a hairpin bend, where another set of marked stairs will lead you into

Sacsayhuamán. Allow 30 to 45 minutes to ascend from the city center. Alternatively, take a taxi ($$) along the longer road.

In Quechua, Sacsayhuamán means "satisfied falcon." As immense as the site seems, what you see is only 20 percent of what existed in Inca times. Beginning in the mid-15th century, thousands of indigenous laborers worked building, cutting, and moving massive stone blocks into place. At its height, Sacsayhuamán may have housed 10,000 people.

A century later, the Spaniards dismantled the site and used the blocks to construct the homes, churches, and other buildings in Cusco. However, they couldn't easily haul off the massive bases that form three impressive tiers of the zigzagging ramparts that stretch more than 1,000 feet (300 m).

With 22 repeated walls, it appears that these zigzags served as a form of defense since any attacker attempting to scale the walls would always have an exposed flank. This layout has given Sacsayhuamán its popular designation as a fortress when, in fact, it functioned as much more than just a military site.

Although only their bases are extant today, three large towers once stood on top of the battlements. One of them was round and may have been used as a water tower for an army garrison. But the other two may have had religious significance and been used by the Inca during ritual ceremonies of celestial devotions and reverence of the sun, moon, stars, thunder, and lightning.

Opposite the ramparts, across a large, flat central area now used for the annual Inti Raymi festival, rises a hill named Rodadero. According to the Spanish chronicles, storehouses, shelters, and other buildings once covered the sides of the hill. Archaeologists have uncovered the foundations of several buildings, and ongoing

Tipón
- Map p. 121
- $ BTC

Pikillacta
- Map p. 121
- $ BTC

Inca & Wari Sites Southeast of Cusco

Paved Highway 3 southeast of Cusco passes several worthwhile sights. The turnoff for **Tipón** is about 13 miles (21 km) from the city followed by a short uphill stretch. Here, locals continue to work a dozen huge Inca terraces. The irrigation system—in perfect working order—begins with a four-spouted fountain and continues for almost a mile through a stone channel with several falls.

The Wari city of **Pikillacta** lies 19 miles (30 km) southeast of Cusco on the north side of the highway. Built around A.D. 1100, it is the only major pre-Inca site in the region. The stonework may be crude, but the size of the city, with long avenues flanked by 20-foot (6 m) walls, still impresses. Just opposite is **Rumicolca,** where a huge Inca gateway atop the foundations of a Wari aqueduct marks the entrance into the Cusco Valley.

In the village of **Andahuaylillas,** a very important Inca settlement 22 miles (37 km) from Cusco, is **La Iglesia de San Pedro,** a Jesuit church built in the late 16th century. Don't be fooled by the unadorned exteriors because its Andean Baroque interior is so sumptuous that the locals call it the "Sistine Chapel of the Americas" (*offer*).

excavations continue to identify more. The carved and polished bench that sits on the hill is known as the Inca's Throne.

Q'enqo: Q'enqo—whose name comes from the Quechua word for "zigzag"—lies on the right side of the road to Pisac about 1.25 miles (2 km) from Sacsayhuamán. This small site is actually a large limestone rock covered with carved, zigzagging channels that the Inca may have used during ritual sacrifices of blood or, more likely, the corn "beer" known as *chicha*. The walls bear carved animal images, and its small amphitheater witnessed solemn religious rituals.

Beneath the rock, the Inca widened one of the natural cracks and carved it into an underground cave with a stone altar large enough to accommodate a reclining adult. Archaeologists do not know the purpose of this dimly lit shrine. Driven by religious zealotry, the 16th-century conquistadores hacked away at the rock, which was likely once much bigger.

Pukapukara & Tambomachay: Named after the pinkish granite from which its buildings were hewn, the small complex of **Pukapukara** (Red Fort) probably served as a *tambo,* or watch post, although archaeologists still debate its purpose. From its 12,140-foot (3,700 m) elevation, the site gives views of the valley around Cusco. Pukapukara—which probably dates to the mid-15th century—lies on the right of the main road at the spot where the bus to Pisac drops you off.

Almost opposite, a dirt road leads about 300 yards (300 m) to **Tambomachay,** a triple-tiered structure built atop a natural spring and popularly known as the Inca's Bath. Whether or not the Inca bathed here is open to debate, but the series of stone water fountains here are beautiful enough to have deserved a visit by ancient nobility.

Opposite the cascades stands a small stone tower perhaps used for signaling purposes. Climb to the top of the tower for a view of Pukapukara. ∎

Discovering Inca Astronomy

To further explore the Inca's worshipful view of the heavens, visit the **Planetarium Cusco** (*Reserva Ecológica Llaullipata, tel 974/782–692, open on request, $$$$ with at least six people, e-mail: info@ planetariumcusco.com, www.planetarium cusco.com*). You can book the desired type of visit online or go to the city office (*Calle Lucrepata E-16*). The planetarium is about 500 yards (449 m) from another Inca site, Sacsayhuamán (see pp. 136–137), and a visit offers a fine way to deepen your knowledge of ancient Peru.

An introductory exhibit hall explains the Inca vision of the sky, while its domed theater presents information about the stars and constellations. Two mounted telescopes track the constellations at night. Many tourists visit at night to see Sacsayhuamán when it is illuminated, usually around 7:30 p.m., but you can also arrange a day visit.

EXPERIENCE: Taking the Train to Aguas Calientes

Unless you are hiking the Inca Trail, you'll need to take the train to Machu Picchu Pueblo (Aguas Calientes) to see Machu Picchu. This journey, an essential component of a visit, now commands first-world prices. Tourist guides on the Inca Trail get home by taking the much cheaper local train, which is reserved for card-carrying Cusqueños only and is not shown on websites.

For die-hard railroaders, the trip from Cusco is the only way to go. The downtown San Pedro Station no longer services tourist trains, which now all leave from **Poroy Station,** a 20-minute drive west of Cusco. The first sight on the rail journey is the huge fertilizer factory of **Cachimayo,** after which the train trundles through the town of **Izcuchaca** and over the high flat Anta plateau, with wide-open views. The train then turns north and drops excitingly along the narrow **Río Pitumayo Valley,** utilizing a switchback before joining the **Río Urubamba Valley** and turning left to Ollantaytambo, about two hours out of Cusco. Note the extensive Inca terracing on the right. During the short stop at **Ollantaytambo,** souvenir sellers hawk their wares through train windows. After leaving the station, you will get a brief glimpse of the Inca site high up to the right, and later the icy ramparts of **Verónica** (18,866 feet/5,750 m), also on the right. The Río Urubamba tumbles steeply on the left side, and you might see colorful torrent ducks standing on rocks surrounded by white water. After the **Llactapata terraces** become visible beyond the river, the whistle-stop at KM 88 is available only on

request with the Expedition train (see below). Here, a footbridge crosses the river to begin the Inca Trail. After a short tunnel the train makes its way steeply through thick vegetation, passing a dam before arriving at Aguas Calientes.

Practicalities

PeruRail travelers have three choices of service: Expedition, Vistadome, and Hiram Bingham (2nd, 1st, and luxury). While all are comfortable, the Vistadome has larger windows than the Expedition and serves a free snack and sodas; most tourists use this one, but Expedition service will suffice.

Both Vistadome ($90) and Expedition ($60) have daily early-morning departures from Cusco, taking about 3–4 hours one way. About 10 more trains depart from **Ollantaytambo,** where hotels will arrange transportation to and from the station. Ticket costs to Machu Picchu (about 1.5 hours) vary depending on departure time, but are about $55 in Expedition and $73–$90 in Vistadome. The internationally acclaimed, luxurious, Hiram Bingham train leaves from **Poroy** at 9 a.m. and arrives at Machu Picchu Pueblo (Aguas Calientes) at 12:25 p.m., returning at

One of the engines on the Ollantaytambo run

5:50 p.m., every day except the last Sunday of the month. The $870 round-trip fare includes transfer and entry to Machu Picchu, a guided tour, on-board brunch and dinner, tea at Machu Picchu, and cocktails.

Because some travelers arrive via the Inca Trail, more people return from Aguas Calientes than go there. Therefore, buy return tickets in advance. All tickets must be bought at the Wanchaq Station, through a travel agent, or online (e-mail: reservas@perurail.com, www. perurail.com). Competitive service is provided by Inca Rail (Portal de Panes 105, Plaza de Armas, Cusco, tel 084/581– 860, www.incarail.com), with 3 types of seats: Voyager ($52– $61), the 360° ($68–$76), and First Class ($159–$185). Trains depart approximately 8 times a day from Ollantaytambo.

EL VALLE SAGRADO

El Valle Sagrado (Sacred Valley) encompasses the small part of the Río Urubamba that stretches from Pisac to Ollantaytambo. In this fertile area, known in Cusco simply as "the Valley," the Inca built important ceremonial and ritual sites, sweeping agricultural terraces, and strategic *tambos* and forts. Today, the valley's small towns provide varied accommodations and interesting markets, making it an essential part of every visitor's itinerary.

 The Inca terracing at Pisac is among the best in Peru.

Pisac
Map p. 121

Pisac

At 21 miles (33 km) northeast of Cusco, the pretty village of Pisac, near the banks of the Urubamba at 9,751 feet (2,972 m), is the closest of the Sacred Valley towns.

Buses usually stop by the bridge over the Urubamba, five blocks south of the main plaza, where the town holds its famed Sunday market. Originally a local affair, with campesinos coming into town to trade and sell their produce, the market has now been overwhelmed by a huge crafts market. Nevertheless, local farming families in traditional dress quietly carry on their business on the west side of the plaza, where you can still buy produce.

The crafts market spills over into the streets around the plaza, and you can buy almost any kind of highland souvenir here. Prepare to bargain hard, but don't expect better prices than in Cusco. The selection is varied, however, and the outdoor setting perhaps more enticing than Cusco's markets. On Tuesdays and Thursdays, the crafts market (but not the locals' produce section) is almost as large as on Sundays, and during the high season you'll find a smaller market every day of the week.

Also on Sundays, the main **church** on the north side of the plaza holds Mass in Quechua at 10 a.m., followed by a grand procession of leaders from surrounding villages, all dressed in finery and carrying silver-plated staffs as they emerge from the church.

The major **Inca site of Pisac** (*BTC*) sits about 1,000 vertical feet (300 m) above the village. Climb for 1.5 to 2 hours up the steep, 2.5-mile-long (4 km) footpath that leaves from the west (left) side of the main church. Or hire a taxi (*$$*) to drive the 6.5 miles (10 km) to the site. On busy tourist Sundays, *combis* ply the route as well. If you take a taxi, make sure the driver takes you to the upper of the two parking areas, where you can take a footpath around the hillside and above the superb terracing to a saddle (*10–15 mins.*). There you will find some restored Inca baths with running water. Beyond the saddle, and across a small valley, is a cliffside riddled with holes, all that remains of some ancient Inca tombs long since looted by *huaqueros* (grave robbers). Today the tombs are off-limits to tourists.

The main trail swings left beneath some buildings, which probably housed important Inca nobles and high priests. It continues for more than half a mile (1 km), through a double-jamb stone doorway, tunnel, and set of stairs—a fine sampling of Inca engineering. Throughout, the terraces continue to sweep away to the left, affording marvelous views. Eventually, the path reaches a stunning overlook with the fine masonry of the main temple buildings spread out below.

The stonework in the central, most important buildings is as perfectly fitted and well made as any in the Inca Empire. At the heart of the site, the rounded wall of an astronomical observatory encircles a carved stone monument called the **Intihuatana** (Hitching Post of the Sun), which the Inca used to make celestial observations. Badly damaged in the 16th century

Fresh Bread

If you find yourself hungry for a snack while in Pisac, take a walk down Calle Mariscal Castilla, heading east from the northwest corner of the plaza. On the first block, look on the left-hand side for the large wood-burning ovens made of adobe. Here you can purchase delicious flat rolls fresh and hot out of the oven. The miniature adobe castle nearby holds *cuyes* (guinea pigs).

by idol-destroying Spaniards, the monument has recently fallen victim to feckless thieves. Nevertheless, the quality and superb setting of the surrounding niches still inspire awe.

Far below flows the Río Urubamba. You might expect it to meander gently through the valley flatlands; instead, it flows

Awana Kancha
☎ 084/203–287
www.awanakancha.com

straight in great stretches. The Inca, masters of hydrology, channeled the river through stone-walled canals, thereby increasing the area available for agriculture while also decreasing soil erosion.

Beyond the central buildings is a rectangular ritual bath, and by continuing straight south, you'll reach the top of the footpath that leads

gets rather crowded on Sunday afternoons; soak in the solitude by visiting the site in the morning on a non-market day.

Awana Kancha—an Andean camelid theme park—lies on the Pisac road 14 miles (23 km) from Cusco, in Taray District. Its well-presented free exhibit includes various breeds of all four South

Quechua Glossary

Peru's second official language, Quechua is widely spoken in the highlands, where many indigenous people speak it as their first language.

Your attempts to speak may amuse the locals, but they are always delighted to help visitors master a few phrases. Remember that *ll* is pronounced like *y* in "yes."

How are you?—*Allillanchu?*
I'm fine. —*Allillanmi.*
Please—*Allichu*
Yes—*Ari*
No—*Manan*
Thank you—*Yusulpayki*
You're welcome.—*Imamanta.*

Where are you from?—*Maymantan kanki?*
I am from the United States.—*Estados Unidos manta kani.*
What is your name?—*Iman sutiyki?*
My name is John.—*Johnmi sutiy.*
 (Or *Juanmi sutiy.*)
How much?—*Hayk'an?*
That's too much.—*Nishun.*
Please give me a good price.—*Allichu allin chaninta qoway.*
How many children do you have?—*Hayk'an wawayki?*
Is this your child?—*Wawaykichu?*
See you later!—*Ratukama!*
Let's go!—*Haku!*

down to Pisac. Otherwise, turn left and loop back on the lower trail through the terraces to a lower parking area where your taxi or tour bus will be waiting. There isn't any public transportation here, so make sure you have pre-arranged for a taxi to wait for you.

The wonders of the temple of Pisac—the fabulous stonework, old Inca paths, and exhilarating views—reward deliberate, leisurely travelers. Allow at least two hours for an enjoyable visit, not including travel time. The temple

American camelids (see pp. 104–105), such as the suri alpaca with wool that grows almost to the ground. Visitors can feed the animals, and watch occasional demonstrations of carding, spinning, and natural dyeing. At the end of the exhibit, a large retail store offers woven goods for sale.

Villages North & West of Pisac

Stretching northwest of Pisac, the Sacred Valley encompasses several small towns, all of which are served by a paved road. The first, **Calca,** is 11 miles (18 km) away. One of the largest towns in the valley, Calca has an important daily produce market but no significant archaeological sites within easy reach. Before his attempt to recapture Cusco in 1536, Manco Inca made this his temporary headquarters. As a result, the town has two main plazas, a feature of Inca rather than Spanish colonial town planning.

Because of the local market, buses from Cusco to Pisac normally continue on to Calca, which means that visitors catching a bus from Pisac back to Cusco may be relegated to standing room only. Calca doesn't have much in the way of accommodations, but there are a couple of bungalow accommodation options in the area (see Travelwise p. 290).

Independent travelers who want to escape the crowds will enjoy a trip to the rarely visited Inca site of **Huchuy Cusco** (or Huchuy Qosco) on the south side of the Urubamba Valley. You can take a three-hour hike along a signed trail from the village of Lamay, about halfway between Pisac and Calca. The zigzagging trail starts at the Lamay Bridge over the Urubamba and involves a 2,600-foot (800 m) gain in elevation. A longer but less steep trail leaves from Calca. Known for its extensive terracing, Huchuy Cusco features several Inca buildings, including a three-story *kallanka* (great hall), as well as spectacular views of the Sacred Valley. There is a campsite located close to the site and trekking tours are available.

Twelve miles (19 km) beyond Calca, the attractive village of **Yucay**—known for some of the best hotels in the Sacred Valley (see Travelwise p. 290)—has two Inca-style main plazas and some **Inca walls** still standing. This has long been an important agricultural area, and local farmers still use the Inca terraces on the north side of the village.

Standing between the two grassy, tree-filled main plazas, the colonial **Iglesia de Santiago** (St. James) has been restored but opens only erratically. At Christmas, Yucay puts on a colorful festival with masked dancers.

Calca
 Map p. 121

Huchuy Cusco
Map p. 121

Yucay
Map p. 121

A crafts market in Ollantaytambo

Urubamba

🏛 Map p. 121

Chinchero

🏛 Map p. 121

Maras

🏛 Map p. 121

Two miles (3 km) beyond Yucay, the town of **Urubamba** spreads out in the middle of the Sacred Valley at the point where the paved road from Cusco via Chinchero joins the valley road. Buses from Cusco take either the route via Pisac and Calca or via Chinchero. Urubamba, whose best attraction is the Seminario Ceramic Studio (see sidebar p. 147), also makes a good center for catching buses to Cusco, Pisac, Chinchero, and Ollantaytambo. Mototaxis ($) get you to Yucay.

Chinchero & Moray: About 18 miles (29 km) northwest of Cusco on the paved road to Urubamba, buses pass the Inca site and colonial town of **Chinchero,** at 12,376 feet (3,772 m) a high point on the drive to the Sacred Valley. Much higher and remoter than Pisac, Chinchero has a well-deserved reputation for traditional weaving and offers family stays and weaving lessons for seriously interested travelers (see sidebar p. 128).

The town's Sunday market, where locals dressed in distinctive traditional clothing sell and barter produce, competes with Pisac's, and an extensive tourist market has all the usual highland souvenirs. The town holds smaller markets on Tuesdays and Thursdays.

If you visit Chinchero on one of the market days, ask the person who collects your entrance fee or punches your BTC to open the town's colonial **church** ($$$ or BTC). Filled with floral murals that extend to the ceiling, the

INSIDER TIP:

Some notable, less frequented valley sites include Moray; the Salineras salt mines; Parque de la Papa, near Pisac; and the hot springs above Calca, which now offer fully refurbished bathhouses.

—JAMES DION
*National Geographic Society,
Director Tourism Programs,
Maps Division*

church sits atop Chinchero's massive Inca walls. The walls have ten trapezoidal niches large enough for a standing person, although archaeologists have not yet determined their purpose. Extensive terraces lie off to the left, as well as occasional rocks carved into stairs or seats.

The road that drops from Chinchero to Urubamba has fabulous views of the snowcapped peaks of the Cordillera Vilcanota on the north side of the Sacred Valley, including Nevado Sahuasiray, the highest at 18,964 feet (5,780 m). Along this road, you will see a turnoff to the small colonial town of **Maras.** Few buses go to Maras; travelers normally take a Cusco-Urubamba bus and get off at the Maras turnoff. From there, it's about a 2.5-mile (4 km) walk to town. Or you can wait at the turnoff for a shared taxi or *combi*; if you are in luck, one will already be there.

From Maras, take a taxi (*$$$*) to the fascinating site of **Moray** (*$$$ or BTC*), 4 miles (7 km) away along a signed dirt road that has some descents and climbs. Allow up to two hours to walk there unless you are very fit and acclimatized.

Moray has no Inca fortresses or temples. Your eyes must travel downward, to three huge, circular or oval-shaped **terraced pits** sunk into the earth, the largest approximately 118 feet (36 m) deep and 722 feet (220 m) long.

All three pits had seemingly been in use before the height of the Inca Empire, but exact dates are unknown. Researchers, who measured natural temperature differences between the highest and lowest terraces, surmised that the ancient Peruvians used them as an agricultural laboratory to monitor optimum growing conditions for their crops. You can walk around the terraces, descend to them, or climb a nearby hill for an overview.

Salineras: The valley's most unique site, indeed, there is nothing like it in Peru and perhaps the world, is Salineras, salt mines on the south side of the Río Urubamba. You can visit either by climbing up from the river or by descending from Maras. Combining Salineras with a visit to Moray makes an excellent day trip off the normal tourist trail. If you want to ride, rent mountain bikes from outfitters in Cusco.

Visitors find the sight of more than 5,000 salt pans glistening in the high-altitude sunlight quite

mesmerizing. Each of the pans is a rectangular depression, approximately 10 feet (3 m) across and 1 foot (30 cm) deep, dug into the ground. A natural spring at the top of the valley feeds the pans with a steady stream of warm water heavily loaded with dissolved salt. Those who lived in the region before the Inca developed a system to divert the water

■ **The mesmerizing salt pans between Maras and Urubamba, in the Sacred Valley**

into the pans using hundreds of narrow channels, most less than a foot (30 cm) wide, dug into the sloping earth. By blocking the channels with bits of wood or bunches of vegetation, they controlled where the salt water flowed and which pans it filled.

Moray
🗺 Map p. 121
💲 $$$

Salineras
🗺 Map p. 121
💲 $

 A farmer in the Sacred Valley uses oxen to plow his potato field.

Ollantaytambo
Map p. 121

Today, several local families continue to mine the salt pans using techniques little changed from centuries ago. Once the pans fill with water, it takes a few weeks for the liquid to evaporate and leave behind a layer of salt. The salt deposit is then scraped up by hand, loaded into sacks, carried out, weighed, and sold mainly for use in animal salt licks.

To reach Salineras from Maras, ask a local to show you the footpath near the church; follow the path downhill to the north for about 3 miles (5 km) to the salt pans. Or hire a taxi in Maras, or at the Maras turnoff, to take you down the longer dirt road to the top of the site. This approach road gives spectacular overviews of the salt pans.

If you want to continue on to the main Urubamba-to-Ollantaytambo highway after you have toured the site, walk along the left side of the pools and continue downhill to the Río Urubamba, almost 2 miles (3 km) away. Turn right and follow the river. Cross the footbridge and continue on the trail for a few minutes until you reach the highway. Visitors to the salt pans from Urubamba should take a mototaxi about 3 miles (5 km) to the footbridge over the river that will take you to the Salineras trail (*el puente para las salineras*). Cross the bridge, turn right, and follow the trail for about half a mile (0.8 km) until you reach the small cemetery of Pichingoto. Turn left and follow the salty stream up the trail; after about 45 minutes, you'll reach the lowest of the salt pans. This route is less spectacular than arriving from the top, but more direct.

Ollantaytambo

The last and most interesting town in the Sacred Valley, Ollantaytambo sits at 9,187 feet (2,800 m) and about 19 miles (30 km) beyond Urubamba. Since very few buses travel here directly from Cusco, take a bus to Urubamba and change to one of the *combis* that travel here several times every hour ($). Public

INSIDER TIP:

The crafts markets at Pisac and Chinchero both take place on Sunday. In the afternoon, tourists crowd nearby Ollantaytambo: We recommend visiting the site at another time of the day.

−ROB RACHOWIECKI
National Geographic author

buses drop you off in the village's Plaza de Armas (also called Plaza Mayor). Tour buses continue 200 yards (183 m) over a narrow bridge crossing the Río Patacancha, a tributary of the nearby Río Urubamba, to a second plaza, with spectacular views of the terracing and fort of the Inca site.

Parts of Ollantaytambo—a real Inca city that has landed in the 21st century—remain almost unchanged despite the passage of several centuries. To stroll around the ancient village, start in the Plaza de Armas with the church behind you; turn right (northeast) and wander for a few blocks along the narrow, cobblestone streets.

Each block consists of two *canchas* (communal dwelling areas), one of the salient features of Inca town planning, each of which has only one door from the street into a central courtyard. Several homes surround each courtyard. Unlike our own homes, and their private street entrances, individual Inca houses did not have doors that opened onto the street; the buildings had to be entered from the courtyard. Thus typical Inca walls are long and unbroken, and doors often date to after the conquest.

A visit to the **Inca site of Ollantaytambo** (*$$$$$ or BTC*) requires stamina. Negotiate your way through the crafts market in the

Peru's Premier Potter

Born in coastal Piura, **Pablo Seminario** has been fascinated by ancient Peruvian pottery since his childhood encounters with *huaqueros* selling looted ceramics to the highest bidder. After earning a degree in architecture in Lima, Seminario moved to Cusco in 1979, but soon found his architectural work overshadowed by his desire to study and re-create the pottery of pre-Columbian peoples using ancient techniques. Seminario met Marilú Behar, a textile artist, and together they moved to Urubamba, where they opened a small ceramics workshop. Natural clays nearby provided Seminario with the same material used by Inca potters.

Developed over three decades, Seminario-style pottery is instantly recognizable and ranges from utilitarian to decorative, jewelry to totems, and vases to wall plaques. Begun as a small, family affair, the **Seminario Ceramic Studio** (*Berriozabal 405, Urubamba, tel 084/201–002, e-mail: kupa@seminarioceramicas. com, www.ceramicaseminario.com*) has now moved to larger grounds and is an important source of income for local artisans. The studio and sales gallery open daily, and Pablo or Marilú often talk to visitors. A guide will lead you through the attractive grounds, which include local plants and a camelid enclosure.

■ **Women on their way to the crafts market carry goods and spin wool with an ages-old drop spindle.**

parking area below the site to the entrance, then climb up the steep Inca staircase, through numerous wide agricultural terraces. As you climb, you'll see remarkable walls and niches with fine stonework; examining them is a perfect excuse to stop and catch your breath.

An unfinished, but exceptional, double-jamb doorway marks the top of the stairs. In fact, apart from the terracing, many of the most important structures at the top of Ollantaytambo were clearly under construction when the Inca abandoned the site.

The superb wall to the left of the door contains ten niches; the footpath in front of it affords marvelous views of the village and beyond. The wall comprises only

half of a building whose outer wall is missing.

Above this wall stands a massive structure consisting of six monolithic blocks united by slim spacer stones, an unusual feature in Inca construction that has long puzzled archaeologists.

The large stones are pinkish rhyolite that were quarried from an outcrop more than two miles (3 km) away as the condor flies, southwest across the Río Urubamba. Using an elaborate system of sleds, log rollers, and levers, the Inca moved these massive blocks from the quarry, across the river, and up the ramp that is still visible today at the back left of the site.

In 1537, after Manco Inca had lost the battle at Sacsayhuamán, he retreated first to Calca then to Ollantaytambo, with its steep and defensible layout. Hernando Pizarro (Francisco's half brother) marched on Ollantaytambo with 70 cavalry and numerous Spanish and indigenous foot soldiers, intent on capturing or killing Manco and ending the uprising.

The Inca, aware of the Spaniards' plans, prepared an ingenious and unexpected defense. When the Spanish troops arrived at the base of Ollantaytambo, Manco rained arrows, spears, boulders, and slingshots down onto the attackers, and opened up channels from the Río Patacancha. This flooded the ground behind, sending the horses of the Spanish into panicked disarray.

Forced to retreat, the chastened Spaniards barely escaped the trap. The battle would prove to be the most important ever won by the Inca against the conquistadores.

Descend the way you came up, or if you have a head for heights, continue up and to the right of the six monoliths, where a narrow path leads through a section of less well-made buildings, probably a residential area.

The trail continues around the cliff rising above the site, with

Buying *Chicha*

Glance at the main entrance of a courtyard in Ollantaytambo and you may find a stick flying a plastic bag or a bunch of flowers. A white "flag" indicates that freshly made bread is for sale, while a red flag, or flowers, advertises *chicha* (corn beer).

Go in to buy some, but note that, unless your stomach has already become well acclimatized to rural Peruvian food, you may find that the chicha has the effect of making you queasy.

Don't accept the drink in one of the large, poorly washed, public glasses. Use your own mug or wide-mouthed water bottle, and you'll be less likely to encounter an upset stomach, although the locals won't know quite what to make of this! Still, so many tourists visit the town that the residents probably find strange foreign habits acceptable.

INSIDER TIP:

Break away from the pack and try to explore beyond the well-worn route from Cusco to Machu Picchu. The Sacred Valley is very underrated; the places are incredible.

—JAMES DION
National Geographic Society,
Director Tourism Programs,
Maps Division

photogenic views of the terraces and walls you have visited framed by trapezoidal windows. This path emerges above another, less well-preserved group of terraces, through which another flight of stairs will take you down to an area called Incamisana.

Containing some of the most recently excavated parts of Ollantaytambo, **Incamisana** includes stone channels and ceremonial baths leading back toward the entrance of the site. The best known bath, **Baño de la Ñusta** (The Princess's Bath), demonstrates two important elements of Inca architecture. First, this elaborate monument was carved out of the existing rock, not made from imported boulders. Second, you will notice three steps skillfully carved into the rock, a motif found in many important sites. The number three reflects the Inca reverence for celestial triads, such as the sun, moon, and stars, or thunder, lightning, and the rainbow. ∎

WALK: THE INCA TRAIL

South America's most famous and popular trek, the Inca Trail passes stunning archaeological sites, winds through exuberant cloud forest, and ascends steep passes below the snowcapped Cordillera Vilcabamba to reach Machu Picchu.

A breathtaking view awaits hikers at the end of their arduous trek.

Regulations

Trekkers along the Inca Trail will find it heavily regulated. You must camp in designated areas as part of a tour organized by a licensed outfitter (see Travelwise pp. 307–308). Authorities limit access to 500 people daily, including guides and porters (300 people), which reduces the number of permits reserved for tourists to a maximum of 200 per day. Nonrefundable permits ($$$$$), which bear your name and passport number, cannot be transferred. Arrangements to receive an advance permit must be made with outfitters, who

charge from $400 to more than $1,000 for the trek from Cusco. The trail closes down in February for maintenance.

Despite the necessary bureaucratic requirements that every visitor must abide by, the Inca Trail remains an unforgettable highlight for all those who attempt it. Although just 24 miles (39 km) long, the trail requires four days to complete because of its steepness and constant changes in elevation. Operators have pre-established campsites along the following route.

The Trek

Groups traditionally start at KM 88 (8,203 feet/2,500 m), which is reached only by the Cusco–Aguas Calientes railway. Others prefer to take a private vehicle from Cusco to KM 82, then hike 4 miles (7 km) along the south side of the Río Urubamba to Llactapata. Near KM 82, Aventours operates a private camp with showers, saunas, and views of glaciated Verónica (18,866 feet/5,750 m).

A 1-mile (1.6 km) uphill hike from KM 88 takes you to **Llactapata** ❶ (8,727 feet/2,660 m), with extensive Inca terracing. Although a campsite overlooks Llactapata, most push on 4 miles (6 km) up the Río Cusichaca Valley to the village of **Huayllabamba** ❷ (9,843 feet/3,000 m), where you can buy drinks and snacks and make camp. (A spur off the trail heads south to **Paucarcancha,** an Inca *tambo*, with a modern campsite, 40 minutes away.) Most, however, stay on the path and climb the narrow Río Llullucha Valley through a fairyland forest of *quenual* trees. Here you will find two small campsites. The main area, **Llulluchupampa** ❸ (12,140 feet/3,700 m) has toilets, sits 2.5 miles (4 km) above Huayllabamba, and offers superb views back to the valley.

NOT TO BE MISSED:

Warmiwañusca • Sayacmarca
• Phuyupatamarca • Huiñay
Huayna • Intipunku

The climb then zigzags to **Warmiwañusca**
❹ (Dead Woman's Pass), at 13,774 feet (4,198
m) the trek's highest point, more than a mile
(1.6 km) above Llulluchupampa. The knee-
searing, 1.25-mile (2 km) descent back to **Río
Pacamayo** ❺ (11,812 feet/3,600 m), a popular
camping area, gives views across to **Runkura-
cay.** Trekkers pass this unusual, oval-shaped Inca
site on the ascent to the second pass (12,875
feet/3,924 m), a little more than a mile (2 km)
above Pacamayo. Once there, enjoy the good
views of the Cordillera Vilcabamba.

Descending again, the trail offers superb
vistas of the wonderful site of **Sayacmarca**
(Dominant Town), perched at 11,598 feet
(3,535 m) on a promontory and reached by
a steep Inca stairway to the left. From the site,
the trail plunges through bamboo forest. Soon

there begins a gentle climb, following an Inca
tunnel, to a barely noticeable third pass (12,140
feet/3,700 m). About a mile (1.6 km) beyond,
the imposing ritual site of **Phuyupatamarca**
❻ (Cloud Level Place) looms into view. The
11,680-foot-high (3,560 m) site features water
flowing through restored ceremonial baths. A
camping area, with views of Salcantay (20,552
feet/6,264 m), is located nearby.

Only 5 more miles (8 km), mainly downhill,
bring you to Machu Picchu. The trail cork-
screws down an astonishingly long stairway
through lush cloud forest, passing left of lovely
Huiñay Huayna ❼ (Forever Young) at 8,859
feet (2,700 m) high. Above it you will find a
small, overcrowded hostel and campsite. The
route contours around and then emerges at
Intipunku ❽ (Sun Gate), with Machu Picchu
spread out magically below.

⛰	See also area map p. 121
➤	KM 88
↔	24 miles (39 km)
⏱	4 days
➤	Machu Picchu

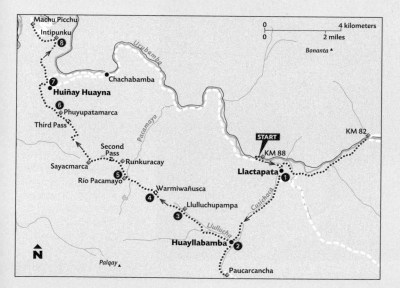

MACHU PICCHU

Peru's most famous attraction lures hundreds of thousands of visitors every year, as well it should. This Inca city, undiscovered during the 16th-century Spanish conquest, forgotten and undisturbed for almost four centuries, has the most spectacular location and architecture worthy of the great South American archaeological sites.

A few local campesinos in the Urubamba Valley knew of the overgrown temple above their farms, but Machu Picchu remained unknown to the outside world until 1911, when American historian Hiram Bingham, searching for Vilcabamba, was guided here by locals.

Unsure what to make of the site, Bingham nonetheless knew right away that he had stumbled upon something of breathtaking importance. He mounted return expeditions in 1912 and 1915, beginning a long process of discovery and speculation that continues today. It is perhaps surprising that archaeologists still cannot explain why the Inca built this legendary lost city.

Logistics

A quick visit from Cusco or the Sacred Valley requires an entire day, beginning with a long train ride to Aguas Calientes in the morning (see p. 139) followed by a shuttle bus to the site, two to four hours of exploring, and a return to town in the evening. It's an excellent excursion and the way most people visit these extraordinary ruins. However, Machu Picchu crowds with tourists in the middle of the day.

If you have the time, stay overnight nearby and spend an entire day investigating some of the exciting side trips or lesser known

The prison group and industrial sector of Machu Picchu

sectors. Only one small, expensive hotel serves Machu Picchu itself. So for more reasonable options, head down to **Aguas Calientes,** where there are dozens of hotels in every price range. Located at a more comfortable elevation of 6,760 feet (2,060 m), this busy town struggles with its recent growth, finding itself crammed into a small area girded by mountains and the Urubamba. There are no taxis in town so be prepared to walk anywhere you need to go. The hot springs, for which the town is named, are about a ten-minute walk above the city center.

Admission: you can buy entrance tickets for Machu Picchu at the **Dirección Regional de Cultura Cusco** (see p. 123), or directly through the website *www.machupicchu.gob.pe* avoiding the price increases of the tourist agencies. For reductions for students it is necessary to physically present themselves at the offices of the Ministry of culture in Cusco (*Calle Garsilaso or Calle Maruri 340*) or that of Machu Picchu Pueblo (*Aguas Calientes*).

The entrance ticket to the citadel, valid for three days from the date of purchase, costs around $40 (*free of charge up to 7 years; reduced to $19–21 up to the age of 25 by presenting a valid identity document and university card*) with entry shifts every hour from 6 a.m. to 2 p.m. The ticket allows a visit of up to 4 hours along defined routes, one of which is designed for elderly or disabled visitors. From the citadel, if you have chosen one of the two additional itineraries by purchasing the $53 ticket, you can continue

climbing the Huayna Picchu or Machu Picchu, the mountains that dominate the site, but only in the first 3 entry turns (*from 6 a.m. to 8 a.m.*), having maximum two hours to visit the citadel.

For a less steep and less dangerous climb, we recommend the second route, which is longer but much easier. (*NB: You can only enter the citadel once*).

Arrival at the Site: the frequent departures of buses (*$$, round trip*) that connect Machu Picchu Pueblo (*Aguas Calientes*) to the archaeological site begin at 5:30 a.m. The road to Machu Picchu meanders for 6 miles

---

INSIDER TIP:

Remember that you may not bring backpacks into the site at Machu Picchu. You can't carry water in disposable plastic bottles nor carry food of any kind.

–KENNY LING
National Geographic contributor

(10 km) up to 7,970 feet (2,430 m) offering thrilling panoramas. Alternatively, follow the marked path; it is steep but it saves you many sharp bends. Buses leave tourists in a small parking lot in front of Machu Picchu Sanctuary Lodge; bathrooms, a bar, and luggage storage are adjacent. Look for guides (*$$$ per person for a 2–3* (continued on p. 156)

Machu Picchu
Map p. 121
www.machupicchu.gob.pe

ALTERNATIVES TO THE INCA TRAIL

The iconic Inca Trail (see pp. 150–151) to Machu Picchu is so popular that it is booked months in advance. So local outfitters have developed numerous other treks in the Sacred Valley area that are much less crowded but equally dramatic. Some can be done by experienced independent backpackers, who should avail themselves of one of several trekking guidebooks for precise directions.

The Inca walls provide inspiration for trekkers.

Precautions

See Parque Nacional Huascarán (see pp. 182–187) for pertinent information about *arrieros*, and remember that, even if you are going independently, hiring a local contributes to the rural economy.

Scores of outfitters operate out of Cusco. They provide equipment and guides for the many trekking opportunities: Some of the best are listed in Travelwise (see pp. 306–307). Getting the cheapest rate is not necessarily a good thing because unscrupulous outfitters cut corners by underpaying and overworking porters and *arrieros*, providing poorly trained guides or inadequate gear, and not properly disposing of waste.

The Trails

The **one-day Inca Trail** leaves on the opposite side, from KM 104 on the railway,
crossing the Urubamba by footbridge to Cachabamba, then climbs about 1,700 feet (500 m) to Huiñay Huayna. From there, continue to Intipunku and Machu Picchu; allow six to nine hours. (Some outfitters break the trip by camping near Huiñay Huayna.)

Two **Salcantay hikes** leave from Mollepata at 9,187 feet (2,800 m), about 60 miles (96 km) west of Cusco off Highway 3. Both begin by heading north toward Salcantay, southern Peru's second highest mountain. One skirts east of the glaciers to join the Inca Trail at Huayllabamba and requires the same permits.

The better choice swings southwest over the superb views of 15,421-foot (4,700 m) Salcantay Pass and drops through several ecological zones to the **Santa Teresa** coffee-growing region, finishing at Aguas Calientes. This is the best of the long treks, ending near

Machu Picchu; allow five to six days. This hike has become so popular that there are now four comfortable but pricey mountain lodges on the route (*tel 084/262–640, www. mountainlodgesofperu.com*).

A fun llama trek around **Huayllanay,** a remote 17,390-foot (5,300 m) peak southwest of Ollantaytambo, is a four-day circuit that visits rarely seen Inca sites, passes through tiny communities, and affords opportunities to see how highland campesinos farm. It ends near the Inca Trail, where you can catch a train to Aguas Calientes. Llama-assisted treks can also be arranged in the **Lares Valley,** north of the Sacred Valley. Hikes of two to five days through this region, known for its remote villages and colorful weaving, visit the important campesino town of Lares, offering an opportunity to see how rural Andean people live.

Another hike near Cusco includes the high and strenuous circuit of 20,907-foot-high (6,372 m) **Apu Ausangate.** Get there from Tinqui, a village 88 miles (140 km) east of Cusco on the Puerto Maldonado road. *Apu* refers to a summit sacred to the Inca and still worshipped by Quechua today. In late May or early June, campesinos throng here for the Qoyllur Riti festival. They climb to more than 15,550 feet (4,750 m) at night to reach the glaciated northern flanks of the Apu and celebrate with music, masks, and costumes. There are no facilities, but tour operators will arrange tented camps for these wild mountain festivities.

Most of the seven-day Ausangate circuit lies at more than 14,436 feet (4,400 m), with some passes exceeding 16,405 feet (5,000 m). It is only for hardy, acclimatized trekkers. In addition to stunning views, highlights include the chance to see vicuñas and condors, natural hot springs, huge herds of alpaca, and few fellow trekkers.

EXPERIENCE: Pursue Active Adventures Near Cusco

Cusco is a mecca for the adventurous: In addition to trekking along the Inca Trail to Machu Picchu, you can arrange expeditions to summit the major peaks of **Ausangate** and **Salcantay.** Also popular are white-water river rafting trips, ranging from day runs on the **Río Urubamba** to multiday adventures descending from the high Andes to the Amazon Basin on the **Ríos Apurímac** and **Tambopata.**

Mountain biking is a newer sport, offering superb panoramas on dirt roads and tracks reaching remote Inca sites. Horseback riding varies from easy walks of a few hours to demanding weeklong rides guaranteed to get you away from the beaten path.

For those who need more adrenaline, try hang gliding over the **Sacred Valley.** Or, if you prefer flying adventures with your feet firmly on the ground, birdwatching expeditions will show you some of Peru's most obscure birds (see Travelwise pp. 307–308).

■ **The Temple of the Three Windows**

hrs. excursion) and entry nearby. (*We reiterate the recommendation to buy entrance tickets in advance*). The ticket includes a site map. Machu Picchu is open 6 a.m.–5 p.m., with large crowds between 9 a.m. and 3 p.m., especially on Mondays and Fridays, and the days preceding the Inti Raymi (*24 Jun.*), the Fiestas Patrias (*28–29 Jul.*), and winter solstice (*21 Jun.*). The site admits a maximum of 5,600 entrances, with a maximum simultaneous presence of 2,500.

Agricultural Area & Royal Sector

From the main entrance a path leads between some small Inca buildings to offer you the first glance on Machu Picchu, a view that is undoubtedly extraordinary. Look around for orientation; you are surrounded by terraces in the agricultural sector, with two main groups of buildings separated by a central square covered with grass.

The buildings on your left belong to the prisons, craftsmen, and residential areas. Behind, toward the northeast, the unmistakable Huayna Picchu stands out. On the left of the central square are the buildings of the royal sector and the most important temples, including the astronomical observatory with the only *intihuatana* (see below) intact surviving in the land of the Inca. At the top, turning your head to your left you will see the arrival point of the Inca Trail to the southwest, and Intipunku in the distance.

Before leaving the agricultural center and starting to explore the city, many visitors climb a long ladder on the left, following the outer wall of the royal sector and turning around it until they reach the Inca Trail. The steps continue zigzagging to the **hut of the keeper of the funerary rock,** an extraordinary place to stop at the beginning or end of the day, with a magnificent view of the city lying at your feet in its entire splendor.

After drinking in the view, return to the top of the wall of the royal sector, entering through a superb and much photographed Inca gateway. Look below you for the only building in Machu Picchu with a rounded wall, the **Temple of the Sun.** Cordoned off from visitors, it is best seen from above. Inside sits a granite altar slab, carved in situ from the rock beneath. A trapezoidal window on the east side of the temple is aligned so that the rising sun of the winter solstice casts its rays along the altar. Another

featuring some of the best stonework in Machu Picchu. Although he found no human remains placed inside the cave, the quality of the architecture led Bingham to pronounce it a royal tomb.

On the north side of the Temple of the Sun begins a long line of **ceremonial baths,** or fountains, 16 in all, with water cascading from one to the next. The highest fountain is also the most elaborate. Taking the stairs that climb above the fountains brings you to a **quarry,** which provided the builders with at least some of the material they needed.

INSIDER TIP:

Hire a guide in Cusco [see Visitor Information p. 123] to visit the remote Vilcabamba region, the area where rebel Inca held off the Spaniards. It is still a place full of mystery and replete with ruins yet to be identified.

–LARRY PORGES
*National Geographic
Travel Books editor*

---

window has holes drilled into it. Although no one knows the purpose of the holes, an early explanation that snakes crawled through them has given the window its popular name, the **Serpents' Window.**

Walking around and below the Temple of the Sun brings you to the **Royal Tomb,** a cave with finely carved step motifs, painstakingly cut niches, and superbly finished walls

Sacred Plaza

Walk across the quarry to the northwest to reach the Sacred Plaza. On the right, the impressively large trapezoidal windows of the **Temple of the Three Windows** give excellent views into the central plaza. Next to it stands the **Principal Temple,** which is sagging and cracked along the right side, one of the few places in Machu Picchu to show substantial damage due to ground settling beneath the massive boulders. At the front left side of this temple, a carved, kite-shaped rock represents the constellation of the Southern Cross.

The west side of the Sacred Plaza has a small, curved lookout point, with views of steep terracing tumbling toward the Río Urubamba far below and the white peaks of the Cordillera Vilcabamba on the distant horizon.

To the left of and behind the Principal Temple, you will find the **Sacristy.** Located near Machu Picchu's ceremonial sites, this room has a rock bench and several niches that would have afforded the Inca high priests a place to prepare for rituals. Two large, polygonal rocks flank the entrance, one of which is said to have 32 angles.

To reach the **Intihuatana** ("Where the sun hooks") take the staircase behind the Sacristy. The big rock presents small niches, presumably used as handholds by the older priest-astronomers as they climbed to this most important carved rock. Exactly how the Inca used the Intihuatana is unclear, but archaeologists agree in affirming that somehow the celestial alignments of the rock enabled the priests to predict with certainty the shortest day of the year. Thus, they reversed the shortening days by "hitching up" the sun.

Prison Group & Industrial Sector

Descend from the Intihuatana and cross the Central Plaza toward the entrance to reach the **Prison Group** above the lowermost of the 16

ceremonial baths. The **Temple of the Condor** was named for a rock carved into the shape of a condor's head. Behind the rock are two more resembling outstretched wings. A small hole behind the condor leads to an underground cell, and above it you can see the adult-size niches that Bingham thought looked like prison cells. In fact, it is unlikely that these niches held prisoners.

From the prison group, head to the farthest eastern walkway along the edge of the **industrial sector,** and look for a cave-like opening into a semi-subterranean room. Named **Intimachay** ("Sun Cave"), this room is lit by a long, narrow window that is aligned with the rising sun during the winter solstice. Outside, look down into the rocky terraces below, where you just might see a family of wild viscachas scampering around.

Other Sites

It takes two to three hours to visit the sights outlined above. Most are

Machu Picchu: an Evolution in Tourism

Regulations governing visits to Machu Picchu and the Inca Trail have changed dramatically since the 1980s. Then, backpackers took a train from Cusco to Aguas Calientes for less than $2, hiked the Inca Trail independently for a fee of $7 (including entrance to the Citadel), and stayed at the site-side hotel for $50. Meanwhile, VIP travelers could clatter into the Central Plaza by helicopter.

Awareness of Machu Picchu's intrinsic importance was raised in 1983 when UNESCO proclaimed it the first of Peru's World Heritage sites. Although helicopter flights were banned and Inca Trail clean-up campaigns initiated, rampant

development and environmental degradation became the watchwords of the next two decades. In 2001, a crane being used to illegally film a Peruvian beer ad chipped off part of the Intihuatana. Meanwhile, a contract was awarded to build a cable car to the entrance, and years of protracted international and local protests were needed to quash this plan. Finally, in 2003, the government began to enforce regulations requiring all trekkers to join guided groups and limiting the number of hikers to 500 per day, and visitors to Machu Picchu to 5,600 per day. This is why reservations must be made in advance and fees have risen.

included on guided tours, but there are hundreds of other buildings to explore, many unnamed. If you have the time, take one of several longer walks outside the city itself for a completely different perspective of Machu Picchu's layout and location.

Many travelers like to climb **Huayna Picchu,** which you can reach by a trail at the far northeast end of the city. The trail's guarded gate, where climbers must register, accepts two groups, one from 7 a.m. to 8 a.m., and one from 10 a.m. to 11 a.m. Tickets are required in advance (see p. 153).

This steep and narrow trail passes through a short but narrow Inca tunnel. The hike takes 45 to 90 minutes one way and rewards with a fine view.

■ **The Central Plaza and residential sector**

INSIDER TIP:

The Citadel and environs are often underappreciated for their amazing biodiversity, with hundreds of species of birds and dense tropical growth just footsteps away.

–CHRISTOPHER
AUGER-DOMÍNGUEZ
*National Geographic
International Editions photographer*

Return the way you came, or take the spectacular trail that hugs the back side of Huayna Picchu to the **Temple of the Moon.** The trail descends steeply to the cave containing the temple and ends below the route that climbs up the mountain. Leave the temple and continue up to the junction with the Huayna Picchu trail; allow an extra three hours. Part of the route involves climbing wooden ladders attached to the cliff.

If this seems too hard, try the less demanding hike to **Puente Inca** (*Inca Bridge, make sure it is accessible*). From the Hut of the Caretaker of the Funerary Rock, a signed trail heads southwest away from Machu Picchu and through high cloud forest. It contours around the mountain to the bridge, about a 30-minute walk away. Or take the end of the Inca Trail as it climbs steadily to **Intipunku.** This route takes about an hour and gives the same first view of Machu Picchu as seen by trekkers along the Inca Trail. Return the way you came.

After visiting the lost city, return to Aguas Calientes via bus. If you need to catch an afternoon train, allow at least an hour for the descent as lines for the buses can get long. ■

A hardy region alive with crafts, markets, festivals, and unspoiled traditions that beckon adventurous travelers

CENTRAL HIGHLANDS

◼ Textiles from the Barrio Santa Ana area of Ayacucho

CENTRAL HIGHLANDS

The rugged central sierra is less touristed than anywhere else in the highlands of Peru. Noted for its crafts, markets, and festivals, this region was once overlooked because of social instability and a lack of resources. Still untrammeled by crowds today, the central sierra is nevertheless growing in popularity, charming visitors with its selfless hospitality, unspoiled traditions, and lovely scenery.

Each of the villages in the Río Mantaro Valley has perfected its own particular *artesanía* (handicraft). One produces fine filigreed silver jewelry, another fabricates homespun and naturally dyed woolen tapestries and ponchos, and yet another offers gourds intricately carved with scenes of daily life in the Andes. Each of the villages also holds its own *feria,* or market day. No matter when you visit, you're sure to run across a feria happening somewhere in the region.

In the markets around the city of Ayacucho, the crafts-loving traveler will find characteristic *retablos,* folding altars once carried by itinerant priests and travelers but now more often used as decorative wooden boxes. The retablos come in many sizes and open to reveal carved religious and Andean scenes. The smaller ones,

barely the size of a deck of cards, make emblematic souvenirs of the region. The area's carpets, clay statuettes, and religious icons are also beautifully crafted.

Eaten more often in the central sierra than anywhere else in Peru, potatoes were an Andean staple for thousands of years before the arrival of grains in the New World. The most popular of the region's many delicious dishes, *papa a la Huancaína,* a cold dish of boiled potatoes covered with a cheese sauce, is now enjoyed as an appetizer all over Peru. Other plates have remained local; only in Ayacucho can you sit down to a hearty meal of *puca picante,* a potato and meat stew in red peanut and pepper sauce, or *patachi,* a thick wheat soup cooked with beans, dehydrated potatoes, and beef or lamb.

History buffs should visit the ruins of the capital of the Wari Empire (A.D. 600–1100), which once spread over several hillsides outside Ayacucho, while fans of colonial architecture will love the famous 18th-century convent of Santa Rosa de Ocopa, in Concepción, and the fabulous churches in Huancavelica and Ayacucho, home of the most spectacular Easter parades in all of Peru.

The only regular, low-priced, non-tourist train service left in Peru runs between Huancayo and Huancavelica, and twice a month during the dry season a tourist train runs from Lima through the highlands to Huancayo, passing through the world's second highest passenger station along the way. Good paved roads connect Lima to Huancayo and Ayacucho; however, travel to other destinations must be done by bus along rough, unpaved roads that present an exciting challenge for the adventurous. ∎

NOT TO BE MISSED:

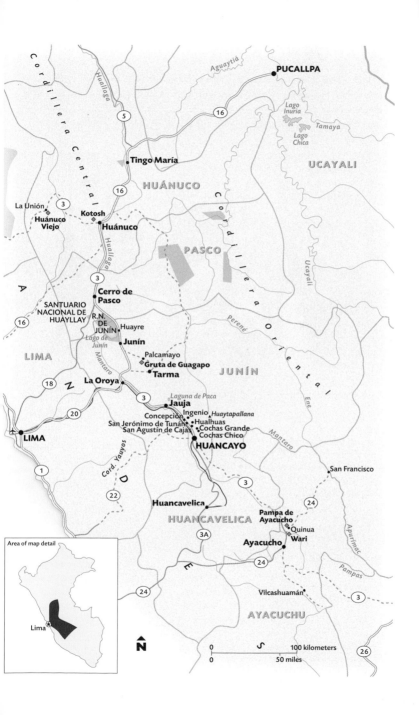

AYACUCHO AREA

In 1539, Francisco Pizarro founded San Juan de la Frontera de Huamanga, a *tambo* (shelter) on the main Inca highway joining Cusco with Quito. Known throughout the colonial era simply as Huamanga, the city changed its name to Ayacucho (Quechua for "corner of the dead") to mark a decisive battle for independence fought in nearby Quinua in 1824.

A street scene in downtown Ayacucho

Ayacucho

Map p. 163

Visitor Information

iPerú, Jr. Cusco 108– Municipalidad Provincial de Huamanga

066/318–305

E-mail: iperuayacucho@ promperu.gob.pe

Because of its altitude of 9,023 feet (2,750 m), temperate climate, and fertile countryside, Ayacucho enjoyed easy success as a colonial city. But its relative isolation made it difficult to attract visitors and slowed economic development.

In the 1970s and 1980s, the Shining Path movement (see sidebar p. 165) capitalized on the region's poverty, finding ready support in a population with few resources. Departmental statistics for 1981 show that there were only 28 miles (45 km) of

paved roads outside the city and that less than 15 percent of its citizens had access to electricity and running water.

As peace slowly returned to the region in the 1990s, more travelers began to visit this most colonial of the highland towns. Unpaved roads made the trip more than a little hair-raising for most, but in 1999, a new paved road from Lima via the coastal town of Pisco made Ayacucho accessible in 10–12 hours by bus from the capital ($$$). Travel from Ayacucho to other cities still necessitates challenging rides on bumpy roads, although the roads to Cusco and Huancayo have recently been paved. Several bus companies, clustered mainly north of Ayacucho's Plaza de Armas, provide travel services in the region. Daily flights to Lima are another good alternative.

Ayacucho

Called the "city of churches," Ayacucho counts 33 colonial churches—or so the locals claim the number to be—among its many impressive old buildings. Several of them are well worth visiting, but opening hours are erratic and few of the churches have telephones. For current information about times, check with the iPerú tourism office.

Colonial buildings, fronted by arched *portales* (arcades) surround the **Plaza de Armas** (locally called the Plaza Mayor). Now used as political or business offices, many of the buildings are open to the public during working hours.

INSIDER TIP:

For authentic handiwork, try the colorful local markets in small towns. They are often full of locals who come to trade goods among themselves.

−JONATHAN B. TOURTELLOT
Geotourism Editor,
National Geographic Traveler

The city's 17th-century **Catedral** anchors the east side (Portal Municipal) of the plaza. Featuring twin towers, the cathedral has a simple facade that belies its rich interior, filled with ten altars covered in gold leaf, an ornate wooden pulpit, and a religious art museum. Major processions held for Semana Santa begin and end at the cathedral, open every day 5:30 p.m.–7 p.m., and also 10 a.m.–11 a.m. Sunday morning.

The Origins of Shining Path

In 1970, Abimael Guzmán (b. 1934), a communist and professor of philosophy at the University of Ayacucho, established the radical Maoist group, Sendero Luminoso (Shining Path). Originally formed to return land and power to disenfranchised campesinos, Shining Path had become a terrorist organization by the late 1970s, paralyzing the nation with car bombings in Lima, roadblocks in the mountains and jungles, and the destruction of major bridges.

The group's activities soon plunged the country into a vicious and poorly delineated civil war that ultimately killed about 80,000 Peruvians. (Visit the Museo de La Nación in Lima for a stirring exhibit; see p. 73.) The conflict hit Ayacucho especially hard and turned the city, and the impoverished countryside around it, into an especially dangerous place to visit.

Captured in 1992 along with several of his lieutenants, Guzmán is now being held in the Naval Prison of Callao in Lima. Without Guzmán to guide it, the movement lost momentum. Today, Shining Path is no longer considered a threat to travelers anywhere in Peru.

**Museo
Arqueológico
Hipolito Unanue**

✉ Independencia
502

☎ 066/312–056

🕐 Closed Mon.

💲 $

On the west side of the plaza, the **Prefectura** (Portal Constitución) has beautiful 18th-century tile work and a cell that held local revolutionary heroine María Parado de Bellido prior to her execution in 1822.

North of the Plaza: A block north of the plaza, along 9 de Diciembre, stands **Iglesia Santo Domingo,** a 16th-century church famed for its role during the Spanish Inquisition; according to one story, heretics were hung from the church's three arches. Inside, the gold-leaf altar shows Andean influence in the form of hummingbirds and a face thought to be that of an Inca. Two statues, the Lord of the Holy Sepulcher and the Virgin of Sorrows, are brought out during the city's impressive Holy Week processions (see sidebar below). Continuing north three blocks along 9 de Diciembre brings you to the

Mercado Artesanal Shosaku Nagase, a well-regarded crafts market.

Leading north away from the plaza, 9 de Diciembre runs parallel with **Asamblea,** a pedestrian-only street for the first two blocks that features restaurants and Internet cafés. About a mile (1.6 km)

INSIDER TIP:

Bring two inexpensive digital cameras; accidents happen and cameras can be stolen.

–BOB BENFER
National Geographic grantee

---

farther north, the **Museo Arqueológico Hipolito Unanue** exhibits mainly local Wari artifacts but also includes some objects from other cultures. It's best to visit this small museum, delightfully set within a cactus garden, in the morning

---

EXPERIENCE: Witness an Easter Procession

Semana Santa (Holy Week) begins on Palm Sunday and continues for the entire week leading up to Easter Sunday. Peruvians mark the week with religious services and processions, none as fervent or spectacular as those in the central sierra, where the devoted carry heavy crucifixes and huge statues of Catholic saints and the Virgin Mary through the streets of the region's cities and villages. The celebrations also include fireworks, costumes, music, bullfights, and fairs.

The most glorious of all Holy Week celebrations takes place in Ayacucho. The city turns off all its lights during

the candlelit procession on Good Friday, and on Holy Saturday, it stages a running of the bulls. The festivities culminate at dawn on Easter Sunday with the image of Christ rising from a pyramid of candles erected at the cathedral. (*Check tourism brochure listing exact routes and times of all events; book accommodations well in advance as hotels fill up quickly.*)

Also known for its Easter processions, **Tarma** (see p. 174) carpets its streets with thousands of flower petals arranged into religious images and other designs, making the solemn march to the cathedral a splendid spectacle to behold.

One of many ornate gold-leaf altars in the cathedral on Ayacucho's Plaza de Armas

since the staff don't always adhere to the posted afternoon hours.

South of the Plaza: Two blocks of 28 de Julio, between the southwestern corner of the plaza and the city market, form a pedestrian-only mall. On the first block, the Jesuit **Templo de la Compañía** has a fine collection of colonial paintings. Begun in the early 17th century and added to several times, the building once housed a school that taught Latin and the arts to indigenous children. Just beyond, **Centro Turístico Cultural San Cristóbal** (*Jr. 28 de Julio 176*), a small but relaxing modern mall, offers Internet cafés, coffee shops, art galleries, and bars.

Opposite the market on 28 de Julio, **Iglesia de San Francisco de Asís,** one of Ayacucho's oldest churches, has the city's largest church bell. Older still is **Iglesia y Monasterio de Santa Clara,** two blocks west on Nazareno, famed for its delicately carved wooden ceiling with Moorish influence.

Museo Andrés Avelino Cáceres, housed in the 17th-century Casa Vivanco, is named after an Ayacucheño marshal who fought Chile in the War of the Pacific. Displays include military maps and other paraphernalia, as well as colonial- and republican-era furniture and art.

Farther south on 28 de Julio, a small plaza holds **Iglesia Santa Teresa,** which boasts an ornamental gold-plated main altar in churrigueresque style. Santa Teresa is a church as well as a Carmelite nunnery, where the sisters make and sell their own candy. If the church is closed, ask politely and they may allow you to enter through their little shop.

Across the small plaza stands little **Iglesia San Cristóbal,** Ayacucho's oldest church (1540) and one of the oldest on the continent. It is frequently closed, but who knows, you may get lucky.

About a mile (1.6 km) uphill and south of the center along

Museo Andrés Avelino Cáceres

✉ Jr. 28 de Julio 508

🕐 Closed Sun.

☎ 066/818-686

💲 $

Wari Culture

Around A.D. 600, the Wari (also spelled Huari)—an expansionist, militaristic, and religious people who imposed their own language and culture to all the conquered communities—established an empire over most of Peru. Some of their best known settlements include: **Cerro Baúl,** northeast Moquegua (see pp. 90–91); the **Toro Muerto** petroglyph fields, 3 hours from Arequipa (see p. 109); **Pachacamac,** southeast of Lima (see pp. 74–75); **Pikillacta,** 19 miles from Cusco (see p. 137); **Wilcahuaín,** near Huaraz (see p. 181); and the capital city outside Ayacucho.

The influence of Wari culture on Peruvian history is unmistakable. The roads that linked far-flung Wari outposts together later formed the basis of the extensive road network maintained by the Inca. Designed to resist earthquakes, Wari buildings were sometimes made from polygonal blocks of stone, a feature characteristic of later Inca architecture. Fine Wari tapestries and other woven textiles are among the best produced by any culture in the world. They have survived well in the dry desert climate and can be seen in several of the region's museums.

Wari culture reached its apogee in the ninth century, and by 1100, the empire had fractured into several subgroups eventually conquered by the Inca.

This may once have been an ancient Wari graveyard site.

Calle Grau, which becomes Calle San Blas, is **Barrio Santa Ana,** a district famed for its artisans. Centered on Plazuela de Santa Ana, it is surrounded with galleries that display and sell textiles, stone carvings, and retablos. A walk along the barrio's traditional cobblestone streets takes you past workshops open to visitors. Take your time, stop in, and have a look.

Beyond Ayacucho

Wari & Northeast: Travel agents in Ayacucho can arrange inexpensive tours with Spanish-speaking guides to visit Wari and Quinua. Independent travelers should catch one of the minibuses (*1 hr., $*) that leave from the Paradero Magdalena at the east end of Avenida Mariscal Cáceres in Ayacucho. Set out early in the morning to visit Wari, continue on to Quinua, and return to Ayacucho in the evening.

The archaeological site of **Wari** (*$*) lies 14 miles (23 km) north of Ayacucho along the paved road toward Quinua. The capital of the Wari Empire (see sidebar opposite), and once home to an estimated 50,000 people, the city covers a total of 8.5 square miles (13.7 sq km). Compared to other Peruvian sites of its size, Wari is little visited; unless you hire a guide, you may find yourself exploring alone.

Begin at the small on-site **museum** (*closed Mon., $*) for an introduction to the ancient city, which has not been well restored. From the museum, a gravel path leads to a crescent-shaped temple near a single massive stone slab that archaeologists believe served as an altar. Some of the impressive walls that line the straight pathways in this area of the site rise to more than 30 feet (9 m) in height; those in the city's upper regions lie buried beneath an almost impenetrable forest of prickly pear cactus. Burial areas discovered in labyrinthine underground tunnels are unsafe for tourists to enter.

From Wari, continue to **Quinua,** a pretty, cobblestoned village 21 miles (34 km) northeast of Ayacucho (*1 hr. by combi, $*). Famed for the miniature churches carved from local stone and used as rooftop ornaments, the city is just a ten-minute walk from the site of the Battle of Ayacucho, which was fought on December 9, 1824, and helped bring an end to colonial rule. A 144-foot-high (44 m) obelisk, its sides carved with scenes from the historic battle, marks the **Pampa de Ayacucho** battlefield. Quinua's small **museum** (*$*) displays military items.

Southeast: Considered by the Inca to be the center of their empire, **Vilcashuamán** lies 75 miles (120 km) southeast of Ayacucho, a five-hour bus ride along unpaved roads. Its five-stepped *usnu* (pyramid) and **Temple of the Sun** demonstrate high-quality Inca stonework. Unfortunately, the current village sits directly atop most of the site's other historic buildings. Ask locals for directions to the thermal springs or the *Puya*

EXPERIENCE:
Learn Crafts, Cooking, & Quechua

Many of the local artisans who live around **Huancayo** offer workshops in some of the traditional crafts of the region, including weaving, gourd carving, and jewelry making. **Quechua language courses** are also available, as well as Spanish for beginners and advanced speakers. Learn **how to cook** typical Peruvian dishes, or attend a **music or dancing class.** Classes take place in small groups or one-on-one. Arrange to stay in the home of a local family, where you can practice your newfound language skills or help out in the kitchen (see Travelwise pp. 308–309).

Huancavelica

⬛ Map p. 163

Visitor Information

✉ Manuel Segura 168, Plaza de Armas

☎ 067/452–938

www.turismo huancavelica.com

Dirección Regional de Cultura/Museo Regional "Daniel Hernández Morillo"

✉ Jr. Antonio Raymondi 193, Huancavelica

☎ 067/453–420

🕐 Closed Mon.

raimondii forest (see p. 178), both an hour's walk away. Stay a night at a village hotel, or arrange a day trip from Ayacucho.

Huancavelica

In 1571, the Spanish established Huancavelica to take advantage of the natural mercury and silver deposits in the surrounding countryside. Today this small city, whose colonial churches deserve a visit, is the eponymous capital of its department.

Because travel to Huancavelica is difficult, few tourists visit this friendly city. If you are coming from or returning to Huancayo, plan a ride on the **Tren Macho** (see p. 172; *tel 064/216–662*), or consider

traveling back to Huancayo by bus, which follows a higher, more scenic route. Continuing on to Ayacucho requires catching an early morning minibus to Rumi-cacha—a hamlet on the main Lima-Ayacucho road—then picking up another minibus to Ayacucho; allow eight to ten hours. You will find the offices for most of the bus companies around Parque Santa Ana, six blocks east of the Plaza de Armas.

The **Dirección Regional de Cultura,** a block west of the Plaza de Armas, has a small archaeology museum and offers useful information for tourists.

Noted for their silver, rather than gold, altars, Huancavelica's colonial churches, with the exception of the cathedral, open for early morning services (*6:30 a.m.–8:30 a.m.*). Open most of the day, the **cathedral** on the Plaza de Armas was built in 1673 and boasts what locals insist is the best colonial altar in Peru. Older still, **Iglesia San Sebastián,** on Plaza Bolognesi, dates to 1662 and has been restored. On the same plaza, the 18th-century **Iglesia San Francisco** has an amazing 11 altars, while **Iglesia Santo Cristóbal,** near the mineral springs, offers good views of the city. **Iglesia Santa Ana,** on Parque Santa Ana, is the oldest church in the city.

Five blocks north of the plaza, a steep flight of steps leads up to the **San Cristóbal Mineral Springs.** The lukewarm sulfurous springs offer the weary traveler private showers and a public swimming pool. ■

EXPERIENCE: Take the Highest Train Ride

Finished in 1908, the railroad to Huancayo was the most important link between Lima and the Central Sierra for much of the 20th century. The fantastic route extends from the coast to an ear-popping 15,681 feet (4,781 m) before reaching Huancayo.

During the 1980s, bridges along the railroad fell victim to attacks by Shining Path. The Ferrocarril Central Andino (*tel 01/390–5858 ext. 222 or 216, www. ferrocarrilcentral.com.pe*) runs the Lima-Huancayo section from April to November, in conjunction with particular holidays, starting from the Estación de Desamparados in Lima. The round-trip ticket costs $180–270 (classic or tourist service), and can be purchased at travel agencies such as Fertur Perú Travel (*www. fertur-travel.com*), which offers packages that also include hotel accommodation.

HUANCAYO AREA

The sprawling commercial capital of Huancayo sits 10,731 feet (3,271 m) above sea level in the agricultural department of Junín. With a population of some 450,000 inhabitants, Huancayo is about three times the size of Ayacucho and, after Cusco, the second largest city in the Peruvian Andes.

Huancayo

Despite being named for the Huanca people, who lived here before the Inca, today's Huancayo has few archaeological ruins or colonial churches. Still, this postcolonial city clings to tradition and delights visitors with the strength of its cultural customs. Its handicrafts, markets, and fiestas are second to none.

In 1839, the Peruvian constitution was signed at **La Merced** (*1st block of Calle Real*), the city's most interesting church. Three blocks away, Huancayo's main plaza, **Plaza de la Constitución,** contains a neoclassical cathedral.

About 1.5 miles (2.4 km) northeast of the plaza along Giráldez, **Cerro de La Libertad** (Liberty Hill) offers nice views of the city, places to eat, arts-and-crafts stands, and a playground. Follow the signed path from Cerro de La Libertad 1.25 miles (2 km) to the eroded sandstone formations at **Torre Torre** (Tower Tower).

The whimsical winding walls and strange statues of **Parque de Identidad Wanka,** about 2 miles (3 km) north of the center, amuse locals and travelers alike. The park's exhibits detail the city's history. Buy some traditional local food at one of several

Terracing above Cochas Chico, a craft village, in Rió Mantro Valley

eateries nearby, and enjoy a pleasant picnic among the park's native plants.

Markets: Huancayo lies in the wide and fertile Río Mantaro Valley, crammed with farms and small villages, some of which are famed for their handicrafts (see sidebars pp. 169 & 173). Sunday is market day, when farmers and craftsmen bring their products to sell in the city. The **crafts market** lies along Calle Huancavelica, five blocks southeast of the Plaza de la Constitución. In addition to the dizzying array of interesting local crafts, there are many other kinds of goods. Be sure to keep an eye out for pickpockets.

NOTE: Huancayo's Main Long-Distance Bus Companies
Cruz del Sur (*Ave. Ferrocarril 151, Sector 1, tel 064/223–367*) to Lima (*7 hrs.*)
www.cruzdel
sur.com.pe

Expreso Molina Union (*Angaraes 334, Chilca, tel 061/224–501*) to Ayacucho (*12 hrs.*)

TICCLAS (*Ave. Ferrocarril 1590, Chilca, tel 979/778–144, WhatsApp also*) to Huancavelica (*5 hrs.*)

Turismo Central (*Jr. Ayacucho 274, tel 064/223–128*) to Huánuco (*6 hrs.*) & Pucallpa (*18 hrs.*)
www.turismo
central.com.pe

Chilca Train Station

✉ Ave. Leoncio Prado 1766 & Ave. Ferrocarril

Santa Rosa de Ocopa

✉ 3 miles (5 km) NE of Concepción

⊕ Closed Tues.

$ $

The colorful daily food and produce market, with delicacies such as pigs' hooves, live guinea pigs, and dried frogs, is located in the covered **Mercado Mayorista** on Ica, a block east of the main Lima train station. At the busy Sunday market, stalls spill out along the train tracks.

Getting Out of Town

Huancayo lacks a central bus terminal but has plenty of bus services. Local minibuses leave from several stops near Plaza Amazonas in the city center, while long-distance companies operate all over town (see note p. 171). For information on the tourist offers in the region,

---

INSIDER TIP:

The Cordillera Yauyos found between Lima and Huancayo possesses lagoons, waterfalls, and appealing villages.

—CELIA CACERES
National Geographic grantee

---

please contact the Dircetur office (*Jr. Pachitea 201, tel 064/222–575, closed Sat–Sun, tourism.junin.gob. pe*). From **Chilca** station trains leave for Huancavelica, the last ones left in Peru at low cost: a spectacular 80-mile (128 km) route, which crosses 38 tunnels and 15 bridges. Trains leave every morning at 6:30 a.m. from Huancayo, while the return from Huancavelica is scheduled for 2 p.m. ($–$$). The journey takes 4–5 hours. This historic railway

section has been nicknamed **Tren Macho.**

Carretera Central

Peru's Carretera Central (Highway 3) extends through the highlands from the Bolivian border at Lake Titicaca to a remote area on the Ecuadoran frontier. The southern sector, from Puno and Cusco to Abancay, is paved; the section from Ayacucho to Huancayo is an unpaved, but major, highway. North of Huancayo, the highway, which is again paved, runs through the picturesque central sierra as far as Huánuco.

Concepción: Located 14 miles (23 km) northwest of Huancayo in the Río Mantaro Valley, Concepción is famed for its 18th-century Franciscan convent, **Santa Rosa de Ocopa.** Founded in 1725 to train jungle-bound missionaries, the convent now has a museum of indigenous artifacts and jungle wildlife collected by the friars. Its fabulous library houses more than 20,000 items, ranging from colonial maps and 16th-century religious books to collections of early photos of mission work. Frequent *colectivos* leave the Concepción Mercado for Ocopa daily.

Jauja: All Peruvian schoolchildren know that Jauja, 25 miles (40 km) northwest of Huancayo, was the first colonial capital of Peru. It was also an important center of Huanca

(continued on p. 174)

EXPERIENCE: Visiting Local Artisans

Villages known for their handicrafts dot the Río Mantaro Valley northwest of Huancayo. Lying mainly on the east side of the river, they can be visited by local minibus or on a tour from Huancayo. Most minibuses leave from near Iglesia la Inmaculada, about six blocks east of Huancayo's Plaza de la Constitución.

If you speak Spanish, wander through the villages and ask where the artisans live and work; many of the craftsmen will welcome you into their workshops. On market day, you may see more food and produce than anything else, but local artisans will be there, too, and you will certainly find beautifully crafted pieces for sale.

The best known of the villages, **Cochas Grande** and **Cochas Chico,** lie just 7 miles (12 km) north of Huancayo along a side road. They produce *mates burilados,* gourds engraved with exceptionally detailed representations of Andean life. The tradition has been around for more than 4,000 years. Craftsmen use wood-working tools to incise the hard rinds of these inedible, ornamental fruits, then scorch them to bring out the color. Depending on their size—which can range from smaller than a tennis ball to as large as a sizable watermelon—and the detail of the carving, the gourds can sell from a few dollars to several hundred. Considered the center of gourd carving in Peru, Cochas Chico holds its market day on Friday.

Market day in **San Agustín de Cajas,** 7 miles (12 km) northwest of Huancayo near the highway to Concepción, falls on Monday. Look for wicker furniture and broad-brimmed hats made of sheep's wool.

A couple of miles away, **Hualhuas** has a Tuesday market filled with superb tapestries, ponchos, and

Alexander Gallardo Pinco weaving in Barrio Santa Ana

rugs woven from alpaca and sheep's wool. Most of the natural dyes come from vegetation, although the red is made from the cochineal insect, a tiny bug that secretes and lives in a cottony white growth on the pads of the prickly pear cactus. Considerably smaller than a pea, the body of the female produces an intense crimson color when crushed.

The Spanish conquistadores exported this precious dye to Spain, where its use was limited to the most important and wealthy people, including Catholic cardinals whose robes were dyed red. Only gold surpassed it as the most important export from the New World.

On Wednesdays, the skilled artisans of **San Jerónimo de Tunán,** about 9 miles (14 km) northwest of Huancayo, sell their silver filigree jewelry and ornamental figurines. Peruvians typically favor handsomely crafted pairs of roosters, representative of cock-fighting, an activity popular throughout Latin America.

Travel another 5 miles (8 km) from San Jerónimo to **Ingenio,** where trout are harvested in Peru's largest fish hatchery. Visitors are welcome to tour the facility and learn how the fish develop from eggs to fingerlings (less than a year old) to adults. Afterward, relax at one of the local restaurants over a meal of fresh trout.

A girl in traditional clothes at the Pampa de Quinua

life. Walk or take a mototaxi ($) to the unnamed site discovered 2 miles (3 km) southeast of town, or visit **Laguna de Paca,** a popular lake 2.5 miles (4 km) north of town. Escape the lakefront noise with an invigorating hike to the ruins in the surrounding hills.

Southeast of Jauja, roads follow both the *izquierda* (left), or east, and *derecha* (right), or west, sides of the Río Mantaro Valley. Most of the crafts villages lie on the *izquierda* side; the *derecha* side has buses to Huancayo.

Visible only on clear days, 18,925-foot-high (5,768 m) **Huaytapallana** is a rarely climbed glaciated peak that lies 15 miles (24 km) northeast of Huancayo. Local outfitters arrange hikes to the base of the glacier, but if you want to reach the summit, you are on your own.

From Jauja, near Huancayo, the highway climbs 50 miles (80 km) to **La Oroya,** an important mining town at 12,241 feet (3,731 m). A major transportation junction, with the road and railway to Lima passing through, the city was identified as one of the ten most polluted in the world in a *National Geographic* article published in 2007.

Fourteen miles (22 km) beyond Jauja, a branch road (Highway 20) heads east away from Highway 3 to the Amazon lowlands. After 22 miles (35 km) the road passes through **Tarma** (10,077 feet/3,050 m), a town famed for its spectacular Easter processions (see sidebar p. 166). Perched on the Andes' eastern edge, Tarma sits alongside a spectacularly steep road that plunges nearly 7,400 feet (2,250 m) to Chanchamayo and the jungle.

Some 16 miles (26 km) to the north is one of Peru's major caves, the **Gruta de Guagapo,** a huge limestone cave about 2.5 miles (4 km) from the village of Palcamayo. Local guides will take you inside for a short way, but you will need technical speleological gear to explore farther.

Lago de Junín: Back on the Carretera Central, it's an additional 21 miles (34 km) to tiny **Junín** situated at 13,534 feet (4,125 m) near the site of an important battle for independence in August 1824. About 8 miles (13 km) north is 19-mile-long (30 km) Lago de Junín, Peru's second largest lake. Known for its unique birdlife, the lake is home to the almost extinct Junín grebe and numerous other highland lake species, all protected here on this national nature reserve. Dedicated birders should ask at the Municipalidad in Junín about renting a boat.

High Places: With an elevation of 14,217 feet (4,333 m), **Cerro de Pasco**—about 47 miles (76 km) north of Junín—claims to be the highest city in the world. The capital of its department, it is a cold and unsightly, but friendly, mining town. To the southwest is **Santuario Nacional de Huayllay** (see sidebar right).

Beyond Cerro de Pasco, the Carretera Central drops along the Río Huallaga Valley for about 70 miles (112 km) to **Huánuco,** at an elevation of 6,214 feet (1,894 m). Rarely visited, the department capital possesses a delightful climate that offers welcome relief for *soroche* (altitude sickness) and cooler temperatures after touring the humid rain forests around Pucallpa (see pp. 254–256).

Other Sites: About 3 miles (5 km) west, on the unpaved road to La Unión, is **Kotosh,** known as the Temple of the Crossed Hands because of its famous mud molding of crossed forearms, dating to 2000 B.C. The crossed hands are now in Lima's Museo Nacional de Arqueología, Antropología e Historia (see p. 72), but you can see a reproduction at the partially restored site.

A mototaxi will take you there (*$, round–trip, including wait*). The entry fee includes a Spanish-speaking guide.

From Huánuco, unpaved Highway 3 continues east to **La Unión** (*6 hrs. by bus from 400 block of Tarapacá*). Then, it's a three-hour hike to the extensive and impressive Inca site at **Huánuco Viejo.** (Or catch a *combi* en route to El Cruce to get within 1.5 miles/2.4 km of

Breathless Bouldering

Locally known as **Bosque de Piedras** (Stone Woods), **Santuario Nacional de Huayllay**, located 25 miles (40 km) southwest of Cerro de Pasco on unpaved Highway 18, features rock formations named after the animals they resemble. A great place for climbing, it has undeveloped camping areas, but you must bring your own climbing gear. Make sure you are acclimatized; the short hiking circuits wind through the boulders at more than 13,452 feet (4,100 m).

the site.) La Unión has basic hotels and buses that serve Chiquián.

North of Huánuco, the road becomes Highway 16 and drops down to Tingo María before continuing to Pucallpa on the Río Ucayali in the Amazon Basin. Take care when traveling through this region. It's a coca-growing area with a reputation for lawlessness. ∎

The best place in all Peru to experience the nation's majestic mountains and demanding treks

HUARAZ & THE HIGH ANDES

■ Mountains have long linked Earth with the realm of the gods for the people of the High Andes.

HUARAZ & THE HIGH ANDES

Huaraz is the premier hiking and climbing destination not only in Peru, but in all of South America. It's easy to see why. Snowcapped mountains dominate the view to the north and east of this highland city. To the west rise the peaks of the Cordillera Negra, to the east, the Cordillera Blanca, a 112-mile-long (180 km) range that is among the most beautiful and impressive in the Andes.

■ **Sheepherder, dog, and flock walk the unpaved roads outside of Huaraz.**

Established in 1975, Parque Nacional Huascarán, a UNESCO World Heritage site, protects an extensive part of the Cordillera Blanca, including Huascarán itself, Peru's highest peak. The park is one of the best places to see the *Puya raimondii,* the world's largest bromeliad (the same family as the pineapple). The inflorescence of this prodigious plant takes up to a century to mature, but when it does—wow! Some 8,000 or more white flowers cover the spike, which can top 33 feet (10 m) in height. Mature plants flower just once, usually in May.

South of the Cordillera Blanca is the Cordillera Huayhuash, a compact group of startlingly steep mountains huddled around 21,766-foot-tall (6,634 m) Yerupajá. Peru's second highest mountain range, the Huayhuash offers excellent opportunities for high-altitude trekking. Pay close attention though: The ascents here are generally more demanding and technical than in the Blanca and present serious climbing challenges even for seasoned mountaineers.

The Cordillera Negra lies to the west of and parallels the Blanca. In between nestles Huaraz, anchoring a string of small towns along the Callejón de Huaylas, the local name for the Río Santa Valley that separates the two ranges. The Cordillera Negra's mountain-biking paths afford stupendous views of the Blanca to the east.

Hidden below the glaciated mountains lie dazzling lakes, their waters sparkling with surreal jade hue, emerald, and turquoise. Home to such highland birds as the Andean goose and puna ibis, the lakes attract a steady stream of birders as well as hikers and climbers, many of whom spend entire

NOT TO BE MISSED:

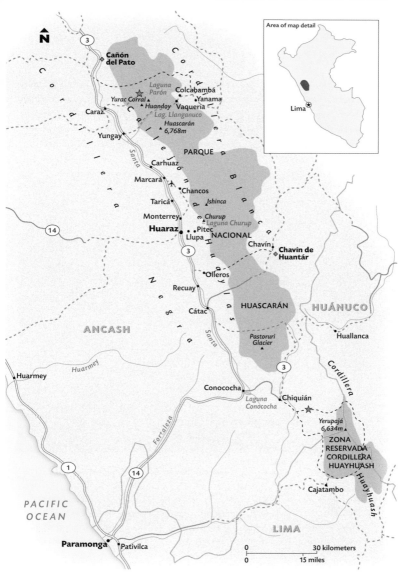

summers ascending one peak after another. Whether an invigorating day hike or epic two-week adventure, there is something here for everyone. Conditions are best in the dry season (*May–Sep.*), and most trailheads are less than three hours from Huaraz. History is just as important in this region as anywhere

in Peru. Located partly underground on the east side of the Blanca, 3,000-year-old Chavín de Huántar is just a two-hour bus ride from Huaraz. Also along the east side, between the Andes and the Amazon Basin, several rarely visited villages still carry on agricultural traditions first developed centuries ago. ∎

HUARAZ

With a population of more than 120,000, bustling Huaraz is the main city in the Callejón de Huaylas and the capital of Ancash Department. Overlooked by mountains, it attracts trekkers and climbers from all over the world, as well as vacationers from the coast eager to spend some time in the shadow of the peaks. The lively, hospitable residents cater well to tourists, and scores of outfitters stand ready to rent equipment or organize entire expeditions.

 Huascarán, the world's highest tropical mountain, dominates the view north from Huaraz.

Huaraz

🗺 Map p. 179

Visitor Information

✉ iPerú, Pasaje Alonso Martel

☎ 043/428–812

E-mail: iperuhuaraz @promperu.gob.pe

NOTE: Huaraz has no central bus station; inquire at iPerú for times and destinations. Lima is 8 hours away by bus.

Orientation

Avenida Luzuriaga, the main street in Huaraz, hums with tourist agencies, outfitters, money changers, and restaurants. It runs north past the Plaza de Armas, with its crafts markets and modern cathedral, and continues three long blocks to the main east-west street, **Avenida Raimondi,** where you will find several bus companies and the central market.

North of Raimondi, Luzuriaga becomes Fitzcarrald, which crosses Río Quilcay after three blocks. Here you can catch one of the *combis* (minibuses) that run north through the Callejón de Huaylas, past the towns of Monterrey, Carhuaz, Yungay, and Caraz.

Extending east from the Plaza de Armas, Calle Sucre climbs several blocks to the residential district of La Soledad. Here the tall spire of **La Iglesia de la Soledad** overlooks small hotels built after the 1970 earthquake. The church houses the patron saint of Huaraz.

Sightseeing

Acclimatize yourself with a pleasant stroll around town. Located on Luzuriaga near the Plaza de Armas, the **Museo Arqueológico de Ancash** has exhibits of stone stelae, sculptures, and monoliths from various cultures. The museum's collection also includes mummies, trepanned skulls, ceramics, and models of local archaeological sites. Some exhibits have printed English explanations.

Walk through **Jirón José Olaya,** the only turn-of-the-20th-century thoroughfare (euphemistically called a colonial street) that remains, with traditional balconies and red-tiled roofs. Then head north on Calle Confraternidad Este, cross the bridge over Río Quilcay, and continue to the **Piscigranja de Truchas** (*tel 043/421–081, $*), a trout hatchery about a 30-minute walk from downtown Huaraz. Fingerlings from the hatchery stock nearby lakes, while grown fish are sold at the restaurant next door. If you get lost along the way, ask locals for the "pee-see-GRAN-ha."

To reach **Monumento Nacional Wilcahuaín,** a well-preserved eighth-century Wari site (*$*), walk north along Fitzcarrald (which becomes Centenario), continue 12 blocks past the Hotel Huascarán, and turn right at the signpost. Signs—and locals—will guide you the rest of the way. Or catch a minibus (*$*) on 13 de Diciembre in Huaraz for the 5-mile (8 km) ride north to the site.

The main attraction is a three-tiered temple platform with labyrinths of windowless rooms that feature advanced stonework and ventilation systems. Nearby stands the smaller site of **Ichiwilcahuaín** For a tip, local kids will give you a guided tour (in Spanish) and show you the footpath to **Monterrey,** an hour's walk away.

The natural hot springs at **Baños Termales de Monterrey** are rich in iron, accounting for their murky brown color. The waters are diverted into two main pools, and several smaller ones, that crowd with locals on weekends. Monterrey is 3.75 miles (6 km) north of Huaraz on the main road. Take a minibus or taxi (*$*) from the city or walk from Wilcahuaín. ▪

Museo Arqueológico de Ancash

- ✉ Ave. Luzuriaga 762
- ☎ 043/421–551
- 🕐 Closed Mon.
- 💲 $

Baños Termales de Monterrey

- ✉ Adjoining Real Hotel Baños Termales Monterrey
- ☎ 043/349–069
- 💲 $

EXPERIENCE:
Enjoy Outdoor Activities

If you're a traveler interested in spending time outdoors, Huaraz has something for you. You can rent equipment at one of the local shops and set out on a **daylong hike** or weeklong **mountain-climbing expedition.** Or join one of the **guided bike tours;** some include a descent to the coastal lowlands. There are also opportunities for horseback riding.

Peru has no dedicated ski areas, but die-hard skiers flock to Huaraz every year for competitions on the region's glaciers. In recent years, low water levels and pollution have curtailed rafting on the Río Santa, although **Class II runs** are available year-round (see Travelwise pp. 308–309).

Casa de Guías (*Jr. Simón Bolívar 680, Huaraz, tel 043/421–811, www.agmp.pe*) has lists of guides approved by Asociación de Guías de Montaña del Peru and arranges mountain rescues.

PARQUE NACIONAL HUASCARÁN

Unparalleled anywhere else in the Americas, Parque Nacional Huascarán covers a spectacular 1,313 square miles (3,400 sq km) of territory in the high Andes. Within its 112-mile (180 km) length, the park includes all but the two northernmost glaciated mountains of the Cordillera Blanca. Massive Huascarán is the tallest, but at least 20 others exceed 19,685 feet (6,000 m), making this area extremely popular with mountaineers.

■ Glaciated peaks dominate the views, even for the sheep.

Parque Nacional Huascarán

🗺 Map p. 179

Visitor Information

🗺 Park Office, Calle Sal y Rosas 555, Huaraz

☎ 043/422–086 (park office)

💲 $ (daily); $$$ (overnight permit)

www.sernanp.gob.pe

The snow-clad peaks of Parque Nacional Huascarán overlook gorgeous lakes and steep-sided *quebradas* (ravines), where footpaths lead trekkers into the heart of the park. Between the mountain massifs, the trails make their way over 15,585-foot-high (4,750 m) passes that afford startlingly close views of impossibly steep ice walls. You can see the most famous of these, **Punta Unión,** on the four-day Santa Cruz trek (see pp. 184–185). From here, tongue-twisting

behemoths such as Taulliraju (19,128 feet/5,830 m), Quitaraju (19,804 feet/6,036 m), Artesonraju (19,768 feet/6,025 m), and Chacraraju (20,053 feet/6,112 m) rule the horizon in all directions. *Raju?* It's the Quechua word for "snow peak."

Multiday Treks

Popular treks in the Blanca in addition to the Santa Cruz include the **Alpamayo Base Camp Route** (*7–12 days*), which goes over several high passes and through the remote Quebrada de los Cedros on the north side of Alpamayo. It finishes in any one of several villages, depending on the length of the trek. The three-day **Olleros to Chavín Trek** goes over one high pass (15,420 feet/4,700 m) and emerges at the archaeological site of Chavín de Huántar (see p. 195). Many other options also exist.

Both climbers and trekkers agree that it is best to visit the Blanca in the dry season, which begins in mid-May and usually lasts into mid-September. This doesn't mean you won't see rain or snow, however; just recently a snowstorm hit Punta Unión in June. Trekking out of season is certainly possible, but bring good rain gear and quality waterproof tents. January through March are the wettest months. If the thought of sleeping in a cold, wet tent doesn't appeal to you, consider a day trip. Or book a night in one of the high-altitude climbers refuges within the park.

Hiring Guides

While hauling a heavy pack over high passes is doable for fit, acclimatized hikers, others may want to hire an *arriero* (wrangler; *$15–20 per day*) and mules (*$5–10 per day*). You will also have to provide food and pay for an extra day (or two) for the *arriero* to make the return trip home with the unloaded mules. If you speak Spanish and have a flexible schedule, visit one of the trailhead villages (especially

Cashapampa on the Santa Cruz Trek) and hire an *arriero* there instead of in Huaraz.

If you want to explore the park with a guide, rates range from $40 for Spanish-speaking trekking guides to well over $100 for certified, climbing guides.

Annie S. Peck

Classicist Annie Smith Peck (1850–1935), who taught at Purdue University, was an insatiable adventurer and traveled extensively in Latin America and Europe. Determined to prove that a woman can do anything a man can, she became a mountaineer, an unheard of pursuit for the women of her day.

In 1908, Peck climbed the north peak of Huascarán, the first successful ascent of the mountain by either man or woman. Three years later she made it to the top of Coropuna, in southern Peru. On its summit she hoisted a suffragist banner that read "Votes for Women."

Cooks charge about $20 to $30 a day. Casa de Guías or the agencies listed in Travelwise (pp. 308–309) can make your arrangements. (Note that park authorities have recently discussed a new law that would make licensed guides mandatory on all climbs and treks.)

Bear in mind that Huaraz is a wildly popular destination

(continued on p. 186)

SANTA CRUZ TREK

The second most popular trek in Peru after the Inca Trail to Machu Picchu, the Santa Cruz trek takes nature lovers through groves of native highland *quenual* trees to the 15,585-foot-high (4,750 m) pass known as Punta Unión, affording one of the most spectacular and accessible views in the Andes. Most hikers can complete the route in four days, but fit, experienced trekkers may finish in three.

Camping with views along the Santa Cruz trail

Although you can follow this moderate route in either direction, most visitors prefer to begin with a long, relatively gentle ascent followed by a demanding, steep descent rather than the other way around. Because of its popularity, the trail is clear and relatively well signed, but it also suffers from litter. Campsites offer pit toilets; unfortunately, most are not maintained and may be unusable.

Begin in Caraz, where you should catch one of the *combis* that make the two-hour journey to the village of **Cashapampa ❶** (9,515 feet/2,900 m). They leave regularly every day from Calle Santa Cruz and Calle Bolognesi. Cashapampa has basic restaurants, mules for rent, and camping areas ($$), but

if you take an early bus from Caraz then you won't need to camp here.

A dirt road heads out of town to the northeast and quickly brings you to a sign that marks the start of the trek. The rocky and slippery trail heads east along the south side of the Quebrada Santa Cruz Valley. It then swings east-northeast, staying on the south side of the valley and becoming less rocky after two to three hours. Five hours after setting out from Cashapampa, you reach a large pampa called **Llamacorral ❷** (11,812 feet/3,600 m), which provides good campsites for your first night on the trek.

The next day, continue east-northeast as the valley widens, passing bogs, lakes, and waterfalls. Stay on the south side of little

NOT TO BE MISSED:

Laguna Jatuncocha • Punta
Unión • Taulliraju • Laguna
Morococha • Quebrada Paria

Laguna Ichiqcocha and the larger **Laguna
Jatuncocha** (12,796 feet/3,900 m), four
hours from Llamacorral. About an hour later,
the trail crosses the Río Santa Cruz and splits
in two directions. (The signed northbound trail
climbs up Quebrada Arhuyacocha, a good side
trip to the south base camp of **Alpamayo.**)

Follow the main trail east along the north
side of Quebrada Santa Cruz for another
hour before crossing back to the south side,
near the flat **Taullipampa 3** (13,944 feet/
4,250 m). Most trekkers camp here, but if
you backtrack for 30 minutes to the little
Quebrada Arteson and climb up a short way,
you will find less used and more scenic sites.

From Taullipampa begins the steep, three-
hour trail to **Punta Unión.** Enjoy the sight of
Taulliraju, overlooking icy Taullicocha Lake to
the left, and **Artesonraju,** behind and to the
right. At the pass, more mountains pop into
sight. A ridge to the south of Punta Unión
gives even better views.

The descent southeast is very steep, passing
north of upper **Laguna Morococha** (15,093
feet/4,600 m) and other small lakes before
reaching the upper Río Huaripampa. Cross the
river two to three hours after the pass, and
head south along the eastern side of the valley
through quenual forests. A couple hours later,
you will find good camping opposite **Quebrada
Paria 4** (12,632 feet/3,850 m). If you want a
closer view of the glaciers, consider taking the
three-hour hike to the west up Quebrada Paria.

From the camp at Paria, continue south
along the east side of the Huaripampa Valley
and swing southeast after two hours, passing
some buildings along the way. About three
hours from Paria, the trail crosses the river
on a well-built bridge. Signs will point you
to the nearby village of **Colcabamba** (10,827
feet/3,300 m), where families offer beds
and basic meals, or to **Vaquería 5** (12,140
feet/3,700 m), an hour's climb above the
river. *Combis* leave Vaquería for Yungay via
the Quebrada Llanganuco every morning.

▲ See also area map p. 179

► Cashapampa

↔ 31 miles (50 km)

⏱ 4 days

► Vaquería

for Peruvians during the Fiestas Patrías National Independence holiday (July 28–29); you may find it hard to book services for several days before and after the celebration.

Day Trips

The park's most popular day trip is to **Lagunas Llanganuco,** east of Yungay, located 50 miles (80 km) from Huaraz. Tours often stop at *campo santo* (see

---

EXPERIENCE:
Climbing High

Fit, acclimatized travelers with little ice-climbing experience can hire a guide who will teach you everything you need to know to summit. The climbing season is May through September, and most beginner's climbs take about three days. Favorite peaks are Pisco (18,872 feet/5,752 m) and Ishinca (18,144 feet/5,530 m).

Three climber's refuges offer meals, hot showers, and comfortable beds for $35 a night per person, including breakfast and dinner. Refugio Peru, a base for climbing Pisco, has 80 beds; Refugio Huascarán and Refugio Ishinca both have 60 beds. Refuges close from October to April. You can get more information from Don Bosco de los Andes (*tel 043/443–061, e-mail: andesdbosco @hotmail.com, www.rifugi-omg.org*) **in Mar-cará, 12.5 miles (20 km) north of Huaraz.**

---

sidebar p. 195) near Yungay before following the road up the narrow Quebrada Llanganuco to two lovely mountain lakes.

At the first lake, **Chinancocha** (Quechua for "female lake"), rent a rowboat to enjoy

time on the water, or go for a 1.5-hour walk along the nature trail at the west end. To the east stands a forest of *Polylepis* trees (locally called *quenuales*), distinguished by their peeling rust-colored bark. Over the years, locals have burned the trees to clear the land for pasture or used them as firewood. Once common in the Andes, this representative highland native species survives only in small pockets today. The second lake, **Orconcocha** (Male Lake), lies nearby.

Huascarán and triple-peaked Huandoy (20,982 feet/6,395 m) dominate the spectacular view on the drive up to the lakes. The road continues for 12 miles (20 km) beyond the lakes, crossing over a high pass called the **Portachuelo de Llanganuco** (15,640 feet/4,767 m), then dropping through Vaquería, past the hamlet of Colcabamba, and on to the town of Yanama.

To reach the 12,796-foot-high (3,900 m) **Yurac Corral** (also known as Cebollapampa), follow the road about 2 miles (3 km) past the lakes. Just after the hairpin turn, look for the entry point for two hiking trails. The first leads 3.5 miles (5.5 km) to the refuge at the **Pisco base camp** (see sidebar left); the other climbs 4 miles (6 km) up the Quebrada Demanda Valley to fabulous **Laguna 69** (15,420 feet/4,700 m) at the base of Chacraraju. Hikers normally use the second trail as a day hike, although you can make it into a two-day trek. Few tours to Llanganuco continue on to Yurac

Corral, which is best reached by taxi ($$$$$) from Yungay.

Pastoruri Glacier makes another good day trip. Travel 44 miles (71 km) southeast via Cátac, then take a dirt road through a *Puya raimondii* stand to arrive near the glacier. If you want to walk on the ice, hike about 1.25 miles farther (2 km). Because it is receding, the glacier is closed to visitors in the low season.

You may also want to take a hike to **Laguna Churup** (14,715 feet/4,485 m), about 11 miles (18 km) directly east of Huaraz at Pitec. Early morning minibuses leave Huaraz from Avenida Caraz, a block east of Fitzcarrald, along the unpaved road to the village of Llupa, 9 miles (14 km) away. From Llupa, continue east along the dirt road to Pitec, where you will see a farm and a huge sign for the national park. Plan ahead; you can hire a taxi to Pitec in Huaraz but not in Llupa.

From Pitec, a signed trail left of the road follows a ridge toward the lake, about 3 miles (5 km) away. Wooden steps and ladders make navigating the steep sections more manageable (*slippery when wet*). The trail eventually reaches the smooth, rocky shore that overlooks the gorgeous lake under glaciated **Nevado Churup** (18,029 feet/5,495 m)—an ideal spot for a picnic lunch.

From Caraz, 41 miles (66 km) north of Huaraz, an unpaved road runs 19 miles (30 km) up a narrow gorge to **Laguna Parón** (13,583 feet/4,140 m). Join a tour in Huaraz or Caraz, or take a taxi from Caraz ($$$$$

■ Clouds obscure mountain views during the rainy season.

round-trip, including wait). Several peaks surround the picturesque lake, including Huandoy, Pisco, and Chacraraju. Most people visit simply to enjoy the views, but if you want to hike, take the trail that follows along the north shore of the lake. ■

Highest Tropical Mountains

Mount Huascarán (22,205 feet/6,768 m), which is located 497 miles (800 km) south of the Equator, boasts the highest peak in the tropics, but it is in good company. Parque Nacional Huascarán—declared a UNESCO World Heritage site in 1985—is home to another 50 peaks that rise to over 18,700 feet (5,700 m) above sea level. With the exception of the Himalaya, the region surrounding the city of Huaraz can truly be considered the roof of the world.

CALLEJÓN DE HUAYLAS

Bounded on the west by the Cordillera Negra and on the east by the Cordillera Blanca, the valley known as the Callejón de Huaylas begins at Laguna Conococha and stretches 93 miles (150 km), roughly following the course of the Río Santa. A trip north along its chief road will take you past small, quiet towns and introduce you to the warm, pleasant traditions of the indigenous Quechua population, all with a breathtaking mountain backdrop.

A field of tarwi

Callejón de Huaylas

Map p. 179

The route from Conococha through the *callejón* first passes through high, grassy terrain suitable for grazing cattle, llamas, and alpacas, which sometimes stop traffic as they cross the road. Twenty-seven miles (43 km) beyond Conococha you will reach **Catac** (11,943 feet/3,640 m), the first town in the valley and the point for crossing the Cordillera Blanca by road to Chavín de Huántar (see p. 195). One of the few towns to have survived the 1970 earthquake (see sidebar p. 195) with little damage, **Recuay** (11,155

feet/3,400 m) lies 6 miles (10 km) beyond. Neither town is much visited today.

After Huaraz (10,138 feet/ 3,090 m), the region's major city, the main road continues north through the village of Monterrey with its hot springs (see p. 181) and on to **Taricá** (9,350 feet/2,850 m), where local potters display and sell their creations.

Next you come to little Anta Airport (*tel 043/443-156*), which services Huaraz. The airport has erratic and, in some years, nonexistent service. LC Perú (*tel*

01/204–1313, www.lcperu.pe) currently runs flights from Lima.

Beyond this small airport lies **Marcará** (9,023 feet/2,750 m), where the **Don Bosco de los Andes Mission** (see sidebar p. 186) has its headquarters. The mission's goal is to train local young people in woodworking. Open to visitors, its workshop showcases pieces in progress, including elaborately carved doors used in the area's churches, as well as altarpieces, household furniture, and other crafts.

From Marcará, minibuses and taxis ply the short route to **Chancos,** 2.5 miles (4 km) to the east. Popular with locals on weekends,

---

INSIDER TIP:

If you find yourself in Peru on July 28, be sure to partake in the Día de la Independencia festivities. Meet the local people and sample some of their most beloved dishes.

–SARAH SHAW
National Geographic contributor

Chancos has hot springs (*$$*) with baking-hot caves used as saunas and cooler pools for soaking.

Carhuaz (8,655 feet/ 2,638 m)—the first major town north of Huaraz—lies 2 miles (3 km) from Marcará. On Sundays, this sleepy town of 6,000 people comes alive with the weekly market, held three blocks

Local Mapmaker

Renowned local cartographer Felipe Díaz owns Carhuaz's **Hotel El Abuelo** (*tel 043/394–456, www.el abuelohotel.com*), which operates in the north corner of the city's pretty Plaza de Armas. The café sells *Cordilleras Blanca & Huayhuash,* a tourist map updated every two years, and a scale model developed by Díaz. You will find its maps of the valley's main trekking routes and major towns invaluable while in the region. In the hotel there is a restaurant, with cuisine also for vegans and vegetarians, and a gift shop.

northwest of the Plaza de Armas and attended by campesinos from nearby villages. Its vibrant annual Fiesta de la Virgen de la Merced takes place around the third week in September with dancing, fireworks, bullfighting, processions, and general mayhem.

About 12.5 miles (20 km) north of Carhuaz lies old **Yungay** (8,203 feet/2,500 m), the scene of Peru's single worst earthquake disaster in 1970 (see sidebar p. 195). Visitors to the old town stroll quietly through flower-filled gardens and bemusedly inspect the tops of the church steeple and palm trees that give silent testimony to Yungay's Plaza de Armas, now buried below. The cemetery is open daily. After the earthquake, new Yungay was

(continued on p. 194)

CORDILLERA HUAYHUASH CIRCUIT

A favorite with hikers, this trek, while demanding, offers the opportunity to walk at consistently high elevations while surrounded by mountain and lake scenery that are unparalleled anywhere else. The entire circuit takes 11 days. Add more for rest or exploration, or walk a half circuit on the spectacular eastern side.

Highland lakes dot the circuit.

NOT TO BE MISSED:

Laguna Jahuacocha • Punta Sambuya • Laguna Mitacocha • Laguna Carhuacocha • Punta Cuyoc

Preparation

To get to the gateway of the Cordillera Huayhuash Circuit at charming **Chiquián** (11,155 feet/3,400 m), take a bus from Huaraz. The most reliable, Transportes El Rápido (*Jr. 28 de Julio 202, tel 043/422–887, $*), makes the three-hour trip two times each day. Once in Chiquián, catch a *combi* for Llamac, 90 minutes away; *combis* leave the main plaza a few times daily. Chiquián has hotels and basic supplies. Llamac has a municipal camping area with water, a basic hostel, and shops selling bottled drinks. (New, unpaved roads built by mining companies allow closer access to the mountains but lack public transportation. Some outfitters use them to get into the area, but the trek described here follows the traditional circuit.)

Every community in the Cordillera Huayhuash collects a user fee from those who pass through. Bring small bills and expect to pay

⚠ See also area map p. 179
► Llamac
↔ Approximately 75 miles (122 km)
⏱ 11 days
► Llamac

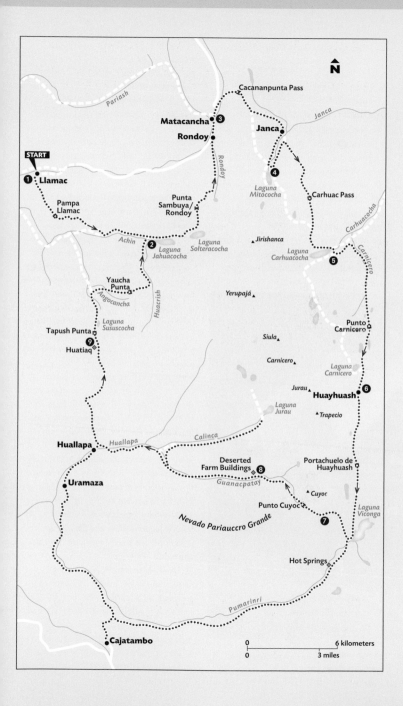

about $65 along the entire circuit. The best topographic map is *Cordilleras Blanca & Huayhuash,* available at Hotel El Abuelo in Carhuaz (see sidebar p. 189).

The Trek

On your first trekking day, leave from the plaza in **Llamac ❶** (10,827 feet/3,300 m) and head southwest to a signed trail that switchbacks steeply, climbing south through fields of huge cactuses. After two to three hours, you will pass water tanks in a saddle then head southeast for 1.5 hours toward the flat **Pampa Llamac Pass** (14,108 feet/4,300 m). Here you will get your first, exciting view of the Cordillera Huayhuash. A clear trail moving east soon enters an enchanting *quenual* forest before dropping

The snow-covered mountaintops of the Cordillera Huayhuash

toward the Río Achin Valley and **Laguna Jahuacocha ❷,** two to three hours below the pass. A crowded camping area, Jahuacocha has fabulous views of the Huayhuash. While there, look for the local women selling beer, soft drinks, baked potatoes, and knitted hats.

The trail heads east along the north shore of Jahuacocha then climbs northeast above Laguna Solteracocha, becoming a steep, zigzagging trail with stunning views. About three to four hours from Jahuacocha, you will reach **Punta Sambuya/Rondoy Pass** (15,585 feet/4,750 m). From here zigzag down, heading northeast to the Quebrada Rondoy, and follow the valley north to a road located two hours from the pass. A few houses mark the communities of Rondoy and **Matacancha ❸** under a thumb-shaped peak to the north. Walk north along the road to a hairpin bend, then leave the road and head northeast for five minutes to corrals, where you will find good camping. (Organized treks with private vehicles may start the circuit here, or you can walk in on this road from Llamac in six to seven hours.)

From the campsite, head northeast to a ridge and follow the obvious mule trail east to the base of the cliffs. The trail follows the cliffs southeast, climbing to **Cacananpunta Pass** (15,388 feet/4,690 m), three hours from camp. Don't be surprised if you see a condor or two soaring by the cliffs. Zigzag steeply east of the pass and contour around south-southeast to the farmhouses of **Janca,** two to three hours from Cacananpunta. You can camp here, but it's better to continue south-southwest for an hour to **Laguna Mitacocha ❹,** with campsites at its north end and unforgettable views of **Jirishanca** (19,994 feet/6,094 m).

Leave Mitacocha and go northeast on the far right of the Janca Valley, then climb east-southeast for three to four hours up the Quebrada Waya Valley toward the sandy **Carhuac Pass** (15,224 feet/4,650 m). Beyond the pass, drop gently south and admire the superb views of the two highest Huayhuash peaks, Yerupajá and Siula (20,815 feet/6,344 m). After an hour, you'll reach the amazing overlook at **Laguna Carhuacocha** ❺. Turn east and hike past the farmhouses at the southeastern end of the lake. Because the area is so beautiful, people often spend two nights camping here.

Leave along the south side of Río Carhuacocha and climb northeast for an hour to the **Quebrada Carnicero Valley.** Work your way southeast; when the trail flattens, stay high on

---

INSIDER TIP:

Hire a local guide whenever possible. A knowledgeable local is a fascinating source for the history of the Inca, facts about wildlife, and insight into present-day life in Peru.

—JAMES DION
National Geographic Society,
Director Tourism Programs, Maps Division

---

the south-southeast side to see remnants of the **Inca Trail.** Continue due south, crossing a stream and passing ponds, to **Punto Carnicero** (15,093 feet/4,600 m), 3.5 hours from the river. The trail descends southward, winding between two lakes then turning southwest and passing another section of the Inca trail. Soon, **Laguna Carnicero** will appear on the right, overlooked by even taller peaks. Camp on the dry southwestern shore, or continue an hour south to the more crowded camping at **Huayhuash** ❻.

After crossing Río Huayhuash, the trail climbs south for 2.5 hours to **Portachuelo de Huayhuash** (15,700 feet/4,785 m). Continue south for 1.5 hours to **Laguna Viconga;** hike above the lake's western shore to a 14,682-foot pass (4,475 m) with views of double-peaked **Cuyoc** to the northwest. The main trail drops to **buildings** ❼ used by dam-control personnel. Camp just northwest of the buildings.

(Here the trail divides; you can opt to head southwest along the Río Pumarinri to the **hot springs** an hour away, where there are campsites. From here, a 12-mile (19 km) trail west along the Pumarinri Valley ends at **Cajatambo,** where you will find simple hotels, restaurants, and buses to Lima.)

From Laguna Viconga, the indistinct main route passes northwest of the dam buildings. After two hours, Cuyoc again looms into view; take the highest northwestern trail to **Punta Cuyoc** (16,405 feet/5,000 m), three to four hours above camp. The trail, once again clearly marked, descends steeply northwest to the long Quebrada Guanacpatay, which it follows westward. Occasionally boggy, but dry, campsites are available, especially 2.5 hours below the pass near some **deserted farm buildings** ❽ on the valley's north side.

Descend west for two to three hours, crossing the river twice. As the water swings north, follow the trail on the east side, descending steeply to the **Río Huallapa**. The main trail goes west. (Turn east to camp at Laguna Jurau and visit the area made famous by Joe Simpson's book and movie, *Touching the Void.*)

Returning to the south bank of the Río Huallapa, continue for two to three hours past the gorgeous tumbling waterfall of **Quebrada Guanacpatay,** toward Huallapa. Just above the village, the trail climbs steeply to the north. (The wider trail continues southwest through Huallapa and the village of Uramaza, finally ending at Cajatambo, seven to nine hours later.)

Or, hike north along the right side of Quebrado Huancho, crossing it twice; camp near the farm of **Huatiaq** ❾. The next day continue northward for three to four hours along the left side of the valley to **Tapush Punta.** Descend north past swampy Laguna Sususcocha. Cross a stream an hour below the pass, and 15 minutes later swing east into Quebrada Angocancha. Begin on the south side, then cross to the north and head east to **Yaucha Punta** three to four hours from Tapush Punta. The trail drops steeply northeast to Quebrada Huacrish, where a southbound trail takes you back to Laguna Jahuacocha, three hours from Yaucha Punta.

■ Local resident draped in colorful blanket

Caraz

🗺 Map p. 179

Visitor Information

✉ Jr. San Martín 112, Municipalidad Provincial de Huaylas

☎ 043/483–860

🕐 Closed Sat.–Sun.

built about 1.2 miles (2 km) away. There you can catch one of the buses that travel east up the Llanganuco Valley.

Although it is located just 7.5 miles (12 km) past Yungay, **Caraz** (7,513 feet/2,290 m), the final town of the Callejón, has seen less earthquake damage than most of its neighbors. It is also the valley's most charming city. The gateway for treks and climbs to Laguna Parón, Quebrada Santa Cruz, and the northern Cordillera Blanca, Caraz promises quieter accommodations than Huaraz while the lower elevation gives the town a spring-like climate. The tourist office is located in the colorful Plaza de Armas.

West of Caraz, an unpaved road climbs for about 25 miles (40 km) to the 13,780-foot-high (4,200 m) **Huinchus Pass** in the Cordillera Negra, near one of the largest known stands of *Puya*

INSIDER TIP:

For a better perspective on the site of Chavín de Huántar, climb the opposite (east) hillside—the higher, the more impressive the view.

—JOHAN REINHARD
National Geographic explorer-in-residence

raimondii. Pony's Expeditions (see Travelwise p. 309) organizes tours that include vehicle transportation up to the pass and a descent back down on mountain bikes.

North of Caraz, the Río Santa drops into the **Cañón de Pato** on the road to Chimbote. After the first few miles of paved road, the unpaved route wends its way through stunning scenery that includes massive cliffs and more than 30 tunnels drilled through the rock. Yungay Express (*Ave. Antonio Raymondi 920, Huaraz, tel 955/041–692*) runs three buses every day to Chimbote (*7 hrs., $$$$*); sit on the right for the best views.

Chavín de Huántar

In the Conchucos Valley on the eastern side of the Cordillera Blanca, the mid-Andean culture of the Chavín emerged around 1200 B.C. and lasted about a thousand years. Known for highly stylized stone carvings of

A large, three-tiered temple fronted by a huge courtyard dominates the area. A landslide in 1945 buried the courtyard and lower temple, but excavation has revealed elaborate drainage systems in the courtyard and superbly engineered passages and ventilation ducts inside the temple, named the Castillo.

At one time, puma heads contemplated the world from the walls of the temple. Today only one remains in place; the rest are stacked up inside the temple or

Chavín de Huántar

Map p. 179

$ $

Earthquakes in the Callejón de Huaylas

The Callejón de Huaylas has experienced three catastrophic earthquakes within living memory. The first, in 1941, loosened an avalanche into Laguna Pomalcocha, which broke its banks and poured down the Cojup Valley into Huaraz, killing 5,000 people and devastating the city. Four thousand people died in 1962, when an avalanche off western Huascarán destroyed the village of Ranrahirca. But the worst event took place on May 31,

1970, when a massive earthquake killed 70,000 people in central Peru. A deadly *aluvión* (a mix of ice, water, earth, and rocks) swept down on the town of Yungay and completely buried it, killing almost all of its 18,000 inhabitants.

Today, the entombed city is a *campo santo* (cemetery) covered over with memorial gardens. The same earthquake destroyed most of Huaraz and killed about half of its 30,000 residents.

feline deities such as jaguars and pumas, and less important such as serpents, condors, and human figures, the Chavín influenced artistic development in much of central Peru, from the highlands to the coast.

The important archaeological site of Chavín de Huántar is the largest Chavín site in Peru. It lies at 10,302 feet (3,140 m) on the outskirts of Chavín, a 2.5-hour drive from Huaraz via the only paved road across the Cordillera Blanca. In 1985, it became a UNESCO World Heritage site.

on display in the site's museum and elsewhere in Peru.

The remarkable Lanzón de Chavín, a slender, 15-foot-high (4.5 m) intricately carved stele, stands in the midst of tortuous underground passageways within the Castillo.

Most people visit the site with a guided tour from Huaraz. Public buses run by Transportes Sandoval (*Ave. Confraternidad Internacional Oeste 640, tel 043/428-069*) and others usually continue through Chavín to Huari, on the east side of the Cordillera Blanca. ■

An unexpected trove of archaeological treasures, time-honored crafts, and coastal seascapes

NORTH COAST

Donkeys are a favored mode of transportation in the remote villages of the Sechura Desert.

NORTH COAST

Unlike its southern counterpart, the north coast is not on the "gringo trail" and thus receives fewer international visitors. However, those that travel the 797-mile (1,283 km) length of the Panamericana Norte between Lima and the Ecuadoran border will not be disappointed by the journey through Peru's northernmost deserts.

■ The green trees of the Sechura Desert

Archaeological sites dot the landscape along the north coast. Little more than sunbaked mud hills at first glance, some of the sites have revealed treasure-laden tombs that are among the richest in the world. Others cover several square miles and comprise dozens of pyramids or massive mud walls extensively decorated with carved reliefs. Archaeologists working in the region today are certain that many more sites lie just beneath the surface waiting to be uncovered.

This ongoing sense of discovery makes exploring the north coast exciting and fascinating. In 1987, archaeologists digging in Sipán, near Chiclayo, discovered the richest burial ever found in South America. Since then they have uncovered more tombs at the same site, most recently in 2007, and they expect to find at least two more. Meanwhile, carbon dating undertaken in 2001 at the newly excavated site of Caral, near Barranco, yielded an unexpected surprise—a city that dates back nearly

five millennia, a thousand years older than any other city in South America. And in 2006, National Geographic–funded archaeologists working near Trujillo found a 1,500-year-old burial of a tattooed female, the first example of a major entombment of an upper-class woman. You never know what may be discovered next.

The region's dry desert conditions have helped preserve many of the cultures that predated the Inca by hundreds or even thousands of years. The best known of these are the Moche (100 B.C.–A.D. 850), but you can tread in the footsteps of lesser understood and far older cultures at Sechín (from 1600 B.C.) and Caral (from 2900 B.C.). The Chimu and Sicán peoples bridged the gap between the Moche and the Inca, and various other smaller groups left indelible traces over the centuries. The region's museums exhibit highlights of the discoveries, the best in the small city of Lambayeque.

Elegant colonial Trujillo, with its well-preserved architecture, is the main city along the north coast and a good base for exploration. Also worth visiting are the colonial towns of Lambayeque and Piura, the center for crafts villages in the region and gateway to the most important center of shamanism in Peru.

If decorated Moche ceramics are any indication, the beaches along the north coast have offered the best places to surf and sun-worship for thousands of years. As they have done for at least two millennia, the fishermen of Huanchaco paddle out to sea and surf back on reed boats that look like swollen surfboards. Today, surfers can rent a reed boat in this popular fishing village or paddle out on their own boards.

Dozens of other surfing areas dot this region, some of which require more expertise than others. Foremost among these, Máncora has the best beaches, climate, and range of accommodations on the entire Peruvian coast. ∎

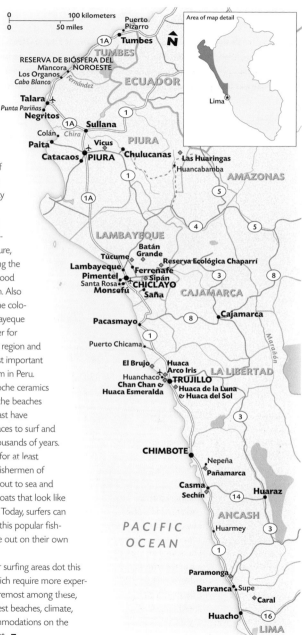

TRUJILLO AREA & SOUTH

Stretching north along the coast, often within sight of the Pacific Ocean, the Panamericana passes some of Peru's most ancient archaeological sites. A great base for exploration, the Spanish colonial city of Trujillo—eight hours by bus from Lima—lies near wonderful Chimu and Moche archaeological sites, as well as the lively little beach town Huanchaco.

■ Huanchaco Beach near the city of Trujillo hosts many surfers and beachgoers.

Trujillo

⛰ Map p. 199

Visitor Information

✉ iPerú, Jr. Independencia 467

☎ 044/294–561

E-mail: iperutrujillo @promperu.gob.pe

Trujillo

Francisco Pizarro arrived in Peru in 1532 intent on conquest. Because the Inca had only recently subjugated the Chimu people, Pizarro decided to ally himself with the Chimu and build a major city in their territory. In 1534 he sent conquistador Diego de Almagro (1475–1538) to found a town near the Chimu capital of Chan Chan. Named after Pizarro's birthplace of Trujillo, Spain, it is one of the oldest colonial cities in Peru.

Without access to timber and stone, the Spaniards built Trujillo with the best material available— adobe. They constructed low, thick walls that kept buildings cool in the desert heat and relatively resistant to earthquakes. However, just as in other areas of Peru, earthquakes have regularly damaged Trujillo's structures. All of the buildings standing today date after 1619, the year one quake completely destroyed the city. The earthquakes of 1759 and 1970 also caused substantial damage.

INSIDER TIP:

Ask around and you'll probably find a local surf pro to give you lessons at a reasonable rate. It's usually less than the prices the surf shops charge, and you may make a surf buddy.

—NEIL SHEA
National Geographic writer

The city's churches and mansions display the bold ornamentation typical of European baroque style, developed even more in the 18th century under the influence of rococo. In the 19th century, the delicate cast-iron railings that covered street windows became the most distinctive feature of Trujillo's architecture. Traditionally painted white, they gleam brilliantly against the multihued pastel shades of the buildings in the city center.

Trujillo declared independence from Spain in 1820, the first city in Peru to do so. In honor of the event, it became the capital of La Libertad Department five years later.

The best way to see Trujillo's colonial center is on foot (see pp. 202–203). A walk along the well-planned streets on a quiet Sunday morning will transport you back in time, but you will have to be satisfied with seeing most buildings from the outside. Midweek, traffic can be consistently noisy, and attempts to make some streets pedestrian-only have met with

resistance from business owners. The traditional names of many of the city's central streets are displayed on large, ornate plaques; the current names (used on maps and in mailing addresses) appear on smaller, simpler signs nearby.

In the heart of the city you will find the **Museo de Arqueología, Antropología e Historia** of the Universidad Nacional de Trujillo (UNT), which houses permanent

exhibitions dedicated to the Moche and Chimu cultures and to the civilizations that developed in northern Peru in pre-Columbian times. Every first Friday of the month, admission to the museum is free.

(continued on p. 204)

Museo de Arqueología, Antropología e Historia

✉ Jr. Junin 682, Trujillo
☎ 044/474–850
🕑 Closed Sun.
💲 $

EXPERIENCE:
Surf's Up

The north coast of Peru is warmer and has more reliable waves year-round than the central and southern coasts. At least 30 beaches in the region boast excellent conditions for surfing. A few are suitable only for expert surfers capable of riding some of the longest waves in the world, such as the 1.2-mile-long (2 km) wave at Puerto Chicama north of Trujillo. More appropriate for beginning and intermediate surfers, the popular coastal villages of **Máncora** (see pp. 219–220) and **Huanchaco** (see p. 204) offer good food and lodging and a limited amount of rental equipment, which is generally lacking in Peru.

Consult *www.perusurfguides.com* to find the best beaches and get a detailed report of the spots. The weather report is available at: *www.surf-forecast.com/countries/ Peru/breaks.*

COLONIAL TRUJILLO WALK

Many of Trujillo's wonderful colonial and republican buildings are privately owned and lack regular opening hours, so a stroll through this historic town requires a sense of flexibility and adventure. Mansions are generally open mornings and evenings on weekdays and Saturday mornings. Church hours are erratic, except for the cathedral, which opens every morning and evening.

The marble statue honoring liberty dominates Trujillo's spacious Plaza de Armas.

Start your walk at the languid **Plaza de Armas ❶**, one of the largest and most relaxed in Peru. Enjoy concerts by the municipal band on Friday and Saturday nights, and at 8 a.m. on Sundays, attend the ceremonial flag-raising, which might include Peruvian *paso* horses or a *marinera* dance performance. German sculptor Edmund Moeller (1885–1958) created the massive marble statue of "La Libertad."

On your left, on the north corner of the plaza, the relatively unadorned **Catedral** (*Calle Orbegoso & Calle Independencia*) dates to 1666. Its museum (*tel 044/231–474, closed Sun., $*) exhibits religious paintings and liturgical clothing. Next door, three walls covered in 17th-century Seville tiles surround the superb courtyard of the **Archbishop's Palace**—which opened to the public in 2007.

On the plaza's south corner, the **Municipalidad,** where Trujillo declared independence from Spain in 1820, houses city offices. Nearby, the elegant **Casa de Urquiaga** (*Calle Pizarro 446*), now a bank, displays Simón Bolívar's writing desk and objects from several cultures. The three courtyards are typical of early Trujillo construction, although the present structure dates mainly to the 19th century.

Continue northeast along Pizarro, and enter **Iglesia de la Merced ❷** (*Calle Pizarro 550*) from a courtyard fronting the Superior Court. Rebuilt in 1630, this church is one of Trujillo's oldest buildings and boasts a baroque facade and superb cupola. **Casa de la Emancipación ❸** (*Calle Pizarro 610*), where Trujillo's leaders once prepared the city's declaration of independence, now houses a bank and features photos of local poet César Vallejo,

NOT TO BE MISSED:

Archbishop's Palace • Casa de Urquiaga • Iglesia de la Merced • Plazuela El Recreo • Monasterio El Carmen • Museo del Juguete

local art displays, and free cultural events. At the block's end the 19th-century **Palacio Iturregui** ❹ (*Calle Pizarro 688*), now the Club Central, is celebrated for its marble statues, interior ironwork, and delicate columns. Guided tours ($$$) are provided on request.

Enjoy lunch in the 700 block of Calle Pizarro, otherwise known as "restaurant row" (Ristaurante Romano is good), then head to **Plazuela El Recreo** ❺, a pedestrian plaza two blocks away with a fountain designed by Gustave Eiffel (see sidebar p. 17) and a stone gateway, once

the town's north exit. Look for remains of the 17th-century city wall and water system here.

Turn right on Calle Estete, then right again onto Calle Bolívar. Walk one block to **Monasterio El Carmen** ❻ (*Bolívar & Colón, $*), an early 18th-century Carmelite nunnery and baroque church. Knock on the door on Bolívar to see Trujillo's best colonial art, or see if the main door on Colón is open to admire the gilded altar. Then head two blocks northwest on Colón and turn left onto Independencia to visit **Museo de Juguete** ❼ (Toy Museum; *Calle Independencia 705, tel 044/208-181, closed Sun. p.m., $*). This fine collection includes 150 examples of children's toys, ranging from ancient Moche rattles to 19th-century lead soldiers.

Casa Ganoza Chopitea ❽ (*Independencia 628*) has a baroque entrance, rococo facade, Moorish balcony, and a 19th-century wrought-iron window. Of the three traditional inner courtyards, the first two are preserved. The Casona Deza café serves superb coffee and snacks.

EXPERIENCE: Ride Peruvian *Caballos de Paso*

Caballos de paso (*paso* horses) are mid-size horses bred for sure-footedness, not for speed. Unlike trotting breeds, paso horses amble evenly with little up-and-down movement, resulting in an exceptionally comfortable ride. Considered the smoothest saddle horses in the world, they are also tough and well suited to demanding trips into the rough, dry, and expansive western Andes.

The National Association of Owners and Breeders of Peruvian Paso Horses proudly claims the breed has its roots in steeds brought by Christopher Columbus. Originally bred on Caribbean islands, paso horses soon appeared in Central America and then in Peru. Today, Trujillo is the capital of the country's *Caballos de Paso*. Arrange rides and exhibitions with a tour agency (see Travelwise pp. 309–310).

Huanchaco

🖪 Map p. 199

Huanchaco

Traveling west on Mansiche Avenue for 6 miles (10 km) you reach Huanchaco. Once a fishing village, it has grown in size and popularity and now boasts dozens of small hotels and restaurants that cater to surfers and travelers who prefer a seaside base for visiting the local sites.

Frequent buses ($) and taxis ($$) ply the route from Trujillo.

Huanchaco fishermen still use *caballitos* (see sidebar p. 207), boats made from the reeds that grow in the marshy area on the port's north end. They paddle out when the fish are biting and surf back a few hours later with their catch, selling the fish immediately on the beach and then stacking their caballitos to dry along the beachfront. Adventurous travelers can rent a caballito for a few soles, ask a fisherman to paddle them out, and then surf back.

Built in 1540, the white **church** on the bluff overlooking Huanchaco is reputedly the second oldest in Peru. The church—which serves as a landmark for pilots

arriving at the Trujillo airport—is usually open during the day. For good views, climb the belfry.

The surf here is gentle enough for caballitos and appropriate for beginning surfers. Wet suits are recommended since water temperatures, warmest from January to March, range from 64° to 72°F (18°–22°C). You can rent a board (see Travelwise p. 309–310), take lessons, or arrange a tour to one of the more difficult areas. Travelers interested in all of these options, and perhaps even volunteering to help homeless children and other projects, should contact Otra Cosa (*Las Camelias 431, tel 044/461–302, otracosa.org*).

Moche & Chimu Sites

All of the major Moche and Chimu archaeological sites scattered around Trujillo open daily from 9 a.m. to 4 p.m. (visitors can stay until 5 p.m.). Allow two or three days to see all the sites thoroughly. The most important and impressive are Huaca de la Luna and Chan Chan, which you can visit together in a day. El Brujo has amazing recent discoveries and also deserves a visit. For an overview in Spanish, visit the **Museo de Arqueología, Antropología e Historia** (see p. 201) before you leave Trujillo.

Chan Chan: Located 3 miles (5 km) west of Trujillo on Avenida Mansique, the way to Huanchaco, Chan Chan is a dusty 20-minute walk off the main road; a taxi is recommended. Valid for two days, the admission ticket includes the site museum, Huaca Arco Iris, and Huaca Esmeralda**.**

A UNESCO World Heritage site, and the world's largest mud-brick city, Chan Chan was the late capital of the Chimu people (A.D. 900–1470), who controlled the north coast from Lima to the Ecuadoran border until the Inca conquest. The huge city once housed as many as 50,000 people and covered some 10 square miles

Chan Chan

- Map p. 199
- Ave. Mansique, Trujillo
- 044/234–862
- $

chanchan.gob.pe

Moche Culture

Although the Moche (100 B.C.–A.D. 850) ruled over a relatively small area of the north coast—mainly from Lambayeque to Nepeña, with some influence as far away as Piura and Huarmey—their tremendous cultural contributions made them one of the most important pre-Inca societies. Contemporary with the Nazca people of the south coast, but unrelated to them, the Moche left behind huge coastal pyramids, fabulously rich jewelry, and artistically superb ceramics.

Moche pottery makers perfected the use of molds, which allowed them to produce many similar pieces quickly and efficiently. Nevertheless, some of their works exhibit such an elaborate sense of individuality and realism—a wad of coca leaves in one cheek, buck teeth, rounded or drawn features—that it is clear they were modeled on specific people.

Moche pottery typically portrays priests and warriors, who were at the apex of society, as well as lower-class fishermen, musicians, prisoners, and even people suffering from disease. More than any other in South America, the Moche culture excelled at the creation of erotic pottery; surviving pieces illustrate a wide variety of sexual positions.

An excavated piece on display at the Musco Tumbas Reales de Sipán

Major Moche archaeological sites include **Huaca de la Luna** (see pp. 208–209), with its fantastic, life-size reliefs; **El Brujo** (see pp. 207–208), where a 1,500-year-old mummy of a tattooed woman was discovered; and the tombs of **Sipán** (pp. 215–216), which have yielded the most important burials excavated on the continent, full of gold pieces and intricate jewelry, as well as thousands of pots that once held food for the afterlife.

(26 sq km) with adobe temples, plazas, terraces, ramps, and buildings. Now, however, about half the city has disappeared due to erosion and modern encroachment.

Chan Chan comprises ten **royal compounds** containing the burial mounds of Chimu rulers. Looted in the early decades of the Spanish conquest, the city was left to decay amid rare but devastat-

to the Chimu. Allow an hour for a stroll through the compound's two ceremonial sectors, walk-in well, mausoleum, and assembly room with superb acoustics.

Archaeologists are slowly investigating the other compounds. The **site museum** is located on Avenida Mansique, about 1 mile (2 km) from the archaeological area. It houses an interesting exhibition

■ **The archaeological site of Chan Chan, the largest pre-Columbian city in South America**

ing floods and rainstorms caused by El Niño. By the 20th century, Chan Chan had turned into a huge sprawl of tumbling, eroded walls with only worn mud reliefs attesting to its former glory.

Archaeologists have restored one of the royal compounds, the **Tschudi Complex** (recently renamed Nik An). Here signs guide visitors past walls decorated with images of sea otters, fish, waves, seabirds, and the moon, all symbols of religious significance

of aerial photographs, ceramics, metal objects and a small light and sound show. From the museum you can decide to undertake the tour of the site by bicycle (*free, duration: 40 mins. round-trip, only Sat. & Sun. 9 a.m.–3:30 p.m.*) thanks to the Bicitour project supported by National Geographic and Sustainable Preservation Initiative (SPI), which involves young Peruvians as companions. **Huaca Esmeralda,** a two-tier temple platform in a dodgy district between Chan

Chan and Trujillo, is best visited with a knowledgeable guide. Better preserved is **Huaca Arco Iris,** off the Panamericana, 2.4 miles (4 km) north of Trujillo. Climb the ramps to see adobe panels and niches.

El Brujo: From Trujillo at the point where Jr. N de Pierola forks with Avenida Mansiche, the Panamericana heads north. An unpaved side road off the highway leads to the remote archaeological site of El Brujo, 37 miles (60 km) north of Trujillo. The highlight of this fascinating coastal complex is **Huaca Cao,** a Moche pyramid from which archaeologists unearthed the 1,500-year-old, tattooed mummy of a woman in 2006.

INSIDER TIP:

Few tourists visit the northern coast, so you can enjoy the region's fabulous sites, great seafood, and towns that retain the old Spanish ambience all to yourself.

–JOE YOGERST
National Geographic writer

La Señora de Cao, as she is called, was wrapped in cotton along with pieces of gold and jewelry that indicate her high status. Her grave contained numerous clubs and spears, unusual in Moche culture. Moche noble-women were typically sacrificed to

Totora Reeds—A Unique Resource

Totora reeds (*Schoenoplectus californicus,* the California bulrush) grow in swampy areas in the Andes, Central America, and the southern United States. Two-thousand-year-old ceramics demonstrate that Moche fishermen used these reeds to construct pointy-prowed boats. Today, fishermen from the coastal village of Huanchaco still build and use the boats, which they call *caballitos* (little horses).

The use of these reeds has nearly disappeared in other parts of the Americas; however, on Lake Titicaca, the Uros people are famed for their large totora-reed boats and houses made from sturdy reed mats. They also use the reeds to make baskets and other items such as fans, while farmers sometimes use them as fodder for livestock.

El Brujo

Map p. 199

939/326–240

$

www.elbrujo.pe

accompany a nobleman into the afterlife. No one yet knows why this woman was tattooed or buried with so many weapons.

The temple platform, where archaeologists found the mummy, is decorated with reliefs similar to those at Huaca de la Luna (see pp. 208–209). From the summit, you can see **Huaca El Brujo,** a larger Moche site that is closed to the public, as well as **Huaca Prieta,** the oldest garbage dump in Peru. Archaeologists have deduced

**Huacas del Sol y
de la Luna**

🅰 Map p. 199

☎ 044/221–269

💲 $$$

**www.huacasde
moche.pe**

much from the 5,000-year-old discards, but you may be happy simply to view the pile from a distance. Access to El Brujo, once a remote site reached by poor dirt roads, has improved since the mummy's discovery in 2006, and a site museum will soon help interpret this find.

Huacas del Sol y de la Luna:
The Moche site, Huaca de la Luna (Temple of the Moon), lies 5 miles (8 km) southeast of Trujillo. Although the smaller of a pair of temple platforms (the other Huaca del Sol), it is the more important because of the polychromatic reliefs that decorate its walls. The temple is a series of superimposed structures built over six centuries. When one temple fell out of use, the Moche built another on top, burying old murals and creating new ones, and leaving behind a mosaic of altars and walls.

Huaqueros have looted the temple, and tombs recently found in the burials belong to sacrificed prisoners rather than important nobility; nevertheless archaeologists suspect that many rich noble tombs await discovery.

The **main temple** has a 245-foot-long (75 m) facade consisting of seven steps, each nearly 10 feet (3 m) high and decorated with a row of larger-than-life images. Some of the images depict humans, such as parades of armed warriors and naked prisoners, but most show mythical beings such as spiders and dragons holding decapitated heads, or Aiapaec, the decapitator god. Smaller temples

on the site feature complicated murals of priests and animals or giant grotesque faces.

Several hundred yards away stands the badly damaged Temple of the Sun–Huaca del Sol, the world's largest adobe structure, composed of an estimated 140 million bricks.

Peruvian Hairless Dog

Except for a tuft between its ears and on the end of its tail, the *viringo* has no hair at all. In spite of the unorthodox look, or perhaps because of it, these dark, medium-size dogs were prized by the Moche, who included them as funerary sacrifices. Because their skin is warm to the touch, many believed the dogs could relieve the pains of arthritis.

After the Spanish conquest, the viringo almost disappeared. In 1996, the United Kennel Club recognized it as a distinct breed, the only Peruvian dog to be so documented. Today, by law, every site along the coast has at least a pair of viringos, considered a national treasure.

The flat area between the two temples contains the foundations of hundreds of rooms dedicated to a variety of industrial, religious, and residential uses. Archaeologists are currently excavating the buildings, which have been used as the model for the Museo Huacas de

Moche site museum. Admission includes a guided tour, usually in Spanish, but several bilingual placards will help English-speaking travelers. Visit early in the morning to avoid dusty afternoon winds and heat.

Other Places

Caral: Historians and archaeologists have known of the ancient city of Caral for more than a century, but excavation did not begin until 1996. In 2001, carbon dating proved that the site was at least 4,700 years old, with some indications that construction may have begun as early as 3000 B.C.

Caral has several stepped pyramids, one of them 100 feet (30 m) tall, and some fronted by a circular sunken plaza, temples, and residential areas. The most important of the 18 ancient sites in the Supe Valley, Caral features an interpretation center and obligatory local guides (*$$$ per group*). Follow the Panamericana to the village of Supe (113 miles/185 km from Lima), and from there take a taxi (*$$$*) along a dirt road for another 14 miles (23 km).

Barranca: Because it offers better accommodations than Supe, consider basing yourself in the seaside town of Barranca 6 miles (10 km) northwest of Supe along the Panamericana. From here, another 6 miles (10 km) north will bring you to the stepped Chimu pyramid of **Paramonga** (*$*), which has eroded but can still be climbed for excellent views of the coast.

Working at Caral on Residencio 12, which housed 20 of the elite in its day

Sechín: Three miles (5 km) southeast of Casma, a sleepy town 225 miles (370 km) north of Lima, is Sechín (*$$*), a 3,600-year-old city built by people for whom torture and death seem to have been a way of life. Currently under excavation, the site features 12-foot-high (4 m) walls that surround three sides of a small temple, their carved reliefs depicting warriors eviscerating scores of prisoners. Because the walls are made of stone, the figures appear much bolder than the eroded reliefs of the Moche and Chimu *huacas*. The museum has information about Sechín and other huacas nearby.

With the same admission ticket, you can visit **Pañamarca,** a weathered Moche pyramid located 7 miles (12 km) from Sechín. Ask to see the murals. ∎

Caral

🅐 Map p. 199

☎ 01/205–2500

💲 $$

www.zona caral.gob.pe

THE COAST NORTH OF TRUJILLO

A mix of past and cutting-edge modern, the cities and sights north of Trujillo offer a rich introduction to the history and culture of Peru's north coast. Here you can relax among the locals in the shade of distinguished colonial buildings or head out to the beach for a day of sun and surf. The region's many remote archaeological sites also beckon visitors, with some of the oldest—and most extraordinary—finds in the country.

The Catedral San Miguel Arcangel de Piura is located in the town of Piura.

Chiclayo

 Map p. 199

Visitor Information

✉ iPerú, Calle San Jose 823, Palacio Municipal

☎ 074/205–703

E-mail: iperu chiclayo@promperu. gob.pe

Chiclayo

Chiclayo, the fast-growing capital of Lambayeque Department and Peru's fourth largest city, is a three-hour express-bus ride north of Trujillo. Although Chiclayo, a modern city, dates to the 16th century, it never became a major colonial center under Spanish rule and wasn't officially founded until 1835.

Unlike most Peruvian towns, Chiclayo lacks a central Plaza de Armas, replacing it instead with an elongated **Parque Central** anchored by a neoclassical cathedral whose construction began in 1869, but which wasn't inaugurated until 1916. Apart from a few main thoroughfares, the city is a hodgepodge of narrow, crooked, cobbled roads that recall the days when donkey paths led to the town center.

Locals refer to Chiclayo as La Ciudad de la Amistad (The City of Friendship), and its businesslike bustle does have a certain charm. However, the city would not appear on most travel itineraries were it not for one thing—the superb archaeological sites nearby, including the Moche site of Sipán,

---

INSIDER TIP:

Practice good etiquette at archaeological sites. Avoid walking on the stonework and outside the stairways and paths. Don't touch the intricate carvings.

—JUSTIN KAVANAGH
*National Geographic
International Editions editor*

---

home of the richest tomb ever discovered in the Americas.

While in Chiclayo, visit the **Mercado Modelo** (see sidebar p. 214), amble along the quiet **Paseo de las Musas** with its neoclassical statues inexplicably harking back to Greek mythology, hang out in Parque Central, and enjoy the laid-back, down-to-earth quality of the city.

To visit the areas around Chiclayo, you can take a guided tour (*$$$$$, plus entrance fees*), hire a taxi (*$$$$$*), or take one of the local buses (*$*) that go almost everywhere. Ask at the visitor information office for schedules.

Lambayeque

A 7.5-mile (12 km) bus ride (*$*) to the northwest brings you to historic Lambayeque, once the

departmental capital but now greatly overshadowed by Chiclayo. Lambayeque has some interesting colonial architecture, but more importantly, it is home to two of the best museums in Peru.

Museo Tumbas Reales de Sipán: Opened in 2002, this world-class museum, the best in northern Peru, is dedicated to the royal tombs of Sipán (see pp. 215–216). To enter the pyramid-shaped building, climb up the ramp to the third floor, where the museum's exhibits begin. Just as archaeologists must enter a pyramid from the

(continued on p. 214)

Museo Tumbas Reales de Sipán

✉ Ave. Juan Pablo Vizcardo y Guzmán 895, Lambayeque

☎ 074/283–978

🕐 Closed Mon.

💲 $

Huaqueros

Huaca is a catchall word meaning "ancient temple," "tomb," or "funeral mound." A huaquero is someone who digs into huacas hoping to profit from buried treasure. Not interested in bones or potsherds, huaqueros search for unbroken ceramics or gold pieces to sell on the black market. They are rarely part of any organized operation, just poor peasants trying to make a little extra cash.

Merchants will occasionally offer travelers ancient objects; the pieces are almost always modern reproductions. Even if an item is the real thing, it is illegal to export it from Peru or to import it anywhere else.

SICÁN CULTURE

Not to be confused with Sipán, the Sicán culture (A.D. 750–1375) bridged those of the Moche and Chimu peoples in what is today Lambayeque Department. The Sicán continued many Moche practices, including ceramics, metallurgy, and the construction of pyramid-shaped funerary platforms. Today you can visit their main sites at Batán Grande and Túcume.

A funerary mask on display at the Museo Nacional de Sicán

Sicán pottery makers used the lost wax technique to create many pieces from a single mold. They extended this practice to the production of gold ornaments, which became a hallmark of Sicán culture. They also developed the idea of strengthening and improving metals with alloys, beginning with arsenic and copper and continuing with gold and silver. Using adobe ovens fired with hard, hot-burning *algarrobo* (carob) wood and cane blowpipes, they could attain temperatures as high as 1,832°F (1,000°C), allowing them to produce some of the most sophisticated metal objects yet made.

Dozens of pyramidal burial mounds cover the Sicán landscape. Unlike the Moche, who buried their dead lying down, the Sicán buried them sitting upright with their legs crossed. Nobles were entombed with oversize gold gloves, precious ritual objects, and gold face masks with slanting *ojos alados* (winged eyes), a reference to the mythological first Sipán king, Naylamp, who was said to have grown wings and flown away after his death.

In Ferrañefe, 11 miles (18 km) north of Chiclayo, the modern **Museo Nacional Sicán** (*9th block Ave. Batán Grande, tel 074/286–469, closed Mon., $$*) has a superb display of artifacts from two Batán Grande tombs, as well as stunning reproductions of the burials. Discovered by Japanese archaeologist Izumi Shimada in 1991, the site's first intact tomb held the body of a nobleman who had been buried upside down with his legs crossed, his decapitated head covered with a gold mask and placed in the grave. The bodies of two women and two boys, as well as a slew of valuable funerary objects, lay next to him. In 1995, Shimada excavated an even larger tomb of a nobleman surrounded by 22 sacrificed young women. A short video (in Spanish) at the museum outlines the significance of the excavations.

Batán Grande, about 20 miles (32 km) northeast of Ferrañefe, lies mostly within the **Santuario Histórico Bosque de Pómac,** a preserve for algarrobo trees, some nearly a thousand years old. You can reach it by tour or taxi. The site contains 36 *huacas,* the tops of their pyramids poking out eerily from the trees. *Huaqueros,* busy searching for gold, have dug an estimated 100,000 holes around the site, yet Izumi Shimada continues to work here.

In 2006, in conjunction with Museo Sicán, Shimada discovered an aristocratic cemetery containing 21 burials and two pits of funerary offerings. Among the exciting objects uncovered were a dozen *tumis* (ceremonial knives) decorated with an image of Naylamp, the first decorated tumis to have been recovered from an intact tomb.

■ **Ceramic figurine on display at the Museo Nacional de Sicán**

Around 1050, Batán Grande fell victim to a severe combination of droughts and other weather events caused by El Niño. Evidence suggests that the buildings on top of and surrounding the pyramids were systematically and concurrently burned, and that the people moved to nearby **Túcume** (*tel 978/977–578, $$*).

Fifteen miles (24 km) north of Lambayeque, Túcume can be reached by bus, tour, or taxi (*$*). **Huaca Larga** is one of 26 pyramids at the site. Around 1375, the Chimu conquered the Sicán but were defeated by the Inca less than a century later. The pyramids exhibit Sicán, Chimu, and Inca characteristics. So far, archaeologists have found only Inca burials.

The pyramids surround Cerro Purgatario, a natural hill. Take the footpath up the hill to a lookout with expansive views over the landscape, locally called the Valley of the Pyramids. A site museum explains the findings of the previous excavations undertaken by Norwegian explorer Thor Heyerdahl (1914–2002), who directed the dig from 1989 to 1994.

top and work their way down, you will descend through the museum, whose muted atmosphere and dim lighting highlight the superb displays. At this time, all of the exhibit plaques are in Spanish.

On the **third floor,** a short video and other presentations will introduce you to the geography and history of the Moche

of Moche metallurgy; many of the copper, silver, and gold items on display were created as the result of improved techniques and advances in technology.

The museum's **second floor** presents visitors with a series of breathtaking exhibits of gold, silver, and turquoise treasures. Highlights include a gold-and-silver necklace shaped like two strings of ten huge peanuts; breastplates made of thousands of tiny blue turquoise and red *Spondylus* shell beads, painstakingly strung onto cotton thread; and gold earplugs decorated with animal mosaics. Archaeologists discovered these fabulous pieces among a pile of disintegrated textiles, corroded copper, rotted wood, and other grave goods. Some of the displays explain the techniques used to save the hundreds of objects within the tombs, and an accurate reproduction of several of the burials as they were uncovered demonstrates clearly how painstaking the recovery and restoration efforts must have been.

The Lord of Sipán, like other Moche noblemen, was buried in a cane coffin surrounded by small pottery vessels containing food such as yams, chilies, sweet potatoes, and corn. But he was not buried alone. The bodies of three women, two soldiers, one boy, and several llamas were also found in the tomb. On the **first floor** of the museum, you can see a reconstruction of the burial—which was distributed over two levels—along with the skeletal remains of the nobleman

EXPERIENCE:
Visit the Market

Chiclayo's **Mercado Modelo** encompasses several city blocks just north of Parque Central. Typical of most Peruvian city markets, it has specific sections for produce, meat, and fish, and small booths selling clothes and everyday household items. Because Peruvians take shamanism seriously, especially in the north, it also has a *mercado de brujos* (witch doctors' market). Along the row of stalls on the market's south side you will find herbs, teas, potions, salves, animal parts, snake skins, amulets, and hallucinogenic cactuses for sale and salespeople who will enthusiastically describe all the uses and benefits of their products. You may even be able to arrange a healing session, but it's advisable to do so only with the help of a reputable guide.

people. The eye-catching pieces of pottery on display have provided historians with an endless source of information about the people, their gods, and their lives. But don't overlook the more mundane items such as seeds and bones, which reveal much about ancient agriculture, wildlife, and fishing. Also on the third floor, you can follow the development

Everything from fruits to amulets can be found at the Mercado Modelo.

and his dazzling riches. You could combine a visit to the museum with a trip to the site of Sipán (see below), where the pyramid (better called a funerary platform mound) has yielded several other burials and work continues to find more.

Museo Brüning: This older museum no longer houses artifacts from Sipán but is well worth a visit anyway. Located five blocks west of the Museo Tumbas Reales de Sipán, the Museo Brüning—with its exhibits labeled in English—has some Moche ceramics on display but also showcases pieces from several other cultures and from the nearby archaeological sites of Túcume and Batán Grande (see pp. 212–213).

Two blocks west of the Museo Brüning lies the **Plaza de Armas,** where the 17th-century **Iglesia San Pedro** has impressive murals

and a baroque altar. A block north, along 2 de Mayo at San Martín, stands the colonial **Casa de Logia o Montjoy,** which boasts a 210-foot-long (64 m) balcony, the longest in Peru.

Sipán

The archaeological site of Sipán lies next to the modern village of the same name, 17 miles (28 km) east of Chiclayo. The road passes through lush sugarcane fields and the village of Pomalca.

Of the two pyramids at the site, the smaller one, **Huaca Rajada** (Split Temple), has yielded all known Sipán burials and work continues today in search of more. Archaeologists believe that upper-class homes topped the larger pyramid, although none have yet been found.

A footpath picks its way past several excavations at the site, which is dotted with signs in English to help guide your way.

Museo Brüning

✉ Huamachuco & Atahualpa, Lambayeque
☎ 074/282–110
$ $

Museo de Sitio Huaca Rajada

▲ Map p. 199
✉ Campiña Huaca Rajada s/n
☎ 9/8/977–622
$ $$, $$$ for guided tour

Although the excavations now contain only reproductions of items discovered by archaeologists, they are well done and give a good impression of how the tombs must have looked just before the dead were buried.

Excavated in 1987 to 1988, the **main tomb** of the Lord of Sipán dates to about A.D. 350. In late 1988, another royal tomb was unearthed at a much deeper level in the funerary mound. The man within this tomb—buried about 300 years before the Lord of Sipán—is known as the Old Lord of Sipán. What happened with this burial mound during the intervening centuries still puzzles archaeologists, but they do know that

---

INSIDER TIP:

For a good view of the archaeological site at Sipán, climb a short way up the larger pyramid to the platform that overlooks Huaca Rajada.

—CHRISTOPHER AUGER-DOMÍNGUEZ
National Geographic International Editions photographer

---

at least one other royal tomb was ransacked by *huaqueros.* A fourth tomb was found in 2007, and it is likely that others are waiting to be discovered.

Archaeologists have also uncovered the burial places of several less important figures at Sipán. One, a high priest, had a tomb almost as impressive as royalty. Another burial contained 1,137 pots in the shapes of warriors, priests, prisoners, musicians, and anthropomorphic deities.

Seaside Villages

Once you have tired of ancient sites, take a tour of the *circuito de playas* (beach circuit). First head to **Pimentel,** Chiclayo's favorite summer (*Dec.–Mar.*) beach resort. Located 7 miles (12 km) southwest of Lambayeque, it has decent surfing conditions, a creaky, century-old pier, an interesting blend of new beach houses and 19th-century buildings, and a fishing port with a few *caballitos de totora* still around.

A few miles south, the traditional, but busy, fishing village of **Santa Rosa** features colorful wooden boats, a few caballitos, and simple but good seafood restaurants serving ceviche and the local specialty, *tortillas de ray* (stingray omelet). The pleasant town is easily reached by frequent minibuses (*$*); walking along the beach isn't recommended.

Return to Chiclayo via the crafts village of **Monsefú,** known especially for its straw hats, baskets, and fans, and for its *chicha,* a local corn drink.

Lying inland 28 miles (45 km) southeast of Chiclayo, **Saña** (or Zaña) was founded in 1563 and became the region's foremost colonial city. Repeatedly sacked by pirates in the 17th century, it was destroyed by El Niño floods in 1720. Today, desert sands surround the walls and arches of the four churches in this ghost town.

Reserva Ecológica Chaparrí

The community of Santa Catalina owns and operates this dry-forest reserve near Chongoyape, 47 miles (75 km) northeast of Chiclayo. Working with biologists and conservationists, Chaparrí protects the region's endangered species, such as the white-winged guan (25 percent of the world's population lives here), Tamandua anteater, and ocelot. Spectacled bears rescued from poachers and other animals live in large natural enclosures on the 141-square-mile (364 sq km) reserve, which offers minimum-impact tourism designed to help the community.

Book in advance a mandatory guide for entry and visit to the reserve (tel 074/796–299, $$$$). The reserve also offers good opportunities for hiking, bird-watching, camping, and horseback-riding.

Built with local materials, Chaparrí Ecolodge (tel 984/676–249, e-mail: info@chaparrilodge.com, www.chaparrilodge.com, from $$$$) has 16 solar-powered rooms, 12 with private facilities. Rates include full board, guides, and use of the natural swimming pool.

Piura Department

Piura: From Chiclayo, the Panamericana heads north then northwest through the wide, sandy, and sparsely inhabited Sechura Desert to the colonial city of Piura. Originally founded by Francisco Pizarro in 1532 near the present-day city of Sullana, the city moved several times until settling at its current location in 1588.

Inland, low, and surrounded by desert, Piura is the hottest city in Peru. It is also prone to floods during bad El Niño years, closing the Panamericana and virtually isolating the city from the rest of the country.

Parts of the **Catedral** (*Plaza de Armas*) date from the 16th century, but most of the structure was added on in bits and pieces later. Inside, its highlights include paintings by local artist Ignacio Merino (1817–1876).

A block southeast of the Plaza de Armas, **Jirón Lima** boasts the most colonial character of any street in town. One block to the southwest stands **Casa Grau,** the birthplace of Adm. Miguel Grau (1834–1879), a hero of the War of the Pacific against Chile. The Peruvian navy has restored the house, which now serves as a naval museum.

Two blocks east of the plaza, the Río Piura barely runs during the dry months but can become a deadly torrent during bad El Niño years. In 1998, the bridge crossing the river on Avenida Bolognesi collapsed, but it has since been rebuilt.

The **Museo Municipal Vicus** houses a fine collection of gold work from the little-known Vicus culture (200 B.C.–A.D. 300), which was a local offshoot of the Moche. Archaeologists are currently excavating a Vicus site with several pyramids that they discovered in the Piura area in early 2008.

Surrounding Towns: Several of the small towns in the Piura Department are of interest. Locals and visitors alike

Piura

🅜 Map p. 199

Visitor Information

✉ iPerú, Jr. Ayacucho 459

☎ 073/320–249

E-mail: iperupiura@ promperu.gob.pe

Casa Grau

✉ Calle Tacna 662, Piura

☎ 073/326–541

🕒 Closed Sat.–Sun.

💲 Donation

Museo Municipal Vicus

✉ Ave. Sullana ang. Jr. Huánuco, Piura

☎ 073/322–307

🕒 Closed Mon.

💲 $

head 7.5 miles (12 km) south-west to the dusty village of **Catacaos,** known for its crafts market, typical restaurants, and elaborate Holy Week festivities. The crafts market is busiest on weekends, when stalls selling panama hats, leatherware, ceramics, wood carvings, and fine silver filigree cover several blocks near the Plaza de Armas. Hole-in-the-wall *picanterías* (typical restaurants) are busiest at lunch, when citizens of

Do-It-Yourself Mud Bath

While in Máncora, head to the hot springs for a little DIY pampering. Here you can soak in the water and give yourself a body and facial treatment at the natural mud baths 7 miles (11 km) east of town up the wooded Río Fernández Valley. There is no one at the springs to help you, but a local will charge you to use the baths and powder-fine mud. Continue up the valley to hike through the dry forest. You can arrange for a mototaxi in Máncora.

Piura come to feast on *seco de cabrito* (stewed kid goat served with rice and yucca or beans), *seco de chavelo* (salted beef and plantain stew), or *copuz* (stewed goats heads).

Plenty of other dishes are also available for less adventuresome eaters.

Chulucanas, 38 miles (60 km) east of Piura, vies with Catacaos for the title of best northern craft village. Unlike Catacaos, which sells a little bit of everything, Chulucanas is famed nationwide for its distinctive, rounded, earthen-colored ceramics depicting people, especially the *chichera,* a large lady that sells chicha.

Coastal Communities:

Out on the coast, the historic but almost forgotten port of **Paita,** 36 miles (57 km) west of Piura, has been an important harbor since before the Spanish conquest. It became a Spanish colonial port and received attention from pirates, buccaneers, and even Sir Francis Drake (1540–1595), the English admiral who first sailed around the world. Manuela Saénz (1797–1856), mistress of liberator Simón Bolívar, lived her last years, destitute, in Paita. Now privately owned, her simple house still stands.

Most visitors continue 9 miles (14 km) north to the popular white-sand beach at **Colán.** Nearby, the Dominicans built **Iglesia San Lucas de Colán** in 1536. Reputedly Peru's oldest church, it is in surprisingly good condition and still in use today; ask around for the church warden, who has the keys. The ocean here is warm year-round, about 76° to 82°F (24.5°–28°C), and the swimming is good. Stingrays enjoy the shallow, sandy conditions, however, so be sure to drag your feet when entering the water. (This caveat applies for all the sandy northern beaches you might visit.)

Farther north, the coastal roads deteriorate into sandy tracks. Most vehicles return to Piura or go inland to **Sullana,** a busy market town 23 miles (37 km) north of Piura on the Panamericana. This is where the Panamericana splits, and travelers have the choice of continuing northeast into the southern Ecuadoran highlands via the border town of Macará, or heading northwest to the oil port of Talara, midway between Piura and Tumbes, and continuing along the coast.

Talara, 3 miles (5 km) off the Panamericana, has little of interest, but a 7-mile (12 km) paved road to the southwest will take you to **Negritos.** This village—with a lighthouse, sea lion colony, and beaches for swimming and surfing—sits on Punta Pariñas, the westernmost point in continental South America (locally called Punta Balcones).

Continuing north will bring you to **Cabo Blanco,** 20 miles (32 km) along the coast by unpaved road or a few miles longer via the Panamericana. An important oil field lies beneath the area, and oil pumps and off-shore rigs blemish the landscape. Peru's most famous deep-sea sportfishing port, Cabo Blanco drew the likes of Ernest Hemingway and Vice President Nelson Rockefeller in the 1950s. In 1953, American oilman Alfred Glassell, Jr., set the world record here for largest marlin caught—a 1,560-pound (709 kg) specimen. The

Pottery at the Catacaos crafts market

fishing has declined since, but the area is now more popular with expert surfers. The perfect 10-foot (3 m) tubular wave crashes onto a wicked reef, however, so beginners shouldn't attempt it.

Continuing 9.5 miles (15 km) to the north you will arrive at **Los Organos,** a small, relaxed beach village with easy surfing year-round. There are a few simple places to stay, but most visitors go to the fishing village of **Máncora,** Peru's most celebrated beach area. Máncora is easy to reach, with the Panamericana dropping you off in the middle of town, just two or three minutes' walk from the ocean. Water temperatures are warm, the surf is suitable

Soccer provides family entertainment in the small villages of the Sechura Desert.

for beginners, the sun stays out year-round, and local fishermen keep the restaurants supplied with fresh fish. Accommodations, ranging from backpackers' hangouts to deluxe bungalows loosely spread out over several miles of beachfront, should be booked well in advance for New Year's and Fiestas Patrias (when prices can double), and on summer weekends. Surfing is acceptable all year but best from November to March. You can rent a board and sign up for a lesson; or try kite surfing.

Huancabamba: The eastern part of Piura Department climbs to heights above 10,000 feet (3,000 m) in elevation. From Piura, a 130-mile (210 km) road heads east to Huancabamba (*8 hrs. by bus*). Built on the unstable banks of the Río Huancabamba, the town—subject to

subsidence and erosion—has been nicknamed "*La Ciudad que Camina*" (The Town That Walks).

Huancabamba is the center of shamanism in Peru (see sidebar opposite). Check with the local tourist center for a list of reliable witch doctors and healers, many of whom live several miles away in Las Huaringas. Their agents in town will arrange horseback transportation for the all-night ceremony. There are no hotels in Huaringas; book basic accommodations in Huancabamba.

Tumbes Department

Peru's northernmost coastal department centers on the small city of **Tumbes.** Located 19 miles (30 km) from the Ecuadoran border, it has access to several beaches and nature reserves. The relatively modern **Plaza de Armas** is surrounded

INSIDER TIP:

Rise early to catch the hundreds of fishing boats as they set out to sea along Máncora beach. The sight of the bright colors of the boats in the morning sun is a truly unforgettable sight.

−KENNY LING
*National Geographic
contributor*

by simple bars and restaurants with shaded outside patios for a cool drink in hot weather.

Several of the most interesting streets in the city ring the plaza. Quaintly dilapidated 19th-century buildings line Grau, east of the plaza. The modern pedestrian thoroughfares of San Martín and Bolívar, north of the plaza, are also worth a stroll. The **Malecón,** a block southwest,

overlooks the Río Tumbes. (*Mosquitoes can be a problem, even in the town center.*)

You can see the only Peruvian population of the American crocodile, *Crocodylus acutus,* at the crocodile sanctuary in **Puerto Pizarro,** 9 miles (14 km) northeast of Tumbes. Local shrimp farms threaten their existence in the wild. Bird-watchers will enjoy renting a boat ($$$$) to visit the mangroves and **Isla de los Pajaros** (Bird Island), with its large breeding colonies of seabirds that return spectacularly at dusk. Lovers may wish to rent a boat ($$$) to **Isla de Amor** (Love Island), where you will find beachside restaurants and hammocks.

The umbrella organization **Reserva de Biósfera del Noroeste** (Biosphere Reserve of the Northwest), based in Tumbes, protects three areas; however, no infrastructure for tourism exists. Arrange for a visit with a local tourist agency. ■

Reserva de Biósfera del Noroeste

🗺 Map p. 199

✉ Panamericana Norte 1739, Tumbes

☎ 072/526–489

**www.sernanp.gob.
pe/reserva-de-
biosfera-noroeste**

Witchcraft

Peruvians from all classes and walks of life believe in the power of *brujos* (witch doctors) and *curanderos* (curers) to resolve myriad problems, including sickness, broken hearts, failing business ventures, and spiritual threats. Using charms, talismans, and a variety of plants, herbs, and potions—including the hallucinogenic San Pedro cactus or ayahuasca vine—shamans work with the afflicted during sessions that normally begin late at night and last until dawn. Chanting, blowing smoke, waving leaves, and

rubbing the body with herbs and stones can all play a part in the curing process.

Witchcraft is practiced in numerous small villages in the coastal, highland, and jungle areas throughout Peru, but none are as well known or respected as Las Huaringas in the highlands near Huancabamba, where a healing session costs $60 or more. Patients are usually Peruvian, but the occasional foreigner does show up. If you take the process seriously, you will be heartily welcomed, but gawkers will receive a frosty reception.

Remote pre-Inca sites, forgotten cloud forests, and charming colonial cities

NORTHERN HIGHLANDS

The carved wooden pulpit of the 17th-century church of Belén in Cajamarca

NORTHERN HIGHLANDS

Well off the "gringo trail," Peru's remote northern highlands make travel difficult, but the region's attractions certainly reward the effort. Here, in a varied—and very challenging—environment of lush green valleys, desert mountaintops, and transcendent cloud forests, some of the most dramatic events in Peruvian history took place.

■ Cerro Santa Apolonia overlooks the colonial city of Cajamarca.

In 1532, Atahualpa, the king of the Inca, relaxed in the famous baths at Cajamarca, gateway to the northern highlands. Little did he realize that Francisco Pizarro and his small band of Spanish conquistadores would soon turn his world upside down.

You can still see the Inca room where Atahualpa sat imprisoned in the days before his execution, but it is Cajamarca's Spanish legacy that really shines. Dozens of colonial

mansions now serve the meager tourist population as delightful little hotels suitable for every budget. Festivalgoers will find the Carnival celebration in Cajamarca— the largest city in the northern highlands— one of the wildest, and wettest, in Peru.

The Río Marañón, one of Peru's major tributaries to the Amazon, winds its way through the Amazonas Department, cleaving the northern highlands in two. Traveling overland east from Cajamarca to the quiet city of Chachapoyas, the capital of the department, can be a heady experience. Beat-up old buses descend wildly along badly maintained roads into the Marañón Valley before climbing into the rugged, poorly explored, and nearly forgotten region of tranquil cloud forests. Named after the pre-Inca culture that built massive citadels and cities in the northern highlands, Chachapoyas is surrounded by many spectacular ruins. The best known, the stupendous fortress city of Kuélap, rivals Machu Picchu in size and scenery. Unlike Machu Picchu, however, only a few dozen travelers visit Kuélap each day during the high season. While not as refined as Inca craftsmanship, the site's stonework bears distinctive designs.

Other ruins in the region hold amazing tombs built impossibly high on sheer cliffs, and archaeologists claim that more sites await discovery. Local anthropologist Peter Lerche estimates there may be as many as 350.

Chachapoyas is so remote that scientists did not measure the 2,531-foot-high (771 m) Catarata de Gocta (Gocta Falls), the second highest waterfall in Peru, until 2006. The falls lie barely 20 miles (32 km) north of Chachapoyas and only now have started to attract visitors. The important archaeological site of La Laguna de Cóndores, near Leymebamba, lies about an equal distance to the south of the city, yet it was not properly explored until 1996. Even the best topographic map of the region, published by Peru's Instituto Geográfico Nacional, shows blank areas, labeled "Insufficient Data," that begin just 15 aeronautical miles (24 km) southeast of the city. You certainly can make your own adventure here. ∎

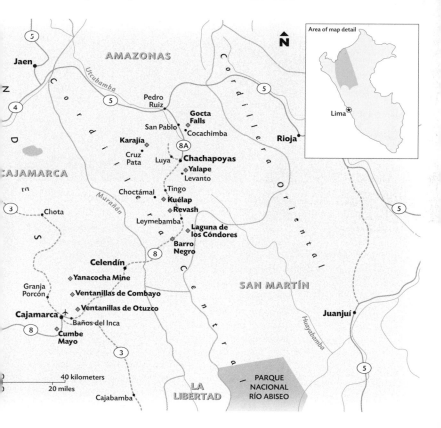

CAJAMARCA

The lovely colonial city of Cajamarca—the most important in Peru's northern Andes—sits at a moderate elevation of 8,695 feet (2,650 m) surrounded by a fertile valley. Dismantled and rebuilt after the Spanish conquest, Cajamarca bears few traces of its distinguished Inca past. Today it is home to the largest gold mine in South America, a source of both wealth and difficult social and environmental problems in a rapidly changing world.

Wide straw hats are typical headgear for campesinos of the Cajamarca region.

Cajamarca

Map p. 225

Visitor Information

iPerú, Jr. Cruz de Piedra 601

076/365-166

E-mail: iperu cajamarca@prom peru.gob.pe

www.municaj.gob.pe

History

The area around Cajamarca contains the ruins of several ancient civilizations, none of them well understood. Some of the ruins date as far back as the Early Horizon (1000–300 B.C.), while others belong to the Cajamarca culture (A.D. 500–1000). The Inca arrived around 1460 under the leadership of the great conqueror Inca Pachacutec and incorporated the region into their growing empire.

In 1525, Pachacutec's grandson, Inca Huayna Capac, died suddenly of smallpox in Quito, Ecuador, leaving the empire unexpectedly divided between two sons: Atahualpa, who ruled the north, and Huascar, who reigned over Cusco and the south.

In the civil war that followed, Atahualpa gained the upper hand, and in 1532, victoriously marched to Cusco, pausing to rest and consolidate his power in the major cities en

INSIDER TIP:

While strife breaks out—as it has on occasion over the last 500 years—conflict is localized. Residents appreciate the economic benefits visitors bring and treat them well.

—JAMES DION
*National Geographic Society,
Director Tourism Programs,
Maps Division*

route, including Cajamarca. Here, Atahualpa, along with many thousands of his troops and attendants, camped at the nearby hot springs now known as Los Baños del Inca.

Meanwhile, Francisco Pizarro and more than 160 Spanish soldiers, about 60 on horseback, pushed inland and reached Cajamarca on November 15, 1532. They settled themselves in stone warehouses near today's Plaza de Armas, where they awaited the arrival of the Inca leader.

Atahualpa appeared the next day, carried on a litter accompanied by thousands of his soldiers. He was met by Friar Vicente de Valverde, who presented Atahualpa with a Bible that the Inca tossed aside as worthless. Incensed, the Spaniards fired their cannon then burst out from their hiding places on horseback, shocking the Inca soldiers who had never heard gunfire or seen horses before that day.

The ensuing battle was violent and bloody, but the small, fearless band of desperately outnumbered Spanish cavalry proved unstoppable. Clad in armor and swinging their swords wildly, they cut down thousands of Atahualpa's tunic-clad men, who tried as best they could to defend themselves with clubs, slings, and axes. In the end, the Inca were defeated and their leader taken prisoner.

Atahualpa realized that what the rough Spaniards really wanted above all else was gold and treasure. So he made a deal with his captors. He would fill a room—up to the height of his outstretched arm—with gold objects and fill it twice more with silverware. In return, the Spaniards would grant him his freedom.

Travel Practicalities

Cajamarca has no central bus terminal. Most bus offices operate along Avenida Atahualpa, 1.25 miles (2 km) southeast of the center. (Don't confuse it with Atahualpa, near the Plaza de Armas.)

Located 2 miles (3 km) northeast of town, the airport (*tel 076/343–757, corpac.gob.pe*) offers daily flights to Lima with LC Perú and LAN Perú.

Word of the bargain spread rapidly, and fabulous ornaments of gold and silver made their way to Cajamarca on the backs of porters and llamas from all over the Inca

El Cuarto de Rescate

✉ Jr. Amalia Puga 750

💲 $

El Conjunto Monumental de Belén

✉ Jr. Belén & Junín

☎ 076/362–601

💲 $

NOTE: A single ticket ($)–the *boleto turístico*–gives entry to El Cuarto de Rescate, El Conjunto Monumental de Belén, and the Museo Etnográfico. Buy the ticket at either of the first two sites. All facilities are closed Mon. (*Spanish guides $$, English tours $$$*).

Empire. Within a few months, the Inca had paid their leader's ransom. An incalculable fortune of precious objects, ranging from gold earplugs to life-size silver statues of corn and llamas, filled three rooms in the city. Uninterested in the artistry of the pieces, the Spanish melted everything down to produce 13,200 pounds (6,000 kg) of gold and 26,400 pounds (12,000 kg) of silver bullion, an astounding treasure that would be worth nearly $200 million today.

Even before they were able to ship the treasures to Spain, the Spaniards reneged on the ransom deal and sentenced Atahualpa to death. On July 26, 1533, the Inca leader was executed near the spot where he had been caught little more than eight months earlier.

EXPERIENCE:
Visit a Working Farm

Of the several working farms in the area around Cajamarca, Granja Porcón (*23 miles/37 km NW of Cajamarca, Jr. Chanchamayo 1355–Fonavi 1, tel 921/752–531 or 976/682–209, e-mail: turismo@granjaporcon. org.pe, www.granjaporcon.org.pe*) **is the best at providing visitors with a good tour, tasty meals, and overnight accommodations. Upon request, opportunities for horseback riding, fishing, and hiking can be provided. Visitors can join in the farming activities during a day tour arranged by a tourist agency, or stay here and discover the various aspects of rural life. The farm offers guided tours of Cajamarca and offers a transport service** (*pick-ups, minivans or combis*) **to/from the airport, or a connection with your hotel if you are not staying in the facility. Please note: It is an evangelical community; therefore it is not suitable for everyone.**

Colonial Cajamarca

The great Inca plaza where the Spaniards captured and executed Atahualpa has long since disappeared, replaced by a smaller, but still sizable, colonial Plaza de Armas. In fact, the Spaniards tore down every Inca building but one and used the stones to rebuild the city. The lone survivor stands near the plaza, **El Cuarto de Rescate** (The Ransom Room), the room that held Atahualpa while the Inca collected his ransom.

INSIDER TIP:

While you expect to see spectacular Inca ruins, the 17th-century Spanish colonial towns are treasures not to be overlooked.

–ADRIAN COAKLEY
National Geographic photo editor

Typical of Inca design, it features trapezoidal niches and solidly constructed doors and walls. A rope prevents visitors from touching the walls.

Just a few blocks away, **El Conjunto Monumental de Belén** comprises a 17th-century church and hospital. The church, built of light-colored volcanic rock, features an elaborate baroque facade, the finest example of its kind in Cajamarca. Enter through the door on the right, which passes

■ Students heading home from school in Cajamarca

into a courtyard. Inside the church, you will find a wooden pulpit decorated with carvings of various saints, a gold-plated altar, and a cupola representing the heavens supported by eight stalwart angels. Look out especially for the unusual depiction of an exhausted Christ sitting with his legs crossed, resting his chin on a miraculously double-jointed hand.

Outside, the offices of the **Dirección Desconcentrada de Cultura** overlook the courtyard. On weekdays, the INC acts as a tourist office. At the back of the courtyard, the church-run **Hospital de Varones** (Men's Hospital) has grim, cell-like cubicles, used by patients well into the 20th century, and a small exhibit of early medical instruments. The hospital's kitchen and dispensary once operated along the building's right-hand side. Now this area serves as an **art gallery,** with a permanent collection of vivid, oversize paintings of campesinos and countryside by the famed Cajamarquiño painter, Andrés Zevallos (1916-2017).

The **Museo Etnográfico** stands one block over, in what used to be the church-run Hospital de Mujeres (Women's Hospital). Also built of volcanic rock, the building's facade bears lovely images of flowers, fruits, birds, and angels. A pair of sculpted women with four breasts each, a potent symbol of fertility, adorns the tops of two high pillars on either side of the front door. Inside, the former hospital has a small collection of artifacts labeled in Spanish.

The iron fountain in the center of the spacious **Plaza de Armas** dates to 1692. Typical of the period, the plaza's **cathedral,** begun in the 17th century, boasts a baroque facade and gold-plated altar. Because Spain levied taxes only on completed churches, Cajamarca's cathedral, deliberately built without a tower, was considered "unfinished," thus avoiding the considerable burden of colonial taxation.

Baños del Inca

🖼 Calle Atahualpa
s/n, Baños del
Inca

☎ 076/348–563
or 076/348–
385

💲 $–$$

Opposite, the more interesting church of **San Francisco** (*museum closed Sun., $*) has a museum and catacombs. Although parts of the church predate the cathedral, the tower wasn't added until the mid-20th century. The museum entrance fee includes a guide, who will show you dozens of religious paintings, primarily from the 17th century, in various stages of disrepair or restoration, as well as furniture and clocks from the 18th and 19th centuries. Visitors to the catacombs should be prepared to crouch as they make their way past the burial pits, now empty, and wall niches still used to entomb Franciscan friars.

The delightful chapel of **Capilla de la Dolorosa** adjoins the right side of the church and features a painting of Virgin Mary, her heart pierced by seven swords.

From the plaza's southernmost corner, Calle 2 de Mayo climbs steeply southwest via zigzagging steps to **Cerro Santa Apolonia,** a restful hilltop with a fine view of the city. There you will also find a small chapel, garden, and carved rocks, one of which is said to have been used by Atahualpa as he reviewed his troops.

Around Cajamarca

Most visitors to Cajamarca enjoy a day trip to the **Baños del Inca,** 4 miles (6 km) east of the city along the road to Chachapoyas. Take a bus from the city center. Local entrepreneurs have developed these natural hot springs—where the Inca Atahualpa and thousands of his soldiers camped before their fateful encounter with Pizarro—into a deservedly popular complex that includes public baths, private pools, saunas, and massages. Many travelers linger to eat lunch at one of the fine restaurants nearby, or indulge in an overnight stay at the luxurious resort hotel.

Several other places around Cajamarca are best visited as part of a guided tour offered by one of the agencies clustered around the city's Plaza de Armas. Be aware that most guides do not speak much English and work hard to

■ A family farm in Cajamarca

relate basic information. Half-day tours ($$$) leave daily. The sites all charge nominal entrance fees.

Located in the highlands approximately 12.5 miles (20 km) southwest of Cajamarca, **Cumbe Mayo** (*tours $$*) is an area of naturally eroded geological formations and man-made canals that date back two millennia. The site's petroglyphs, decorating the walls of some nearby caves, are even older. Many travelers make the four-hour walk to this popular pre-Inca attraction, but a guided tour is probably the best way to experience the site since its highlights lie spread out along a dirt road.

The pre-Inca necropolis of **Ventanillas de Otuzco** includes 338 niches carved into a rocky hillside that lies 5 miles (8 km) northeast of town on the road that passes the local airport. Catch a *combi* along Del Batan near the

city center, take a taxi, or walk to the site.

Historians do not know exactly when the niches were built but estimate that the first one likely appeared around 300 B.C., with more added gradually over the next several hundred years. Not every niche could accommodate an entire body; some are just big enough for a partial skeleton.

The **Ventanillas de Combayo,** a similar but larger site 16 miles (26 km) beyond Otuzco, has about 800 niches and is much less often visited by tourists.

Celendín

A good place to take a break during the demanding bus journey along the rough road to Chachapoyas, this sleepy town lies about four hours east of Cajamarca. Here you will find simple hotels and a bright blue **church** on the main plaza. Visit the Saturday market, famed for its exceptional straw hats.

Buses run from Cajamarca to Celendín regularly, but travel onward to Chachapoyas is limited to just a few buses each week. And the trip is difficult. After climbing to about 10,500 feet (3,200 m) outside Celendín, the road drops precipitously to the Río Marañón then labors up to the 12,068-foot-high Barro Negro (Black Mud) Pass, descends to Leymebamba, and finally climbs slowly to Chachapoyas at 7,661 feet (2,335 m). Hardy travelers will be rewarded with a cross section of Peru that few tourists ever see. ■

CHACHAPOYAS REGION

The Amazonas Department is so remote that only one paved highway crosses it, and just two roads reach its small capital city, Chachapoyas. Despite the challenges it presents, this wonderfully exciting region—filled with a wealth of ancient sites hidden among breathtaking cloud forests—will enchant anyone eager to venture off the beaten path.

A traditional hillside home in the Chachopoyas region

Chachapoyas
🗺 Map p. 225

Visitor Information
✉ Iperú, Jr. Ortiz Arrieta 582
☎ 041/477-292

E-mail:
iperuchachapoyas
@promperu.gob.pe

Museo Ministerio de Cultura
✉ Jr. Ayacucho 904
☎ 041/477-045
🕐 Closed Sat.–Sun.

Chachapoyas, or Chacha as the locals call it, is a quiet, pleasant town with some attractive little churches and balconied 19th-century buildings. Although founded in 1538, the city has lost all of its early colonial structures. The **Plaza de Armas** has a tourist office and the small archaeological museum **Ministerio de Cultura.** A 10-minute walk west along Calle Salamanca will take you to **Mirador Guayamil,** which offers good views over the town. Locals enjoy an evening

paseo (stroll) around the plaza in the early evening.

A block north of the plaza, the streets near the market swarm with trucks and *combis* headed to many of the nearby villages. There are few specific bus stops or terminals; ask the friendly locals for information about where and when to pick up transportation.

Outfitters in town (see Travelwise p. 310) can provide you with information and arrange tours to the Gocta waterfall and nearby archaeological areas. Some tours require several days of trekking on foot or horseback. Many agencies in Chachapoyas pool their clients for day trips (and longer) to Kué-lap (see pp. 234–235), by far the best known site.

North & West of Chachapoyas

Karajía: Made of stone in other areas, the larger-than-life-size sarcophagi at **Karajía,** about 30 miles (48 km) northwest of Chachapoyas, were created with mud, wood, and straw. These bullet-shaped structures, each topped with an oversize head colorfully painted with an image of a human face, were placed in ledges high on cliffs, where the dead could "look out" over the valley below. Some of them once held the remains of Chachapoya nobility, but all of the mummies and funerary offerings have long since been removed by *huaqueros* and archaeologists. The sarcophagi remain, however, eerily staring out into the distance in several places. Karajía, with six intact sarcophagi, is the easiest to visit.

Catch a *combi* in Chachapoyas to the hamlet of Luya (*1 hr.*), then hike for three hours to Karajía. Or take another *combi* from Luya to Cruz Pata (*1 hr.*) for a 45-minute walk. Locals in the villages act as guides, or you can join a tour in Chachapoyas. Ask about the numerous other sites in the area.

Catarata Gocta: Farmers living in the remote hamlets north of Chachapoyas knew that the surrounding cloud forests hid the huge **Catarata Gocta**

(Gocta waterfall), but local legends prevented villagers from visiting or even talking about them. Few people outside the area knew about the falls until 2002, when a German hydro-engineer named Stefan Ziemendorff saw them. Four years later his preliminary measurements indicated that the double-tiered falls were an astounding 2,531 feet (771 m) in height, making them the third highest in the world, as claimed by the official Peruvian tourism office.

Numerous measurements taken since 2006 cast doubt

INSIDER TIP:

Hiring a guide or taking a tour is the best way to see the attractions in the Chachapoyas region: Most are poorly signed and not well served by public transportation.

–KENNY LING
National Geographic contributor

---

upon this claim. Nevertheless, the World Waterfall Database rates Gocta Falls among the top ten in the world; other measurements name it the 16th highest. No matter what the rank, the recently discovered falls are a magnificent sight that few people have actually experienced.

Gocta Falls is located on the Río Cocahuayco near the hamlet of **San Pablo,** east of the main

(continued on p. 236)

KUÉLAP

Beautifully located at about 10,000 feet (3,000 m) above sea level, and affording superb views of the surrounding countryside, this ruined city is the largest and most important Chachapoya site. At this elevation, the wet cloud forest supports a rich growth of bromeliads and orchids that plaster its walls. Although it is the most accessible in the region, Kuélap is the least visited of the major archaeological sites in Peru and can still give the traveler that exciting frisson of being an explorer.

■ Rhomboid-shaped stone decorations are a hallmark of Chachapoya architecture.

Although some remnants near the main entrance have been carbon-dated to the sixth century A.D., the Chachapoya constructed most of Kuélap from A.D. 900 to A.D. 1100. The Inca added a few buildings after they conquered the Chachapoya in the 1470s. But for three centuries after the Spanish conquest, this urban citadel lay forgotten by the outside world until its rediscovery in 1843 by a local judge named Juan Crisóstomo Nieto.

The city's main structure is an awe-inspiring **stronghold** almost 2,000 feet (600 m) long and 400 feet (120 m) wide. At times, its massive wall, built of large limestone blocks, reaches more than 50 feet (17.5 m) high, although much of it stands at half that. Each of the wall's three entrances are narrow and highly defensible. The main entrance, still used today, slopes upward and becomes increasingly narrow, with

high walls on either side, ending in a section that allows only one person to pass through at a time. This layout made it easy to fend off would-be attackers, who would soon realize the futility of trying to enter the city.

Inside are the remains of more than 400 **round buildings** once covered with steep, conical thatched roofs. The city's estimated 3,000 inhabitants used many of the buildings as private dwellings. Some of their walls bear tiled friezes in the rhomboid or zigzag patterns that are a hallmark of Chachapoya architecture. Either the Inca or early colonialists during their brief stay added five square, or rectangular, buildings. Charred beams indicate that someone torched the thatched roofs just before the city was finally abandoned.

The inverted, cone-shaped *tintero* (inkwell), with a face carved in bas-relief on its eastern side, has puzzled experts for decades. No one quite understands the function of this 18-foot-high (5.5 m) **temple** located at the south end of the site. Some have proposed that it served as a solar observatory, water tank, and jail, among other possibilities. The recent discovery of offerings nearby has led many archaeologists to consider this Kuélap's main ceremonial temple.

At the other end of the citadel, a 23-foot-high (7 m) D-shaped **torréon** (lookout tower) dominates the wall. In its base, archaeologists discovered a cache of 2,500 rocks that would have been the perfect size to use in slingshots. Most of the site's other buildings still lie in ruins, but many of them are slowly being restored as part of a project begun in 1999.

The 1,000-year-old defensive walls of Kuélap soar over the surrounding cloud forest.

Visiting Kuélap

Most visitors arrive in Kuélap on a guided excursion from Chachapoyas (*$$$*). Alternatively, you can take a minibus, leaving every hour from Terminal Terrestre (*Triunfo 223, Chachapoyas*), to reach the station of the small village of Nuevo Tingo (*$*). The bus managed by the concessionaire of the new cable car that connects to the site leaves from here (*30 mins., bus + cable car, www.telecabinaskuelap.com, closed Mon., $$ including entrance*). At the top, continue for 20 minutes on foot to the fortress. From Tingo it is also possible to continue on foot along a steep path that climbs for 6 miles (10 km) up to Kuélap; allow 4 hours for the ascent and 2 hours for the descent.

■ **Corn of Gold is found along the hillsides and near the hot springs.**

Chachapoyas–Pedro Ruíz road. Because of extremely limited public transportation, visitors must take taxis or a tour to San Pablo, where a two-hour hike along a marked trail will lead you to a good view of the upper falls. To see the falls from the bottom, you'll have to backtrack and take another taxi to the tiny community of **Cocachimba,** then hike about three hours through the cloud forest, where you might see cock-of-the-rock and yellow-tailed woolly monkeys on your way to the falls.

Gran Vilaya: American explorer Gene Savoy first applied the name to the extensive area from the Río Utcubamba west to the Río Marañón. Covering a wide range of ecological zones, Gran Vilaya, which harbors some 30 archaeological sites, is not easily explored and requires fitness, resourcefulness, and patience. It is recommended that you join an organized tour in Chachapoyas. The nice lodge in Choctámal, close to Kuélap, makes for a good starting or finishing point.

South of Chachapoyas

Levanto Area: Catch an early morning ride near the Chachapoyas market for a day trip to Levanto, 14 miles (22 km) south of town. Settled by Spaniards before they moved on to Chachapoyas, this pretty village has an unrestored early colonial church. Once the visit is complete, go down the wild Inca Trail from Levanto to Chachapoyas (*ask for directions on site, or hire a guide*). Allow four to five hours for the return hike back to Levanto.

About a 30-minute walk north of Levanto along the road back to Chachapoyas, the great pre-Inca site of the Chachapoyas culture of **Yalape** features numerous round buildings adorned with friezes. Built after Kuélap, Yalape rivals it in overall size, which you can see in the distance to the southwest.

Revash: The Late Chachapoya funerary site lies near the village of Santo Tomás, 37 miles (60 km) south of Chachapoyas. Constructed of rock and adobe, then plastered and painted pink and cream, the *chullpas* constructed high into the limestone cliffs look like little houses but are, in fact, tombs. Most were ransacked long ago; a few yielded some bones and funerary offerings for archaeologists to study. Revash is difficult to reach; take any bus from Chachapoyas to Leymebamba and get off at Yerbabuena, the turnoff to Santo Tomás. From here, it takes almost four hours to climb to the ruins on foot along marked trails.

Leymebamba: The most important colonial village on the road to Celendín is about 46 miles (75 km) south of Chachapoyas. A half-hour walk by footpath (*ask locals for directions*), or 3 miles (5 km) southwest by the road toward Celendín, will bring you to the **Museo Leymebamba,** a superb community-run rural museum. Its impressive collection includes

more than 200 mummies and their accompanying funerary offerings, all recovered in 1997 from cliffside tombs at Laguna de los Cóndores. Many of the mummies are still wrapped and on display in protective glass cases. The museum also has an orchid garden with more than one hundred species. Regional architectural traditions influenced the construction of the building, which is made of local materials. Simple accommodations are available in town.

The long and strenuous uphill climb from Leymebamba to **Laguna de los Cóndores** takes 10 to 12 hours by foot or on horseback. In 1997, experts removed the mummy bundles from the site's funerary niches and chullpas for safekeeping. Today only the structures remain, perched high on cliffside ledges overlooking the lake. A very simple lodge provides shelter; bring your own food. ■

Museo Leymebamba

Ave. Austria s/n, San Miguel

971 / 104–909 or 971 / 104–907

$$

museo leymebamba.org

Cloud Forests

In Peru, cloud forests are known as *la ceja de la selva* (the eyebrow of the jungle). These narrow strips of land—found on mountainsides rising above rain forest—are dominated by huge trees that soak up moisture from clouds. Constantly bathed in fine mist, cloud forests combine rugged topography with brusque changes in temperature and elevation, the perfect setting for micro-environments within which different species can evolve.

Perched above the Amazon Basin, cloud forests cover much of Peru's eastern Andes and yield some of the greatest

biodiversity and endemism on the planet. This excitingly remote ecosystem teems with myriad birds and beetles, flowers and fungi, mosses and monkeys. It also contributes to Peru's record-producing numbers of wildlife and is where scientists often discover new species.

Cloud forests can be difficult regions to penetrate, primarily because the terrain makes building roads a challenge. However, many loggers have found their way in, methodically working up from river valleys and posing an environmental threat for this very important ecosystem.

Home to indigenous peoples; countless unnamed plants, insects, birds, and animals; and once-in-a-lifetime experiences at a jungle lodge

AMAZON

◼ The brown-throated three-toed sloth (*Bradypus variegatus*) is active in the rain forest by both day and night.

AMAZON

The Peruvian rain forest offers quintessential moments: watching a family of giant river otters playfully frolic outside their den overlooking an oxbow lake; hiking through the "emerald forest" on a spongy jungle path, light softly filtering through branches a hundred feet above your head; and making your way along a steamy jungle river in the late afternoon as the sun slowly sinks over the distant Andes.

Only about one-sixth (16 percent) of the massive Amazon Basin lies within Peru, but the significance and impact of the land comprising its portion of the basin far outweigh the actual size. Stretching back to the early 1970s, Peru has often been more proactive than some of its neighbors in serving as caretaker of the region's flora, fauna, and indigenous peoples. While logging, mining, and slash-and-burn agriculture do take place, this long-term conservation effort is readily apparent in satellite photos of the region: The Peruvian Amazon stands out as a bright green swath against russet-color deforested regions just across the border.

Preserved beneath this verdant canopy is one of the world's great stores of biodiversity, a treasure chest of nature that is far from being fully catalogued or understood. According to the Instituto de Investigaciones de la Amazonía Peruana (IIAP), Peru boasts more bird species (around 1,800) than any other nation on the planet. It's also near the top of the charts in mammals, freshwater fish, amphibians, and flowering plants; about a fifth of the world's butterflies flit through Peruvian forests and glades. Even though these numbers apply to the country as a whole, the Amazon accounts for the vast bulk of these creatures.

No one knows for sure how long humans have occupied the Amazon, but some estimates suggest it is as long as 7,000 years or even more. The ancient Inca actively traded with the Amazon tribes for foodstuffs, bird feathers, jaguar skins, turtle oil, and medicinal ceremonial plants like coca leafs. The Inca may have never reached the Amazon proper, but they certainly knew their way around major tributaries flowing down from the Andes. Their name for the Madre de Dios was Amarumayu (River of the Great Serpent) after the giant anaconda that dwelled along its banks.

Francisco de Orellana, one of Pizarro's officers, led the first Spanish expedition down the Amazon in 1541 to 1542, an epic journey that included a leg down the Río Napo in northern Peru to its confluence with the Amazon River near present-day Iquitos. The Spaniards then ignored the region for the next 300 years. Despite the lure of El Dorado and endless riches, travel through the Amazon was just too difficult and dangerous.

It wasn't until the mid-19th century that Europeans ventured into the region with any consistency in order to tap the native rubber trees, pan for gold in the riverside silt, and harvest the area's seemingly endless forests. Modern times have also brought oil and gas exploration, settlers intent on farming the jungle, missionaries piloting their own small prop planes, and tourists seeking the archetypal Amazon experience that Peru delivers so well. ∎

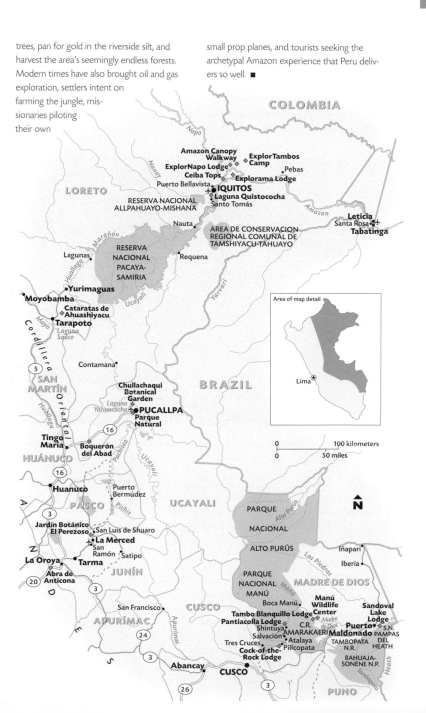

NORTHERN AMAZON

Peru's Amazon lies predominantly in northern Loreto, the country's largest department by sheer extent of its roadless rain forest. Three major rivers, the Ucayali, Marañón, and Napo, form the major tributaries to the Amazon River, but the area is braided by countless smaller waterways—some of which have been barely explored. Peru's most important jungle city is Iquitos, reached only by air or boat.

■ Houses in the rain forest are often elevated to keep animals and floodwater out and open-sided to let in cooling breezes.

Iquitos

🅰 Map p. 241

Visitor Information

✉ iPerú, Jr. Napo 161

☎ 065/236–144

E-mail: iperuiquitos @promperu.gob.pe

Roads from Lima reach Pucallpa on the Río Ucayali, and Yurimaguas on the Río Huallaga, from where travelers continue by iconic decked riverboats (see sidebar p. 246).

Iquitos

With a population of about 450,000, Iquitos is the largest city in the world that cannot be accessed by road. It is a major Amazon port, and boats from here can reach the Atlantic,

although most travelers these days change vessels at the border, where Peru meets Brazil and Colombia. Boat docks are found along Avenida La Marina north of the center (see sidebar p. 246). The airport (*Ave. Abelardo Quiñones км 5, tel 065/260–532 or 065/260–182*) is about 4 miles (6 km) southwest of town. Most flights are to and from Lima, but a few go to Tarapoto or Pucallpa.

Founded as a mission by Jesuits in 1757, Iquitos was a tiny outpost until the 1880s, when the rubber boom transformed it into a bustling city of 25,000 entrepreneurs. During the following decades, some of the city's most opulent buildings were constructed (see Iquitos walk pp. 244–245). After endemic rubber tree seeds were smuggled out of the Amazon to Malaysia, where they were grown in plantations, the bottom dropped out of the rubber market. Iquitos suffered an economic decline after World War I, replacing rubber with less lucrative logging, agriculture, and animal hunting for zoos. The

---

INSIDER TIP:

When packing for the Amazon, along with your binoculars, sunscreen, and bug repellent, take a plastic bag to keep the humidity off your camera electronics.

—ADRIAN COAKLEY
National Geographic photo editor

---

discovery of oil in the 1960s revitalized the area, and the resulting wealth seeded the tourism industry, which remains an economic mainstay today.

Since mototaxis ($) are the favored mode of local transportation, Iquitos is chaotically noisy, but what it lacks in peace and quiet it makes up for with an exuberantly welcoming and laid-back atmosphere.

North of Iquitos: A couple of miles (3 km) north of the center of Iquitos, **Puerto Bellavista,** on the Río Nanay, is a suburban port easily reached by Bellavista–Nanay buses heading north along Próspero. A market here sells freshly grilled fish, and thatched-roofed bars overlook this midsize Amazonian tributary. During the low-water months (June–Nov.), the sandy beaches that appear are popular with the locals.

Boats can be hired from Puerto Bellavista for various short trips, including to **Pilpintuwasi Butterfly Farm,** a 20-minute boat ride away, followed by a well-marked 20-minute walk through Padre Cocha village if the water is low. There are two separate projects here—a butterfly farm where you can learn about lepidopteran life cycles, and a wildlife refuge with a changing family of mammals and birds rescued from poachers. Several monkeys and an anteater wander freely around the grounds, authorized (but not funded) by Peruvian authorities. Contact the farm about volunteer opportunities that may be available here.

Beyond Padre Cocha is the loose-knit village of **San Andrés,** with small communities of Bora and Yagua Indians easily reached by boat from Puerto Bellavista. Tourist-oriented indigenous dances and handicrafts are available.

South of Iquitos: Local buses going south of the city leave mainly from around Plaza 28 de Julio, seven blocks southeast of (continued on p. 246)

**Pilpintuwasi
Butterfly Farm**

✉ Padre Cocha

☎ 935/443–248 (WhatsApp also)

🕐 Closed Mon.

💲 $$

**www.amazonanimal
orphanage.org**

HISTORICAL HIGHLIGHTS OF IQUITOS WALK

The mansions built after the 1880s rubber boom were decorated with opulent *azulejos* (glazed tiles) shipped up the Amazon from Italy, Spain, Portugal, and Morocco. These aging, tiled buildings offer interesting sightseeing and are a source of inordinate pride for Iquiteños. The two streets with the most memories of the past are the waterfront Malecón Tarapacá (locally called the Boulevard) and busy Calle Próspero, parallel to it.

Iquitos's famed Iron House, designed by Gustave Eiffel, is on the Plaza de Armas.

NOT TO BE MISSED:

Plaza de Armas • Malecón Maldonado • Museo Amazónico • Malecón Tarapacá • Belén Market and Belén Village

Begin at the **Plaza de Armas** ❶, just a block east of the riverfront. The roar of mototaxis makes the plaza sound like a racetrack; visit on Sunday morning when a flag-raising ceremony and parade close the plaza to vehicles. Iquitos's **Iglesia Matriz** (Main Church), on the southwest corner, was built from 1911 to 1924 in neoclassical style. The church is also known as Iglesia San Juan Bautista (St. John the Baptist), for the patron saint of Iquitos. The whole region has a huge fiesta on his feast day, June 24.

The plaza's most celebrated structure is **La Casa de Fierro** (Iron House) on the

southeast corner at Calle Putumayo and Próspero. Designed by Gustave Eiffel (see sidebar p. 17) as a prefab building for the 1889 Paris Exhibition, it caught the eye of a rubber baron who had the building dismantled, shipped up the Amazon, and reassembled in Iquitos. What remains today is half of the original; the rest has since been dismantled. The Iron House looks like you might expect—metal sheets bolted together—but its unique origin draws the visitor's attention. It's been occupied throughout its tenure on the plaza as a grocery store, house, factory, restaurant, social club, even the British consulate. In 2007, the second floor became the Amazon Café, where you can now have a drink and look out over the plaza.

On the plaza's northeast corner, the tumble-down Clay House, **Casa de Barro** (*Calle Napo 200–212*), built of adobe, has a wooden balcony, and predates the rubber boom. View it from the outside.

From the plaza, head east one block along Jirón Napo toward the riverfront. You'll pass the **iPerú Tourist Information Office** (*Jr. Napo 161, tel 065/236-144*) on your right. To your left is **Malecón Maldonado ➋**, a riverside pedestrian parkway stretching two long blocks. It has pleasant restaurants and bars with outdoor patios and gets busy on weekend nights with strolling families, plus musicians, magicians, and street performers. Turn right (south) on Malecón Tarapacá, which is gentrified now with small plazas, statues, and a rotunda. One block away, at Malecón Tarapacá 208, is the former **Hotel Palace ➌**, built in 1908 and then the most luxurious hotel in Iquitos. Now it is the site of a military base, its art nouveau flourishes and period azulejos remain.

Another block south is **Biblioteca Amazónica ➍** (*Malecón Tarapacá 354*), adjoined by **Museo Amazónico** (*Calle Tarapacá 386, closed Sun., $*). Built in 1873 and 1863 respectively, these are among the city's oldest buildings, both highly decorated with tiles. The museum features dozens of fiberglass casts made directly from members of Amazonian tribes, standing within period carved wooden walls, ceilings, and furniture. The library archives historical material and is open to the public.

Turn right on Calle Morona for one block. On your left is **Casa Cohen ➎** (*Jr. Próspero & Calle Morona 401*), covered with azulejos, now Los Portales Supermarket. A block farther south, **Casa Morey ➏** (*Calle Próspero 502*) is also worth a look. Six blocks south along Calle Próspero to Calle 9 de Diciembre is the **Belén Market ➐**, stretching

over several blocks to the left, open daily, and best visited in the morning. Here, stalls teem with jungle produce of all kinds, ranging from live turtles to dozens of fish species. Pasaje Paquito is an alley where medicinal herbs, potions, unguents, and talismans are sold. **Belén Village,** behind the market, houses thousands of inhabitants in floating huts, and locals give tours in canoes.

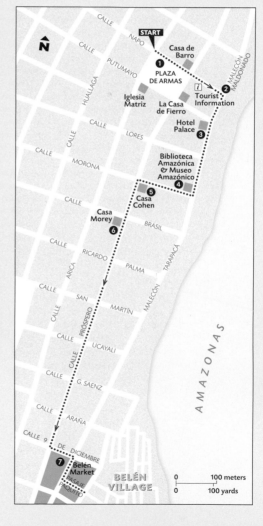

🗺 See also area map p. 241
➤ Plaza de Armas
🕐 45 minutes
↔ 1 mile (1.6 km) one way
➤ Belén Village

EXPERIENCE: Voyaging the Amazon

Three-decked vessels, with the lowest deck reserved for cargo and the upper decks for hammocks and a few cabins, traditionally have plied the wide rivers of northern Peru, linking Yurimaguas and Pucallpa with Iquitos and the Colombian-Brazilian border. They're a great way to get to know the *ribereños* (river dwellers).

Prospective passengers go to the docks where chalkboards indicate when and to where each boat is departing. The destination is reliable; the departure time is not. Sailings are usually postponed by hours or days until the captain gets a profitable cargo. Watching cattle, cars, cement, or sacks of corn being loaded, and later unloaded in tiny communities, is all part of the experience.

Fares are inexpensive, typically less than $10 per day in hammock class, up to $20 for cabin passengers; prices are negotiable. Basic meals are included, but finicky eaters may want to bring their own food. Bottled drinks and snacks are sold aboard. Cabins, usually with four bunks, are tiny and airless; bathrooms, including cold showers, are shared. Hammock passengers bring and sling their own; you can buy one in markets throughout the Amazon. Don't hang your hammock near the engine room (very noisy) or under a light (hard to sleep and attracts insects).

Once you select a boat, go aboard and speak to the captain or owner about a passage and get a receipt. Don't hand over your fare to anyone else! Leave your bags in a hotel until you find the right boat, rather than wandering around the docks with luggage. Then watch your baggage in the chaotic loading and unloading process.

The length of voyages depends on the river's height and whether you are going with or against the current. From Iquitos, allow two to three days to the Brazilian border, three to four days to Yurimaguas, and four to six days to Pucallpa.

Another alternative to the border are open launches, called *rápidos* or *expresos*, charging about $70 for an uncomfortable, all-day trip from Iquitos. If you want more comfort, ships operating out of Iquitos offer luxury travel with naturalist guides, good food, air-conditioned cabins, and higher prices (see Travelwise pp. 310–311).

the city center (ask the friendly locals for the exact bus stops, which are rarely marked), or take one of the ubiquitous mototaxis to visit beyond the city.

A popular local getaway is **Laguna Quistococha** (*$; by mototaxi $$, by bus $*), about 30 to 40 minutes southwest of the city. This jungle lagoon features a zoo of local animals, an aquarium, and a protected swimming area with paddleboats, beachside restaurants, picnic areas, and bars.

The zoo has been much improved in recent years, with reasonably sized enclosures for capybaras, jaguars, monkeys, tapirs, and more. The 6-foot-long (2 m) paiche fish, one of the world's largest freshwater species and currently suffering from overfishing because of the delicacy of its flesh, can be seen in a fish hatchery project which is working to reverse the decline in its numbers.

Marked trails through the zoo and around parts of the lake take visitors past labeled rain forest trees and flowers; one trail ends up at a Tarzan-like rope swing. Though it might not be the "real rain forest," hanging out with local families and getting good views of the zoo animals is a fun way to spend a weekend afternoon.

The village of **Santo Tomás,** about 9 miles (14 km) southwest of Iquitos (but not on the road to Quistacocha), is famed for its ceramics, including pots and masks. There is a beach here in the low water season. Nearby **Santa Clara** has the largest and most popular expanse of white-sand beach from June to October.

Downriver from Iquitos

Away from Iquitos, travelers should make every effort to stay in one of the numerous jungle lodges, most of which are charmingly rustic with kerosene lanterns, mosquito nets, and cold showers. An exception is **Ceiba Tops** (see Travelwise p. 301), one of the few lodges with private hot showers and air-conditioned rooms, located 25 miles (40 km) from Iquitos and run by Explorama, Iquitos's oldest outfitter. They also operate the **Amazon Canopy Walkway** (see sidebar p. 248) and offer increasingly rustic accommodations such as the **Explorama Lodge,** 50 miles (80 km; see Travelwise p. 301) from Iquitos, the **ExplorNapo Lodge,** on the Río Napo, 98 miles (157 km; see Travelwise p. 301) from Iquitos, and open-sided, palm-thatched sleeping platforms, for the more adventurous traveler. At the **ACTS Estación de Campo,** tourists can share the scientific

investigations carried out by researchers. Overnight stays at any of these places can be combined with visits to the Canopy Walkway.

The Río Napo's headwaters are in Ecuador; this was the route that Francisco de Orellana used to descend the Amazon in 1541. It is the major Peruvian tributary into the Amazon downriver from Iquitos. Beyond this confluence is the village of **Pebas** (also

One of the thousands of species of butterflies found in the Peruvian Amazon

called Pevas) about 90 miles (145 km) from Iquitos. Founded in 1735, the oldest town on the Peruvian Amazon now has 3,000 inhabitants, the most famous of whom is Peruvian artist Francisco Grippa, who welcomes visitors to his home/studio/gallery, which towers over the town. Guests interested in his lively, jungle-themed paintings are served beer and bananas by the friendly Grippa, who was born in coastal Tumbes and studied in the United States and Europe, but has made Pebas his home since the early 1990s.

Most of the town's inhabitants are mestizos, members of the four main local tribes—the Bora, Huitoto, Yagua, and Ocaina. Many of the region's villages are home to small groups of one of these tribes. Tours of the villages can be arranged in Iquitos. They welcome tourists with dance performances, and accept both Peruvian and U.S. currency in their crafts markets. Pebas is a regular stop for ships and boats traveling between Iquitos and the border, and has a couple of basic hotels.

At the border with Colombia and Brazil, the biggest town is Colombia's **Leticia,** with many hotels and daily flights to Bogotá. A short walk connects the town with the smaller Brazilian port of **Tabatinga,** from which ships continue down the Amazon to

INSIDER TIP:

Look for barges full of huge jungle trees along Río Ucayali showing evidence of logging. Depending on the season, you may also see locals farming fast-yielding crops on the floodplains.

–NEIL SHEA
National Geographic writer

Manaus (one week), also reached by air from Tabatinga. Ships from Leticia to Iquitos take about three days; uncomfortable *rápido* boats take about 12 hours. Launches connect Leticia with the Peruvian border post at Santa Rosa, where passports are stamped.

EXPERIENCE: Walk Atop the Amazon Canopy

In the 1970s, biologists began exploring the rain forest canopy, experimenting with tree-climbing gear, platforms, and even hot-air balloons to study little-known plants and animals that lived only in the treetops. Two decades later, the naturalists at Explorama's field station began constructing canopy platforms linked by hanging bridges near the **Río Napo,** 100 miles (160 km) from Iquitos. With 14 platforms supporting a series of treetop suspension bridges, the 2,640-foot-long (805 m) walkway is now among the longest anywhere.

The walkway, enclosed in netting, gives superb and unique views of the rain forest canopy undulating off to the horizon. The

opportunities for seeing treetop birds, lizards, and orchids are excellent, but mammal sightings are rare. For many visitors, ascending into the canopy, accessible to anyone able to climb stairs and with a head for heights, is the highlight of their Amazon experience. Binoculars, water, and sun protection are essential.

Since the building of Explorama's Canopy Walkway, Inkaterra has built a seven-platform walkway at its **Reserva Amazónica Lodge** on the Río Madre de Dios near Puerto Maldonado (see p. 264). You can also access the canopy via the platforms at Rainforest Expedition's Posada Amazonas and Refugio Amazonas lodges on the Río Tambopata (see Travelwise p. 304).

Upriver from Iquitos

Diverse ecosystems, including a white-sand jungle, are protected within the 223-square-mile (577 sq km) **Reserva Nacional Allpahuayo–Mishana** (*Carretera Iquitos–Nauta, km 26.5, $$$, overnight $$$$*).

Once reached by boat from Puerto Bellavista via the Río Nanay, it can now be accessed by bus ($) from the new Nauta road, although infrastructure is numerous ongoing Peruvian and international research projects. Further information is available from Instituto de Investigaciones de la Amazonía Peruana (*IIAP, Ave. A Quiñones km 2.5, tel 065/265-515, www.iiap.org.pe*).

The ecologically diverse **Area de Conservacion Regional Comunal de Tamshiyacu–Tahuayo** (ACRCTT) comprises a 1,600-square-mile (2,575 sq km) reserve in the headwaters of Ríos

■ A canopy walkway overlooks the Peruvian Amazon.

limited. (*Carry water and insect repellent.*)

The reserve exhibits a high degree of both endemism and biodiversity. Bird-watchers have recorded almost 500 species here, including the Allpahuayo antbird and Mishana tyrranulet, found nowhere else. Also recorded are about 150 mammal species, including the rare equatorial saki and Lucifer titi monkeys. Herpetologists are delighted by 120 different reptiles, and other animals and plants are equally widely represented. Much more is being discovered in Tamshiyacu and Tahuayo, Amazonian tributaries upriver from Iquitos. In 2003, a rapid biology inventory conducted by Chicago's Field Museum found more species of mammals and trees in the ACRCTT than in any natural area of its size in the world. This superb reserve is best visited by staying at the **Tahuayo Lodge,** 90 miles (145 km) from Iquitos and operated by Amazonia Expeditions (*tel 800/262-9669 U.S., www.perujungle.com*). In 2007, this company opened the Tahuayo River Amazon Research Center

(TRARC), a collaborative conservation project run by Peruvian authorities and Yale University, among other institutions. Lodge guests can visit the research center, as well as take part in adventures ranging from easy wildlife walks or extreme jungle survival courses.

The riverside town of **Nauta** on the Río Marañón lies 7 miles (12 km) from its confluence with the Río Ucayali; where these two rivers meet, the Amazon is formed. Founded in 1830, Nauta has been dragged into the 21st century by the recent construction of a paved road to Iquitos. What used to be a half-day river journey is now barely a two-hour minibus ride, and boat passengers from Yurimaguas often disembark here to shave a few hours. Conversely, folks in Iquitos enjoy the longest road trip available to them—about 63 miles (101 km). Visit the **main church,** which has a superb crucifix carved from a huge tree trunk, and stop by the **bustling market.**

Several minor tributaries join the Amazon between Nauta and Iquitos, and most have lodges built on them. Among the most noteworthy is the **Treehouse Lodge** (*tel 801/797-2777, treehouselodge. com*) inside the Reserva Nacional Pacaya–Samiria. The intimate **Muyuna Amazon Lodge** (*tel 065/242-858, www.muyuna.com*) is 86 miles (140 km) away on the Río Yanayacu, where dolphins abound.

Reserva Nacional Pacaya–Samiria

Reserva Nacional Pacaya–Samiria lies in the wedge of rain forest bounded by the confluence of Ríos Marañón and Ucayali. Covering a massive 8,031 square miles (20,800 sq km), this is the largest reserve in Peru. It is among the best places to see both pink and gray river dolphins (see sidebar right), as well as manatees, giant

A pink dolphin, formally known as the Amazon River Dolphin

river otters, turtles, and numerous reptiles. Birds are varied and abundant, and land mammals such as monkeys, sloths, and various rodents are common. Harder to spot jungle cats and tapirs are also found here.

The reserve is home to more than 40,000 people, who live in about 90 communities. They are freely allowed to fish and hunt, but visitors are strictly controlled; entrance from Iquitos or Nauta is limited and often disappointing. Although the biodiversity is undeniably high, the areas near the edges of the reserve have been hunted out, and you'll need to get deep into Pacaya–Samiria to see abundant wildlife.

The best way to see the reserve is to take a riverboat to **Lagunas,** 10 to 12 hours from Yurimaguas or a day and a half from Iquitos. Here you will find basic hotels; allow at least 5 days to reach good observation areas. Alternately, stay at the **Pacaya–Samiria Amazon Lodge** (tel 065/226–137, www.pacayasamiria.com.pe) on the Río Marañón, 118 miles (190 km) from Iquitos, which is on the outskirts of the reserve and offers day trips by small boat. The entrance ticket to the reserve ranges from $16 to $40 based on the number of days of stay. For detailed information on sustainable tourism, accommodation, and excursions in the reserve, visit www.pacaya-samiria.com.

Moyobamba, Tarapoto, & Yurimaguas

These three small but important cities lie in the Amazon Basin near the end of the paved road which stretches from the Panamericana north of the coastal city of Chiclayo, across the northern Andes, and down to Yurimaguas on the Río Huallaga, with frequent ship connections to Iquitos, two days away. This is northern Peru's main road route.

River Dolphins

Surprisingly, two species of dolphins live in the freshwater Amazon basin. The smaller gray dolphin (*Pontoporia blainvillei*) is found throughout the Amazon and along parts of the Atlantic coast, while the larger pink dolphin (*Inia geoffrensis*) is truly freshwater and found only in the Amazon Basin. A new river species (*Inia araguaiaensis*) was discovered in Brazil's Araguaia river basin in 2014.

Among many Amazon tribes, folklore passed down for generations about the pink dolphin has the common thread of dolphins being transformed into handsome young men. These dolphins are sometimes blamed for an unexpected pregnancy!

In Peru, dolphins are more common in the north, especially where two rivers merge. Many rivers in and near the Reserva Nacional Pacaya–Samiria have good populations. Oxbow lakes such as Lake Yarinacocha near Pucallpa are also good dolphin-watching spots.

NOTE: Moyobamba's bus terminal (Terminal Terrestre), on the southern outskirts of town (Ave. Grau), is served by direct bus lines to Tarapoto, Yurimaguas, Chiclayo, and Lima.

Canoes are the only way to get around the floating houses of Belén in Iquitos.

Moyobamba

🗺 Map p. 241

Visitor Information

✉ Municipalidad, Jr. Pedro Canga 262, Plaza de Armas

☎ 042/562–191

www.munimoyo bamba.gob.pe

Dircetur

✉ Jr. San Martín 301, Plaza de Armas

☎ 042/562–043

www.turismosan martin.gob.pe

Dirección Desconcentrada de Cultura

✉ Ave. Benavides 380

☎ 042/562–281

💲 $

🕐 Closed Sat.–Sun. (small museum and local information)

www.cultura.gob.pe/ es/ddc/san-martin

Moyobamba: The capital of San Martín Department, Moyobamba has a population of about 45,000. Located about 12 hours by bus from Chiclayo, it is the oldest town in the Amazon Basin, having been established as an Inca outpost in the late 15th century. The Spaniards founded a town here in 1542, but nothing is left of those early days due, in part, to devastating earthquakes in 1990 and 1991 that demolished most of the city.

At an altitude of 2,820 feet (860 m), this town has a humid, hot, Amazonian climate, and the exuberant surroundings are rich in flora and waterfalls. Locals call it "the city of orchids" and claim that about 3,500 species have been identified in the area. Several gardens and plantations sell or exhibit orchids, including **Jardín Botánico San Francisco** (*www.jardinbotanico moyobamba.com, $*), reached easily by a 1.25-mile (2 km) mototaxi ride from the center.

Other nearby destinations include **Baños Termales San Mateo,** 3 miles (5 km) south of the city center, especially popular with locals on weekends and accessible by mototaxi (*$*). Of various waterfalls, the most popular are **Cataratas del Gera** and **Cascadas Paccha,** both reachable by a mototaxi ride followed by a short walk through rain forest.

The airport, 2 miles (3 km) west of the city center, has flights to Lima and Iquitos; it's the region's main air gateway. There is no central bus terminal, but many companies have offices on the 6th to 8th blocks of Salaverry, 2 miles (3 km) northwest of the center.

Tarapoto: With more than 100,000 inhabitants, Tarapoto is the largest and fastest growing city in this region. The city is located 70 miles (112 km) beyond Moyobamba by paved Highway 5, which follows the Río

Moyo valley. It was founded on August 20, 1782, a date commemorated by a weeklong annual fiesta.

During the 1970s and 1980s, Tarapoto became a haven for drug runners and terrorists, giving it a reputation for danger. This situation was brought firmly under control during Fujimori's presidency in the 1990s. These days, the only danger you are likely to experience is a headache from the earsplitting noise of the mototaxis circling the central streets. Traveling south along the upper Huallaga river valley to Tingo María is still not recommended, but otherwise Tarapoto has a nascent but welcoming tourism industry.

Whereas Moyobamba is the delicate city of orchids, Tarapoto robustly calls itself "the city of palm trees." Certainly, the surrounding countryside, about 1,000 feet (300 m) lower than Moyobamba, is lush with palms and many other rain forest trees growing in the convoluted landscape of the last and lowest Andean foothills before the flatlands of the Amazon. The beautiful surroundings make up for the lack of interesting sights within the city.

Foremost among the region's lakes is **Laguna Sauce** (also called Laguna Azul), 32 miles (51 km) southeast of town. Getting there involves crossing the Río Huallaga on a raft; all the *colectivo* minibuses and taxis use this method and take about 2.5 hours to get to the lake, where the intrepid traveler will find camping, fishing, canoe rental, and hotel facilities.

Tarapoto is surrounded by dozens of waterfalls, which can be visited through arrangements with local tour agencies (see Travelwise p. 311). The best known is

Tarapoto

⛰ Map p. 241

Visitor Information

✉ Jr. Ramirez Hurtado

☎ 042/526–188

EXPERIENCE: Visiting the Asháninka Indians

The largest Peruvian Amazonian Indian group, the Asháninka (also known as the Campa) has about 55,000 people living in 200 scattered and mainly remote communities. They suffered greatly during the 1980s, when villagers were caught between Sendero Luminoso activities and Peruvian Army reprisals. Now, a generation later, the Asháninka are claiming title to their lands to safeguard them against oil and logging interests, and are opening community-based tourism projects.

Marankiari Bajo (*tel 964/283–802, e-mail: osbaldo62@hotmail.com*), 16 miles (26 km) from La Merced on the paved road to Satipo, is an Asháninka village that welcomes ecotourists and has simple accommodations with local families.

Camping is permitted, and villagers will guide you on walks and boat rides.

Puerto Bermúdez is a village on the Río Pichis-Pachitea about seven hours from La Merced along unpaved roads. Public trucks leave from La Merced Bus Terminal daily around 4 a.m. Puerto Bermúdez has a rarely-used airstrip (for chartered flights). A very poor road, which is impassable in the rainiest months, goes north to Pucallpa.

Expeditions to visit more remote Asháninka villages can be organized at Albergue Humboldt (*tel 963/722–363, e-mail: humboldt49@hotmail.com, www.alberguehumboldt.com*), an inexpensive backpackers' hostel (and the best accommodation available).

Yurimaguas

 Map p. 241

Cataratas de Ahuashiyacu, about 9 miles (14 km) north on the road to Yurimaguas. Nearby, **Laguna Venecia** is a popular place for a swim and the two sights are often visited together.

White-water rafting and canoeing are offered on the Río Mayo and the lower reaches of the Río Huallaga from June to October.

Yurimaguas: This friendly port of about 45,000 inhabitants, 80 miles (129 km) beyond Tarapoto on Highway 13, is literally the end of the road. It is the most northeasterly city in Peru that is connected with the rest of the country by road. The route from Tarapoto has long been famed as a potholed, car-swallowing monster, but paving has now been completed. The journey, which until recently took six to eight hours, can now be done in less than three hours.

Founded by Jesuit missionaries in 1710, the town is named after two Indian groups, the Yoras and the Omaguas, who no longer exist. As the main port on the lower Río Huallaga, with direct fluvial connections to Iquitos, Yurimaguas grew during the rubber boom, and a few buildings on Avenida Arica in the center boast imported tilework dating from that period.

The main reason to visit, apart from getting to the end of the road (and what traveler can resist that often Quixotic challenge?), is to take a boat along the Amazon to Iquitos. The main port is located at the north end of town, with large three-decked vessels leaving several times a week for the voyage that takes from one to four days, depending on type of ferry and river conditions. Fares range from about $30 in a lower deck hammock to $60 for a cramped cabin bunk with basic meals included. Stops are made at Lagunas, which takes 10 to 12 hours to reach (for the Pacaya–Samiria reserve, see pp. 250–251), or Nauta (to catch a bus and reach Iquitos a few hours before the boat), as well as numerous tiny riverside settlements.

Shipibo Indians

Famed for the distinctive geometric designs that they use to decorate their handmade ceramics and textiles, the Shipibo Indians are a matriarchal society. They can be found wandering the streets of central Pucallpa selling their crafts.

Many Shipibo live in open-sided, thatched-roofed houses on stilts in villages such as Santa Clara, San Francisco, and Nuevo Destino, on the Yarinacocha. These villages can be reached in about an hour by boat from Puerto Callao; the first two now are linked by dirt roads to Pucallpa.

Pucallpa & Around

The capital of the Ucayali Department and an important logging and agricultural center, Pucallpa is a growing city of more than 300,000 inhabitants. Though it is hard to imagine that the population in 1900 was only 200 people, the arrival of the highway from Lima in 1930 made this Peru's major Amazonian city after Iquitos. The 158-mile (255 km) section of Highway 16 between **Tingo María** and Pucallpa is mostly paved, with beautiful cloud forest scenery as it climbs from Tingo's 2,150 feet (655 m), over a 5,292-feet (1613 m) pass in the Boquerón del Abad, and down to Pucallpa at 505 feet (154 m). Because of the views and

---

INSIDER TIP:

When visiting Pucallpa, check out the hallucinogenic, *ayahuasca*-inspired works of local artist and shaman Pablo Amaringo. Although he died in 2009, you can still admire his visionary art at *www.ayahuasca visions.com*

–JUSTIN KAVANAGH
National Geographic International Editions editor

---

recent reports of armed holdups of buses at night, the six-hour journey should be done during the day.

Pucallpa is not without its attractions, however. A famed local shaman worth looking up is woodcarver **Agustín Rivas.** His **former family home** (*Calle Tarapaca 861, tel 061/571–834, closed Sun.*) contains an exhibition of his work, carved from natural roots

■ A bromeliad, one of perhaps 80,000 plant species in the Amazon Basin

and branches gathered from the jungle. His art is now on display in many parts of the world, including a figure of Christ at the Vatican. After a wood-collecting accident damaged his hands, obligating him to stop carving, Rivas returned to his childhood home of Tamshiyacu, where he now works as a shaman for the Sacha Runa Collective (*sacharuna.com*).

Parque Natural (*Jose Balta, tel 961/606–042, $*) has a small zoo, botanical garden, picnic area, playground, and lake with rowboats, plus a museum exhibiting fossils and cultural artifacts from local tribes. It can be reached by the airport bus or mototaxi (*$*).

Pucallpa
◬ Map p. 241

Pucallpa's most famed attraction is **Yarinacocha,** a beautiful, oxbow lake 5 miles (8 km) from the city center. Buses along Tarapaca go to **Puerto Callao,** the lake's ramshackle port from where boats can be hired to see dolphins and to visit Shipibo Indian villages

(see sidebar p. 254). Boatmen charge about $5 to $7 an hour in boats accommodating several passengers. Many of these watercraft are locally called *peki-pekis,* because they are powered by what looks like a lawn mower engine attached to a 10-foot-long (3 m) propeller shaft, which makes a characteristic *pekipekipeki* noise.

Navigating the Pucallpa Area

There is no central bus terminal in Pucallpa, but most companies have offices around the 600–800 blocks of Raimondi (*2 blocks SW of Plaza de Armas*).

The airport (*tel 061/595–529*) is located 3 miles (5 km) northwest of town and has daily flights to Lima and Iquitos. Chartered aircraft go to various Amazonian towns.

The boat docks move locations depending on water levels. High water (Jan.–Apr.) brings them to six blocks southwest of the Plaza de Armas; in low water they can be found almost 2.5 miles (4 km) away at La Hoyada, reached by mototaxi.

Puerto Callao has rustic lakeside eateries serving fish and very basic accommodations. A couple of more comfortable, but still simple, lodges are across the lake.

The slow ships taking four to six days to cruise down the **Río Ucayali** north of Pucallpa to Iquitos carry both cargo and passengers. They are an essential link between Iquitos and the rest of Peru. Although there are no luxury cruises in this area, rápidos link the main towns along the river. The most important are **Contamana** and **Requena,** both of which have simple but adequate places to stay and eat for adventurous travelers. Alternately, sling your hammock on the boat in Pucallpa and spend the best part of a week in intimate contact with life on the river all the way to Iquitos.

Chanchamayo Region

This important coffee-growing region is the closest jungle area to Lima, only 180 miles (290 km) and seven hours of ear-popping bus travel away, making it a popular getaway for Limeños looking for a change of pace and climate. It is reached by precipitous paved Highway 20, which climbs steadily from the coast to the cold 15,890-foot (4,843 m) **Abra de Anticona Pass** before continuing on through La Oroya and Tarma (see p. 174) and then plunging down to 2,600 feet (800 m) above sea level at San Ramón. The last hour of the journey is particularly spectacular.

INSIDER TIP:

Pucallpa is a major Amazon gateway.
If you have extra time, visit Parque Natural de Pucallpa.

Its friendly experts can help prepare you for what you'll see in the wild.

—NEIL SHEA
National Geographic writer

Chanchamayo is comprised of two main towns, **San Ramón** and, 7 miles (12 km) farther along the highway, **La Merced,** both with several hotels and restaurants. The **Jardín Botánico El Refugio** in the El Refugio hotel in San Ramón (see Travelwise p. 300) is open to the public. San Ramón has an airport where light aircraft can be chartered for trips throughout the Selva Central (Central Jungle); showing up at the airport in the morning and asking will often result in securing yourself a flight on a space-available basis. La Merced has the central bus terminal.

Some Asháninka (see sidebar p. 253) come to La Merced to sell handicrafts or trade at the daily market. Travelers are more likely to see Asháninka, however, in the village of **San Luis de Shuaro,** 14 miles (23 km) beyond **La Merced** on the road to Puerto Bermúdez, where there is a weekend market. A few miles before this village is the **Jardín Botánico El Perezoso** (Sloth Botanical Garden), where you will find more than 10,000 plant species are represented. ∎

Villagers doing laundry along the Río Yanayacu, an Amazon tributary

SOUTHERN AMAZON

Centered around the watershed of the Río Madre de Dios, the southern Amazon region includes a huge swath of rain forest between the Andes and the Bolivian and Brazilian frontiers. Much of the land is preserved within the confines of national parks and nature reserves, some of which double as refuges for both animals and indigenous peoples.

A black caiman, one of the residents of Manú National Park

The untamed nature of the southern Amazon is what makes it so compelling; the region is one of the best places in all of South America to see rain forest creatures in their natural habitat. The region is one of the holy grails of world bird-watching, especially the riverside clay licks that attract scarlet macaws and the oxbow lakes that provide a habitat for the strange, primitive hoatzin bird. Another oxbow denizen is the giant otter, which lives in family groups in lakeside dens.

But the area is not easy to reach or explore. Other than the newly paved highway between Cusco and Puerto Maldonado, there are a few daily flights from Cusco. While buses from Cusco take 12 hours, boats are often the quickest and easiest way of traveling around the region, but even that mode of transportation has its limitations. Rapids make the Madre de Dios unnavigable for much of its length, effectively dividing the river into upper and lower portions. In fact, a good pair of hiking boots, a responsible and knowledgeable guide, and a sharp machete are the only means to explore much of the region.

Manú National Park

Peru's premier jungle sanctuary is the remote Parque Nacional Manú, which sprawls across 7,260 square miles (18,800 sq km) of rain forest northeast of Cusco. Together with adjacent parks like **Amarakaeri** and the recently established **Alto Purús,** the region is one of the largest protected spaces in the tropics— an area nearly as big as Portugal. The park is accessed via the ragtag riverside village of **Boca Manú,** which lies about an hour by plane or two days by road and river from Cusco. All travel into the national park is by river and overnight accommodation is camping, which visitors must prearrange with a local outfitter before venturing into the park, or in one of the few lodges (see Travelwise pp. 302).

Manú's ecosystems vary from stunted elfin forest and cloud forest around Tres Cruces in the southern part of the park, where the elevation soars to 13,700 feet (4,175 m), to the steamy tropical lowlands along the Río Manú, where the forest canopy reaches high into the sky and the terrain is studded with oxbow lakes that mark the previous path of the river. The biodiversity is astounding. Manú harbors something on the order of a million insect species (most of which are still unnamed), 15,000 different plant varieties, more than a thousand bird species (more than 10

percent of the global total), and 200 mammal species, including spectacled bear, jaguar, giant otter, puma, tapir, and 13 different types of monkey.

More than 30 indigenous groups from at least half a dozen tribes also inhabit the park, including ancient cultivators like the Machiguenga and Piro, and the nomadic Mashco Piro and Yaminahua, who continue to spurn contact with the modern world. So elusive are the Mashco Piro that no one really knows how many there are. Tribal warfare flared inside the park as recently

---

INSIDER TIP:

Tour operators in Lima or Cusco will reserve lodges in the Amazon and often find cheaper flights than you can find on your own.

–MILES BUESST
National Geographic contributor

---

as the 1980s, and government helicopters have sometimes been greeted by a fusillade of arrows. The vast majority of the estimated 2,000 Indians who dwell inside the boundaries of Manú National Park exist on primitive hunting, gathering, and fishing.

Upriver from Boca Manú along the Alto Madre de Dios are several indigenous villages, the site of an old Spanish mission, and a small riverside inn called the **Pantiacolla Lodge** (*tel 084/238–323, pantiacolla.com*),

NOTE: Transportation alternatives around the southern Amazon include:

Flights: Charter— Cusco to Manú Andes Servicios Aeros (*www.losandescorp. com*).

Scheduled—Cusco to Puerto Maldonado Lan Perú (*tel 866/435–9526 U.S. or 01/213–8200 Peru, www.lan.com*)

Buses: Cusco to Pilcopata Unancha (*Calle Huáscar 222, Cusco*)

Gallito de las Rocas (*Ave. Diagonal Angamos 1952, Cusco, tel 084/226–895*)

EXPERIENCE: Take an Amazon River Trip

Unlike the late 19th-century explorer and rubber baron Carlos Fitzcarrald, one doesn't have to haul a steamship up and over a mountain to navigate the Peruvian Amazon. Nowadays there are a number of aquatic options, from the long motorized canoes (*peki-pekis*) that provide "taxi" service along many of the rain forest waterways to the comfortable triple-decked cruise boats that operate out of Iquitos.

Getting to the River

There's nothing quite as exciting as organizing your own Amazon expedition. Several adventure travel companies based in Cusco and Lima offer customized boat trips to Manú National Park via the Río Alto Madre de Dios. In addition to the boat—usually the same type of vessel as the water taxis—the cost includes tents and camp chairs, gas stove and cooking utensils, battery and generator to run the radio, extra outboard engine, plus ample food, drink, and fuel to last however long you wish to stay on the river.

The boats are fast, but not especially comfortable. The wood-slat seats require some padding—like a spare life jacket or a stadium seat cushion. Bring your own sleeping bag, pillow, and towel. The boat engines are also noisy, making earplugs a good investment.

At a minimum, the crew normally entails a boatman/driver (who can do basic repairs if the motor should fail) and a cook to look after the supplies and prepare meals. While not required, a jungle expedition is infinitely better in the company of a naturalist guide who can describe the flora and fauna and find creatures lurking in the foliage.

Those short on time can book a charter flight from Cusco to the dirt airstrip across the river from Boca Manú, just outside the park. A more time-consuming but intriguing method of reaching the river is driving over the Andes from Cusco to a small port called Atalaya on the Alto Madre de Dios. One could conceivably make this drive in a very long single day, but many people choose to break the overland trip into two days, with an overnight stop at Cock-of-the-Rock Lodge.

From the muddy banks of Atalaya, it takes two or three days (depending on stops) to reach Boca Manú, where the Madre de Dios merges with the smaller, wilder Río Manú. You can stay at Pantiacolla Lodge, the private Manú Wildlife Center, or villages like Diamante (see Travelwise pp. 300–304). But going up the Río Manú into the park, choices are limited to a simple lodge or riverside camping.

Typical Day on the River

The day starts with breakfast and hot coffee around the campfire that takes the edge off the surprisingly chilly morning air. After breaking camp and packing up, a full day of exploration begins. This might entail simply cruising up a stretch of river or something more adventurous like hiking along a rain forest trail to an oxbow lake or lagoon to search for creatures like giant otters, macaws, or monkeys.

There's always time for a cooling dip in the river—the piranhas and caimans rarely trouble humans—and lunch is usually eaten in the boat as it moves up- or downstream. Around an hour before sundown, the boatman finds a good place to make camp. In the fading afternoon light, passengers swim, read, or scan the forest canopy with binoculars until dinner is ready.

Incredibly dark Amazon nights bring a different ambience. Clay licks are a good place to watch a tapir, largest mammal of the South American rain forest. Sweeping a flashlight across the water reveals dozens of red eyes—caimans resting on the mudflats or opposite bank. And there is no shortage of sounds: the drone of countless cicadas, primates screaming in the dark, and maybe even the far-off roar of a jaguar.

Asociación Reserva Ecológica Chontachaka (*eco logiaperumanu.com*) offers tours that include a boat trip to the Manú reserve. **Inka Natura Travel** (*tel 971/427-346, www.inkanatura.com*) from $ 1,300 per person (group travel) to $ 4,700 per boat (private excursions).

Small aluminum boats are used to visit Amazonian tributaries.

which arranges hikes into parts of the park that cannot be reached by boat. Pantiacolla Peak, a good three-hour walk from the lodge, offers one of the few viewpoints over this part of the rain forest.

Farther upstream is the sleepy riverside hamlet of **Atalaya,** where the road over the Andes used to end (terminus is now Intahuanía). Although there is public transportation between Atalaya and Shintuya, there is no through bus: One must hop a shared taxi from Atalaya to Pillcopata (*1 hr.*), where there are buses three times a week to Cusco (*9 hrs.*). A couple of hours up the road is the private **Cock-of-the-Rock Lodge** and nature reserve, home of the eponymous jungle bird, known for its bright black-and-red plumage and lively mating dance, which can be viewed from strategically placed blinds (*$$*) along the Río Kosñipata.

Downstream from Boca Manú

are several other private reserves including the **Tambo Blanquillo Lodge** and the long-established **Manú Wildlife Center.** Both lodges feature food and overnight accommodation, as well as canopy towers, nature trails, and oxbow lakes with floating platforms. The center also boasts a tapir lick, where guests can sleep overnight on mattresses inside a blind. Along this same stretch of river is the **Colpa Blanquillo** clay lick, an ocher bank where scarlet macaws and other birdlife gather daily to lick minerals from the cliff face.

Puerto Maldonado

The largest city of the southern Amazon region, Puerto Maldonado (pop. ca. 56,000) lies far downstream from Manú and is actually easier to reach by doubling back through the Andes than trying to proceed down the

(continued on p. 264)

Cock-of-the-Rock Lodge
✉ Petit Thouars 3811, Lima
☎ 01/730-6565
www.inkanatura.com

Tambo Blanquillo Lodge
☎ 01/249-9342 or 987/939-992

E-mail: info@tambo blanquillo.com

www.tamboblan quillo.com

Manú Wildlife Center
✉ Rió Madre de Dios
☎ 971/427-346
www.inkanatura.com

BIRDS OF THE AMAZON

Lists of Peru's birdlife are constantly increasing, as new species are discovered, taxa are rearranged, and birds from other countries are found within Peruvian borders. Ornithologists agree that more than 1,800 species are found here, approximately a fifth of the world's total, a number exceeded only in Colombia. Counting just breeding birds, not migrants or accidentals, Peru leads the world.

Red-and-green macaws (*Ara chloroptera*) are the rarest of the Peruvian macaws.

More than half of these bird species are found in the Amazon, with **Parque Nacional Manú** clearly representing the country's most biodiverse region. Here, at **Cocha Cashu Biological Station,** ornithologists recorded a world-record 331 species in one day without using motorized vehicles. Though this station is for scientists only, travelers can see many of the park's approximately 1,000 birds on camping and lodge-based expeditions. You might notice at the **Limonal Park Ranger Station,** a Muscovy duck, green ibis, rufescent tiger-heron, and white-winged swallow in a single binocular field.

Every trip in the Amazon Basin is accompanied by more sightings of birds than all other vertebrates combined. Even visitors who aren't dedicated birders cannot help but be attracted to the colorful beauty of these animals gliding across the river in front of their boat.

Diversity

Perhaps the most quintessential tropical birds are the related macaws and parrots. In captivity, they live 80 years or longer, and in the wild, they mate for life. They are rarely seen in pairs, however, preferring to fly in loose-knit, loud, raucous flocks. Ranging from sparrow-size parrotlets to 3-foot-long (1 m) macaws, they tend to stay in groups of their own species, but sometimes several different species are found together on clay licks. These mineral-rich, riverside, soil cliffs attract hundreds of macaws and parrots who feed on the salty soil to aid digestion.

The most splendid are the blue-and-yellow macaw (*Ara ararauna*) and the scarlet macaw

---

INSIDER TIP:

When birds awake, they call loudly to protect their territory. Known as the dawn chorus, it's the best time for birding.

–ROB RACHOWIECKI
National Geographic author

(*Ara macao*), both of which sport blue upper wings, and have yellow or scarlet underparts respectively. With their long, tapering tails, strident screams, and slow, deliberate wingbeats, they are unmistakable. Many species, such as the mealy parrot (*Amazona farinose*), are largely green; when a flock lands in a tree they blend in so well they're almost invisible. Others are distinguished by colorful heads or wing bars.

Toucans, with their unwieldy banana-shaped beaks and psychedelic colors, are another emblematic Amazonian group. Among the largest is the 2-foot-long (0.6 m) Cuvier's toucan (*Ramphastos cuvieri*), a black bird with white breast and yellow, red, and blue accents. This toucan often sits solitarily atop the highest rain forest trees, giving loud yelping calls. Smaller toucans, called aracaris, are often seen skittishly crossing rivers, undulatingly swooping across one by one in a ragged column.

The prehistoric-looking hoatzin (*Opisthocomus hoazin*) is the favorite bird of many visitors. A brown, goose-size bird in its own family, the hoatzin has a blue face and punkish long feathers sticking up from its scalp. It's not much of a flyer, preferring to scramble around in the

vegetation of swampy lake banks. Hatchlings have a unique claw on each wing and are able to dive underwater; when threatened, they fall into the lake, swim away, and later clamber back to their nest using the claws. Both their swimming ability and wing claws are lost as they mature.

Road trips to Manú often stop in the low cloud forest, where the Andean cock-of-the-rock (*Rupicola peruviana*), Peru's national bird, can be seen. Males, with bright orange-red plumage topped by a bizarre helmet, gather to dance around a small forest clearing; the best dancers attract a female. These mating-dance areas, called leks, are well established and are used by the birds from season to season.

More than a hundred members of the hummingbird family are found in Peru, many of them in the Amazon. Bearing flamboyant names such as golden-tailed sapphire (*Chrysuronia oenone*), they'll come to lodge feeders or surprise you with a sudden buzz as you hike through the rain forest.

True to its name, the pale-winged trumpeter (*Psophia leucoptera*) has a deep trumpeting call.

Explorer's Inn

✉ 36 miles (58
    km) upriver on
    Rió Tambopata

☎ 082/573–029

**www.explorersinn.
com**

Madre de Dios. There are several daily flights from Cusco (*45 mins.*) as well as long-distance bus service from Cusco (*about 11–12 hrs. on the newly paved road*) and Juliaca (*16–18 hrs. if the road is in good condition*).

Close to the Bolivian border and astride what is now the Inter-Oceanic Highway between Atlantic and Pacific, this is a thriving market and transportation center, as well as a government hub. Populated mostly by immigrants from the Andes and coast, Puerto Maldonado was originally founded as a rubber collecting center at the confluence of the Madre de Dios and Tambopata Rivers. Logging, gold, and Brazil nut booms also came and went. These days the primary sources of income are river transport and ecotourism.

The **Plaza de Armas,** with its trademark clock tower, is worth a stroll, as is the main street **(Calle Leon de Velarde),** where several shops sell locally made hammocks and other rain forest trinkets. Restaurants serve local dishes like *patarashca* (river fish steamed in banana leaves) and *timbuche* (fish soup). A couple of blocks northeast of the plaza, the bustling riverside port area can be picturesque, especially at dusk and dawn when the water turns molten silver. There is another port on the Río Tambopata at the south end of town. But for most travelers, Puerto Maldonado is little more than a transit point between the airport or bus terminal and nearby eco-lodges and nature reserves.

Much of the rain forest to

the south and east of Puerto Maldonado is now parkland, with the popular Reserva Nacional Tambopata–Candamo and huge Parque Nacional Bahuaja–Sonene as the primary units. These parks are contiguous with Bolivia's Parque Nacional Madidi, forming one of the largest protected areas in the entire Amazon region. Researchers have long flocked to the area, but tourism here is still relatively undeveloped.

The jungle starts right outside the city, with the trail head to **Lago Sandoval** approximately half an hour by motorboat from the Puerto Maldonado waterfront.

INSIDER TIP:

Many consider Tambopata's Explorer's Inn ground zero for studies in rain forest ecology. The 138-foot [42 m] Canopy Tower offers great perspectives on the Amazon rain forest.

—KAI TIEDEMANN
National Geographic field researcher

The huge lake is a mecca for bird-watchers but also a great place to spot caimans, capybaras, and giant otters in the swampy lakeside vegetation (*aguajales*). **Sandoval Lake Lodge** (*tel 01/730–6565, www.inkanatura. com*), a joint venture between an international ecotourism company and a group of local Brazil nut farmers, crowns a bluff above the lake. Other main wildlife areas are reached via boat up the Río Tambopata, or the Heath River, that marks the divide between Peru and Bolivia. Most of the jungle lodges are situated along the Tambopata, around two to seven hours by water outside the city. Most visitors book multiday stays at these lodges (see Travelwise pp. 300–304) before arriving in the Amazon. Though local travel agencies in Puerto Maldonado may also be able to help with reservations for the lodges, it's best to plan ahead.

Tambopata National Reserve

The reserve protects a huge swath of lowland rain forest along the south bank of the Río Tambopata. Like Manú, the area is known for its incredible biodiversity—more than 600 bird species, 200 fish species, 160 different types of reptiles and amphibians, and an astounding 1,200 varieties of butterfly. The park is also known for its large jungle animals like capybaras, howler monkeys, tapirs, and caimans, as well as the **Colpa Colorado,** a clay lick where as many as six different bird species (including macaws) gather each morning. Some of the park's scientific research stations, including the **Explorer's Inn** and the **Tambopata Research Center,** double as eco-lodges.

Farther upstream along the Río Tambopata is the expansive **Parque Nacional Bahuaja Sonene,** which can also be reached via the Heath River in the east.

■ **One of the eco-lodges in Tambopata National Reserve**

This is a completely different type of Amazon landscape—Peru's only tract of tropical humid savanna, intermittently flooded grasslands similar to the Pantanal of Brazil. While much of the wildlife is the same as that found in the rain forest zone, the **Pampas del Heath** also attracts far different creatures, like the giant anteater, marsh deer, and maned wolf. Other than a couple of lodges along the Heath River, the massive park offers little in the way of visitor facilities, apart from the **Heath River Wildlife Center,** located about five hours by boat from Puerto Maldonado. As the Heath marks the international frontier, visitors will need to obtain a Bolivian visa before cruising up the river. ■

Tambopata Research Center

✉ Upriver on Río Tambopata

☎ 984/705-266

www.perunature.com

Heath River Wildlife Center

✉ Downriver on Heath River

☎ 084/255-255

www.inkanatura.com

TRAVELWISE

Riders astride a *caballo de paso*

PLANNING YOUR TRIP

When to Go

Most travelers plan to visit the highlands, if for no other reason than to see Machu Picchu. The best time to go is during the highland dry season (late May–mid-Sept.), although these are the coldest months with freezing nighttime temperatures in the Andes. Unfortunately, the dry season coincides with the June to August high season, when North Americans and Europeans take their vacations, and when Peruvians celebrate some of their most important holidays. So, to avoid the crowds and increased hotel rates, consider traveling in the shoulder seasons of May and

September to November. In the wettest months (Jan.–Apr.), bus transportation may be delayed or canceled, and hikers will find muddy trails, wet tents, and cloudy skies.

In the Amazon rain forest, by definition, it rains all year. The north is generally wetter than the south, especially from October to May, but it rarely rains for very long, even on the wettest days. Torrential tropical downpours lasting an hour or two are the norm; then the sun comes out again.

The coast generally suffers from a gray mist known as *garúa* from May to December, except in the north where it is sunny and hot year-round. Limeños flock to the beaches from Christmas to Easter.

What to Take

Pack as you would for travel to any wet, hot place if you are going to the Amazon, but if you are exploring the highlands, bring warm clothes as it can freeze at night. You can buy almost anything in Peru's major cities, so you can usually replace something you forget. As always, make sure that you bring all prescription medications in your carry-on luggage.

People with big feet will find it difficult to buy shoes larger than American size 12, so they should bring all the footwear they need. To save space when packing, wear your hiking boots onto the plane if you are planning a trek. In the event of an emergency in Peru, all camping gear can be rented but you'll want your own comfortable, broken-in boots for those long trails. In order to take advantage of the discounts, especially in the Cusco area, students must show a valid university card and identity document.

Insurance

Most Peruvian health-care providers expect to be paid at the time of service, and it is up to you to get reimbursed through your health insurance after a medical procedure. They won't do it for you, as in U.S. emergency rooms or doctors' offices. You'll need to call your insurance company as soon as possible from Peru, not after you return. Be aware that some policies exclude certain "dangerous" activities such as mountaineering or white-water rafting.

Consider having a provision to be flown back to your home in an emergency, as this contingency may be the most expensive part of a hospitalization.

Entry Formalities

Visas

Citizens of most countries require only a valid passport to enter Peru as a tourist. Upon arrival, you will fill out an immigration form that you should keep inside your passport, as you will need to return it to authorities upon departure. Both the form and your passport are stamped with your date of entry and the number of days that you are permitted to stay. Tourists are automatically given 183 days. If you need more, ask the official for as many days as you need. It is not possible to extend this amount within Peru. For longer stays, you can travel to a neighboring country and return, to begin the process again.

Customs

Peruvian customs formalities are normally straightforward. Visitors can import about 3 quarts (3 L) of alcohol, 20 packs of cigarettes, and up to $300 in gifts duty free. Laptops, cameras, musical instruments, and sports equipment for personal use are permitted duty free. It is illegal to export pre-Columbian artifacts or items that are more than a hundred years old from Peru. It is legal to take coca-leaf tea out of Peru but not to import it into most other countries (including store-bought boxes of coca-leaf tea bags).

Peru Embassies

United States
Embassy of Peru
1700 Massachusetts Ave., NW,
Washington, D.C. 20036, US
Tel 202/833–9860
Fax 202/659–8124
E-mail: digitaldiplomacy@
embassyofperu.us
www.embassyofperu.org

United Kingdom
Embassy of Peru
52 Sloane St.
London SW1X 9SP, UK
Tel 020/7235–3802
E-mail: postmaster@peru
embassy-uk.com
www.peruembassy-uk.com

Canada
Embassy of Peru in Ottawa
130 Albert St., Ste. 1901
Ottawa, Ontario
Canada, K1P 5G4
Tel 613/238–1777
Fax 613/232–3062
E-mail: embassy@
embassyofperu.ca
www.embassyofperu.ca

Australia
Embassy of Peru
40 Brisbane Ave., Ground floor
Barton ACT 2600
Canberra, Australia
Tel 02/6273–7351
E-mail: embassy@embaperu.
org.au
www.embaperu.org.au

Vaccinations

No vaccinations are officially required to enter Peru (see pp. 272–273).

HOW TO GET TO PERU

By Airplane

From North America, you'll find direct, nonstop flights to Lima from Miami, Los Angeles, Dallas, Houston, Atlanta, New York, and Toronto with several airlines. From Europe, nonstop flights depart from Amsterdam, Madrid, and Paris. Flying from the U.K. or other European cities requires changing flights.

All intercontinental flights to Peru land in Lima's modern Jorge Chavez International Airport (LIM; *tel 01/517–3100, www.lima-airport. com*). From the luggage claim/ customs area, it is only a few steps to taxis, so you don't really need a porter.

Taxis from the airport to hotel areas cost up to $25 if you grab the first one outside of the arrivals gate. Walk a few steps outside and into the taxi parking area for much cheaper fares, especially if you speak Spanish and are used to bargaining.

Hotel buses from the airport charge about $9 but can be slow as they stop at several hotels en route. Allow an hour to get from the airport to most hotels during the day when traffic is heavy. There is only one good hotel next to the airport itself (Wyndham Costa del Sol Lima Airport).

The airport has one terminal building with two levels. Domestic Arrivals is on the ground floor at the right end (as you enter from outside) and International Arrivals is at the left end. Both Domestic and International Departures lounges are entered through the same gate upstairs on the first floor. There is a left luggage deposit next to the domestic flight arrivals area. A food court, restaurants, and shops are available, with a limited 24-hour selection. Money-changing facilities and ATMs are inside the International Arrivals area and in several other parts of the airport. Internet service is available upstairs over Domestic Arrivals.

By Boat

Cruise lines sailing along the Pacific coast stop at the ports of Salaverry (for Trujillo), Callao (for Lima), and San Martín (for Pisco), and shore excursions can be arranged. Companies sailing along the Peruvian coast include Princess Cruises, Holland America, Cunard, Norwegian, and several others.

Travelers sailing along the Amazon from Brazil can enter Peru at the tri-border with Colombia and continue to Iquitos.

By Bus

Because of the Darién Gap, an area without roads on the border between Panama and Colombia, it is not possible to drive or take buses from North or Central America to South America. Buses enter Peru via paved highways at six main border crossings: two from Ecuador, one from Chile, two from Bolivia, and one from Brazil.

The busiest Ecuador/Peru border crossing is at coastal Aguas Verdes/Huaquillas (Hwy. 1A, Panamericana Alternativa), with another important entry point at highland Macará/La Tina (Hwy. 1, Panamericana). From Chile, near the coast, the Panamericana joins Arica with Tacna. The two main border crossings from Bolivia are via Desaguadero (Hwy. 3) at the south end of Lake Titicaca, and at Copacabana/Yunguyo via the Strait of Tiquina in the middle of the lake; both of these link up with the Bolivian capital of La Paz. There is busy and frequent bus traffic at all these points.

It is also possible to enter Peru from Brazil via the newly-paved Interoceanic Highway from Assis Brasil to Iñapari and on to Puerto Maldonado. There are also a few minor entry points via unpaved roads at other places on the Ecuadoran, Chilean, and Bolivian borders.

GETTING AROUND
By Airplane

Lima is by far the most important hub of Peru's domestic airline network. Usually, flying from one major Peruvian city to another will entail a transfer in Lima. There are no flights linking the northern Amazon (Iquitos) with the southern Amazon (Puerto Maldonado or Cusco) without returning to Lima.

Airlines often overbook, and in Peru, it is important to reconfirm flights 72 and 24 hours in advance, especially during the peak season. This can be done on the phone, in a local office, through the travel agent where you bought your ticket, or even by your hotel on request. Airport lines can be slow and checking in two hours early is recommended.

Peru has a well-deserved reputation for short-lived airlines due to financial, political, and legal problems. The three main airlines from the 1980s and 1990s no longer exist in the 21st century; the best ones today may be gone tomorrow. That said, LATAM Perú, part of the international LATAM chain, has provided the most reliable, extensive, and comfortable service in recent years; Star Perú and LC Perú have also been fairly reliable, albeit with services to a limited number of cities. Peruvian Airlines is a relative newcomer, but has been well received. It has no sales offices and sells tickets either online or through bank deposits. Aerocondor suspended its flights in 2008. Other airlines have yet to prove themselves over the long haul. New ones pop up

like mushrooms and last for a few months or years.

Local travel agents have information about these options.

LATAM Perú
José Pardo 513, 1st floor
Miraflores, Lima
Tel 01/213–8200
www.latam.com

LC Perú
Ave. Pablo Carriquirry 857
San Isidro, Lima
Tel 01/204–1313
www.lcperu.pe

Peruvian Airlines
Tel 01/716–6000
E-mail: reservas@peruvian.pe
www.peruvian.pe

Star Perú
Comandante Espinar 331
Miraflores, Lima
Tel 01/705–9000
www.starperu.com

By Bus

Bus service throughout Peru is frequent and reasonably efficient. Few Peruvians own cars, so traveling by bus is the most common way of getting around.

Costs on long-distance buses range from about $1 to $3.50 per hour of travel, depending on class of service. The cheapest buses make frequent stops, take meal/toilet breaks at simple roadside restaurants, and are slow. Better buses have bigger seats, onboard toilets, and snacks included in the price. The best services, often called *bus-cama* (bus-bed), have deeply reclining seats and extra legroom. Some have two decks, with the most expensive lower-deck seats stretching out almost into beds.

In some major cities (e.g., Cusco, Arequipa, Puno), there are bus terminals that service dozens of small and large bus companies and many destinations. Within the terminal, each company has a ticket counter, often with people shouting out the destination of their next departure. It's a lively scene with snack bars, pharmacies, ATMs, telephones, even Internet cafés on the premises. In other cities, including Lima, Trujillo, and Huaraz, bus companies have their own individual terminals at different addresses.

Tickets can be bought just before departure time, in advance at the terminals, or from some travel agents for a commission. Buying advance tickets gives you the opportunity for best seat selection. Front-row seats are often separated from the driver's cab by a glass wall and curtain, so your feet are up against a bulkhead and you can't see anything. The back row is the bumpiest and next to the toilet.

When traveling at night, beware of theft, on all services. Don't fall asleep with unsecured hand luggage in an overhead rack or with an expensive camera loosely around your neck. Locked bags tagged with a ticket and stowed by bus company employees in the luggage compartment are normally safe.

Around major holidays, Peruvians love to travel and visit families, buses are booked up days in advance, and fares can double. Think ahead, especially around Christmas, Easter, and Fiestas Patrias. Conversely, discounts are offered during slow travel periods.

Expect delays if traveling in the highlands during the rainy months, especially when visiting remote towns that are reached by unpaved roads. Even good, paved highways can occasionally be closed for days by landslides.

Of Peru's hundreds of bus companies, the following are among those with the best reputations and services. Phone numbers and addresses are for Lima ticket offices, but reservations can be made for travel from other cities. Several also have more than one office

or terminal in Lima. Always check where your bus will leave from—it might not be from where you buy the ticket. If a company isn't on this list, it does not imply its services should be avoided.

Cruz del Sur
Javier Prado Este 1109
La Victoria, Lima
Tel 01/311–5050
www.cruzdelsur.com.pe
This is the best and most expensive company, with several classes of service. You can safely book online. Routes along the coast and from Lima up to Cusco, Puno, Ayacucho, Huancayo, Huaraz, and Cajamarca.

Websites for the following companies provide information about itineraries, destinations, and fares. Booking online can be problematic, but it is improving. During busy periods, extra departures may be available that are not listed online.

CIVA
Paseo de la República 575
La Victoria, Lima
Tel 01/418–1111
civa.com.pe
The coast, Cusco, Puerto Maldonado, Chachapoyas, and Tarapoto.

Movil Tours
Javier Prado Este 1093,
La Victoria, Lima
Tel 01/716–8000
www.moviltours.com.pe
The north coast, Huaraz, northern highlands, Arequipa, Tarapoto, and Yurimaguas.

Oltursa
Aramburú 1160
San Isidro, Lima
Tel 01/708–5000
www.oltursa.com.pe
The coast, Cusco, Huaraz.

Ormeño
Javier Prado Este 1059

La Victoria, Lima
Tel 01/472–1710
The coast, Cajamarca, Huaraz, Cusco, and Puno.

Tepsa
Javier Prado Este 1091
La Victoria, Lima
Tel 01/617–9000
www.tepsa.com.pe
The coast, Cajamarca, Cusco, Nazca.

Palomino
Luna Pizarro 343
La Victoria, Lima
Tel 01/202–0600
www.grupopalomino.com.pe
Cusco, Abancay, and Andahuaylas.

Transportes Linea
Paseo de la República 979
La Victoria, Lima
Tel 01/424–0836
www.linea.pe
Luxurious bus line offering various on-board comforts and VIP waiting rooms at the terminals. Among the destinations: the northern coast, Huaraz, and Cajamarca.

By Car
Car rental companies have offices in Lima and major Peruvian cities. Rental rates are higher than in Europe or North America, and rarely include unlimited *kilometraje* (mileage in kilometers).

Generally speaking, car rental is a poor idea. In Lima, as in other cities, traffic is very congested and frightening to negotiate for the uninitiated. Outside of Lima, distances are great, roads are potholed and poor, road signs are erratic at best, and driving at night is not recommended because of slow-moving, poorly lit vehicles mixed with fast-moving buses. It's cheaper to take buses between cities and then use taxis locally. Hiring a taxi for a whole day is often cheaper than renting a car.

If you insist on renting a car, you can use your own driver's license. You'll need a passport and credit card, and should be over 23 (25 in some cases). Peruvians drive on the right. Be aware that if you are involved in an accident that causes an injury, you might end up in jail for several days or even weeks. In Peru, you are presumed guilty until proven innocent.

Therefore, it's recommended that you take out local insurance that provides coverage for third-party injuries when you rent a car. Park cars overnight in guarded lots (better hotels have them). During the day, car minders miraculously appear if you park on the streets; these folks generally watch the same patch day after day, and tipping them to watch your car is expected.

Police can and will pull over drivers for any reason. Even if you have done nothing wrong, they can inspect your passport and driver's license. Sometimes, police may suggest that there is a problem, hoping that a bribe will be offered to solve the problem. Locals simply smooth things along by slipping the officer S/10 ($3–$4) with their papers. If you politely and steadfastly refuse, you'll eventually get your papers back.

Roads & Maps: All paved and many unpaved roads have highway numbers that can be seen on some maps. Highway numbers are infrequently posted on roadsides, and locals don't normally refer to numbers. Instead, a road is known by its destination, as in *la carretera a Cusco* (the road to Cusco). The main exception is La Panamericana, which roughly follows Peru's coast from Ecuador to Chile via Lima. Although labeled Highway 1 on maps, it is always called La Panamericana.

By Taxi

Meters are not used so a price should be negotiated with the driver before you get in. Short rides in most cities are about $1 (S/3), except in Lima where a short ride is usually S/5. Longer rides go up to S/12. Tipping isn't necessary.

Taxis aren't regulated, so anyone can moonlight by sticking a red-and-white "Taxi" sticker in a car window. Usually, the biggest problem with these drivers is that they don't know their way around very well; rarely, they might attempt to drive visitors down an unlit street to rob or possibly rape them. It's not common, but it happens. Single women often prefer to use registered taxis that can be called from hotels, restaurants, or other sites of interest. These cost twice as much but are safe.

By Train

Train service is limited to frequent daily services from Cusco to Aguas Calientes for Machu Picchu (see p. 139), three trains a week between Cusco and Puno, and occasional trains from Lima to Huancayo (see sidebar p. 170).

By Water

Two remarkably different regions of Peru require boat travel: Lake Titicaca, the world's highest navigable lake, and the vast lowland rain forested Amazon Basin. In both cases, there are no regularly scheduled departures or itineraries, but many boats ply these waters every day. Uber-adventurous travelers just show up at the docks of Puno or Pucallpa and hop on board with the locals. Guidance is provided in the Lake Titicaca (see pp. 112–117) and Amazon (see pp. 238–265) sections of this book. Travelers with a keen sense of organized adventure can arrange their departures with tour operators listed in the Outdoor Activities section (see pp. 306–310).

PRACTICAL ADVICE

Addresses

Many street addresses are followed by "s/n." This notation means *sin numero* (without a number), for buildings that don't have a number.

Communications

Internet Access: Internet access is cheap and easy. Throughout the country, you'll find Internet cafés charging as little as 1 to 2 nuevos soles per hour to get online. Just look for Internet signs. Many Internet cafés have cheap "net-to-phone" capabilities. Online access in hotels can be expensive, especially in higher-price business hotels, many of which now offer Wi-Fi.

Mail: The post office is privately run by Serpost (*www.serpost.com.pe*). The service is reliable but pricey—mailing a postcard anywhere in the world costs 6 nuevos soles. Post offices (*correos*) are found in every town, and postcards are sold by vendors near the entrance.

Telephones: Public telephones work with either phone cards or coins. There are many brands of phone cards (*tarjetas telefónicas*), most of which require a lot of dialing. Call the card company, wait for a reply (in Spanish), enter your pin number (which you scratch off the card), listen to another message telling you how much money you have left on the card, and then dial the number. A few phones take electronic chip cards, which are easier to use but harder to find.

Peru's 24 departments have three-digit area codes beginning with 0, with the exception of Lima, which has an 01 area code. When dialing within a department, don't use the area code.

If calling Peru from abroad, dial the international access code 0051, followed by the area code without the 0, followed by the number. Peruvian numbers have seven digits in Lima, six digits outside of Lima, and nine digits (all beginning with 9) for cell phones. These numbers have no area codes. The cell phone system changed from seven to nine digits in mid-2008, so you may find older brochures, books, etc., with seven-digit cell numbers. They won't work.

To call abroad from Peru, the international access code is 00, and English-speaking international operators can be reached on 108.

Conversions

In almost all cases, Peru uses the metric system. The main exception is with gasoline, which is dispensed in U.S. gallons.

Electricity

Peru uses 220V, 60HZ AC electricity. Outlets have two holes and accept both flat and round prongs.

Etiquette & Local Customs

Peruvians consider politeness to be important. Beginning any transaction with *buenos días* (good morning) or *buenas tardes* (good afternoon) is always a good start. Men who are friends often give one another an *abrazo* (a back-slapping hug) on meeting or parting. Women exchange "air kisses" with almost anyone. After a meal, a belch is considered the height of rudeness.

Holidays

The country shuts down on the following national public holidays. Businesses, including most museums and some restaurants, close. Buses are overcrowded, and buying tickets well in advance is recommended.

January 1–New Year's Day
March/April–Easter Thursday, Good Friday
May 1–Labor Day
July 28–29–Fiestas Patrias (National Independence)
August 30–Saint Rose of Lima
October 8–Battle of Angamos
November 1–All Saints' Day
December 8–Feast of the Immaculate Conception
December 25–Christmas Day

Other important holidays, such as Cusco's Inti Raymi (*June 24*), are held only in specific areas, and not throughout the country.

Liquor Laws

The drinking age is 18, although IDs are almost never checked. *Ley seca* (dry law) requires that all alcohol sales in restaurants, bars, and shops are banned on the Friday, Saturday, and Sunday around a government election.

Media

The main Peruvian newspapers are the conservative *El Comercio* (*elcomercio.pe*) and the investigative *La República* (*larepublica.pe*). The best weekly news magazine is *Caretas* (*caretas.pe*).

The Peruvian TV channels, all in Spanish, have a rather bland range of programming. Most hotels offer cable TV, which includes international news networks such as CNN and BBC.

Money Matters

The Peruvian currency is the nuevo sol (S/), divided into 100 céntimos. It comes in bills of S/10, 20, 50, 100, and 200, and coins of S/5, 2, 1, and 1, 5, 10, 20, and 50 céntimos.

The nuevo sol has oscillated in value between S/3 and 4 per U.S. dollar. The U.S. dollar is the favored foreign exchange currency, followed by the Euro. Other hard currencies such as pounds sterling and

Canadian dollars can be exchanged at fewer places and at poor rates.

The best places to change money are *casas de cambio* (exchange houses), which are faster than bureaucratic banks, stay open longer (including weekends), and give better rates. Lima, Arequipa, and Cusco have the best exchange rates. It is essential that cash dollars are in excellent condition; worn, slightly torn, and heavily marked notes are not accepted.

Cajeros automáticos (ATMs) are found outside banks and inside major airports, bus terminals, and shopping malls. They are linked with Plus (Visa), Cirrus (Master-Card), and sometimes American Express. Expect to pay a fee both in Peru (2 percent–10 percent) and at your home account. Withdrawals can be received in either nuevos soles or dollars.

Tarjetas de crédito (credit cards) are widely accepted in better hotels, restaurants, and businesses, but a surcharge of up to 7 percent is often charged.

Opening Times

Banks are generally open from 9:30 a.m. to 5 p.m., Monday to Friday, and some on Saturday mornings. Casas de cambio are often open until 8 p.m. or later weekdays and are open on weekends. Businesses and government offices often close for lunch.

Few shops are open on Sundays. Lima and other major cities have a few 24-hour supermarkets and at least one all-night pharmacy. Cab drivers are good sources of information about late night openings.

Religion

Peru's population is more than 80 percent Roman Catholic, although Protestant, Mormon, and Evangelical missions are making inroads. Many indigenous inhabitants, while outwardly Catholic, combine a degree of traditional animism or worship of natural phenomena such as mountains and plants with their church-based religion.

Time Differences

Peru is five hours behind Greenwich Mean Time (GMT) and the same as Eastern Standard Time (EST). Daylight Savings Time is not used.

Tipping

Cab drivers are not tipped. In better restaurants, a 19 percent tax and 10 percent tip is included in the bill, and adding another 5 percent is normal. In inexpensive places, tips aren't included or expected, but giving the waiter a few coins is a nice gesture. Tip porters 50 cents per bag. Tip tour guides about 1 to 2 dollars per person for a short tour and about 5 to 10 dollars for a full day (more if it's a private tour). On a trekking trip, tipping porters, mule drivers, cooks, and guides is expected. Allow about 15 percent of their wages.

Travelers With Disabilities

Facilities for travelers with disabilities are few and far between. Only a few first-class hotels have rooms that are wheelchair accessible. Peruvians with disabilities generally rely on others to help them get around.

Visitor Information

The national tourism website (www.peru.travel) is quite good for information about Peru's sights and cities. Its tourist information offices, called iPerú, are found in major cities.

For detailed information on hotels and restaurants visit www.andeantravelweb.com/peru.

EMERGENCIES
Crime & Police

Peru is relatively safe if you take sensible precautions—avoid displays of wealth, don't wear expensive jewelry, and carry money hidden in a money belt or pouch. Divide your funds into more than one place to avoid losing it all if you are pickpocketed, which is by far the most likely crime to happen. Keep expensive cameras inside a bag when you aren't using them. Make photocopies of the ID pages of your passport and carry those—leave your passport in the hotel safe when you don't need it. Avoid ill-lit streets at night, and be alert to your surroundings. See other precautions suggested above under the Bus, Car, and Taxi sections (see pp. 268–270).

The police are generally helpful, although in large cities, it's best to deal with the *policía de turismo* (tourist police), who wear white shirts and blue uniforms (as opposed to the dark olive uniforms of ordinary police). Some of them speak English.

Embassies
U.S. Embassy

Ave. La Encalada block 17
Surco, Lima
Tel 01/618–2000
E-mail: lima_webmaster@
state.gov
pe.usembassy.gov

U.K. Embassy

Ave. José Larco 1301
Torre Parque Mar, 22nd fl.
Miraflores, Lima
Tel 01/617–3000
www.gov.uk

Canadian Embassy

Bolognesi 228
Mirafores, Lima
Tel 01/319–3200
E-mail: lima@international.gc.ca
www.canadainternational.gc.caa

Australian Embassy

Ave. La Paz 1049
Miraflores, Lima
Tel 01/630–0500
E-mail: consular.lima@dfat.
gov.au
peru.embassy.gov.au

Emergency Telephone Numbers

The following numbers work in most of Peru:

Ambulance 106
Red Cross 115
Fire 116
Police 105
Tourist Police Headquarters
01/460–1060
iPeru 24-hour Travelers' Hotline
01/574–8000.

Health

Peru has good private clinics and doctors, which are better than state-run hospitals. Pharmacies sell most of the medicines that you use at home, many without a prescription. If you get sick, ask your hotel for a recommendation for the best local facility. Calling the iPeru 24-hour Travelers' Hotline (*tel 01/574–8000*) also yields good recommendations.

Vaccinations are not normally required for entry into Peru. Vaccinations against hepatitis A and typhoid are recommended, as is yellow fever if traveling to jungle regions. Hepatitis B vaccination is suggested for extended independent travel. Malarial tablets are suggested for jungle trips, although sleeping under a fan or mosquito net, wearing long sleeves and pants especially during the dawn and dusk mosquito hours, and using repellent is adequate protection. Altitude sickness can be a common complaint when flying from coastal Lima to highland towns (see sidebar p. 129 in the Cusco chapter for further information.)

Tap water is not safe to drink. Always use bottled or boiled water, widely available throughout Peru. In better restaurants, ice is made with boiled or filtered water; in cheap places, ice is best avoided.

Lost Property

Most insurance policies require a police report to be made within 24 hours of a loss. The tourist police are the most efficient choice in major cities. Otherwise, go to the local police station and be prepared to speak Spanish or bring a translator. If your passport is stolen, contact your embassy.

FURTHER READING

An exhaustive list is impossible, but the following titles will offer the traveler some interesting perspectives on Peru.

Nonfiction

History & Archaeology

Lost City of the Incas by Hiram Bingham (1948)
The Ancient Kingdoms of Peru by Nigel Davies (1998)
The Conquest of the Incas by John Hemming (2003)
The Last Days of the Incas by Kim MacQuarrie (2007)
The Incas and Their Ancestors by Michael Moseley (1993)
Machu Picchu: Exploring an Ancient Sacred Center by Johan Reinhard (2007)
Art of the Andes: From Chavín to Inca by Rebecca Stone-Miller (1995)

Outdoors

Trekking in Peru: 50 Best Walks and Hikes by Hilary Bradt and Kathy Jarvis (2014)
Classic Climbs of the Cordillera Blanca by Brad Johnson (2003)
Running the Amazon by Joe Kane (1989)
Trekking in the Central Andes by Rob Rachowiecki, Greg Caire, and Grant Dixon (2003)
Touching the Void by Joe Simpson (2004)

Nature

A Field Guide to the Birds of Peru by James Clements and Noam Shany (2008)
Neotropical Rainforest Mammals by Louise Emmons and Francois Feer (1990)
Tropical Nature: Life and Death in the Rainforests of Central and South America by Adrian Forsyth and Ken Miyata (1987)
A Neotropical Companion by John Kricher (1997)
The Ecotravellers' Wildlife Guide: Peru by David Pearson and Les Beletsky (2001)
A Parrot Without a Name: The Search for the Last Unknown Birds on Earth by Don Stap (1990)
Peruvian Wildlife: A Visitor's Guide to the Central Andes by Barry Walker (2008)
Birds of Machu Picchu by Barry Walker and Jon Fjeldså (2015)

Travel

Along the Inca Road: A Woman's Journey into an Ancient Empire by Karin Muller (2001)
Keep the River on Your Right by Tobias Schneebaum (1994)
Cochineal Red: Travels through Ancient Peru by Hugh Thomson (2006)
A Sacred Landscape: The Search for Ancient Peru by Hugh Thomson (2007)
The White Rock: An Exploration of the Inca Heartland by Hugh Thomson (2003)
Cut Stones and Crossroads: A Journey in the Two Worlds of Peru by Ronald Wright (1984)

Fiction

At Play in the Fields of the Lord by Peter Matthiessen (1965). This was adapted as a 1991 epic drama directed by Héctor Babenco.
Aunt Julia and the Scriptwriter by Mario Vargas Llosa (1977)
The Time of the Hero by Mario Vargas Llosa (1963)

Culture & Miscellaneous

Weaving in the Peruvian Highlands: Dreaming Patterns, Weaving Memories by Nilda Callañaupa Alavarez (2007)
Exploring Cusco by Peter Frost (1999)
Woven Stories: Andean Textiles and Rituals by Andrea Heckman (2003)
The Exotic Kitchens of Peru by Copeland Marks (1999)
Eat Smart in Peru: How to Decipher the Menu, Know the Market Foods and Embark on a Tasting Adventure by Joan Peterson and Brook Soltvedt (2006)
The Peru Reader: History, Culture, Politics by Orin Starn, Carlos Iván DeGregori, and Robin Kirk, (1995)

HOTELS & RESTAURANTS

Peru has a huge array of places to stay and eat, and the selection given in this book is limited to some of the best or most interesting choices in varied price ranges. Many other places are good, and lack of a listing in this section does not mean you should not stay or eat there.

Hotels

Accommodations vary widely in Peru, ranging from plenty of scruffy places with shared showers charging as little as $3 per person to a few luxury establishments where a room may cost more than $1,000. This extensive range reflects the fact that Peru is a Third World country with world-class attractions and visitors of all economic backgrounds. The cheapest places are used by ordinary Peruvian travelers and backpackers; they aren't necessarily bad if you only need four walls and a lumpy bed. However, they are not listed in this guide, although in small, remote villages, they may be all that is available.

Hotels of all kinds have varied titles including *hospedajes, pensións, hostals, hosterías, casas, posadas, albergues, residenciales,* lodges, inns, hotels, or they may have no designation. Hospedajes and pensións are nearly always the cheapest places, with shared bathroom facilities. The other names are ambiguous and can vary greatly in quality; a hostal can be a comfortable hotel while a hotel can be a seedy dive, for example, so don't go by the tag. Campgrounds for RVs or tents don't exist in cities, and are limited to tenting areas in some national parks and scenic areas.

A single room is a *habitación simple.* A double room with two beds is a *habitación doble,* while a double with one large bed is a *habitación matrimonial.* First-class hotels may have two large beds in a double room, or one king. All rooms in this section have

private bathrooms with hot showers, with the exception of some jungle lodges where showers are room temperature—which is not exactly cold.

It is strongly recommended that reservations are made during the June-to-August peak season, especially in the most popular tourist towns of Cusco, Aguas Calientes, Arequipa, and Puno. Demand is very high nationwide during Christmas, Semana Santa (Holy Week before Easter), and Fiestas Patrias *(on and around July 28–29).* Local fiestas, especially Inti Raymi in Cusco, fill hotels to capacity. Hotels may charge a premium over the peak-season rate during these times.

Reservations can be made online, by phone, or through a travel agent. Walk-in rates are often cheaper.

Travelers in less visited towns such as Chachapoyas, Piura, Huancayo, or Ayacucho will find that rates are usually much lower than in the most popular towns.

First-class hotels charge an 18 percent tax to Peruvian guests, but this is waived for foreign visitors who must present a passport and immigration form when checking in. The hotel will make photocopies of these. A 10 percent service charge may be added to the most expensive hotels; this amount is not refunded. Cheaper hotels don't bother with the tax.

Restaurants

Restaurants in hotels may often be your best choice in smaller towns that don't have restaurants listed below. Budget travelers should always inquire

about *el menu del día* (menu of the day), which is a set two- or three-course meal at half the price of eating à la carte, and is often tasty and of excellent value.

In many towns, finding early breakfast is a problem, as restaurants rarely open before 8 or 9 a.m. Better hotels often include breakfasts (served early) in their rates. Hotel breakfasts vary from toast, jam, and a hot beverage to a huge buffet spread, depending on the price of the establishment. Hotel restaurants will normally be happy to serve the general public.

Dinners tend to be served late. If you arrive at a fine restaurant at 7 p.m., it may be empty, but most tables will be taken by 8:30 p.m. In the heavily toured towns, earlier meals are served in restaurants frequented by travelers. Until recently, most better restaurants had nonsmoking and smoking areas; now, many of the best places are completely nonsmoking or have smoking sections in separate rooms.

Restaurant Prices

It is impossible to give precise price ranges for restaurants because menus vary tremendously in price to provide diners with an affordable range. First-class restaurants will have a few entrees around $10 (baked chicken, lasagna) and some well over $20 (lobster, fine steak cuts, gourmet *novo-Andino* plates) on the same menu. Combine this with less expensive set meals, and price bands become no more than very approximate guidelines for meals.

🏨 Hotel 🍴 Restaurant 🛏 No. of Guest Rooms 💺 No. of Seats 🅿 Parking 🕐 Closed 🛗 Elevator

PRICES

HOTELS

The cost of a double room with private bath and hot water in the peak season is given by **$** signs. Low-season rates can be considerably lower, especially in the cheaper establishments.

$$$$$	Over $200
$$$$	$100–$200
$$$	$50–$100
$$	$25–$50
$	Under $25

RESTAURANTS

The average cost of a two-course meal for one person, without tax, tip, or drinks is given by **$** signs.

$$$$$	Over $30
$$$$	$21–$30
$$$	$14–$20
$$	$7–$13
$	Under $7

Credit Cards

Visa (V) and MasterCard (MC) are widely accepted; American Express (AE) and Diners Club (DC) are accepted less often. Discover cards are almost never accepted. To cover bank fees incurred, most establishments will add a surcharge averaging 7 percent when you pay bills with credit cards. Cash is preferred.

Listings

Hotels and restaurants are organized by chapter, then by price, then in alphabetical order, with hotels listed first followed by restaurants.

Inquire in advance at the hotel or restaurant concerning what disabled-access facilities they offer.

▶ LIMA & ENVIRONS

Hotels

▦ MIRAFLORES PARK HOTEL
$$$$$
MALECÓN DE LA RESERVA 1035, MIRAFLORES
TEL 01/610–4000
E-MAIL: PERURES.FITS@ORIENT-EXPRESS.COM
www.mirafloraspark.com.pe
This is Lima's most upscale hotel, with ocean views from most of its opulent suites (about $500) and a presidential suite for $3,500 if you're feeling flush. The modern, glass high-rise is furnished with antiques and 20th-century art. The top floor features an infinity pool. Services such as a bath butler and spa are extra indulgences for the tired businessperson and luxury traveler alike.
🛈 80 🅿 ⬛ 🅂 🅂 ⬛ 🄰
🅂 All major cards

▦ WYNDHAM COSTA DEL SOL LIMA AIRPORT
$$$$$
ELMER FAUCETT S/N, AEROPUERTO JORGE CHAVEZ
TEL 01/711–2000
wyndhamhotels.com
This modern hotel adjoins Lima's international airport and is the only good hotel close to the airport. It has all the facilities that business travelers need while waiting for their connecting flights.
🛈 192 🅿 ⬛ 🅂 🅂 🄰
🄰 🅂 All major cards

▦ SONESTA HOTEL EL OLIVAR
$$$$–$$$$$
PANCHO FIERRO 194, SAN ISIDRO
TEL 01/712–6000
E-MAIL: RESERVAS.SONESTA OLIVAR@GHLHOTELES.COM
www.sonesta.com/Lima
Across from peaceful Parque El Olivar, full of centuries-old olive trees, this hotel is favored by businesspeople and travel groups. Guests have complimentary use of the adjoining fitness club, among the nation's best. Rates include an extensive buffet breakfast in the Peruvian-international restaurant and welcome drinks in the comfortable bar; there is also a fine Japanese restaurant. Well-equipped rooms vary in size; huge suites feature sauna and Jacuzzi.
🛈 134 🅿 ⬛ 🅂 🅂 ⬛ 🄰
🄰 🅂 All major cards

▦ CASA ANDINA STANDARD MIRAFLORES SAN ANTONIO
$$$$
28 DE JULIO 1088, MIRAFLORES
TEL 01/241–4050
E-MAIL: CAC-SANANTONIO @CASA-ANDINA.COM
www.casa-andina.com
Part of a local chain covering most of southern Peru, this hotel offers natural color environments, spacious, well-lit rooms with cheery bedspreads, modern bathrooms, and a buffet breakfast included in its rates. There are three other (more expensive) Casa Andinas in Miraflores.
🛈 52 🅿 ⬛ 🅂 🅂
🅂 AE, MC, V

▦ HOTEL ANTIGUA MIRAFLORES
$$$$
GRAU 350, MIRAFLORES
TEL 01/201–2060
E-MAIL: RESERVAS@ANTIGUA MIRAFLORES.COM
www.antiguamiraflores.com
This mansion set in a charming garden features elegant public areas. Rooms and suites (some with kitchenettes and Jacuzzi) have comfortable colonial-style handcrafted

furniture, attractive art and antiques, sumptuous tiled bathrooms with tubs, and Wi-Fi. English-speaking staff caters to guest needs. Rates include breakfast.

🛏 39 🅿 🆂 🅰 AE, MC, V

🛏 HOSTAL EL PATIO
$$$

DIEZ CANSECO 341–A, MIRAFLORES
TEL 01/444–2107
E-MAIL: RESERVA@HOSTAL ELPATIO.NET
www.hostalelpatio.net

Varied comfortable rooms, some with kitchenettes, surround flowery patios in a charming, clean, and quiet spot near the heart of bustling Miraflores. Cheerfully decorated with Peruvian crafts, this is a colorful place to recharge. The helpful owner speaks English, and continental breakfast is included in the rates.

🛏 23 🅿 🆂 MC, V

🛏 HOSTAL TORRE BLANCA
$$$

AVE. JOSÉ PARDO 1453, MIRAFLORES
TEL 01/447–3363 OR 447–0142
E-MAIL: RESERVAS@TORRE BLANCAPERU.COM
www.torreblancaperu.com

The "white tower hostal" is actually a comfortable, mid-range, four-story, salmon-colored hotel near the coast. A coastal cliff-top path is just a minute's walk away. Rooms are bright and modern with mini-fridges; suites have a balcony. Some staff speak English, and guests with reservations can arrange an inexpensive airport pickup ($6). Public areas have free Wi-Fi, and there is a courtyard. The hotel overlooks a small, grassy park, but rooms with park views may be too noisy for sensitive ears.

🛏 30 🅿 🆂 All major cards

🛏 HOTEL SAN ANTONIO ABAD
$$$

RAMÓN RIBEYRO 301, MIRAFLORES
TEL 01/447–6766
E-MAIL: RESERVAS@HOTEL SANANTONIOABAD.COM
www.hotelsanantonioabad.com

Rates include buffet breakfast and airport pickup, making this hotel a good value. Rooms are good size and look out on a grassy patio. The helpful staff arranges tours, and Wi-Fi is available throughout the hotel.

🛏 24 🅿 🆂 All major cards

🛏 HYATT CENTRIC SAN ISIDRO LIMA
$$$

AVE. JORGE BASADRE 367,
TEL 01/611–1234
www.hyatt.com

Luxurious and elegant hotel of the international Hyatt chain located in the San Isidro district. It houses the Isidro Bistró Limeño restaurant, the result of the experience of Chef Carlos Testino, who offers his guests French-Peruvian bistro-style cuisine. In the evening, go up to the hotel terrace to enjoy a cocktail at the counter of the futuristic Celeste Solar Bar, with a beautiful view of the city.

🛏 250 🅿 🆂 🅰 All major cards

🛏 LA POSADA DEL PARQUE
$$

PARQUE HERNÁN VELARDE 60, SANTA BEATRIZ
TEL 01/433–2412
E-MAIL: POSADA@INCA COUNTRY.COM
www.incacountry.com

Located on a quiet cul-de-sac off the first block of Petit Thouars, this attractive, homey hotel is well located for getting to downtown

PRICES

HOTELS

The cost of a double room with private bath and hot water in the peak season is given by **$** signs. Low-season rates can be considerably lower, especially in the cheaper establishments.

$$$$$	Over $200
$$$$	$100–$200
$$$	$50–$100
$$	$25–$50
$	Under $25

RESTAURANTS

The average cost of a two-course meal for one person, without tax, tip, or drinks is given by **$** signs.

$$$$$	Over $30
$$$$	$21–$30
$$$	$14–$20
$$	$7–$13
$	Under $7

Lima. Rooms have art deco touches, hot water, and cable TV. A sitting room decorated with colonial art features a DVD player, and the dining room has free continental breakfast and Internet booths. The staff is helpful, and some speak English.

🛏 11 🅿 🆂 None

Restaurants

Lima's best restaurants are more expensive than in the rest of the country, but there are hundreds of cheap, simple, unassuming places that aren't listed here. Even in the better restaurants, ask for *el menu del día;* these set meals are often not on the menu but represent great deals if you are watching your budget. Call ahead if dining on Sundays; some places may be closed or do not serve dinner.

ASTRID Y GASTÓN
$$$$$
PAZ SOLDÁN 290,
SAN ISIDRO
TEL 01/442–2777
www.astridygaston.com
Favorite restaurant for many connoisseurs, opened by the famous Peruvian chef Gastón Acurio. A few years ago he moved to Casa Moreyra, in a hacienda built between the 17th and 18th centuries. In the kitchen the chef directs a team of talented young people; the service is impeccable and the wine list well elaborated. The German Astrid takes care of the rich menu of generous and irresistible desserts. The selection of *pisco* at the bar is unmatched.

🛏 120 🅿 🚭 ❄ 🔌 All major cards

EL SEÑORIO DE SULCO
$$$$–$$$$$
MALECÓN CISNEROS 1470,
MIRAFLORES
TEL 01/441–0183
www.senoriodesulco.com
With ancient Peruvian motifs in the dining room and lovely sea views from the terrace, this is an inviting place. The menu is evenly balanced between traditional seafood and meat dishes rooted in coastal culture. A lunch buffet features dozens of items for you to sample. Desserts include homemade ice creams with traditional and exotic flavors, including coca leaf.

🛏 180 🅿 🚭 ❄
🔌 All major cards

HUACA PUCLLANA
$$$$–$$$$$
GENERAL BORGOÑO CUADRA 8,
MIRAFLORES
TEL 01/445–4042
www.resthuacapucllana.com
The restaurant overlooks the eponymously named archaeological site, atmospherically illuminated at night. The faux-rustic building has attractive colonial-style

furniture and a charming patio next to the huaca. Food is *nuevo-criollo,* tending toward meats with some seafood plates.

🛏 160 🅿 🚭 ❄
🔌 All major cards

LA TIENDECITA BLANCA
$$$$
LARCO 111, MIRAFLORES
TEL 01/241–1124
www.latiendecita
blanca.com.pe
Café restaurant inspired by Swiss culinary specialties. Excellent for breakfasts or light meals. They serve excellent coffee and delicious desserts. Do not miss the fondue, served late hours.

🛏 100 🚭 🔌 All major cards

SAQRA
$$$$
LA PAZ 646, MIRAFLORES
TEL 01/654–8884
www.saqra.pe
This cheerful space, decorated with mischievous devils (*saqras* in Quechua) and other art, offers a good variety of Peruvian seafood, meats, vegetarian pastas, and desserts prepared in the popular and contemporary *novo-Andino* style. Their chocolate truffles with banana crème brûlée have been much praised. Most seating is indoors but a terrace beckons on a sunny day. An unusual feature is that almost anything in the house is for sale—so if you like your plate or your chair, a lamp or a piece of art, you can probably buy it.

🛏 85 🕐 Closed Sun.
🚭 🔌 All major cards

LAS BRUJAS DE CACHICHE
$$$–$$$$$
BOLOGNESI 472,
MIRAFLORES
TEL 01/447–1133
www.brujasdecachiche.
com.pe

The name means "the witches of Cachiche," a village on the south coast, and the restaurant works to prepare coastal dishes, some using ancient recipes. The result is an exceptional menu of the best of *criollo* cooking, ranging from potatoes stuffed with shellfish to beef heart kebabs to kid goat stew. The menu helpfully pairs plates with local and imported wines. There is also an extensive lunch buffet.

🛏 200 🅿 🚭 ❄
🔌 All major cards

WA LOK
$$$–$$$$
PARURO 878
TEL 01/427–2750
www.walok.com.pe
Located in the heart of Lima's Chinatown, it is one of Peru's finest high level *chifas.* You can taste traditional dishes such as the typical dim sum and Peking duck, which you will not find in other ordinary Chinese restaurants. Wa Lok, given its popularity, has also opened a new place on Angamos Oeste 700, Miraflores.

🛏 60 🚭 🔌 None

ANTICA PIZZERIA
$$–$$$
2 DE MAYO 732, SAN ISIDRO
TEL 01/422–7939
www.anticapizzeria.com.pe
Red-and-white tablecloths, wooden benches, and candles honor Antica's Italian origins. Wood-fired pizzas, calzones, homemade pastas, and reasonably priced wines are satisfying features. There's also a branch in Barranco at Alfonso Ugarte 242.

🛏 100 🅿 🔌 All major cards

COMO AGUA PARA CHOCOLATE
$$–$$$
PANCHO FIERRO 108,
SAN ISIDRO
TEL 01/222–0174
If you saw the movie *Like*

Water for Chocolate, you'll know that this is a Mexican restaurant—the best one in Lima. Meals are as authentic as you'll find so far south of Mexico City. The ambience is cheerily colorful, and imported tequila livens up the evening.

🔟 90 🅿 ⬛ ♿ All major cards

🍴 HAITI
$$–$$$
DIAGONAL 160, MIRAFLORES
TEL 01/446–3816
www.haitimiraflores.pe
The outside patio overlooks the north end of Parque Central, and this age-old but modernized café is a prime people-watching and meeting place. While the meals are nothing special, locals come to schmooze over pisco sours or coffee while grabbing a sandwich. It's open very late.

🔟 100 🅿 ⬛ ⊘ Closed Sun.
♿ All major cards

🍴 LA RED
$$–$$$
LA MAR 391, MIRAFLORES
TEL 01/441–1026
www.lared.com.pe
A modern-style redbrick exterior opens into airy gray-and-white stone walls set off by bamboo walls and skylights in this *cevichería.* A full menu features *criollo* food, but the seafood is well presented and an excellent value. Open since 1981, it has a well-deserved following of locals in the know. Open 12 p.m. to 5 p.m. only.

🔟 130 🅿 ⬛
⊘ Closed Tues.
♿ All major cards

🍴 SEGUNDO MUELLE
$$–$$$
CONQUISTADORES 490,
SAN ISIDRO
01/635–5555
www.segundomuelle.com
This two-story restaurant

overflows at lunchtime (the only time it's open) and is famed for its award-winning mixed shellfish in three-pepper-sauce ceviche prepared by a chef who claims to be a seafood fanatic. The fabulous menu wanders wildly over the world's oceans, with Japanese and Italian influences. There are other San Isidro branches at Canaval y Moreyra 605, and in Barranco on Costa Verde at Playa las Cascadas.

🔟 200 ⬛ ♿ MC, V

🍴 T'ANTA
$$
PANCHO FIERRO 115, SAN ISIDRO
TEL 01/421–9708
tantaperu.com
Opened by Astrid (of Astrid y Gastón), this deli café has modern furniture and glassed walls for good lighting. Innovative sandwiches and rich desserts are the main offerings (which you can have to go), but locals manage to draw out a visit into a long conversation over the excellent coffees. There are also nine other branches in the city, including one in the historic center (*Pasaje Nicolás de Rivera 142*) and another in Miraflores (*Ave. Vasco Núñez de Balboa 660*).

🔟 90 🅿 ⬛ ♿ All major cards

▶ SOUTHERN LOWLANDS

CHALA

🏨 HOTEL PUERTO INKA
🍴
$$$
PANAMERICANA SUR KM 610
TEL 054/752–079
E-MAIL: PUERTOINKA@PUERTO INKA.COM.PE
www.puertoinka.com.pe
On an attractive bay near the Inca ruins, this place offers basic meal plans or à la carte

choices, kayak and Jet Ski rentals, horseback riding, camping, and swimming. There is a disco on weekend nights.

ℹ 38 🅿 ⬛ ♿ AE, MC, V

HUACACHINA

🏨 HOSTERÍA SUIZA
$$$
MALECÓN DE HUACACHINA 264, ICA
TEL 056/238–762
E-MAIL: RESERVAS@HOSTERIA SUIZA.COM.PE
hosteriasuiza.com.pe
Descendants of Swiss immigrants run this lakeside hotel and speak German, French, Italian, and English. Sand dunes overlook a quiet garden that surrounds the large pool set behind an attractive house. The rooms are cozy with views over the lake, garden, or dunes. Dorms

and apartments with kitchen are also available. Breakfast is included.

ⓘ 23 🅿 Ⓢ ⃗
🅢 All major cards

🏨 HOTEL MOSSONE
$$$
LAGUNA DE HUACACHINA, ICA
TEL 056/213–629
www.dmhoteles.pe
A hotel since 1891, this spacious desert hacienda has public areas with cast-iron chandeliers and a classic wood-paneled bar that hark back to earlier times. The rooms feature parquet floors and elegant simplicity. Internal garden, restaurant with terrace, meeting rooms, and swimming pool.

ⓘ 39 🅿 Ⓢ 🅒 ⃗
🅢 All major cards

🏨 EL HUACACHINERO
$$
AVE. PEROTTI,
BALNEARIO DE
HUACACHINA, ICA
TEL 056/767–608
E-MAIL: INFORMES@
ELHUACACHINERO.COM
www.elhuacachinero.com
This small hotel has simple, functional rooms overlook-ing a pool and bar shaded by palm trees, and is the best value budget option. The hotel has a fleet of green dune buggies, and staff can arrange all local tours.

ⓘ 21 🅿 Ⓢ ⃗ 🅢 None

ICA

🏨 HOTEL LAS DUNAS
$$$$
LA ANGOSTURA 400
TEL 056/256–224
E-MAIL: RECEPCION@LAS
DUNASHOTEL.COM
www.lasdunashotel.com
A sprawling property with large, modern rooms, many with garden views, and good service make this the area's best hotel. Tours to

fly over the Nazca Lines or visit dunes by jeep, sand-board, mountain bike, or horseback, can be arranged. A planetarium ($$$) gives multilingual shows about the Nazca Lines and stars.

ⓘ 146 🅿 Ⓢ 🅒 ⃗ 3
📺 🅢 All major cards

MOQUEGUA

🏨 HOTEL EL MIRADOR
$$$
ALTO DE LA VILLA S/N
TEL 053/461–765
www.dmhoteles.pe
On a hill 2 miles (3 km) from the city center, El Mirador has excellent views and is Moquegua's best hotel. Bun-galows and cheaper standard rooms are available. Breakfast is included in the rates.

ⓘ 28 🅿 ⃗ 🅢 All major cards

NAZCA

🏨 HOTEL NUEVO
CANTALLOC
$$$$
CANTAYO
TEL 056/522–264
E-MAIL: RESERVAS@HOTEL
NUEVOCANTALLOC.COM
www.hotelnuevo
cantalloc.com
This tranquil hotel within a restored 19th-century hacienda by the Cantallo aqueducts boasts the largest rooms in the Nazca area. From the entrance to the spacious, plant-filled garden with an oversize pool, the Nuevo Cantalloc exudes relaxation. Walk or horseback ride around the magnolia-scented grounds while enjoy-ing the company of peacocks, ostriches, deer, and alpacas. Note that the Cantallo aque-ducts are 4 miles (7 km) away from Nazca, so you'll need a car or taxi to get into town.

ⓘ 40 🅿 Ⓢ 🅒 ⃗ 📺
🅢 All major cards

🏨 CASA ANDINA
NASCA
$$$
BOLOGNESI 367
TEL 056/523–563
www.casa-andina.com
This is the best hotel in central Nazca, featuring a restaurant with Peruvian and international dishes and a small, shaded, circular pool. Three floors of quiet, comfortable, modern, colorfully decorated rooms overlook a long, airy, palm-filled courtyard. All tours are arranged.

ⓘ 60 🅿 Ⓢ 🅒 ⃗
🅢 All major cards

🏨 HOTEL ALEGRÍA
🍽 $$
LIMA 166
TEL 056/522–702
E-MAIL: INFO@HOTEL
ALEGRIA.NET
Three floors of spick-and-span rooms surround a pleasant garden anchored by a kidney-shape pool. Over the past two decades, Hotel Alegría has developed a reputation as a great place to meet other travelers wanting to share costs on local tours. The hotel's travel agency is happy to oblige.

ⓘ 60 🅿 Ⓢ 🅒 🈁
🅢 All major cards

🏨 HOSPEDAJE YEMAYA
$
CALLAO 578
TEL 056/523–146
E-MAIL: NASCAHOSPEDAJE
YEMAYA@HOTMAIL.COM
This friendly, helpful, family-run hostal attracts backpackers and budget travelers. Simple but bright tiled rooms have hot showers, and public areas include Wi-Fi and a laundry machine. A rooftop terrace is available for drinks and snacks.

ⓘ 14 🅿 🅢 MC, V

🅢 Nonsmoking 🅒 Air-conditioning Ⓢ Indoor Pool ⃗ Outdoor Pool 📺 Health Club 🅢 Credit Cards

PARACAS

SOMETHING SPECIAL

HOTEL PARACAS RESORT
$$$$$
PARACAS 173
TEL 056/581–333
www.marriott.com
For decades, this was the well-known but aging Hotel Paracas, the grand dame of the south coast. The 2007 earthquake destroyed it, and the newly rebuilt Hotel Paracas Resort is a luxurious upgrade, the Marriott chain, firmly retaining its position as the best coastal hotel south of Lima. The new hotel enjoys the same location on one of the prime spots on the Peruvian coast, just in front of the Paracas National Reserve. The extensive property boasts beach access and local boat tours, two swimming pools, and a spa with beauty treatments (Peruvian cocoa skin packs) and a relaxing water circuit. The **Ballestas restaurant** offers a mixed Peruvian-Mediterranean menu while the **Chalana Restaurant**, located on the hotel's private dock, offers freshly caught fish. The area for the little ones makes the structure suitable for families, although it remains a first choice among newlyweds looking for privacy. Flights over the Nazca Lines and 4WD dunes tours are arranged.
(i) 120 P S S ⊠ All major cards

HOTEL EMANCIPADOR
$$$$
PARACAS 25
TEL 056/532–818
E-MAIL: PARACAS@HOTEL EMANCIPADOR.COM
www.hotelemancipador.com
A renovated complex with rooms and housing units with kitchen that can accommodate up to 6 people. Parking, swimming pool, green areas, and breakfast included. All bedrooms have sea-view balconies.
(i) 49 P ⊠ ⊛ MC, V

HOTEL MAR AZUL
$$
ALAN GARCÍA B–20, LOTE 20, CHACO
TEL 056/534–542
E-MAIL: INFO@HOTEL MARAZUL.COM.PE
www.hotelmarazul.com.pe
This is a good-value budget hotel one block from the beach and four blocks from the dock. It features bright, tiled rooms with large windows and balconies, some with a sea view. Rates include breakfast, and Ballestas tours are easily arranged.
(i) 16 ⊛ MC, V

EL CHORITO
$$
PARACAS S/N
TEL 056/545–045
The catch of the day is the main feature in this airy, white restaurant with ceiling fans. Service can be slow.
⊞ 80 ⊛ None

PISCO

POSADA HISPANA HOTEL
$$
BOLOGNESI 222
TEL 056/536–363
E-MAIL: RESERVAS@POSADA HISPANA.COM
A block from the Plaza de Armas, the colorfully decorated Posada Hispana features cozy rooms, some with a loft, and a restaurant serving Spanish and Peruvian food. Wi-Fi and a barbecue are available, and local tours are easily arranged.
(i) 24 P ⊠ ⊛ V

RESIDENCIAL SAN JORGE HOTEL
$$
BARRIO NUEVO 133
TEL 056/532–885
E-MAIL: HOTEL_SAN_JORGE_ RESIDENCIAL@HOTMAIL.COM
www.hotelsanjorgeresi dencial.online
Rooms vary in size and views—some have balconies onto the street while others overlook the swimming pool. Light-toned colors brighten the interior, and bright paintings by local artist Cospy Franco (b. 1968) grace the walls.
(i) 38 P ⊠ ⊛ MC, V

AS DE OROS
$$
SAN MARTÍN 472
TEL 056/532–010
E-MAIL: CONTACTO@ ASDEOROS.COM.PE

⊞ Hotel ⊞ Restaurant (i) No. of Guest Rooms ⊞ No. of Seats P Parking ⊕ Closed ⊟ Elevator

www.asdeoros.com.pe
A modern, cool sports
bar with an outdoor patio
overlooking a swimming pool,
the As de Oros has the best
seafood in town. The pool is
open to the public.

🍽 150 🕐 Closed Mon.
🅿 🚭 ❄ 🌊 ⛲ MC, V

TACNA

🏨 DM HOTELES
TACNA
$$$–$$$$
BOLOGNESI 300
TEL 052/424–193
E-MAIL: TACNA@DMHOTELES.PE
www.dmhoteles.pe
Many comfortable rooms
have balconies overlooking
the pool in a garden. Tacna's
best hotel.

🛏 75 🅿 🌊
❄ All major cards

▶ SOUTHERN HIGHLANDS

AREQUIPA

SOMETHING SPECIAL

🏨 CASA ANDINA
🍽 PREMIUM
AREQUIPA
$$$$$
CALLE UGARTE 403
TEL 054/226–907
www.casa-andina.com
Casa de la Moneda is an 18th-
century mansion that opened
in 2008 as Arequipa's most
elegant hotel. The colonial
building features a flower-filled
public patio surrounded by
reception, gourmet **Restau-
rante Alma,** and a bar. Other
parts of the mansion have
been converted into three
suites and a rooftop terrace
with monastery and mountain
views. Standard rooms are in a
new addition, but all maintain
a colonial style.

🛏 40 🅿 🚭 🚭 ❄
❄ All major cards

🏨 CASA ANDINA SELECT
🍽 AREQUIPA PLAZA
$$$$
PORTAL DE FLORES 116,
PLAZA DE ARMAS
TEL 054/412–930
www.casa-andina.com
With a fabulous location
on the Plaza de Armas, this
comfortable, modern hotel
features the balcony **La Plaza
Bar & Grill,** Arequipa's best
plaza-view restaurant. Rates
include a full buffet-style
breakfast. A petite rooftop
swimming pool surrounded
by a sundeck gives glimpses
of snowcapped mountains.
Book early for rooms with
plaza views.

🛏 58 🚭 🚭 ❄ 🌊
❄ All major Cards

🏨 LA GRUTA
HOTEL
$$$
LA GRUTA 304, SELVA ALEGRE
TEL 054/289–899
E-MAIL: LAGRUTA@LAGRUTA
HOTEL.COM
www.lagrutahotel.com
Large-windowed rooms, all
different, looking onto a
quiet suburban garden give
La Gruta the air of an elegant
B&B. Some rooms have a
private garden entrance or a
fireplace. The helpful English-
speaking staff provides airport
pickup and tour information
on request; laundry and
room service are also offered,
and American breakfast is
included.

🛏 15 🅿 🚭 ❄ All major
cards

🏨 SELINA
🍽 $$$
CALLE JERUSALÉN 606
TEL 170/977–87
www.selina.com
In Arequipa, La Casa de Mi
Abuela hotel has been an
institution for travelers on
a budget for decades. Now
renovated, it has been part of
the Selina chain since
April 2019. The comfortable

beds and the tree-lined
gardens continue to confirm
its success. It maintains
a good quality/price
ratio.

🛏 40 🅿 🚭 🌊 ❄ All major
cards

🏨 LA CASA DE MELGAR
$$
CALLE MELGAR 108
TEL 054/222–459
E-MAIL: RESERVAS@LACASA
DEMELGAR.COM
www.lacasademelgar.com
This charming 18th-century
casa features three patios
and a garden. Rooms all
differ from one another and
emphasize classic architecture
with sillar walls or redbrick
vaulted ceilings. Rates include
breakfast.

🛏 34 🚭 ❄ V

🍽 RESTAURANT ZIG ZAG
$$$$
ZELA 210
TEL 054/206–020
E-MAIL: INFO@ALPANDINA.COM
www.zigzagrestaurant.com
A colonial house with two
stories linked by an ironwork
circular staircase designed by
Gustave Eiffel, this restaurant
offers a Swiss-Peruvian fusion
menu termed Alpandino.
Ostrich and alpaca are
low-cholesterol choices, and
seafood, beef, fondue, and
quinoa are offered. The staff
and menu make a meal a
learning experience.

🍽 70 🚭 ❄ All major cards

🍽 CHE CARLITOS/
EL MONTONERO
$$$–$$$$
ALAMEDA PARDO 123
TEL 054/270–528
www.consorciobon
gourmet.com
Sharing a riverside location
by the Bolognesi Bridge, the
Montonero and Che Carlitos
serve authentic Arequipeño
and Argentine food. The gar-
den is popular with the lunch
crowd for its extensive menu

of traditional dishes, while several upstairs dining areas are dedicated to the upscale steak house. A spacious playground (with a nanny) keeps the youngsters happy.

🍴 300 🅿 🚳
🚳 All major cards

🍴 SOL DE MAYO
$$$–$$$$

JERUSALÉN 207, YANAHUARA
TEL 054/254–148
E-MAIL: RESERVAS@
RESTAURANTSOLDEMAYO.COM
www.soldemayo.com.pe

Sitting quietly in a suburb, Sol de Mayo has been the grande dame of Arequipa's restaurants for more than a century. It's especially popular at lunch, when the flower-filled garden and surrounding patios draw locals for traditional food; weekend reservations are recommended. The Sol de Mayo *ocopa* is unique, relying more on fried cheese than potato, and the homemade milk-and-cinnamon ice cream melts deliciously in your mouth.

🍴 300 🅿 🚳
🚳 All major cards

🍴 EL TURKO II ART RESTAURANT
$$–$$$

SAN FRANCISCO 223
TEL 059/740–291
E-MAIL: MARKETING@IMPERIO
OTOMANO.COM.PE
www.elturko.com.pe

A mouthwatering blend of Turkish, Middle Eastern, Italian, and Peruvian cuisine combined with international breakfasts makes this place an intriguing hit. Set inside romantic, high-arched rooms, with sillar walls enhanced by frescoes, the restaurant has amiable service and is the best of El Turko's local branches. A large window looks out of the kitchen onto the street so you can wave at the chefs as you pass. Their branch at Calle San Francisco

223 does take-out and delivery.

🍴 40 🚳 MC, V

🍴 ARY QUEPAY
$$

JERUSALÉN 502
TEL 959/741–585
E-MAIL: RESTAURANT
@ARYQUEPAY.COM
www.aryquepay.com

With traditional Peruvian dishes, multilingual menus, folkloric musicians wandering through in the evenings, a tropical flower and bamboo ambience, and friendly service, Ary Quepay is popular with tourists. This is the best place to sample *cuy* (a highland, not Arequipeño dish), and they do good, more typical local plates such as *rocoto relleno* and *adobo*.

🍴 150 🅿 🚳 🚳 DC, MC, V

🍴 CREPÍSIMO
$$

SANTA CATALINA 208
TEL 054/206–620
www.crepisimo.com

With almost one hundred delicious varieties of crêpes, books and board games, a fireplace, a balcony, excellent coffee, and a superb location near Monasterio de Santa Catalina, this place is a winner. Run by the Restaurant Zig Zag folks, their crêpes give a nod to Peru with alpaca and quinoa, and then continue with sweet, savory, meat, vegetarian, and dessert options.

🍴 60 🚳 🚳 All major cards

CHIVAY

🏨 CASA ANDINA
🍴 STANDARD COLCA
$$$–$$$$

HUAYNA CÁPAC S/N
TEL 054/531–020
www.casa-andina.com

This well-run hotel has

semidetached stone bungalows set in a garden with views of snowcapped peaks. The restaurant often features live folkloric musicians during the peak season.

🛏 52 🅿 🚳 🚳 All major cards

COLCA CANYON

🏨 BELMOND LAS CASITAS
$$$$$

PARQUE CURIÑA S/N, YANQUE
TEL 959/672–688
E-MAIL: RESERVAS.CASITASDEL
COLCA@GHLHOTELES.COM
www.belmond.com

These luxurious *casitas* (little houses) are spread out for seclusion, and each features a heated outdoor plunge pool in a private terrace, fireplace, heated stone floors, and a stargazing window over the bathtub. Rates include full breakfast. Available activities (some at extra cost) include guided hiking, zip-lining, and bicycle and horseback riding. Cooking and bird-watching lessons are also offered. A vegetable garden, farm, and health spa are on the premises.

☐ 20 ☐ ☐ MC, V, AE

 COLCA LODGE
$$$$$
FUNDO PUYE-YANQUE
TEL 054/531–191
AREQUIPA RESERVATIONS:
TEL 054/202–587
E-MAIL: RECEPCION@COLCA-LODGE.COM
colca-lodge.com
A rustic adobe, stone, and thatch hotel, the comfortable Colca Lodge is known for having the best natural hot springs in the region, cascading through four rock pools (*may be closed Jan.–Feb.*). Spa services are available both outdoors and inside. Non-guests can bathe here if they buy a meal. Horseback riding, biking, and hiking tours are offered, and fishing rods and inflatable boats are available. The rooms all have outdoor terraces with fine valley views. Rates include breakfast, and other meals are available in three restaurants and two bars.

☐ 45 ☐ ☐ All major cards

COLCA TREK LODGE
$$$$
SAN SEBASTIAN, PINCHOLLO
TEL 054/206–217
E-MAIL: COLCATREKLODGE@GMAIL.COM
www.colcatreklodge.com
All guest rooms have floor-to-ceiling windows with panoramic canyon views, and hot-water bottles slipped into the beds each evening are a nice touch. Andean decorations brighten the lodge, and there are crackling fireplaces in the dining room where breakfast and dinner are served, included in the rates.

There are almost no dining choices in the village. Arequipa to Cabanaconde buses will stop by the lodge and walk-in guests receive discounts. Run by Colca Trek (see p. 307) this is an excellent base for exploring. Mountain bikes and guided all-day hikes to geysers and hot springs are available, or explore the trails yourself with maps sold at the lodge. Hikers can cross the canyon via a hanging bridge to Madrigal on the north side of the canyon. Equipment to climb a snow-capped volcano is rented.

☐ 48 ☐ ☐ ☐ All major cards

LA CASA DE MAMA YACCHI
$$$
PUEBLO DE COPORAQUE
TEL 959/662–705
E-MAIL: RESERVAS@LACASADEMAMAYACCHI.COM
lacasademamayacchi.com
Stone-walled, wood-beamed, and thatched, the hotel exudes southern highland charm. Bike riding, hiking, and horseback riding can be arranged. Rates include buffet breakfast taken in the restaurant with Colca Valley views, and the fireplace in the lobby is an evening gathering spot.

☐ 28 ☐ ☐ ☐ MC, V

JULIACA

SUITES DON CARLOS JULIACA
$$$
MANUEL PRADO 335
TEL 051/321–571
E-MAIL: RESERVASLIMA@HOTELESDONCARLOS.COM
www.hotelesdoncarlos.com
On a quieter street a few blocks from the center, this hotel offers good-size rooms with heaters, which you'll need at this elevation. Airport transfers, Internet, and room service are offered. It's the best place in Juliaca.

☐ 45 ☐ ☐ MC, V

PUNO

HOTEL LIBERTADOR LAGO TITICACA
$$$$$
ISLA ESTEVES, LAGO TITICACA
TEL 051/367–780
E-MAIL: RESERVASPUNO@LIBERTADOR.COM.PE
www.libertador.com.pe
Sitting prettily on its own island 5 miles (8 km) from the city center, linked to the mainland by a causeway, the sparkling white hotel features 11 suites and many rooms with lake views. Furnishings are elegant if somewhat bland. A private dock gives access to all tours, and alpacas wander around the 25-acre (12 ha) island. Rates include breakfast. A taxi (*about $5*) is needed to get into Puno.

☐ 123 ☐ ☐ ☐ ☐ All major cards

CASA ANDINA PREMIUM PUNO
$$$$
SESQUI CENTENARIO 1970
TEL 051/363–992
www.casa-andina.com
On the shores of the lake, about a ten-minute cab drive from the center, this new, modern, two-story hotel features fabulous lake views from its public areas and about half of its rooms; the other rooms have views over the hotel gardens and beyond into the altiplano. The rarely used Cusco-Puno railway line comes by the hotel, where there is a train stop if you are coming from Cusco on the thrice-weekly PeruRail service. Many rooms have balconies and all of them have bathrooms with bathtubs, free Wi-Fi, and oxygen on request. The pricey but excellent restaurant provides buffet breakfast (included) and contemporary Andean dining throughout the day.

☐ 45 ☐ ☐ ☐ All major cards

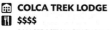 ☐ Nonsmoking ☐ Air-conditioning ☐ Indoor Pool ☐ Outdoor Pool ☐ Health Club ☐ Credit Cards

🏨🍴 SONESTA POSADA DEL INCA-LAKE TITICACA
$$$$
SESQUICENTENARIO 610
SECTOR HUAJE
TEL 051/364–111
E-MAIL: RESERVAS.SONESTA
PUNO@GHLHOTELES.COM
Three miles (5 km) from central Puno and on the shores of Lake Titicaca, this hotel offers various lake tours. The steamship *Yavari* (see sidebar p. 113) is moored outside. Passengers traveling by train between Cusco and Puno can be dropped off at the hotel's private station. Rooms are soundproofed and colorfully furnished, half with lake views. Rates include a bountiful buffet breakfast in the restaurant with a lake view.
🛏 70 🅿 ♿
♦ All major cards

🏨 PLAZA MAYOR HOSTAL
$$$
DEUSTUA 342
TEL 051/366–089
E-MAIL: RESERVAS@PLAZA
MAYORHOTEL.COM
plazamayorhotel.com
This comfortable hotel has a large lobby with a fireplace, friendly staff, heated rooms, bathrooms with tub, showers, hair dryers, and a great location a half block from the Plaza de Armas.
🛏 34 🔌 ♦ All major cards

🏨🍴 HOSTAL PUKARA
$$
LIBERTAD 328
TEL 051/368–448
E-MAIL: PUKARA@TERRA.COM.PE
www.pukaradeltitikaka.com
Heat, hot showers, in-room cable TV, free breakfast in a scenic rooftop dining room, a central location, and free transfers from bus or train stations make this hostel a value.
🛏 14 🅿 ♿
♦ AE, MC, V

🏨 HOSTAL LOS PINOS INN
$
TARAPACÁ 182
TEL 051/367–398
E-MAIL: HOSTALPINOS@HOTMAIL.COM
www.lospinosinnpuno.com
Basic but clean, large rooms with warms showers. Friendly staff make this a budget-traveler's favorite.
🛏 16 ♦ None

🍴 INCABAR
$$–$$$
LIMA 348, 2ND FL.
TEL 051/368–031
Local food such as alpaca and Titicaca trout is served with an international flair. Sauces run the gamut from creamy to curried to colorful. The restaurant is open for breakfast, lunch, and dinner, and serves a variety of snacks and light meals throughout the day. It also has a couch bar in the back, which is popular with travelers.
🪑 100 ♿ ♦ All major cards

🍴 MOJSA RESTAURANT
$$–$$$
LIMA 635, 2ND FL.
TEL 051/363–182
www.mojsarestaurant.com
Overlooking the Plaza de Armas, and with impressive cathedral views from its small balcony, this restaurant is one of Puno's most popular. The menu is varied without being overly long–salads and sandwiches for lighter refreshments; hearty soups, pastas, pizzas, trout, and meats for a main meal; and desserts and espresso coffee and cocktails to finish it all off.
🪑 100 ♦ All major cards

🍴 RESTAURANTE LA CASONA
$$–$$$
LIMA 423, 2ND FL.
TEL 051/351–108
www.lacasona-restaurant.com

PRICES

HOTELS
The cost of a double room with private bath and hot water in the peak season is given by **$** signs. Low-season rates can be considerably lower, especially in the cheaper establishments.

$$$$$	Over $200
$$$$	$100–$200
$$$	$50–$100
$$	$25–$50
$	Under $25

RESTAURANTS
The average cost of a two-course meal for one person, without tax, tip, or drinks is given by **$** signs.

$$$$$	Over $30
$$$$	$21–$30
$$$	$14–$20
$$	$7–$13
$	Under $7

This upstairs restaurant has rooms featuring colonial art, antique irons, and pots of colorful flowers. One wall is a picture window with tables overlooking the pedestrian sector of Lima. A beehive fireplace warms diners. The menu has a good selection of regional fish dishes, alpaca, *cuy*, as well as more standard fare. Desserts are recommended.
🪑 120 ♿ ♦ All major cards

🍴 PIZZA E PASTA
$–$$
AREQUIPA 320
TEL 051/365–434
Of many pizza places in Puno, this is one of the better ones, appealing to locals and travelers alike with its line of Peruvian-style pies—think chilies and Andean herbs instead of bell peppers and basil. Each

---

🏨 Hotel   🍴 Restaurant   🛏 No. of Guest Rooms   🪑 No. of Seats   🅿 Parking   🕐 Closed   🔌 Elevator

is made to order, and you can ask the friendly staff to add or hold ingredients to your taste. The salads are good and vegetarian stuffed calzones are a big hit.

⊞ 60 ⑤ None

🍴 LA CASA DEL CORREGIDOR
$
DEUSTUA 576
TEL 051/351–921
www.cafebar.casadel
corregidor.pe
Excellent local organic coffees and a reduced choice of dishes (salads, sandwiches and desserts) served inside a 17th-century building that now hosts a cultural center and offers Wi-Fi. The outdoor patio is relaxing on a sunny day. The bar offers local punches and various cocktails.

⊞ 24 ⏰ Closed Sun. ⑤ ⑤ None

🍴 RICOS PAN
$
MOQUEGUA 326
www.ricospan.com.pe
This small local bakery chain started at Moquegua 326 and has been so successful that a few more have opened. Eat in or take out the best baked goods in town, with excellent coffees and even pisco sours in the evening. Box lunches are available for picnics. There are two branches: in Jirón Arequipa 332 and Avenida Laykakota 171.

⑤ ⑤ None

PUNO AREA

SOMETHING SPECIAL

🏨 ISLA
🍴 SUASI
$$$$
LAGO TITICACA
TEL 051/351–102
E-MAIL: RESERVAS@ISLA
SUASI.PE
www.islasuasi.pe

This is the most comfortable, isolated, and peaceful hotel on Lake Titicaca (see p. 117), located on a private island 4 hours by boat from Puno. Built of local stone, adobe, and totora reeds, the eco-lodge has rooms with lake views and fireplaces and a two-room private cottage with butler service. The restaurant serves traditional cuisine based on quality ingredients. There is also a library and a small museum on the history and geology of the area.

⊡ 25 ⑤ ⑤ All major cards

▶ CUSCO REGION

AGUAS CALIENTES

🏨 EL MAPI
🍴 $$$$$
PACHACUTEC 109
TEL 01/610–0400
www.inkaterra.com
This is Inkaterra's latest hotel—a modern place that is centrally located near the plaza with large, comfortable superior rooms and suites. Rates include breakfast and dinner.

⊡ 130 🚩 ⑤ All major cards

🏨 MACHU PICCHU
🍴 PUEBLO HOTEL
$$$$$
TEL 01/610–0400
www.inkaterra.com
Cottages are nestled in cloud-forested, orchid-laden gardens a short walk out of town. The hotel is the area's most luxurious, with its own railway stop. Spacious, flagstoned, wood-beamed casitas with alpaca blankets and fireplaces, gourmet restaurant, spa, traditional ceremonies, and guided nature walks are offered. The hotel is part of a private reserve of over 29 acres (12 ha) where, in addition to orchids, you can spot numerous species of birds

and butterflies. Rates include breakfast, cocktail hour, and dinner; children under 12 are free. One caveat—there are lots of steps in the gardens to the cottages.

⊡ 83 ⑤ ⑤ ⑤ All major cards

🏨 GRINGO BILL'S
🍴 $$$$
COLLA RAYMI 104
TEL 084/211–046
E-MAIL: RESERVAS@GRINGO
BILLS.COM
www.gringobills.com
Founded in 1979, this is one of the original backpackers' hotels that has now been upgraded. Rambling rooms have plenty of wooden architecture and are decorated with cosmic murals by a Cusqueño artist. The higher rooms have better views and are newer, but require a lot of stair-climbing. Breakfast is included.

⊡ 40 ⑤ AE, MC, V

🏨 HOSTAL LA CABAÑA
$$$$
PACHACUTEC 805
TEL 084/211–269
E-MAIL: BOOKING@LACABANA
MACHUPICCHU.COM
lacabanamachupicchu.com
A nice wooden hotel several blocks up the Pachacutec hill, this place has some rooms with great views. Helpful hosts add to the attraction. Breakfast is included. Rooms vary in size and price.

⊡ 22 ⑤ ⑤ DC, MC, V

CUSCO

Hotels

SOMETHING SPECIAL

🏨 BELMOND HOTEL
🍴 MONASTERIO
$$$$$
PLAZOLETA NAZARENAS 337
TEL 084/604–000
www.belmond.com
The heavy wooden colonial

entrance doors and antique-filled public areas opening onto a courtyard with a simple but centuries-old fountain, give a hint of something special. The hotel is a carefully preserved 16th-century monastery, with a beautiful church, colonial colonnades, and period art and furniture. The 21st century is not forgotten, but it remains unobtrusive. The hotel offers spa service, bath butlers, and some oxygenated rooms designed to minimize *soroche*. The **Illariy Restaurant** is top-notch, and the adjacent Deli Monasterio offers great traditional Peruvian snacks to go. Guests here have the best chance of scoring a room at the only hotel next to Machu Picchu.

🛏 122 ➖ 🔊 🔲
💳 All major cards

🛏 **PALACIO**
🍽 **DEL INKA**
$$$$$

PLAZOLETA SANTO DOMINGO 259
TEL 084/231–961
www.marriott.com

Right next to Qorikancha and four blocks from the Plaza de Armas, this is a great hotel with exceptional service. It was one of Cusco's earliest mansions, built on Inca walls that can be seen in parts of the expansive lobby and the elegant bar. There is overlying colonial architecture throughout. Rooms are spacious with period furniture, bathtubs, and many have balconies in traditional blue shuttered style. The included breakfast buffet is magnificent. Local taxi drivers know this by its traditional "El Libertador" name.

🛏 154 ➖ 🔊 🔲 📺
💳 All major cards

🛏 **CASA ANDINA**
PREMIUM CUSCO
$$$$

PLAZOLETA DE LIMACPAMPA CHICO 473

TEL 084/232–610
E-MAIL: TRAVEL@CASA-ANDINA.COM
www.casa-andina.com

This is the best of a half dozen Casa Andina hotels in Cusco and the Sacred Valley. Comfortable rooms lead into courtyards where local weavers sometimes ply their trade. The **Restaurant Alma** is one of the best in town, and service is as helpful as it can be. All the Andina hotels offer an extensive buffet breakfast included in their rates.

🛏 94 ➖ 🔊 🔲
💳 All major cards

🛏 **CASA SAN BLAS**
🍽 **$$$$**

TOCUYEROS 556
TEL 084/254–852
TOLL–FREE USA
1–800–569–1769
E-MAIL: RESERVATIONS@CASASANBLAS.COM
www.casasanblas.com

The best lodging in the artisan district of Plaza San Blas, set back on a pretty cobblestone alley three blocks from the Plaza de Armas, this small hotel prides itself on personal service with complimentary breakfast, Wi-Fi, and helpful information. The upper-floor suites, with kitchenettes and city views, are the best value. A rooftop terrace gives great views over Cusco. Standard rooms feature extra-long beds and are named after the textiles that decorate the walls.

🛏 18 🔊 🔲 💳 AE, MC, V

🛏 **XIMA CUSCO HOTEL**
🍽 **$$$$**

EL SOL 1010
TEL 084/581–270
E-MAIL: INFO@XIMAHOTELS.COM
www.ximahotels.com

This modern hotel has a relaxing, uncluttered, flagstone courtyard with a waterfall and a single tree. Spacious rooms have soothing pastel colors

and flat screen cable TVs. It's a 15-minute walk from the Plaza de Armas, and refreshingly makes no attempt to cash in on anything colonial or Inca. Restaurant open from early morning with a buffet of organic products. Buffet breakfast and free Wi-Fi are included.

🛏 167 🅿 ➖ 🔊
💳 All major cards

🛏 **HOTEL RUMI PUNKU**
🍽 **$$$–$$$$**

CHOQUECHACA 339
TEL 084/221–102 OR 236–957
E-MAIL: INFO@RUMIPUNKU.COM
www.rumipunku.com

The Quechua name means "stone doorway" and refers to the double-jambed Inca entrance to this colonial building surrounding two courtyards, one with an Inca

---

PRICES

HOTELS

The cost of a double room with private bath and hot water in the peak season is given by **$** signs. Low-season rates can be considerably lower, especially in the cheaper establishments.

$$$$$	Over $200
$$$$	$100–$200
$$$	$50–$100
$$	$25–$50
$	Under $25

RESTAURANTS

The average cost of a two-course meal for one person, without tax, tip, or drinks is given by **$** signs.

$$$$$	Over $30
$$$$	$21–$30
$$$	$14–$20
$$	$7–$13
$	Under $7

🛏 Hotel   🍽 Restaurant   🛏 No. of Guest Rooms   🔊 No. of Seats   🅿 Parking   🕐 Closed   ➖ Elevator

wall. A lounge has a fireplace, games, and Internet, while rooftop terraces offer city views. Airy rooms with hardwood floors have heaters and thermal blankets. Rates include a buffet breakfast.

🛈 43 P 🚭 🍽
🏧 All major cards

🏨 AMARU INCA
🍽 HOSTAL
$$$

CUESTA SAN BLAS 541
TEL 084/225–933
E-MAIL: RESERVAS@AMARU
HOSTAL.COM
www.amaruinca.com
Some rooms have excellent city views and private bathrooms; a few have shared bathrooms, but all have friendly service. There is a TV lounge, book exchange, and sunny courtyard, and breakfast is included.

🛈 27 🏧 All major cards

🏨 ROYAL INKA I
🍽 $$$

PLAZA REGOCIJO 299
See Royal Inka II below.

🏨 ROYAL INKA II
🍽 $$$

SANTA TERESA 335
TEL 084/222–284 OR 233–037
E-MAIL: RESERVAS@ROYAL
INKAHOTEL.PE
www.royalinkahotel.pe
These sister hotels, a block apart, are good mid-price choices within two or three blocks of the Plaza de Armas. The Royal Inka I is in a 300-year-old building with a lovely courtyard while the newer Inka II has a sauna open to guests of both. Good restaurants.

🛈 58 (Royal Inka I)
🛈 45 (Royal Inka II)
🔁 🚭 🏧 All major cards

🏨 LOS ATICOS
$$–$$$

PASAJE HURTADO–ALVAREZ
QUERA 253

TEL 084/229–772 OR 254–852
E-MAIL: INFO@LOSATICOS.COM
www.losaticos.com
At the end of a quiet alley, Los Aticos serves breakfast in the communal kitchen that guests are welcome to use. Coffee and tea are available all day, and Peruvian cooking classes can be arranged. Free Internet access, use of a washing machine, and a book exchange make this a homey place. The best units are apartments with kitchenettes and sitting rooms, suitable for long stays. A spa and sauna are conveniently situated next door.

🛈 18 🏧 None

Restaurants

🍽 MAP CAFÉ
$$$$$

MUSEO DE ARTE
PRECOLOMBINO,
PLAZOLETA NAZARENAS 231
TEL 084/242–476
www.cuscorestaurants.com
In a futuristic glassed-in section of the courtyard of the Museo de Arte Precolombino, this is the city's best gourmet Peruvian food. During the day, they have a cheaper selection of sandwiches and light meals, but at night (when reservations are strongly recommended), the restaurant shines with its intricately designed novo-Andino menu, including a prix-fixe dinner.

🍴 50 P 🚭 🏧 All major cards

🍽 TUNUPA CUSCO
$$$$$

PORTAL CONFITURIA 233
2ND FL., PLAZA DE ARMAS
TEL 084/252–936
tunuparestaurante.com.pe
Every night at 7:30 p.m., there's a show with mainly highland music and dancers that draw the crowds. (Of several tourist-oriented dinner and show restaurants,

this is the best.) Diners have choices: Sit in front of the stage or at a balcony table with a plaza view. Eat à la carte or sample the wide-ranging buffet of traditional and novo-Andino Peruvian food. It's all good. Peak-season reservations are recommended.

🍴 150 🚭 🏧 All major cards

🍽 LE SOLEIL
$$$$–$$$$$

SAN AGUSTÍN 275
TEL 084/240–543
E-MAIL: MARCINART@
HOTMAIL.COM
www.restauranteleesoleil
cusco.com
This elegant and authentic French restaurant has taken Cusco by storm. Service is impeccable, and the food wouldn't be out of place in Paris. The wine list features only French vintages that range from $35 to more than $100 per bottle. Apart from a short menu of a la carte selections that include ratatouille, duck, quail, and snails, the chef turns out fantastic tasting menus of five to eight courses for foodies who can't make up their minds.

🍴 40 🏧 V

🍽 UCHU PERUVIAN
STEAKHOUSE
$$$$

CALLE PALACIO 135
TEL 084/246–598
E-MAIL: UCHU@CUZCO
DINING.COM
cuscodining.com
This new and popular steakhouse is among the best carnivore places in town. Your choice of meat is cooked on a highly heated volcanic stone—you get to watch it cook until it reaches the perfect doneness for you. Then you can add or dip into a variety of highland sauces. Appetizers and soups are innovative blends of Andean ingredients. Lamb,

---

🚭 Nonsmoking 🅰 Air-conditioning 🏊 Indoor Pool 🏊 Outdoor Pool 🍽 Health Club 🏧 Credit Cards

beef, alpaca, chicken, shrimp, and various fish dishes predominate; there are many vegetarian options.

🛏 75 ⓢ ⓢ All major cards

🍴 CICCIOLINA
$$$–$$$$
TRIUNFO 393, 2ND FL.
TEL 084/239–510
E-MAIL: RESERVAS@CICCIOLINA
CUZCO.COM
www.cicciolinacuzco.com
The restaurant, always crowded, is beyond the tapas bar. In the room with dark red walls and heavy carved wooden chairs, a fusion menu of Mediterranean, Asian, and Peruvian cuisine is offered together with an extensive wine list. Tapas are served at the bar, where you can also choose from the menu. Those who sit in the dining room ($2) cannot order tapas, but the dishes served with care do not disappoint. Open for breakfast, lunch, and dinner.

🛏 80 ⓢ ⓢ All major cards

🍴 INCANTO RISTORANTE
$$$–$$$$
SANTA CATALINA ANGOSTA 135
TEL 084/254–753
E-MAIL: INCANTO@CUSCO
RESTAURANTS.COM
www.cuscorestaurants.com
Once this was an Inca palace, but now it is a fabulous contemporary Italian-Peruvian restaurant with more than 80 dishes. If you have a hankering for pizza, pasta, barbecue, or fine wines, this is the best choice in town. You can also order from a traditional Andean menu or select one of the many vegetarian offerings.

🛏 140 ⓢ ⓢ All major cards

🍴 INKA GRILL
$$$–$$$$$
PORTAL DE PANES 115
PLAZA DE ARMAS
TEL 084/262–992
www.cuscorestaurants.com
A few tables have plaza views at this exceptional grill

serving creative *novo-Andino* food, including alpaca and *cuy*. Pastas and a vegetarian selection are also on the menu, and the desserts are among Cusco's best. An unobtrusive band often plays at night. Reservations are recommended.

🛏 130 ⓢ ⓢ All major cards

🍴 BACO
$$$
RUINAS 465
TEL 084/242–808
E-MAIL: BACO@BACO
CUZCO.COM
www.cicciolinacuzco.com/
baco.html
This hip wine bar (sample a flute of three sommelier-chosen wines) prides itself on pizzas cooked in a terra-cotta oven and sophisticated bar munchies, as well as steaks, salads, and pastas. Iron buckets of fresh flowers and colorful canvases of local art make this a cheerful place to learn about South American wines. Open for dinner only.

🛏 60 ⓢ ⓢ All major cards

🍴 PACHA PAPA
$$$
PLAZOLETA SAN BLAS 120
TEL 084/241–318
E-MAIL: PACHAPAPA@
CUSCORESTAURANTS.COM
www.cuscorestaurants.com
This rustic cobblestoned restaurant features indoor and outdoor dining with Cusqueño food cooked with ancient techniques such as *pachamanca* (under the earth), wood-fired ovens, and clay pots. The Andean soups and stews will warm you on a cold highland evening. Varied pizzas include alpaca among the toppings. You can watch traditional live music.

🛏 45 ⓢ ⓢ All major cards

🍴 GREENS ORGANIC
$$–$$$
SANTA CATALINA ANGOSTA
135, 2ND FL.

PRICES

HOTELS

The cost of a double room with private bath and hot water in the peak season is given by **$** signs. Low-season rates can be considerably lower, especially in the cheaper establishments.

$$$$$	Over $200
$$$$	$100–$200
$$$	$50–$100
$$	$25–$50
$	Under $25

RESTAURANTS

The average cost of a two-course meal for one person, without tax, tip, or drinks is given by **$** signs.

$$$$$	Over $30
$$$$	$21–$30
$$$	$14–$20
$$	$7–$13
$	Under $7

TEL 084/243–379
E-MAIL: GREENS@CUSCO
RESTAURANTS.COM
www.cuscorestaurants.com
The name refers to the wide range of local organic products (some coming from its own garden) served in this semi-vegetarian restaurant upstairs from Incanto (see above). A small but well-chosen selection of chicken, alpaca, and trout dishes keeps carnivores happy, but it is the world-beat vegetarian selections that stand out.

🛏 65 ⓢ ⓢ
ⓢ All major cards

🍴 KUSIKUY
$$
AMARGURA 140
TEL 084/262–870
An excellent mid-range choice for typical Peruvian highland food, this is famed

as one of the best places in town to try *cuy*. If you want to order, call one hour in advance.

🛏 60 📅 Closed Sun. 🆂 🆂 None

🍴 PUCARA
$$
PLATEROS 309
TEL 084/222-027
Just off the Plaza de Armas, built on Inca foundations, this decorous restaurant has wooden tables, white walls, and art with archaeological themes. The menu has pictures to help you decide between the Peruvian, Asian, and international choices.

🛏 50 🆂 🆂 MC, V

🍴 GRANJA HEIDI
$-$$
CUESTA SAN BLAS 525, 2ND FL.
TEL 084/238-383
www.granjaheidicusco.com
A German café famed for huge and varied breakfasts, as well as good lunchtime menus. They produce their own dairy products in their *granja* (farm) outside of Cusco.

🛏 40 📅 Closed Sun. 🆂 None

🍴 JACK'S CAFÉ
$-$$
CHOQUECHACA 509
TEL 084/254-606
www.jackscafecusco.com
This popular artful café serves breakfast all day, offers gourmet sandwiches and salads, and has an international bistro-style menu. Diners often line up outside waiting for a table.

🛏 44 🆂 🆂 None

🍴 KINTARO
$-$$$
PLATEROS 334, 2ND FL.
TEL 084/260-638
This spare but friendly restaurant serves authentic Japanese and vegetarian fare at great prices. Sushi, ramen,

udon, and sake are on the menu.

🛏 100 🆂 🆂 None

🍴 QUINTA EULALIA
$-$$
CHOQUECHACA 384
TEL 084/224-951
A *quinta* is a country house offering a small menu of traditional Andean cooking. This one was slightly more rural when it opened in 1941, although it's only six longish blocks from the Plaza de Armas. Dining is on a covered patio surrounding a tranquil courtyard and the menu is written, in Spanish, on a chalkboard; the most popular items get erased as they become unavailable. This is a great local place to try a bowl of *chairo*, a thick and hearty soup of beef, lamb, and varied highland vegetables. Guinea pig (*cuy*) and suckling pig (*lechon*) are both favorites, and trout, tamales, and stuffed bell peppers are usually on offer.

🛏 80 📅 Lunch only 🆂 None

🍴 EL ENCUENTRO
$
SANTA CATALINA ANCHA 384
TEL 084/247-977
restaurantelencuentro.
blogspot.com
Popular and recommended vegetarian restaurant offering a variety of soups, salads, omelets, and local dishes. Open for breakfast, lunch, and dinner.

🛏 35 🆂 🆂 None

MACHU PICCHU

🏨 MACHU PICCHU 🍴 SANCTUARY LODGE
$$$$$
MACHU PICCHU
ARCHAEOLOGICAL SITE
TEL 984/816-956 (LODGE)
E-MAIL: TRAVELCONCIERGE.
MPS@BELMOND.COM
www.belmond.com

This is the only hotel at Machu Picchu, and you pay a heavy premium for the location. Comfortable rooms with mountain views are more than $1,000; those without views aren't much cheaper. Massages and private guides are available. During the peak season, the hotel is booked solid with groups (who arrange discounts). Rates include meals and drinks. Day visitors can eat the lunch buffet here ($$$$$).

🛏 31 🆂 🆂 🆂 All major cards

OLLANTAYTAMBO

🏨 PAKARITAMPU 🍴
$$$$
FERROCARRIL 852
TEL 084/204-020
E-MAIL: HOTEL@
PAKARITAMPU.COM
www.pakaritampu.com
Set in flowery gardens with mountain and archaeological views, this solid-looking hotel is comfortable and friendly. Local tours and adventure activities can be arranged. The large, airy lobby has a fireplace and cable TV lounge, and the restaurant serves *novo-Andino* food. Rates include breakfast, and box lunches can be purchased.

🛏 40 🅿 🆂 All major cards

🏨 EL ALBERGUE B&B 🍴
$$$
OLLANTAYTAMBO TRAIN
STATION
TEL 084/204-014
E-MAIL: RESERVATIONS
@ELALBERGUE.COM
www.elalbergue.com
You won't miss the train if you stay at Wendy Weeks' B&B. Artist Weeks has owned this tastefully simple place for more than four decades and knows the area well. The B&B has a rustic sauna for guest use. The restaurant,

---

Café Mayu, beside the railway platform, is among the best in town.

🛈 15 🛇 V

🍴 HEARTS CAFÉ

$$

AVENDIO VENTIDERIO
TEL 084/436–726
www.heartscafeperu.com
This indoor/outdoor café serves breakfast, lunch, and dinner including homemade bread and baked goods, quinoa porridge, sandwiches, salads, soups, snacks, box lunches, and vegan food. Proceeds benefit a local children's project, and volunteers are welcome.

🪑 47 🅿 🛇 🛇 None

🍴 MAYUPATA

$$

CONVENCIÓN S/N
TEL 084/610–258
With a fireplace inside and a garden with riverside view, this relaxing restaurant serves pizza, Peruvian staples, sandwiches, and some international plates.

🪑 40 🅿 🛇 🛇 None

URUBAMBA-YUCAY-CALCA AREA

🏨 SOL Y LUNA
🍴 $$$$$

URUBAMBA
TEL 084/201–620
E-MAIL: INFO@HOTELSOL
YLUNA.COM
www.hotelsolyluna.com
Characteristic casitas in local stone are scattered through flowery gardens. The lodge offers horseback riding from its own stable, mountain biking, paragliding, hiking, and other adventures. A full-service spa and tennis court are available. Two restaurants: **Killa Wasi,** more refined, and **Wayra,** enriched by the colorful creations of local artists. Pizza nights and *pachamancas* are favorites.

🛈 43 🅿 🛇
🛇 All major cards

🏨 SONESTA POSADA
🍴 DEL INCA

$$$$$

PLAZA MANCO II 123, YUCAY
TEL 084/201–107
E-MAIL: RESERVAS.SONESTA
YUCAY@GHLHOTELES.COM
www.sonesta.com
Originally an 18th-century monastery, this hotel has attractive new colonial-style bungalow blocks scattered through a large village-like garden with stone paths, fountains, and a chapel. Some rooms are in the creaky original building that houses the lobby, souvenir shops, and a private museum. Sonesta's signature breakfast buffet is included in the rates.

🛈 87 🅿 🛇 🛋
🛇 All major cards

🍴 MIL CENTRO

$–$$

VÍA A MORAY, MARAS
TEL 926/948–088
EMAIL: RESERVAS@MIL
CENTRO.PE
milcentro.pe
The structure, which previously housed a vicuña breeder, has been renovated to host this modern restaurant surrounded by greenery. The view is truly unique: The ruins of Moray are in fact a few steps from here. Chef Virgilio Martinez, who manages the kitchen, offers reinterpretations of typical Peruvian dishes made strictly with organic products. The courses are accompanied by infusions and natural herbal teas.

🪑 50 🛇 MC, V

▶ CENTRAL HIGHLANDS

AYACUCHO

🏨 HOTEL SANTA MARIA
🍴 $$

AREQUIPA 320
TEL 066/314–988
jianhoteles.com.pe

Comfortable, spacious, modern bedrooms with TVs and good views from the rooftop terrace. Breakfast is included in the rates, and room service is available from the restaurant.

🛈 22 🅿 🛇 MC, V

🏨 HOTEL SANTA
🍴 ROSA

$$

LIMA 166
TEL 066/314–614
In a 17th-century mansion, with rooms surrounding two courtyards, one with a large fountain, this atmospheric hotel features large double rooms and bathrooms, and friendly, helpful staff.

🛈 40 🅿 🛇 None

🍴 LA CASONA

$–$$

BELLIDO 463

TEL 066/312–733
Big portions of typical highland Peruvian food served in
a clean, bright dining room or
around a flowery patio attract
locals and travelers alike.

🔲 90 🏷 MC, V

HUANCAVELICA

🏨 HOTEL PRESIDENTE
$$$–$$$$

PLAZA DE ARMAS S/N
TEL 067/452760
E-MAIL: HUANCAVELICA
@HOTELPRESIDENTE.COM.PE
huancavelica.hotel
presidente.com.pe
This is Huancavelica's only
decent hotel in an attractive
old building on the plaza.
Rooms are fairly spartan,
but the beds are comfort-
able. Rates include a buffet
breakfast.

🛈 80 🏷 All major cards

HUANCAYO

🏨 HOTEL TURISMO
$$$$

ANCASH 729
TEL 064/231–072
E-MAIL: HTURISMO@HOTEL
PRESIDENTE.COM.PE
turismo.hotel
presidente.com.pe
In an elegant early 20th-
century building overlook-
ing the civic center, this is
considered Huancayo's best
hotel. Rooms vary in size and
cost, but all have solid beds,
heaters, and cable TV. Rates
include buffet breakfast in the
old-fashioned dining room.

🛈 80 🅿 🔄 🏷 All major
cards

🏨 HOSTAL EL MARQUEZ
$$$

PUNO 294
TEL 064/219–026
E-MAIL: RESERVAS@EL
MARQUEZHUANCAYO.COM
www.elmarquezhuancayo.
com
Centrally located behind
the cathedral, modern El

Marquez has comfortable
carpeted rooms and helpful
staff. Rates include continental breakfast, room service
is available, and three suites
have Jacuzzis.

🛈 28 🅿 🔄
🏷 All major cards

🏨 HOTEL CONFORT
$

ANCASH 237
TEL 064/233–601
Very basic but large rooms
are a good value if you just
need a decent bed for the
night and a hot shower. The
Confort has a central location, and the staff is friendly.
Avoid the noisy rooms in
the front.

🛈 100 🅿 🏷 None

🍴 LA CABAÑA
$–$$

JOSE GALVEZ 400
TEL 064/393–298
Popular with tourists and
locals for its pizzas and
calientitos (hot toddies),
La Cabaña also does sand-
wiches, pastas, barbecue,
and snacks. Musicians bring
the place alive Thursday to
Saturday, when there may
be dancing. The place is very
popular and appreciated by
families with children.

🔲 80 🏷 None

🍴 COQUI CAFÉ
$

PUNO 294
TEL 064/234–707
www.coquicafe.com
This bright, modern bakery
serves good coffee, snacks,
sandwiches, and pastries
all day long. A deli sells
picnic supplies.

🔲 48 🏷 All major cards

TARMA

🏨 LOS PORTALES
🍴 **$$$$**

RAMÓN CASTILLA 512
TEL 01/611–9001

RESERVASHOTELES@
LOSPORTALES.COM.PE
www.losportales
hoteles.com.pe
Easily Tarma's best hotel,
Los Portales sits in a secluded
location about a mile (1.6 km)
from the center on the
western outskirts of town.
The hotel has a grilled chicken
restaurant and a more formal
dining area, as well as a children's playground and a disco
on weekends.

🛈 45 🅿 🏷 MC, V

🏨 HACIENDA LA FLORIDA
$$–$$$

CARRETERA CENTRAL KM 39
TEL 064/341–041
E-MAIL: RESERVAS@HACIENDA
LAFLORIDA.COM
www.haciendalaflorida.com
This working hacienda,
run by a Peruvian-German
couple, gives guests opportunities to feed chickens, milk
cows, pick vegetables, ride
tractors, pet rabbits, and help
with whatever is happening
seasonally. Rates include
breakfast; other meals are
available on request. Camping
is also available.

🛈 12 🅿 🏷 None

▶ HUARAZ & THE HIGH ANDES

CARAZ

🏨 O'PAL SIERRA RESORT
$$$

CARRETERA CENTRAL KM 466.2,
FUNDO SAN LUIS 51–43
TEL 994/583–473
E-MAIL: RESERVAS@OPAL
SIERRARESORT.COM
www.opalsierraresort.com
The resort has several cabins
immersed in a garden. The
units range from cabins for
two people to family-sized
ones for eight people.
Most have an equipped
kitchenette, living room, and
fireplace. A few rooms are

just bedrooms. Horseback rides are available and there is a children's playground. Restaurant service is iffy in the low season, when self-catering could be a better option. You'll need your own transportation or else be at the mercy of infrequent taxis.

[i] 20 P S 🏊 🏠 MC, V

🍴 CAFÉ DE RAT
$–$$
SUCRE 1266
TEL 043/391–642
One table overlooks the Plaza de Armas in this cozy little restaurant that serves breakfasts, pizzas, sandwiches, pastas, and coffees. Maps adorn the walls, and this is an excellent planning center for treks. A fireplace, book exchange, and dartboard make this a good place to hang out.

🪑 28 S 🏠 None

🍴 LA PUNTA GRANDE
$–$$
DANIEL VILLAR 595
TEL 043/391–131
On the outskirts of this small town, La Punta Grande is set around a garden with a playground and serves hearty Peruvian campesino fare—chunky soups, suckling pig, *cuy*, tamales, trout, and barbecue. It's especially good at lunchtime. It also includes a small two star hotel.

🪑 75 P S 🏠 None

CARHUAZ

🏨 HOTEL EL ABUELO
$$$
9 DE DICIEMBRE 257
TEL 043/394–456
E-MAIL: INFORMES@ELABUELO
HOTEL.COM
www.elabuelohotel.com
Rates include breakfast with food from the *hostal's* garden and orchard. Rooms are immaculate, have hair dryers,

and overlook the garden. A terrace has Cordillera Negra views.

[i] 24 P S 🏠 MC, V

CHAVÍN DE HUÁNTAR

🏨 HOTEL INCA
$
WIRACOCHA 170
TEL 044/754–021
Whitewashed walls and a red-tile roof surrounding a central courtyard distinguish this friendly, family-run hotel.

[i] 16 P 🏠 None

CHIQUIAN

🏨 HOTEL LOS NOGALES
🍴 **$**
COMERCIO 1301
TEL 043/447–121
E-MAIL: INFO@LOSNOGALES
DECHIQUIAN.COM
www.losnogalesdechiquian.
com
This attractive, rustic, family-run hotel surrounds a courtyard filled with *nogales* (walnut trees). Rooms have TVs, and the restaurant serves meals on request at any time. Wi-Fi is available.

[i] 28 P 🏠 None

HUARAZ

🏨 ANDINO CLUB HOTEL
🍴 **$$$$–$$$$$**
PEDRO COCHACHÍN 357
TEL 043/421–662
E-MAIL: ANDINO@HOTEL
ANDINO.COM
www.hotelandino.com
Easily Huaraz's best hotel, the impeccable Swiss-run Andino has been housing climbers, hikers, and trekkers for decades. Rooms have garden or mountain views, huge amounts of hot water, and the more expensive suites boast fireplaces and a sauna. Guests enjoy free Internet and fine Swiss and Peruvian dining in the **Chalet Suisse** (*$$$$*), open

to the public. Rates include breakfast.

[i] 54 P 🚪 ♿
🏠 All major cards

🏨 LAZY DOG INN
$$$–$$$$
2 MILES (4 KM) E OF HUARAZ
TEL 943/789–330
E-MAIL: RESERVATIONS@
THELAZYDOGINN.COM
thelazydoginn.com
This lovely eco-lodge built of local materials features four cabins and two rooms in the main lodge. Some units have a fireplace, deck, or private balcony; all have great mountain views. Rates include breakfast and dinner, with produce grown in the garden and greenhouse. The lodge offers horses, bikes, sauna, a bouldering area, outdoor activities, and the

friendly Canadian owners are involved in local community projects.

ⓘ 5 🅿 🆂 🅰 None

🏨 HOSTAL COLOMBA
$$$

FRANCISCO DE ZELA 210
TEL 043/421–501
E-MAIL: RESERVAS@HOTEL
COLOMBA.COM.PE
www.huarazhotel.com

Quietly located in a converted hacienda north of the Río Quilcay, about a ten-minute walk from the center, the Colomba features bunga-lows in a grassy garden. A children's playground, small gym, 19th-century chapel, game room, Internet, and free breakfast buffet are available.

ⓘ 20 🅿 🅰 All major cards

🏨 MORALES GUESTHOUSE
$$

JOSÉ OLAYA 578
TEL 043/425–105
E-MAIL: RESERVAS@MORALES
GUESTHOUSE.COM
www.moralesguesthouse.com

A cozy three-story building with a rooftop dining terrace (with mountain views) and a comfortable lounge on each floor, this guesthouse is run by a local family renowned for trekking and climbing. Rates include breakfast and bus station pickup. Meals, travel confirmation, Internet, and treks or climbs are available on request.

ⓘ 8 🅿 🆂 🅰 None

🏨 OLAZA'S BED & BREAKFAST
$$

JULIO ARGUEDAS 1242
TEL 043/422–529
E-MAIL: INFO@OLAZAS.COM
www.olazas.com

Rates in this charming little hotel include free Internet and continental breakfast served on a rooftop terrace

with one of the best moun-tain views in Huaraz. Kitchen facilities, a book exchange, laundry, and a TV lounge with DVDs are on the premises. The owners specialize in arranging biking and hiking trips and will pick you up at the bus station.

ⓘ 10 🅿 🅰 AE, V

🏨 CHURUP GUEST HOUSE
🍴 $–$$

AMADEO FIGUEROA 1257
TEL 043/424–200
E-MAIL: CHURUPHOTEL
HUARAZ@GMAIL.COM
www.churup.com

This family-run backpackers' hostal has 13 rooms and two cheaper dormitories with private baths. Fireplaces in the lobby and in the top-floor res-taurant with mountain views gather trekkers. A kitchen is available for guests' use, and tours are arranged.

ⓘ 15 🅿 🅰 V, MC

🍴 BISTRO DE LOS ANDES
$$

LUZURIAGA 702
TFL 943/663–508
bistrodelosandes.com

French-Peruvian–run, this spacious restaurant has a fine international menu ranging from curries and pastas to local trout and vegetarian options. There's a book exchange and windows over-looking the Plaza de Armas.

🍴 60 🕐 Closed Sun.
🆂 🅰 MC, V

🍴 CAFÉ ANDINO
$–$$

LUCAR Y TORRE 530, 3RD FL.
TEL 043/421–203
E-MAIL: CAFEANDINO@
HOTMAIL.COM
www.cafeandino.com

Humorously advertising itself as "the third best café in Huaraz," the American-run Andino has exceptional

home-roasted coffees, innova-tive sandwiches and light meals, beers, piscos, the best library in northern Peru, maps, information, a huge fireplace, patio, great views, couches, board games, good music, Wi-Fi, and gorgeous waitstaff.

🍴 60 🆂 🅰 MC, V

MONTERREY

🏨 EL PATIO DE 🍴 MONTERREY
$$$

CARRETERA HUARAZ–CARAZ
S/N
TEL 043/424–965
E-MAIL: RESERVAS@ELPATIO.COM.PE
www.elpatio.com.pe

Set back just enough from the highway to minimize traffic noise, this hotel is Monterrey's best, and it's only a few minutes' walk from the hot springs (see p. 181). Four cabins with a fireplace and 25 nice rooms with stone walls and beamed ceilings, some with balconies, are set around an attractive patio/garden.

ⓘ 29 🅿 🅰 All major cards

▶ NORTH COAST

CASMA

🏨 INN EL FAROL
$$

TÚPAC AMARU 450
TEL 043/411–064
E-MAIL: RESERVAS@EL
FAROLINN.COM
www.elfarolinn.com

A simple but pleasant option and perhaps the town's best, El Farol has a relaxing garden and a lobby covered with maps and photos to plan your archaeological excursions.

ⓘ 24 🅿 🌊 🅰 MC, V

CHICLAYO

🏨 CASA ANDINA SELECT 🍴 CHICLAYO
$$$$

🆂 Nonsmoking   🆂 Air-conditioning   🏊 Indoor Pool   🌊 Outdoor Pool   🏋 Health Club   🅰 Credit Cards

FEDERICO VILLAREAL 115
TEL 074/234–911
E-MAIL: CAS-CHICLAYO
@CASA-ANDINA.COM
www.casa-andina.com
The largest hotel in town, and recently renovated, this is the choice of businesspeople and upscale tour groups. There's a first-class restaurant, a 24-hour snack bar, and a bar. Rates include buffet breakfast and Internet use. A sauna and hairdresser are available.

🛈 123 🅿 ⬍ 🚫 ⬛ 🏊
🍽 ⬜ All major cards

🏨 🍽 WYNDHAM COSTA DEL SOL CHICLAYO
$$$$
BALTA 399
TEL 074/227–272
www.wyndhamhotels.com
A modern, comfortable, central hotel, with large Peruvian art in the lobby, and city views from the shaded rooftop pool and Jacuzzi, this is the best in downtown. Spacious rooms have noise-resistant windows, and some have bathtubs and sitting areas. Buffet breakfast is included.

🛈 82 🅿 🏊 ⬍ 🚫 🍽 🚫
⬜ All major cards

🏨 PARAISO HOTEL
$$–$$$
PEDRO RUIZ 1064
TEL 074/228–161
E-MAIL: RESERVASCIX@
HOTELESPARAISO.COM.PE
www.hotelesparaiso.com.pe
This hotel has simple but clean rooms with fans. The pricier rooms are larger and have Internet connection, but there are public booths in the lobby. Breakfast is included in the 24-hour café. Walk-in guests can get discounted rooms without breakfast.

🛈 65 🅿 ⬍ 🚫
⬜ All major cards

🍽 FIESTA CHICLAYO GOURMET
$$$–$$$$$
SALAVERRY 1820
URBANIZACIÓN 3 DE OCTUBRE
TEL 074/201–970
www.restaurant
fiestagourmet.com
A place for those in the know—no sign, knock to enter this large house. Sit on the patio if the weather is good. Seafood and local dishes including goat and duck are the specialty; it's among Chiclayo's best.

🪑 120 🅿 🚫
⬜ All major cards

🍽 HEBRON RESTAURANT & GRILL
$$
BALTA 605
TEL 074/222–709
www.hebron.com.pe
Large, well-lit restaurant with a long menu of pasta, fish, sandwiches, and local dishes. The windowed area is brighter and more pleasant. Open all day, from 7 a. m. to midnight.

🪑 220 🅿 🚫 ⬜ MC, V

🍽 LA PARRA
$$
MANUEL MARÍA IZAGA 752
TEL 074/227–471
This restaurant has an odd combo of a Chinese section with red-curtained booths and an upstairs grill—both menus are available in both sections served by one kitchen. Busy, varied, popular, with large portions and good value.

🪑 200 🚫 ⬜ All major cards

🍽 RESTAURANT ROMANA
$$
BALTA 512
TEL 074/223–598
This has long been a locally popular place for Peruvian breakfasts, sandwiches, and

full meals. Try *chirimpoco* (goat tripe stew), which is a local breakfast dish. It has three floors; the top floor has a balcony with street views.

🪑 60 ⬜ None

🍽 EL FERROCOL
$–$$
LAS AMERÍCAS 816
TEL 074/236–875
About ten blocks southeast of the center, this locally popular place serves excellent ceviche and inexpensive Peruvian dishes.

🪑 24 ⬜ None

HUANCHACO

🏨 🍽 BRACAMONTE HOTEL
$$$
LOS OLIVOS 160
TEL 044/461–162
E-MAIL: RESERVAS@

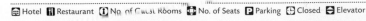

HOTELBRACAMONTE.COM.PE
www.hotelbracamonte.
com.pe
Clean, cozy rooms with Wi-Fi
and cable TV. Children's playground and an indoor game
room featuring billiards, table
tennis, foosball, and board
games. With the ocean a five-
minute walk away and a sizable pool on the premises, this
is a safe family-oriented hotel.
🛈 33 🅿 �... ▩ All major
cards

🍴 RESTAURANT BIG BEN
$$$
LARCO 1312, EL BOQUERÓN
TEL 044/461–378
E-MAIL: RESERVAS@BIGBEN
HUANCHACO.COM
www.bigbenhuanchaco.com
This three-story picture-
windowed restaurant delivers
ocean views from the north
end of Huanchaco. The best
views are from the rooftop
terrace, shielded from the
sun by tabletop parasols. It's
the town's priciest restaurant,
specializing in a long, varied
menu of the freshest seafood
and is open only for lunch.
🍴 160 🅿 ▩ 🕐 Closed
Dinner ▩ All major cards

🍴 OTRA COSA
$$
LARCO 1312,
EL BOQUERÓN
TEL 044/461–346
A vegetarian restaurant using
local products serves on a
patio with ocean views or
in front of a fireplace. The
Dutch-Peruvian owners make
a great apple pie, and the
coffee is excellent. Some of
the profits go to charity, and
volunteering and alternative
tourism projects are available.
🍴 50 🅿 ▩ ▩ None

LAMBAYEQUE

SOMETHING SPECIAL
🏨 LOS HORCONES
DE TÚCUME

$$$$
CASERIO SAN ANTONIO,
TÚCUME
TEL 951/831–705
E-MAIL: RESERVAS@LOS
HORCONESDETUCUME.COM
www.loshorconesde
tucume.com
This rural lodge is in a carob
grove on the outskirts of
Túcume archaeological site.
The thick, cool walls and
interior designs reminiscent
of pre-Inca friezes won first
prize in a biennial architecture competition. Don Victor
Bravo, a famed *curandero*
from a nearby village, can be
hired for traditional healing
ceremonies. Horseback and
jeep tours to various archaeological sites are arranged.
Rates include breakfast and
other meals on request.
🛈 12 🅿 ▩ ▩ MC, V

🍴 EL CÁNTARO
$$
DOS DE MAYO 180
TEL 074/282–196
E-MAIL: JUANA@RESTAURANT
ELCANTARO.COM
www.restaurantelcantaro.
com
Decorated with huge earth-
enware pitchers after which
it is named, this rustic restau-
rant serves a varied menu of
well-prepared local specialties
and is popular for breakfast
and lunch with visitors to the
Lambayeque museums.
🍴 200 🅿 ▩ 🕐 Closed
Dinner ▩ MC, V

MÁNCORA

🏨 DCO SUITES, LOUNGE,
🍴 AND SPA
$$$$$
PLAYA LAS POCITAS
TEL 073/258–171 OR
9947094–128
E-MAIL: INFORMES@HOTEL
DCO.COM
www.hoteldco.com
The area's most exclusive
hotel has just a handful

of stylish sea-view suites
designed for discerning
couples looking to get away
from it all—think honeymoon.
The name DCO—pronounced
"de-se-o"—is a seductive wink
to the Spanish for "desire."
This hotel will appeal to
romantics who wish to be
pampered. Suites have airy
balconies, and bedrooms
have nice touches like
Japanese-style bathrobes.
The rooftop spa allows for
open-air, yet private, couples
massages, and a small infin-
ity pool allows a dip if you
don't feel like getting salty
in the ocean, which is a few
steps away. The **Restaurant
DCO** menu is dominated by
superbly prepared seafood,
though die-hard meat lovers
can order a steak and there
are vegetarian options.
🛈 10 🅿 ▩ 🚿
▩ All major cards

🏨 MÁNCORA BEACH
BUNGALOWS
$$$
PANAMERICANA KM 1215
ANTIGUA NORTE
TEL 073/258125
LIMA RESERVATIONS:
TEL 01/201–2060
E-MAIL: RESERVAS@MANCORA-
BEACH.COM
www.mancora-beach.com
About 2 miles (3 km)
south of Máncora, these
bungalows are either doubles
or family-size. Two separate
beachfront swimming pools
cater to either adults only
(bar and Jacuzzi) or families
(waterslide and waterfall).
Rooms have patios and sea
views. Hammocks, a game
room, a children's playground,
and beach volleyball are on the
premises. Tours are arranged.
Rates include continental
breakfast.
🛈 32 🅿 🚿 ▩ MC, V

🏨 DEL WAWA
$$–$$$
PIURA 139

TEL 073/258–427
E-MAIL: INFO@DELWAWA.COM
www.delwawa.com
With surfing right out the doorstep, surfboard rental and tours to the best northern beaches, kite surfing and windsurfing equipment and lessons, and offshore fishing trips, this place appeals to serious ocean sports enthusiasts. The owner is a champion Peruvian surfer who knows how to keep the most demanding surfer happy.

[i] 14 [P] [MC, V]

🍴 LA SIRENA D'JUAN
$$$
PIURA 316
TEL 073/258–173
Chef Juan Seminario, born in Máncora and trained in Lima's Cordon Bleu school, has opened a chic two-story coastal-rustic restaurant in his hometown, which has fast become one of the top eateries in town. While the seafood is the first attraction, with fresh local tuna prepared in a variety of hot and cold ways, the innovative pasta dishes and traditional coastal plates such as *cabrito* (baby goat) will keep you coming back to try something new. The wine list is among the best in town.

[🪑] 70 [MC, V]

🍴 ANGELA'S PLACE
$
PIURA 396
TEL 073/258–603
E-MAIL: ANGELA.MANCORA
@YAHOO.COM
In a land of seafood, Austrian Angela serves vegetarian meals, heavy European breads and pastries, goulash, and vegan dishes. Open for breakfast, lunch, and dinner.

[🪑] 40 [P] [None]

PIURA

🏨 LOS PORTALES
🍴 $$$$

LIBERTAD 875
TEL 01/611–9001
E-MAIL: RESERVASHOTELES
@LOSPORTALES.COM.PE
losportaleshoteles.com.pe
Elegantly situated on the Plaza de Armas, this is Piura's best hotel. Lemon-color walls with white accents and black iron grill-work hark back to its colonial heritage. The building has been refurbished with tiled or hardwood floors, high ceilings, Wi-Fi in every room, an elegant restaurant, café, and casino. A modern bar features weekend entertainment.

[i] 87 [P] [All major cards]

🏨 COSTA DEL SOL
🍴 WYNDHAM PIURA
$$$–$$$$
LORETO 649
TEL 073/302–864
E-MAIL: RECEPCIONPIURA@
COSTADELSOLPERU.COM
www.costadelsolperu.com
A cool, white, modern building houses an airy lobby and comfortable rooms. The restaurant is among Piura's best, and a casino attracts a local crowd. Rates include breakfast.

[i] 95 [P] [All major cards]

TRUJILLO

🏨 WYNDHAM COSTA DEL
🍴 SOL
$$$$–$$$$$
LOS COCOTEROS 505
TEL 044/484–150
E-MAIL: RESERVAS@
LIBERTADOR.COM.PE
www.wyndhamhotels.com
Luxurious Wyndham hotel with swimming pools, gym, spa, and fitness center. The rooms are spacious, elegant, and modern. The excellent Paprika Restaurant serves Peruvian specialties.

[i] 120 [P] [All major cards]

PRICES

HOTELS
The cost of a double room with private bath and hot water in the peak season is given by $ signs. Low-season rates can be considerably lower, especially in the cheaper establishments.

$$$$$	Over $200
$$$$	$100–$200
$$$	$50–$100
$$	$25–$50
$	Under $25

RESTAURANTS
The average cost of a two-course meal for one person, without tax, tip, or drinks is given by $ signs.

$$$$$	Over $30
$$$$	$21–$30
$$$	$14–$20
$$	$7–$13
$	Under $7

🏨 CASA ANDINA
🍴 STANDARD TRUJILLO
PLAZA
$$$$
ALMAGRO 586
TEL 044/201–044
www.casa-andina.com
A fine, modern, centrally located hotel with friendly, helpful staff, this recently remodeled place includes airport transfer, Wi-Fi, and breakfast in its rates. Completely modernized in recent times, it offers comfortable standard and superior rooms with excellent value for money and service worthy of the chain to which it belongs. Among the attractions are also a bar, restaurant, and laundry service.

[i] 46 [P] [All major cards]

🏨 Hotel 🍴 Restaurant [i] No. of Guest Rooms 🪑 No. of Seats [P] Parking ⊕ Closed ⮂ Elevator

HOTEL COLONIAL
$$$
INDEPENDENCIA 618
TEL 044/258–261
Three floors of rooms with iron-grill windows surround a small colonial-style courtyard in this simple, good-value option; rates are at the bottom of the price range and include Wi-Fi. The hotel is just a block from the Plaza de Armas. Reasonably spacious units have hot showers, fan, and a writing desk, but do vary, so check yours before you unpack to make sure you are satisfied.

🛏 90 🚫 None

EL MOCHICA
$$$
SANTA MARIANA 1462
TEL 044/659–214
E-MAIL: RESERVASMDF @ELMOCHICA.COM.PE
www.elmochica.com.pe
Two restaurants in two different areas of the city: one in the historic center (Independencia 610), one in the La Merced district. Modern furniture and very professional service. The *platos criollos* are among Trujillo's best; try goat, yucca, *tacu tacu*, fried bananas, *cuy*, sweetbreads, and ceviche. Straightforward meat, chicken, and fish dishes are also available.

🍴 550 🅿 🚫
🚫 All major cards

RESTAURANT TOURÍSTICO CANANA
$$$
SAN MARTÍN 791
TEL 044/295–422
The rustic, twisted wooden furniture and a jungle of hanging plants take you away from the desert in this steak house with evening shows. Open only for dinner, the music gets underway around 11 p.m., when a $6 cover is charged. Bands play salsa, meringue, *folklórico*, and rock,

often with a dance show before guests join in the fun.

🍴 250 🅿 🚫 Closed L & Sun.–Tues. 🚫 All major cards

CAFÉ BAR MUSEO DEL JUGUETE
$
INDEPENDENCIA 701
TEL 044/208–181
In a restored colonial house, this old-fashioned café gleams with a polished wood bar, antique cash register, and walls adorned with photos of Peruvian luminaries and intellectuals. Sophisticated yet unpretentious, this is a great spot for a coffee, snack, dessert, or cocktail.

🍴 50 🚫 Closed Sun.
🚫 None

SALÓN DE TÉ BUENOS AIRES
$
PIZARRO 332
TEL 044/205–255
This hole-in-the-wall just off the Plaza de Armas has been a favorite of generations of locals for its typical *criollo* breakfasts. The menu features pork tamales, corn *humitas*, and roast pork or turkey sandwiches on fresh baguettes. Don't expect bacon and eggs.

🍴 68 🚫 None

TUMBES

CASA CÉSAR
$$–$$$
HUÁSCAR 311
TEL 072/522–883 OR
954/912–236
E-MAIL: RESERVAS@CASA
CESARTUMBES.COM
www.casacesartumbes.com
Once known as Hotel César, for decades a Tumbes budget accommodation, Casa César has been completely refurbished and is now an attractive mid-range hotel with contemporary rooms and helpful service. Each

bright, unpretentious unit is named after and decorated with artwork of local fauna by Tumbesian painter José Madrid. Executive rooms cost a few dollars more than standards, but offer a little more space and a mini-fridge. Both include breakfast in their rates and Wi-Fi is available.

🛏 20 🅿 🚫

▶ ## NORTHERN HIGHLANDS

CAJAMARCA

HOTEL & SPA LAGUNA SECA
$$$$
MANCO CÁPAC 1098
BAÑOS DEL INCA
TEL 076/584–300
LIMA TEL 01/514–2222
lagunaseca.com.pe
This hacienda-style resort is located near the Baños del Inca. It has a private source of geothermal water that also reaches the rooms. The rooms are spacious and equipped with large bathtubs. Restaurant with Peruvian and international cuisine, two outdoor pools with thermal water, horseback riding shows, mini zoo, and spa treatments. Rates include buffet breakfast and airport transfers.

🛏 42 🅿 🚫 🏊 🎯
🚫 All major cards

POSADA DEL PURUAY
$$$$
CARRETERA A PORCÓN
HUALGAYOC KM 4.5
TEL 076/367–028 OR
976/683–837
posadapuruay.com.pe
Built in 1822 in the open countryside, 3 miles (5 km) north of Cajamarca, this perfectly restored rural refuge is ideal for a relaxing stay. The rooms are large, decorated with period elements, and offer spacious bathrooms. In the surrounding grounds

there is a children's playground and you can go for hikes and rides. The gourmet restaurant on weekends draws many *cajamarqueños*. Transfers to the airport and to the Baños del Inca are available free of charge.

[i] 14 **[P] [S] [⟨⟩]** MC, V

🏨 COSTA DEL SOL WYNDHAM CAJAMARCA
$$$–$$$$

CRUZ DE PIEDRA 707
TEL 076/362–472
E-MAIL: LALIAGA@COSTADEL
SOLPERU.COM
www.costadelsolperu.com

Next to the cathedral on the plaza, this is the swankiest modern hotel in Cajamarca. Free airport transfer service. Spacious rooms have archaeological motifs and soundproof windows; some bathrooms have tubs. The bar features karaoke, a dance floor, and pool table. Spa treatments are available.

[i] 71 **[P] [S] [S] [S] [⟨⟩] [T]**
[⟨⟩] All major cards

🏨 EL PORTAL DEL 🍴 MARQUÉS
$$$

DEL COMERCIO 644
TEL 076/368–464
E-MAIL: RESERVAS@PORTALDEL
MARQUES.COM
www.portaldelmarques.com

Housed in a renovated colonial mansion, carpeted rooms offer Wi-Fi and are decorated with local art. Rooms vary in size and age. The restaurant is among the best in town. Internet cabins, casino, and bar with happy hour are available.

[i] 41 **[P] [⟨⟩]** MC, V

🏨 EL CABILDO HOSTAL
$$

JUNÍN 1062
TEL 076/367–025
E-MAIL: RESERVAS@ELCABILDO
HOSTAL.PE

www.elcabildohostal.pe

A lovely, large, cobblestone-and-tile courtyard surrounds a fountain in this quaint colonial building, a long block from the Plaza de Armas. Rooms are varied; some have a loft, and all have a modern bathroom within the old-fashioned decor. Continental breakfast is included.

[i] 28 **[T] [⟨⟩]** All major cards

🍴 QUERUBINO
$$

AMALIA PUGA 583
TEL 076/340–900
E-MAIL: RESERVAS@
ELQUERUBINO.COM

Simple and cozy, it offers an Italian-inspired menu. Many great classics (in the Peruvian way, however), especially pasta, lasagna, soups, and many types of pizza. Service and environment certainly pleasant.

[⊞] 50 **[S] [⟨⟩]** DC, MC, V

🍴 RESTAURANT SALAS
$–$$

AMALIA PUGA 637
TEL 076/362–867
E-MAIL: RESTAURANTSALAS@
YAHOO.ES

This cavernous Plaza de Armas eatery has been feeding Cajamarqueños for generations. Founded in 1947, the popular place offers everything from huge chicken and beef platters to regional plates such as *omelette de sesos* (cow-brain omelette), *cuy*, and tamales.

[⊞] 120 **[S] [⟨⟩]** MC, V

🍴 HELADERIA HOLANDA
$

AMALIA PUGA 657
TEL 076/340–113
E-MAIL: HELADOSHOLANDA@
HOTMAIL.COM

About 20 ice cream flavors are locally made and excellent.

PRICES

HOTELS

The cost of a double room with private bath and hot water in the peak season is given by **$** signs. Low-season rates can be considerably lower, especially in the cheaper establishments.

$$$$$	Over $200
$$$$	$100–$200
$$$	$50–$100
$$	$25–$50
$	Under $25

RESTAURANTS

The average cost of a two-course meal for one person, without tax, tip, or drinks is given by **$** signs.

$$$$$	Over $30
$$$$	$21–$30
$$$	$14–$20
$$	$7–$13
$	Under $7

Pies and coffees are also on offer. Disadvantaged and handicapped people are employed in this ice creamery—they give great service.

[⊞] 30 **[S] [⟨⟩]** None

🍴 SANGUCHON
$

JUNÍN 1137
TEL 076/343–066

Open from 6 p.m. until late, this bar and burger joint serves more than a dozen kinds of burgers, plus other sandwiches (some vegetarian), and attracts a hip young crowd.

[⊞] 28. **[S] [⟨⟩]** None

CHACHAPOYAS

🏨 CASA HACIENDA 🍴 ACHAMAQUI
$$$$

CARRETERA PEDRO RUÍZ KM 39

TEL 933/189-144
E-MAIL: RESERVAS@
ACHAMAQUI.PE
achamaqui.pe
This rural hotel in a two-story,
red-tile-roofed, balconied
hacienda lies in a lovely location on the banks of the Río
Utcubamba, about 12 miles
(20 km) west of the city
center by road. Recently
renewed, it makes ecology
its main value. For authentic
and non-invasive knowledge,
guests are offered activities
that are sustainable and in
harmony with the culture and
environment of the area. Restaurant with exclusive use of
homegrown or local products
and typical handicraft shop.
[i] 31 [P] [S] [≈]
[S] All major cards

LA CASONA DE CHACHAPOYAS
$$$
CHINCHA ALTA 569
TEL 041/477-353
E-MAIL: RESERVAS@LACASONA
dechachapoyasperu.com
This late 19th-century man-
sion has been converted
into a quaint hotel with
distinctive all-different rooms,
one with a fireplace. Rates
include breakfast and Internet
use. All the local tours can
be arranged.
[i] 12 [S] MC, V

LA CASONA MONSANTE
$$
AMAZONAS 746
TEL 041/477-702
E-MAIL: INFORMES@
CASONAMONSANTE.COM
www.casonamonsante.com
This 19th-century mansion
with spacious rooms sur-
rounding a plant-filled patio
has been declared a national
cultural site by the Institute of
National Culture. Orchids and
hummingbirds can be seen
from rooms.
[i] 13 [S] V

REVASH HOSTAL
$-$$
GRAU 517
TEL 041/477-391
Inside an 18th-century building on the Plaza de Armas,
rustic rooms look over a tree-
filled courtyard; a few have
plaza views. Rates include
breakfast. A tour agency
offers cheap local tours.
[i] 20 [S] None

LA TUSHPA
$-$$$
ORTIZ ARRIETA 753
TEL 041/477-478
While rather characterless,
this is the best place in town
for steak and grills, and is
popular with the locals, who
joke about the slow service.
Take it or leave it.
[≈] 52 [S] MC, V

CAFÉ FUSIONES
$
AYACUCHO 952
TEL 990/285-862
This is a deservedly popular
breakfast place serving travel-
ers who gather to exchange
travel stories and information.
Coffee is local fair trade and
organic—a pretty hearty brew.
During the rest of the day,
sandwiches, desserts, and
other snacks are available,
and there is free Wi-Fi and
a book exchange. They have
local crafts on the walls and a
gift shop, and can put you in
touch with local guides and
arrange massages.
[≈] 28 [S] [⊕] Closed Sun.
[S] MC, V

KUÉLAP AREA

HOSTAL ESTANCIA EL CHILLO
$$$
CARRETERA DE LEYMEBAMBA
TEL 979/340-444
Rates at this working haci-
enda include breakfast and

dinner. Rustic rooms have
hot water on request, and all
local tours are arranged by
the knowledgeable Spanish-
speaking owner.
[i] 17 [P] [S] None

MARVELOUS SPATULETAIL LODGE CHOCTAMÁL
$$-$$$
CHOCTAMÁL, AMAZONAS
TEL 995/237-268
E-MAIL: LOSTAMBOS@MSN.COM
www.marvelousspatuletail.
com
The spatuletail is a spectacular hummingbird, and
this small, locally sustainable
lodge is popular with birders.
Balconies off rooms give
good birding views. This is
the closest comfortable lodging to Kuélap, a 40-minute
drive away, and the Gran
Vilaya region. This lodge and
the one in Levanto are both
run by Chachapoyas Tours
(see p. 310).
[i] 7 [P] [S] MC, V

LEVANTO

MARVELOUS SPATULETAIL LODGE LEVANTO
$-$$
LEVANTO, AMAZONAS
TEL 995/237-268
E-MAIL: LOSTAMBOS@MSN.COM
www.marvelousspatuletail.net
This tiny lodge has rooms
built in circular Chachapoya
style with two shared, hot-
water bathrooms. Built to
sustainably support locals, it
is a comfortable place to stay
in Levanto.
[i] 4 [P] [S] MC, V

LEYMEBAMBA

LA CASONA
$$$
AMAZONAS 223
TEL 041/830-106
E-MAIL: INFORMES@CASONADE
LEYMEBAMBA.COM

www.casonadeleymebamba.com

The best offer in town, with balconies, tiled roof, lime walls, and a courtyard entirely available to customers. It is available to organize excursions in the area, with guides and mules.

🛏 22 🅿 ⛵ **None**

🏨 LA PETACA
$

AMAZONAS 426
TEL 041/830-140

This is a nice, simple hostal on the Plaza de Armas; some rooms have plaza views.

🛏 7 ⛵ **None**

▶ ## AMAZON

The lodges listed outside of cities and towns may be remote and lack amenities such as modern plumbing, telephone service, and hot showers. The telephone numbers and addresses listed are for the business office, not the lodge itself; check facility locations. Rates for lodges include local and river transfers, meals, and guided jungle tours.

CHANCHAMAYO

🏨 LODGE EL REFUGIO
$$$

EL EJÉRCITO 490
SAN RAMÓN
TEL 961/030-314
E-MAIL: ECOLODGEEL
REFUGIO@GMAIL.COM
lodgeelrefugiochanchamayo.com.pe

The best hotel in the region, El Refugio has varied rooms and bungalows that sleep from two to six people. The on-site botanical gardens attract birds, butterflies, and human visitors. Rates include breakfast.

🛏 22 🅿 ⛵ ⛵ **None**

IQUITOS

🏨 DORADO PLAZA
🍴 HOTEL

$$$$–$$$$$
NAPO 258
TEL 065/222-555
E-MAIL: RESERVAS1@GRUPO-DORADO.COM
www.eldoradohoteles.com

On the Plaza de Armas, the city's most opulent hotel has a Jacuzzi, sauna, casino, two restaurants, and spacious rooms with views over the pool or plaza. Rates include airport transfer and breakfast buffet.

🛏 65 ⛵ ⛵ ⛵ ⛵ ⛵ ⛵
⛵ **All major cards**

🏨 VICTORIA REGIA
🍴 HOTEL & SUITES
$$$–$$$$
RICARDO PALMA 252
TEL 065/231-983
E-MAIL: RESERVAS.VICTORIA
REGIA@TERRAVERDE.PE
www.terraverde.pe
www.victoriaregiahotel.com

Perhaps the second best hotel in town, Victoria Regia is set on a quiet street four blocks from the center. Spacious rooms overlook the indoor pool, and rates include breakfast and airport transfer. Wi-Fi is available.

🛏 61 ⛵ ⛵ ⛵ ⛵
⛵ **AE, MC, V**

🏨 THE GARDEN HOUSE
$
PEVAS 133
TEL 065/231-679

Freshly renovated, it offers rooms of different capacities, all with private bathrooms and hot water. Wi-Fi in public areas, buffet breakfast included in the price.

🛏 14 ⛵ **MC, V**

🍴 FITZCARRALDO
$$–$$$
NAPO 100
TEL 939/155-869
E-MAIL: FITZCARRALDO_VIA
GOURMET@YAHOO.ES

This waterfront restaurant in an older building with a patio is a good place to

people-watch on weekend nights. The food is good and varied, including pastas, pizzas, Peruvian fare, and salads.

🪑 72 ⛵ **MC, V**

🍴 GRAN MALOCA
$$–$$$
SARGENTO LORES 170
TEL 965/607-000

One of the few air-conditioned restaurants in town, Gran Maloca is located in a tiled, rubber-boom era mansion. The menu ranges from international to Amazonian, and features wild game, local fish, palm hearts salad, and an above-average wine list.

🪑 80 ⛵ **MC, V**

🍴 EL MESÓN
$$
MALÉCON MALDONADO 153
TEL 065/231-857

This waterfront restaurant serves an excellent selection of Amazonian game including alligator, peccary, and venison. Turtle has been offered—avoid this dish because some species are endangered.

🛏 90 🚭 🏧 MC, V

🍴 HUASAI
$

FITZCARRALD 131
TEL 065/242–222
E-MAIL: SERVICIOALCLIENTE@
HUASAIRESTAURANT.COM
www.huasairestaurant.com

Regional dishes, lunches, vegetarian options, and barbecue attract a mainly local crowd to this central restaurant. Excellent value for money, especially if you order a menu of the day, and the possibility of home delivery.

🛏 60 🏧 None

IQUITOS AREA LODGES

Lodges

Lodge rates typically include river travel from Iquitos, all meals, and jungle excursions. Rates per night drop for longer visits or groups.

🏨 CEIBA TOPS
$$$$$

M 40 KM FROM IQUITOS
DOWNRIVER ON AMAZON
IQUITOS OFFICE: LA MARINA 340
TEL 065/252–530
E-MAIL: AMAZON@
EXPLORAMA.COM
www.explorama.com

One of four properties run by Explorama, Ceiba Tops is the most luxurious. All rooms and five suites have hot showers, patios, and free Wi-Fi, but no TVs. Landscaped gardens feature a waterslide and hammock house; local musicians play evenings in the bar. Jungle excursions to the Canopy Walkway are offered at extra cost.

🛏 75 🚭 🏊 🏋 🏧 AE, MC, V

🏨 EXPLORAMA LODGE
$$$$$

M 80 KM DOWNRIVER
ON AMAZON
IQUITOS OFFICE:
AVE. LA MARINA 340
TEL 065/252–530
E-MAIL: AMAZON@
EXPLORAMA.COM
www.explorama.com

This is Explorama's original Amazon lodge, built in 1964 and recently updated. Kerosene lamps romantically light rows of thatched wooden rooms, and mosquito netting covers beds. Bathrooms en suite have solar-heated showers and flush toilets. Covered walkways join the rooms, and numerous tours are offered.

🛏 40 🚭 🏧 None

🏨 EXPLORNAPO LODGE
$$$$$

M 157 KM DOWNRIVER
ON RÍO NAPO
IQUITOS OFFICE: LA MARINA 340
TEL 065/254–428
E-MAIL: AMAZON@
EXPLORAMA.COM
www.explorama.com

A half-hour hike from the Canopy Walkway (see sidebar p. 248), this remote rustic lodge is a gateway to still more remote areas. Rooms share bathrooms. There is a field station at the walkway, and the lodge is near an ethnobotanical garden curated by a shaman. Naturalist guides ensure plenty to do. Reservations in this lodge usually start from a minimum of 4 nights and include access to the walkway.

🛏 30 🚭 🏧 None

🏨 PACAYA-SAMIRIA AMAZON LODGE
$$$$$

M 190 KM UPRIVER ON THE
RÍO MARAÑÓN
LIMA OFFICE: TARAPACA 228
TEL 01/469–4521
QUITOS OFFICE: JOSÉ GÁLVEZ 546
TEL 065/226–137

OR 965/720–021
E-MAIL: RESERVAS@PACAYA
SAMIRIA.COM.PE
www.pacayasamiria.com.pe

Separate thatched wooden bungalows have private tiled showers and evening electricity. Hardy travelers can arrange guided camping in nearby Pacaya-Samiria reserve and bird-watchers can arrange weeklong birding tours.

🛏 8 🚭 🏧 V

🏨 TAHUAYO LODGE
$$$$$

M 145 KM DOWNRIVER ON
RÍO TAHUAYO
IQUITOS OFFICE: LA MARINA 100
TEL 800/262–9669
perujungle.com

This is the only lodge adjoining the Tamshiyacu-Tahuayo conservation area and has a high ratio of guides to clients. It arranges personalized itineraries, ranging from jungle survival courses to honeymoon trips, bird-watching expeditions to shamanism. Bedrooms are LED lit, and most have private solar showers. A large, circular, hammock house invites relaxation and socializing.

🛏 15 🚭 🏧 MC, V

🏨 MUYUNA JUNGLE LODGE
$$$$–$$$$$

M 140 KM UPRIVER ON
RÍO YANAYACU
IQUITOS OFFICE: PUTUMAYO 163
IQUITOS RESERVATIONS:
TEL 065/242–858
E-MAIL: RESERVAS@MUYUNA.
COM
www.muyuna.com

Guests love the jungle rooms in stilted, thatched bungalows with a river balcony and hammock. When the water runs high, fish from rooms with private bathrooms, screened with wraparound netting, and lit by kerosene. Welcoming local villagers staff the family-run lodge, and the well-versed guides speak English.

 17 MC, V

MANÚ

Guided tours arrive partly by ground from Cusco over the Andes, then by boat or by expensive chartered light aircraft from Cusco to Boca Manú airstrip, then boat. Alternatively, charter flights are taken from Cusco to the airstrip. Because of the high transportation costs, Manú is more expensive than Iquitos. Rates include all transportation and an overnight at a cloud forest lodge on road trips. Outfitters sometimes offer tented camps on platforms in the park. Area salt licks attract fewer birds from March to June.

COCK-OF-THE-ROCK LODGE
$$$$$
LIMA OFFICE: PETIT THOUARS 3811
TEL 01/730–6565
OR 971/427–346
E-MAIL: POSTMASTER@ INKANATURA.COM.PE
www.inkanatura.com
At 5,000 feet (1,600 m) near Pilcopata, 110 miles (176 km) northwest of Cusco, this cloud forest lodge offers remarkable bird-watching opportunities, including a cock-of-the-rock lek. The lodge is on the edge of the Manú cultural zone (a buffer area for the park) and is often used in combination with trips to the rain forest. Rooms have private bathrooms and balconies.

 12 All major cards

MANÚ LODGE
$$$$$
COCHA JUAREZ
MANÚ NATIONAL PARK
CUSCO OFFICE: PARDO 1046
TEL 084/252–721
E-MAIL: INFO@MANUNATURE TOURS.COM

www.manuperu.com
In the only lodge within the national park, comfortable beds in screened rooms and good meals are available, but bathrooms with cool showers are shared. An extensive network of trails is nearby, and giant river otters often visit Cocha Juarez, an oxbow lake 656 yards (600 m) from Río Manú. Adventurous visitors can use a rope-climbing system to ascend a huge Ceiba tree to a canopy platform for an extra charge. The lodge also owns the Manú Cloud Forest Lodge with six rooms. This can be used as an overnight stay for the land/river trip to Manú Lodge.

 12 MC, V

MANÚ WILDLIFE CENTER
$$$$$
RÍO MADRE DE DIOS
CUSCO OFFICE: LOS GERANIOS 2–G, URBANIZACION MARISCAL GAMARRA
TEL 084/225990
E-MAIL: SALES@MANU EXPEDITIONS.COM
www.manuexpeditions.com
Individual bungalows with large screened windows overlooking an Amazonian garden, mosquito-netted beds, and private hot showers are provided. The Blanquillo salt lick, 25 minutes by boat, attracts scores of parrots. A nocturnal blind at a mammal salt lick is nearby, and tapirs often visit. Two canopy platforms are near the lodge, which is built in one of the region's most biodiverse areas. Manú Expeditions also goes into Manú National Park.

 22 V

PANTIACOLLA LODGE
$$$$–$$$$$
CUSCO OFFICE: CALLE GARCILASO 265, 2ND FL.
TEL 084/238–323
E-MAIL: PANTIACOLLA

MANU@GMAIL.COM
pantiacolla.com
Near Shintuya, close to the end of the road from Cusco toward Manú, this lodge offers rooms with mainly shared showers in a private reserve in foothills on the edge of Manú. You can get there with a 5-hour boat trip from Boca Manú.

 11 P All major cards

PUCALLPA

HOTEL SOL DEL ORIENTE
$$$–$$$$
SAN MARTÍN 552
TEL 061/575–154
E-MAIL: HOTELPUCALLPA@ HOTELESSOLDELORIENTE.COM
www.hotelessoldeloriente. com
Comfortable rooms and a few Jacuzzi suites make this Pucallpa's best central hotel, with a decent restaurant, spacious

---

PRICES

HOTELS
The cost of a double room with private bath and hot water in the peak season is given by **$** signs. Low-season rates can be considerably lower, especially in the cheaper establishments.

$$$$$	Over $200
$$$$	$100–$200
$$$	$50–$100
$$	$25–$50
$	Under $25

RESTAURANTS
The average cost of a two-course meal for one person, without tax, tip, or drinks is given by **$** signs.

$$$$$	Over $30
$$$$	$21–$30
$$$	$14–$20
$$	$7–$13
$	Under $7

---

shaded public areas, and gardens. They'll arrange local tours, including overnights in a lodge on Yarinacocha.

[i] 65 [P] [S] [K] [≋]
[K] All major cards

PUERTO MALDONADO

⊞ WASAI ECO LODGE MALDONADO
$$$

BILLINGHURST S/N
TEL 082/572290
LIMA OFFICE: TEL 01/436–8792
E-MAIL: RESERVAS@WASAI.COM
wasai.com

This thatched-roof hotel has a jungle feel, overlooking the Río Madre de Dios, yet just a block from the Plaza de Armas. Rooms feature refrigerators, hot showers, TV, air-conditioning, and fans. The restaurant is the town's best. The hotel arranges boat tours, and this is a good midpoint between an area lodge visit and catching a flight.

[i] 18 [S] [K] [≋]
[K] All major cards

⊞ ANACONDA LODGE
$$–$$$

CARRETERA AL AEROPUERTO
TEL 082/792–726, 982/6110–39 OR 982/728–518
www.anacondajungle lodge.com

Ten large bungalows, some with two stories, are set in tropical gardens and sleep from two to six people. Six smaller bungalows have two rooms that share a bathroom. The restaurant's Thai chef features Thai and Peruvian cuisine, or you can use the barbecue.

[i] 22 [S] [≋] [K] MC, V

⊞ BURGO'S
$$

26 DE DICIEMBRE 195
TEL 082/573–653
EMAIL: RESERVAS@BURGOS RESTAURANT.COM
www.burgosrestaurant.com

Perhaps the best restaurant in town, it serves meat, fish and vegetarian dishes in a cozy environment. Indoor room and outdoor in contact with nature. The service is friendly and local Amazonian ingredients dominate the menu. If you are lucky you can attend live local dance shows.

[≣] 80 [K] MC, V

⊞ EL CALIFA
$

PIURA 266
TEL 082/571–119

This tropical eatery in a not too attractive building attracts locals for lunch. Specialties such as *juanes* (rice with chicken or fish and olives steamed in banana leaves), venison, fried bananas, and ceviche are served.

[≣] 50 [K] None

PUERTO MALDONADO AREA LODGES

⊞ EXPLORER'S INN
$$$$$

M 58 KM UPRIVER ON RÍO TAMBOPATA
PUERTO MALDONADO LIMA OFFICE: CIRCUNVALACIÓN S/N, TERMINAL TERRESTRE, 2° FL.
TEL 082/573–029
E-MAIL: SALES@EXPLORERS INN.COM
www.explorersinn.com

The oldest lodge on the Tambopata has seven thatched-roof cabins, each containing several screened rooms with private showers. A resident naturalist program for international researchers and university students provides visitors with multilingual guides. Birding is excellent, and the trails are an adventure.

[i] 30 [S] [K] AE, MC, V

⊞ HEATH RIVER WILDLIFE CENTER
$$$$$

4 HOURS DOWNRIVER ON HEATH RIVER

LIMA OFFICE: PETIT THOUARS 3811
TEL 01/422–6743
E-MAIL: POSTMASTER@ INKANATURA.COM.PE
www.inkanatura.com

Heath River lies south of the Madre de Dios on the Peru-Bolivia border in a remote area combining rain forest with tropical grasslands. Nearby is one of Peru's biggest salt licks and an Eseíeje Indian village. Rooms have private bathrooms. Sandoval Lake Lodge can also be visited en route.

[i] 10 [S] [K] AE, MC, V

⊞ RESERVA AMAZONICA
$$$$$

24 MILES (15 KM) DOWNRIVER ON RÍO MADRE DE DIOS
TEL 082/573–534
LIMA OFFICE: ANDALUCÍA 174
TEL 01/610–0400
E-MAIL: CENTRAL@INKATERRA. COM
www.inkaterra.com

A short river trip brings you to the region's most upscale resort featuring rooms and suites with private hot showers, thick towels, electricity, fans, draped mosquito netting, covered patios, and hammocks. Services include spa treatments, honeymoons, and access to a 500-yard-long (457 m) canopy walkway, 100 feet (30 m) above the ground.

[i] 35 [S] [K] All major cards

⊞ SANDOVAL LAKE LODGE
$$$$$

M 30 KM DOWNRIVER ON RÍO MADRE DE DIOS
LIMA OFFICE: PETIT THOUARS 3811
TEL 01/422–6743
E-MAIL: POSTMASTER@ INKANATURA.COM.PE
www.inkanatura.com

A 2-mile (3 km) hike through the rain forest on a boardwalk followed by a dugout canoe ride across the beautiful palm-edged lagoon leads to this impressive hilltop lodge. Rooms have electricity, fans, and private hot showers. This is among the most comfortable lodges in the area.

ⓘ 25 Ⓢ Ⓐ All major cards

⌂ TAMBOPATA RESEARCH CENTER
$$$$$
8 HOURS UPRIVER ON RÍO TAMBOPATA
PUERTO MALDONADO
OFFICE: AVE. AEROPUERTO, LA JOYA KM 6
TEL 984/705–266
U.S. TEL 1–877–231–9251
E-MAIL: SALES@PERU NATURE.COM
www.perunature.com

This remote, rustic lodge with 24 rooms with private restrooms is the farthest from Puerto Maldonado and close to the region's biggest salt lick. Run by Rainforest Expeditions (see p. 310), which works with local villagers to promote sustainability, the journey that can be combined with an overnight stay at one of their two closer lodges on the Tambopata, the **Posada Amazonas** (30 rooms with private baths, 4 hours from Puerto Maldonado) or **Refugio Amazonas** (32 rooms with private baths, 45 minutes from Puerto Maldonado). Rooms in the latter two have an open wall to the rain forest. Various expeditions are offered including photography, kayaking, bird-watching, and various family programs lasting up to eight nights.

ⓘ 24 Ⓐ V, MC

TARAPOTO

⌂ TUCAN SUITES APARTHOTEL
$$$–$$$$
JR. 1 DE ABRIL 315
LA BANDA DE SHILCAYO
TEL 042/528–383
OR 994/547–606
E-MAIL: INFO@TUCAN SUITES.COM
www.tucansuites.com

Near the Río Shilcayo, in a quiet district about 10 or 15 minutes' walk southeast of the noisy center, the modern Tucan Suites offers a rather sunny peaceful selection of rooms, all with kitchenettes, surrounding a central pool. There is a decent restaurant. Their sister property, **Pumarinri Amazon**, (www.pumarinri.com) is a thatched-roof but comfortable rural lodge about 19 miles (30 km) east of town.

ⓘ 24 Ⓟ Ⓢ ⓐ Ⓐ MC, V

YURIMAGUAS

⌂ HOSTAL EL NARANJO
$–$$
ARICA 318
TEL 065/351–504

Some rooms have fans instead of air-conditioning, but all are clean with private showers. Friendly owners and a central location make this a good place to wait for the next riverboat to Iquitos.

ⓘ 45 Ⓟ ⊕ Closed Sun. Ⓢ ⓐ Ⓐ MC, V

ENTERTAINMENT

Peru's *peñas* (local music clubs) and fiestas (festivals of all kinds) are the most popular forms of national entertainment and are guaranteed to keep travelers amused. Visitors will also find cinemas screening the latest international blockbusters and modern nightclubs (locally called *discotecas*) with a young clientele. Theater, symphony, and ballet have a limited following.

Peñas usually feature *música folklórica* or *música criolla*. The first is Andean music, while the latter tends toward coastal styles, with much variety within and fusion between these two branches. The music is often accompanied by dancing, both participatory and for show. A cover is usually charged, and things get under way late and go to the wee hours. Thursday through Saturday nights are the busiest.

Andean folkloric music is based on centuries-old tradition, including melancholic-sounding *zampoñas* (bamboo panpipes), *quenas* (wooden or bamboo flutes), *ocarinas* (small, oval, clay whistles), and *tambóres* (drums) much like what would have been played in pre-Columbian times. The Spanish conquest resulted in the introduction of stringed and brass instruments. The small, ten-stringed *charango*, once made using armadillo shells for a sound box, is a blend of indigenous and Spanish influences and has become an essential component of any folkloric group.

Andean music gained international renown with the 1970 recording of the Peruvian standard "El Cóndor Pasa" by U.S. duo Simon and Garfunkel, and this instantly recognizable tune is played in peñas where international travelers gather. In touristed cities such as Cusco, Arequipa, and Puno, the peña often comes to travelers, with groups of poncho-clad musicians wandering from restaurant to restaurant, playing a few tunes, and passing a hat. Some restaurants offer a dinner show (see restaurant listings).

Criolla music has a more recent history blending mainly Spanish and African styles, the latter from slaves brought by the Europeans and later freed to form their own distinct, small communities along the coast, the best known of which is Chincha (see Southern Lowlands chapter pp. 76–91). It includes Caribbean influences as well, in music and dance such as salsa.

The Peruvian national dance is the coastal *marinera,* with romantic handkerchief fluttering, macho posing, and coy skirt swirling. The nation's foremost dance competition attracts 1,500 dancers to Trujillo during the annual Fiesta de la Marinera, held during the last week of January. Trujillo also is famed for its Festival Internacional de la Primavera (International Spring Festival) during the last week in September when everything *norteño* (*marinera, paso* horses, gastronomy, beauty contests, parades, dances, and surfing competitions) entertains Peruvians and visitor alike.

In the highlands, fiestas are ingrained from Inca times, when the population was regularly expected to attend ritual seasonal festivals during which huge amounts of *chicha* (corn beer) and food were consumed. Today, throughout the highlands, but especially in the southern highlands (see sidebar p. 103), fiestas are frequent and fabulous, with expensive, elaborate costumes, and parades of dancers and musicians taking to the streets.

Popular Peruvian Peñas

Apart from restaurants, the following are recommended.

La Estación de Barranco
San Pedro de Osma 112
Barranco, Lima
Tel 01/247–0344
www.laestaciondebarranco.com
Criolla Andean, jazz, and comedy shows.

La Quinta & La Troica
Jerusalén 522
Arequipa
Tel 054/200–964
Adjoining peñas with a variety of live shows on weekends and other days, June–Aug.

Las Brisas del Titicaca
Wakulski 168
Plaza Bolognesi
Lima
Tel 01/715–6960
www.brisasdeltiticaca.com
Spectacular folkloric dance and music shows; popular with Limeños. Tues.–Sat., $15–$45.

Las Quenas
Santa Catalina 302
Arequipa
Tel 054/281–115
Mainly folkloric music.

Usha-Usha
Puga 142,
Cajamarca
This is a tiny, hole-in-the-wall bar, with impromptu musical evenings led by the guitarist/owner. Closed Sundays and some Mondays.

OUTDOOR ACTIVITIES

Peru's variety of activities is commensurate with its scenic diversity, and there is something for all interests, abilities, levels of fitness, and pocketbooks. From archaeological adventures to wildlife-watching, from surfing to white-water rafting, from mountain biking to mountain climbing, from day hikes to long treks, the list goes on and on.

Outdoor enthusiasts can climb or hike among scores of dazzling snow peaks, surf the world's longest left-handed wave, paraglide startlingly close to Lima's skyscrapers, descend almost 2 very fast miles (3 km) by mountain bike, or white-water raft from the Andes to the Amazon. Birding and wildlife-watching are rewarding throughout the country, but nowhere more so than in the upper Amazon Basin. Less frequently practiced activities include horseback riding, kayaking, and the unusual sport of sand-boarding (like snowboarding on sand dunes).

Most chapters of this book have information briefly highlighting the activities that are of most interest in that region. This section is a guide to the agencies and outfitters who can arrange your activities; it is arranged by region and then alphabetically within sections. A few outfitters with very specialized or localized operations are mentioned in the chapters. Those listed here have brief basic information about the kinds of services they offer.

Many hotels offer adventure tours and activities; see the hotel listings for other possibilities.

■ SOUTHERN LOWLANDS

Hotels in Nazca, Ica, Huacachina, Paracas, and Pisco offer activities such as jeep tours into the desert, sandboarding, desert flights, and wildlife-watching

boat trips. There are few stand-alone operators; a couple of exceptions are listed under Huacachina in the text (see pp. 87–88).

■ SOUTHERN HIGHLANDS

The following outfitters specialize in adventure tours in the Arequipa and Colca Canyon areas:

Carlos Zárate Aventuras
Jerusalén 505
Arequipa
Tel 054/202–461
E-mail: carlos@zarate
adventures.com
www.zarateadventures.com
Climbing specialists.

Colca Trek
Jerusalén 401–B
Arequipa
Tel 054/206–217
E-mail: colcatrek@gmail.com
www.colcatrek.com.pe
The best maps, rental gear, trekking, climbing, rafting, mountain biking, and Colca Canyon tours. English is spoken.

Cusipata
Jerusalén 402–A
Arequipa
Tel 054/203–966
or 952/700–717
E-mail: reservas@cusipata.com
www.cusipata.com
Kayaking classes and rafting trips.

The following agents specialize in tours to Colca Canyon, usually by bus and hotel:

Giardino Tours
Jerusalén 604–A
Arequipa
Tel 054/200–100
E-mail: web@giardinotours.com
www.giardinotours.com

Pablo Tours
Jerusalén 400–AB–1
Arequipa
Tel 054/203–737
E-mail: pablotour@hotmail.com
www.pablotour.com

For visiting Lake Titicaca, the following companies are recommended (see also sidebar p. 114):

All Ways Travel
Deustua 576
Puno
Tel 051/353–979
E-mail: allwaystravel@titicaca
peru.com
www.titicacaperu.com

Edgar Adventures
Lima 328
Puno
Tel 051/353–444
E-mail: sales@edgar
adventures.com
www.edgaradventures.com

Nayra Travel
Lima 419
Puno
Tel 051/364–774

■ CUSCO REGION

With the Inca Trail nearby, and other hikes and activities, Cusco has more outfitters than any other Peruvian city. The following are some of the best. Note that Cusco outfitters specializing in trips to the southern Amazon region are listed under the Amazon (see pp. 310–311).

Amazonas Explorer
Collasuyo 910
Urbanización Miravalle
Cusco
Tel 084/252–846
E-mail: info@amazonas-explorer.com
amazonas-explorer.com
The safest, high-quality river trips; also trekking, biking, horse riding, and other activities.

Aventours
Saphi 456
Cusco
Tel 084/224–050
E-mail: treks@aventours.com
www.aventours.com
Very experienced, high-quality llama treks, a private Inca Trail camp, all Cusco area treks, and cultural trips.

Ecotrek Peru
Urbanización Quispicanchi F–3
Cusco
Tel 084/247–286
or 974–216–074
E-mail: info@ecotrekperu.com
ecotrekperu.net
One- to five-day bike trips, treks, cultural tours, and moderate rates.

Enigma
Fortunato L. Herrera 214
Urbanización Magisterio, Primera Etapa, Cusco
Tel 084/222–155
E-mail: info@enigmaperu.com
www.enigmaperu.com
Customized small group treks, bike rides, cultural adventures, and mountain climbing.

Explorandes
San Fernando 287
Miraflores, Lima
Tel 084/245–700
E-mail: info@explorandes.com
www.explorandes.com
Peru's pioneering outfitter with deluxe trips. See website for offices in Lima, Huarez, and Puno.

Mayuc
Portal Confiturias 211
Plaza de Armas, Cusco
Tel 084/242–824
or 232–666
E-mail: info@mayuc.com
www.mayuc.com
Moderately priced one- and two-day white-water rafting on the Urubamba with private camp, and trekking to Machu Picchu.

Milla Turismo
Urbanización Lucrepata E–16
Cusco
Tel 084/231–710
U.S. Tel 1–720–212–0813
E-mail: info@millaturismo.com
www.millaturismo.com
Maximum flexibility and customized experiences, even trespassing in neighboring countries.

Mountain Lodges of Peru
Cusco Office: Tel 084/262–640
U.S. Office: Tel 1–877–491–5261
E-mail: info@mountainlodges ofperu.com
www.mountainlodgesofperu.com
Specializes in trekking and horseback riding to Machu Picchu using comfortable, expensive lodges.

■ CENTRAL HIGHLANDS

For some unusual local activities, see sidebar p. 169.

Incas del Peru
José Galvez 400, Huancayo
Tel 064/393–298
E-mail: incasdelperu@gmail.com
www.incasdelperu.org
Mountain and jungle trips, biking, cultural courses and trips, all local info, and English is spoken.

■ HUARAZ & THE HIGH ANDES

These outfitters arrange adventure activities:

Galaxia Expeditions
Parque del Periodista 1
Huaraz, Ancash
Tel 043/425–355
or 943/644–737
E-mail: galaxia_peru@hotmail.com
www.galaxia-expeditions.com
It offers climbing, mountain bike routes, information, equipment, and passages for those who climb independently.

Lazy Dog Inn
5 miles (8 km) east of Huaraz
Tel 943/789–330
E-mail: reservations@thelazy doginn.com
The best horses near Huaraz.

Montañero
Parque Ginebra 30–B,
Huaraz, Ancash
Tel 043/422–306
E-mail: andeway@terra.com.pe
www.trekkingperu.com
This company is run by the multilingual founder of the Casa de Guías (House of Guides).

Monttrek Viajes y Aventura
Luzuriaga 646, 2nd fl.
Huaraz, Ancash
Tel 043/421–124
E-mail: info@monttrek.com.pe
monttrek.com.pe
River rafting on the Río Santa, rock climbing, trekking, and mountaineering.

Mountain Bike Adventures
Jr. Lucar y Torre 530
Huaraz, Ancash

Tel 043/424–259
E-mail: julio.olaza@gm⌐⌐\ⅬⅢ
www.⟨h⟩l⌐ ⅢⅢⅢperu.com
The best biking company; also arranges treks.

Peruvian Andes Adventures
José Olaya 532
Huaraz, Ancash
Tel 043/421–864
E-mail: info@peruvian
andes.com
www.peruvianandes.com
Features acclimatization hikes to climbing expeditions. Highly professional, family-run, with two generations of mountain experience.

Pony's Expedition
Sucre 1266
Caraz, Ancash
Tel 043/391–642
or 944/941–214
E-mail: info@ponyexpeditions.
com
www.ponyexpeditions.com
Trekking, climbing, mountain biking.

Skyline Adventures
Industrial 137, Cascapampa
Huaraz, Ancash
Tel 043/427–097,
406/322–2065 (U.S.),
or 943/919–850
E-mail: info@skyline-
adventures.com
www.skyline-adventures.com
Mountaineering expeditions and courses.

The following agencies arrange day trips such as city tours, Chavín de Huántar, Llanaganuco, and tours to other lakes, Pastoruri, and *Puya raimondii:*

Pablo Tours
Luzuriaga 501,
Huaraz, Ancash
Tel 043/421–145
or 943/788–360
E-mail: pablotours@terra.com.pe
www.pablotours.com

■ NORTH COAST

The following agencies specialize in archaeology and local tours:

Clara Bravo & Michael White
Cahuide 495, Urbanización Santa Maria, Trujillo
Tel 044/243–347
E-mail: microbewhite@yahoo.
com
Individualized tours in private vehicles or public transportation. English is spoken.

Colonial Tours
Independencia 616
Trujillo
Tel 044/291–034
www.colonialtoursnorte
peru.com

Consorcio Turístico del Norte
Almagro 301
Trujillo
Tel 044/233–091
E-mail: ffreire@contunor.com
www.contunor.com

Moche Tours
7 de Enero 638, Chiclayo
Tel 074/224–637, 232–184,
or 979/973–203
E-mail: reservas@moche
tourschiclayo.com.pe
www.mochetourschiclayo.
com.pe

Sipán Tours
7 de Enero 772
Chiclayo
Tel 074/229–053
E-mail: sipantours-reservas@
hotmail.com
www.sipantours.com

Trujillo Tours
Diego de Almagro 301
Trujillo
Tel 044/257–518
or 998/398–647

E-mail: ttours@trujillotours.com
www.trujillotours.com

The following specialize in horseback riding:

Asociación Nacional de Criadores y Propietarios de Caballos de Paso
Ruta al Aeropuerto 670
Victor Larco Herrera, Trujillo
Tel 948/315–055
www.ancpcpp.org.pe

Rancho Santana
Pacora Lambayeque
Tel 979–712–145
E-mail: rancho_santana_peru@
yahoo.com
www.cabalgatasperu.com

Other useful north coast agencies:

My Surf Camp Peru
Mz 86 Lote 12 Puerto Malabrigo
La Libertad
Tel 994/088–564
E-mail: info@mysurfcamp
peru.com
www.mysurfcampperu.com
Historic surfing tour operator with two locations: in Chicama and Punta Hermosa. It offers surfing camps that provide lesson packages, accommodation, board and equipment rental.

Otra Cosa
Las Camelias 431
Huanchaco, La Libertad
Tel 044/461–302
E-mail: volunteer@otracosa.org
www.otracosa.org
Arranges volunteering with kids and work at Los Mochicas Surf School and at the restaurant Otra Cosa.

Pacífico Adventures
Rivera del Mar, Talara, Piura
Tel 998/391–428 or
998/176–199

E-mail: reservas@pacifico
adventures.com
Discovering the marine fauna
of the Pacific Ocean through
naturalistic boat tours, deep sea
fishing, and whale-watching.

Surf School Muchik
Independencia 100
Huanchaco
Tel 044/633–487
or 983/430–076
www.escueladetablamuchik.
com
Board rentals and surfing lessons.

◼ NORTHERN HIGHLANDS

Chachapoyas Tours
Santo Domingo 432
Chachapoyas, Amazonas
Tel 941/963–327 or
U.S. 407/583–6786
E-mail: kuelap@msn.com
www.kuelapperu.com
Features day or multiday tours
to Kuélap and northern Peru;
volunteer work and locally
sustainable lodges; and Peruvian
biologists. English is spoken.

Kajachos Trek
2 de Mayo 569
Cajamarca
Tel 076/345–350
or 967/756–743
E-mail: kajachostrek@
hotmail.com
www.kajachostrekperu.com
All Cajamarcan tours; private
English-speaking guide is
available.

Turismo Explorer
Grau 549
Chachapoyas, Amazonas
Tel 041/478–162
E-mail: contacto@turismoex-
plorerperu.com
www.turismoexplorerperu.com
Daily tours to Kuélap and Gocta.

Vilaya Tours
La Merced 1096
Chachapoyas, Amazonas
Tel 941/708–798
E-mail: info@vilayatours.com
www.vilayatours.com
First-class trekking, horseback
riding, hotel-based archaeology and ornithology tours, and
personalized itineraries. English
is spoken.

◼ AMAZON

Definitely check out the Amazon
lodges in the Hotels & Restaurants section—a stay in one of
these lodges, many miles from
any city, is an outdoor activity
in itself.

Explorama
La Marina 340, Iquitos
Tel 065/252–530
E-mail: amazon@explorama.
com
www.explorama.com
Offers Amazon lodges, camps,
and the Canopy Walkway.

Inkanatura
Petit Thouars 3811,
San Isidro, Lima
Tel 01/422–6743
or 971/427–346
www.inkanatura.com
Offers camps in Manú, and
lodges within southern Amazon.

La Patarashca
San Pablo de la Cruz 362,
Tarapoto, San Martín
Tel 962/851–887
or 042/527–554
E-mail: chankas@terra
mail.com.pe
lapatarashca.com
Offers tourism and trekking
in northern Peru.

**Los Chancas
Expeditions**
Rioja 357
Tarapoto, San Martín

Tel 042/522–616
E-mail: chankas@terra.com.pe
chancas.tripod.com
Runs river trips on the lower
Río Huallaga and Río Mayo.

Manú Expeditions
Jiron Los Geranios 2–G
Urbanizacion Mariscal Gamarra
Primero Etapa, Cusco
Tel 084/225–990 or 224–135
E-mail: sales@
manuexpeditions.com
www.manuexpeditions.com
They organize expeditions,
observations and photo safaris in
the Amazon for several days and
programs for true bird-watchers
in the wildest nature. It also
proposes more classic itineraries
on horseback along the Inca Trail.

Manú Nature Tours
Pardo 1046
Cusco
Tel 084/252–721
E-mail: info@manunature
tours.com
www.manuperu.com
Offers tours to Manú Lodge
within Manú, and the cloud
forest lodge.

Pantiacolla Tours
Calle Garcilaso 265, 2nd fl.
Cusco
Tel 084/238–323
E-mail: pantiacollamanu@
gmail.com
pantiacolla.com
Tours to cloud forest and Manú
rain forest lodges and camps.

Paseos Amazonicos
Pevas 246, Iquitos
Tel 065/231–618
www.paseosamazonicos.com
Organizes tours with complete
packages of a good standard,
ensuring hospitality in 2 lodges,
one along the Sinchicuy, a
tributary of the Amazon River,
and the other at the Hawk
Ravine, in a breathtaking

setting. All guides speak English and Spanish.

Quiquiriqui Tours
San Martín 373, 2nd fl.
Tarapoto, San Martín
Tel 940/185–850

E-mail: operaciones@qtperu.com
www.qtperu.com
Offers full-service travel agency with all Tarapoto area tours.

Rainforest Expeditions
Puerto Maldonado Office:

Ave. Aeropuerto, La Joya км 6
Tel 984/705–266
or 01/719–6422
E-mail: sales@perunature.com
www.perunature.com
Offers four excellent lodges on the Río Tambopata.

INDEX

ACKNOWLEDGMENTS

National Geographic Books wishes to thank PromPeru for their assistance in preparing this book, especially Michelle Szejer, Marco Peña, Nancy Ferradas, and Sandra Araujo Urrunag. Additional thanks go to Vladimír Kocerha, former press counselor, Embassy of Peru, Washington, D.C.

ILLUSTRATIONS CREDITS

All the images are by Vance Jacobs except for the following:

12, lia_mistral/Shutterstock; 20–21, Dafercito/Wikimedia Commons; 37, Brooklyn Museum/ Wikipedia Commons; 39, Wikimedia Commons; 42, Jess Kraft/Shutterstock; 100, Mark Green/ Shutterstock; 150, Fabio Lamanna/ Shutterstock; 154, Alejandro Balaguer/PromPeru; 184, Antonio Salaverry/ Shutterstock; 192, Mikadun/Shutterstock; 206, Milton Rodriguez/ Shutterstock; 212, Velvet/Wikimedia Commons; 213, Enrique Jara/Wikimedia Commons; 234, Puririy/Shutterstock; 235, Audioboxeir/Shutterstock; 249, Pere Rubi/Shutterstock; 250, Christian Vinces/Shutterstock; 258, Kletr/Shutterstock; 262,Dan Baciu/Shutterstock.

National Geographic
TRAVELER
Peru
THIRD EDITION

Since 1888, the National Geographic Society has funded more than 14,000 research, exploration, and preservation projects around the world. National Geographic Partners distributes a portion of the funds it receives from your purchase to National Geographic Society to support programs including the conservation of animals and their habitats.

National Geographic Partners, LLC
1145 17th Street NW
Washington, DC 20036-4688 USA

Get closer to National Geographic explorers and photographers, and connect with our global community. Join us today at nationalgeographic.com/join

For rights or permissions inquiries, please contact National Geographic Books
Subsidiary Rights: bookrights@natgeo.com

Third edition edited by White Star s.r.l.
Licensee of National Geographic Partners, LLC.
Update by Iceigeo, Milan (Francesco Filippini, Renata Grilli, Cynthia Anne Koeppe, James Schwarten)

Map illustrations drawn by Chris Orr Associates, Southampton, England.
Cutaway illustrations drawn by Maltings Partnership, Derby, England.

The information in this book has been carefully checked and to the best of our knowledge is accurate. However, details are subject to change, and the publisher cannot be responsible for such changes, or for errors or omissions. Assessments of sites, hotels, and restaurants are based on the author's subjective opinions, which do not necessarily reflect the publisher's opinion.

ISBN: 978-88-544-1711-3

Printed by
Rotolito S.p.A. - Seggiano di Pioltello (MI) - Italy